Kierkegaard's Muse

Kierkegaard's Muse

THE MYSTERY OF REGINE OLSEN

Joakim Garff

Translated by Alastair Hannay

PRINCETON UNIVERSITY PRESS

Princeton and Oxford

Library of Congress Cataloging-in-Publication Data

Names: Garff, Joakim, 1960– author.
Title: Kierkegaard's muse : the mystery of Regine Olsen / Joakim Garff ; translated by Alastair Hannay.
Other titles: Regines gåde. English
Description: Princeton : Princeton University Press, 2017. | Includes bibliographical references and index.
Identifiers: LCCN 2017014677 | ISBN 9780691171760 (hardcover : alk. paper)
Subjects: LCSH: Olsen, Regine, 1822–1904. | Denmark—Biography. | Kierkegaard, Søren, 1813–1855.
Classification: LCC DL204.O47 G3713 2017 | DDC 198/.9 [B]—dc23
LC record available at https://lccn.loc.gov/2017014677

British Library Cataloging-in-Publication Data is available

This book has been composed in Minion Pro

Printed on acid-free paper. ∞

Printed in the United States of America

1 3 5 7 9 10 8 6 4 2

Contents

Translator's Acknowledgment ix

Preface xi

TUNING IN 1

PART 1

1855

The Painful Departure 13

"You my heart's sovereign mistress" 16

The Virgin Islands 24

Governor J. F. Schlegel and His Wife 29

The Attack on the Church 34

"The flies are to such a degree impertinent out here" 37

Patient No. 2067 41

1856

His Last Will and Testament 51

"My Regine! . . . Your K." 55

"She nodded twice. I shook my head." 70

Repetition and the Repetition 71

Regine Frederikke Olsen's Death 80

Cane Garden's Blessings 82

"Food for worms and that's the end of it" 88

". . . for you know how little fuss there is with Fritz and me" 91

Henrik Lund and "Uncle Søren" 95

Regine's First Letter to Henrik Lund 102

The Sealed Letter to Mr. and Mrs. Schlegel 107

The Secret Place in Regine's Heart 114

The Plague's Paradise 118

Contents

The First Love 126

". . . it's exactly a matter I'd like to take up a little: blind love!" 128

"But I am constantly afraid of her passion" 130

". . . so she eggs the merman on" 132

". . . an unsettled point between us"—Regine's Second Letter to
Henrik Lund 135

"One unnamed whose name will sometime be named" 138

"Then I return to you . . ." 143

1857

"The Seducer's Diary" 146

Tropical Yuletide 153

The White Gold—A Dark Chapter 154

"We have had a Negro-uprising on St. Croix!" 158

Regine and "the Blacks" 163

Birch and His Brother 168

"Meet her without being observed" 172

". . . I am an exceptional lover" 176

Either/Or 178

"The priest people in Hellevad" 181

"The day is bad, but the night is worse" 183

". . . then I stand there so untouched by it all" 186

1001 Nights 188

1858

"You imagined it was Cornelia" 194

"What does this silence mean?" 195

". . . I shall the second time with God's help become more cruel" 201

". . . my besetting sin, making eternities!" 204

"God preserve me from their Christianity" 208

". . . as though I were 16 again and not 36" 212

"What an enormous loss, that Mrs. Heiberg has left the theater!" 215

Fritz and His Tormentors 217

"—and when I grew dizzy through gazing down into her infinite devotion" 220

Contents

1859
〜〜〜

"They played mostly dance music" 224

The French Officer—A Little Weakness 227

The Collectively Unutterable and Some Stolen Reflections 229

Birthdays—and Other Fatalities 234

PART 2

1860–1896
〜〜〜

". . . I am not looking forward to coming to Copenhagen" 241

Homecoming and the Time That Followed 242

Regine's Copenhagen and Environs 246

". . . a word or two about the dear Fritz" 250

"I cannot be quit of this relationship" 252

"so close to me that it was almost a collision" 256

". . . my heart is deeply grieved over my poor native land" 259

Regine's Boarding House 262

The Schlegels' "Place on the Corner" 263

"Alas, I am indeed somewhat spectral" 267

Regine's Myth and Brandes's Biography 271

Fireburn: Fritz's Reencounter with the West Indies 276

Exit to Eternity 279

PART 3

1897–1904
〜〜〜

"Then comes a dream from my youth's spring . . ." 285

The Right to Regine's Love Story 287

". . . he is the riddle, the great riddle" 290

" 'our own dear, little Regine' " 293

Contents

Postscript and Acknowledgments 297

Notes 299

Illustration Credits 309

Name Index 311

Translator's Acknowledgment

I would like here to express my deep gratitude to Joakim Garff for invaluable help in finalizing the text and for saving me from more than one serious blunder in translation. I thank my editors, Hannah Paul for initiating the project, and Natalie Baan for guiding it through the final stages. I owe special thanks to Eva Jaunzems for making and prompting innumerable improvements in word and style, and to Brit Berggreen, whose knowledge of Nordic language has been a constant aid throughout.

Preface

> If you went out to Nørrebro, there was a house where one was
> welcome on the first floor. . . . The master of the house was
> a quiet, slender man, whose appearance was always proper
> and dignified. He had served with honor in a high post in the
> government. His wife had, in her youth, been very captivat-
> ing and had become white-haired while still young. Now, she
> was pretty with snow-white curls and a fresh face. To me it
> was as though she bore an invisible mark, for as a very young
> woman she had been loved by a great man. She showed true
> kindness and was genuinely friendly. But you didn't get much
> from her acquaintance; she was far too restless in company
> for that. When the house held an evening reception, she re-
> mained too briefly with any group properly to grasp what was
> being discussed. After a minute, she hurried over to the other
> corner of the room, said a few words there, half listened to the
> topic of conversation, and went off to take care of the tea.[1]

So wrote the well-known Danish literary critic and historian
Georg Brandes, in a retrospective glance at some unforgettable meetings with
the Schlegels in their home at 8 Nørrebrogade. At the time, Brandes was only
twenty-five, but his eyes ever wide open, he had, on that evening too, captured
some characteristic traits of the host couple—seen from the outside. Johan
Frederik Schlegel is the discreet, subdued, and correct host, keeping an eye on
things, always calm. His wife, Regine Schlegel, is otherwise ambiguous; there
is something sphinxlike about her but also fascinating, and even tempting. It is
she who had been the object of Kierkegaard's love, and it is the weight of this
historic romance that Brandes can see in her face, and what moves him to describe her as invisibly marked.

The expression "invisibly marked" is well chosen, but in all its contradictori-
ness it also testifies that while expecting to meet Kierkegaard's delightful young
true love, Brandes was received instead by Schlegel's lawfully wedded wife, who
with her snow-white locks politely went round and served tea. No doubt, as

so many before and since, Brandes had hoped that if only Regine would open the door even just a tiny crack into her spectacular past, he might be nearer to grasping the red thread in the Kierkegaardian labyrinth. But Brandes was let down, because that woman, who holds invaluable knowledge of the man behind the genius, is herself no less of a mystery, an enigmatic and elusive figure who denies herself the calm needed to listen or converse. Without warning, she breaks off from the group because, obviously, she wants to be anywhere but here, anywhere but standing in a room with Brandes, face to face with all the burning questions on the tip of his tongue.

It is not known what the inquisitive Brandes brought home from the meetings in the house on the corner out at Nørrebro; nor does one know whether he ever confided to Regine his long-standing preoccupation with Kierkegaard's writings and his plan to write the most comprehensive biography of the man. One that would delve into his most private experiences with Regine, including the tense drama into which their mutual passion not only developed but, to properly focused eyes, seemed to continue long after the apparent end of their relationship.

Whereas young Brandes tried in vain to catch the attention of Mrs. Schlegel, a sequence of events brought me in touch with Regine in earnest. One summer evening in 1996 I found myself in the small Lolland town of Søllestad, where I gave a talk on Kierkegaard for high school pupils and interested locals. At the reception that followed, I was introduced to a well-preserved elderly couple, she with carefully arranged hair framing a pair of lively eyes, he unassuming and immaculate, with bowtie and a dark blue blazer, newly pressed, with shining brass buttons. The lady proved to be the grandchild of Regine's elder sister Cornelia, and without warning she made me an offer that took my breath away. If interested, I was more than welcome to read the over one hundred letters that Regine had exchanged with Cornelia during her stay in the Danish West Indies, where her husband had occupied the position of governor for a five-year period. If interested!

A week later the man with the bowtie and the blue blazer arrived in my office and placed on the desk an unostentatious cardboard box that had once held wares which, according to the dark green type on its lid, were to be stored at minus eighteen degrees, but which now contained the letters that Regine had written to her favorite sister in blistering tropical heat on the other side the globe. The box confirmed in the oddest way the suspicion that Kierkegaard places before his reader in the preface to *Either/Or*: that the inward is not always the outward, nor the outward always the inward.

In the carton there were a number of newer and larger envelopes labeled with the years from 1855 to 1878. Inside these were some small envelopes bearing, in an elegant hand, the address "Regina Schlegel, Sankt Croix." The postage stamps had all been clipped, presumably by some enthusiastic philatelist. In most cases the envelopes too were missing, which was why the letters were simply held together by a piece of rectangular paper of the kind used in the cheap college exercise books familiar to us from school days. The letters were written on the thinnest of thin paper, usually gray or light blue, and they bore clear signs of having been folded twice before fingers, tired from writing, had coaxed them into their envelopes.

Little by little, as I found moments on free evenings when I could occupy myself with the fragile documents that emerged one by one from the box, Regine and Cornelia began to be resurrected from their silent epistolary realm. Regine left no diary, so to find out who she was one had either to rely on Kierkegaard's account of her, or try putting together a portrait based on the remarks she made after her husband's passing in 1896, when, under the alias "Wife of Privy Councillor Schlegel," she spoke on a couple of occasions of her engagement to Kierkegaard. In those statements, however, she confined herself diplomatically to repeating the official version of the story, and between the very young *Miss* Regine Olsen and the ageing *Mrs. Privy Councillor* Schlegel there are roughly six decades. It was these, the unknown years, to which I had now been given access.

The world that Regine brought with her to my writing desk was in several ways alien, perhaps not least geographically. For me, the Danish West Indies were a *terra incognita*, a land upon which I looked with the adventurer's incorrigible curiosity, but very much also with that periodic dizziness induced by a sense of losing one's orientation, and of the ground giving way under one's feet.

The three small islands of St. Thomas, St. John (Danish St. Jan) and St. Croix, which up to 1917 were Danish possessions, enter into a colonial history as dramatic as it is problematic, where slave trading, piracy, corruption, poisoning, and deadly diseases such as yellow fever and cholera were the *dis*order of the day. That the islands are nevertheless called something as innocent as the "Virgin Islands" may seem ironic, but is due primarily to the untouched, paradisiacal state of their nature, something that also enchanted Regine when she bathed from a chalk-white beach in a small bay, or when on horseback she admired the island's eruptive luxuriance in the pleasant morning hours, before the tropical heat took over or distant signs of bad weather suddenly loomed over the azure sea.

Regine's meeting with West Indian reality was as much nature-shock as culture-shock, but more especially the latter, since she was to appear in the role of the colony's first lady and in reality ranked directly under Denmark's queen, and must face all of the material blessings and social curses then associated with such a status. No less complicated were the everyday challenges that awaited Governor

Preface

Johan Frederik Schlegel, who took over not only Peter von Scholten's imposing palace but also responsibility for the West Indian administration, which following von Scholten's 1848 proclamation of freedom for the slaves was more complicated than ever, marked as it was by an economic crisis and by reforms in the administration of justice, the funding of poor relief, and the educational system.

The principal persona in this story is as much the woman who for more than a generation was married to Johan Frederik Schlegel as it is the girl who was for one year engaged to Søren Kierkegaard. The book therefore deals, also, with the life that awaited Regine on the other side of Kierkegaard; it follows her doings, secret moods, and states of mind, and through these tells everyday stories from a vanished time. Often it is a scene from everyday life that best reveals a person's worldview, their character being most distinctly drawn from their relation to others. Regine's world is a relational world of that kind, filled with friends and acquaintances and loved ones, and the missed as well as the insufferable. But first and last, it is a world sustained by relationship to the family, to the sisters and brothers and their spouses, with whom Regine corresponds in the liveliest way. If this book were a novel, which it by no means is, one could perhaps consider calling it straightforwardly a family novel.

When faced with such rich material, one must of course be selective, something I am certain Regine herself would have applauded. Not everything in a letter can be equally interesting, and I have let lie what to my eyes is less relevant. To the best of my ability I have tried to *represent* Regine and have made every effort accordingly to find and present her from as many sides as possible, so that she does not become yet again a decorative figure in porcelain, lacking an interior, but is shown instead as the woman of flesh and blood, and opinions and desires, that she really was. I am fully aware that it is I myself who function in several of the these connections as stage manager, and I have on occasion introduced stage props that allow Regine to act and be understood against a meaningful background; but I have not been a prompter whispering alternative lines to her. In other words, I have never gone beyond the facts, let alone against them, but have respected the material at hand as being what it is, speaking when it spoke, but also remaining silent when it did not speak.

"God has given me the strength to live as a riddle," remarks Kierkegaard in his journal from 1848, and allows in these words that riddles are not there just to be solved but are in certain cases to remain riddles and to derive their "strength" precisely from their enduring perplexity. The main female character of this book ostensibly comes to no final and definitive understanding of the "power" that issued from that love in her youth, but she is nonetheless drawn more and more in its direction. And it is the nature and scope of this fascination rather than the riddle's solution that preoccupies me; not the definitive diagnosis, but rather the symptoms of a long-lasting amorous fever by which the relationship was marked.

It is with as much relief as sorrow that I bring the following work to a close. "Nulla dies sine linea," Kierkegaard writes somewhere: no day without a line. I have been able to say for some time: "Nulla dies sine Regina," no day without Regine. My wife Synne has patiently come to terms with my years-long passion and has winked at my perpetually disturbed nights. She has listened to my many monologues, read several versions of the manuscript, and contributed to many improvements and no fewer cuts. For this perseverance I owe her my deepest thanks. For any mistakes and shortcomings still lurking in the text, I of course take full responsibility.

Kierkegaard's Muse

TUNING IN

ON THE THIRD TUESDAY IN APRIL 1851, SØREN KIERKEGAARD MOVES OUTSIDE Copenhagen's old ramparts and establishes himself on the first floor in a newly built villa toward the end of Sortedammsøen (Sortedam Lake). His residence is in an almost country setting, surrounded by pleasant private gardens and large commercial market gardens that are spacious and pleasant. From his dayrooms he can follow the comings and goings along the path beside Sortedam Lake, one of the three narrow lakes which once were part of the city's fortifications facing the land, but which already in Kierkegaard's time had become mainly decorative. The two other lakes, Peblingesøen and St. Jørgens Sø, from which generations of citizens have drawn their drinking water, served the same peaceful purpose.

On his regular excursions into and out of Copenhagen Kierkegaard often happens to encounter his former fiancée Regine. Since the 12th of October 1841, when, with much drama and in full view of the public eye, their engagement was broken off, he had exchanged not a single word with her. The breakup almost cost both of them their lives, but they withstood the horrors; each found a new foothold and, much the richer in experience, was able to start over again: Kierkegaard became author of one of history's most profuse, remarkable, and unbridled bodies of writing, while on the 28th of August 1843, Regine became engaged to departmental head Johan Frederik Schlegel, known as Fritz, whom she married on the 3rd of November 1847, in the Church of Our Savior at Christianshavn.

This might well have meant that Regine's relationship to her former fiancé was a closed chapter. But that is just what it was not. These two people, Søren and Regine, proved enigmatically bound to each other and therefore they had to find pretexts and opportunities to meet as often as possible, preferably so as to make it look as if they were meeting quite by chance. Their encounters by the lakes are always wordless but, maybe for that very reason, exceptionally intense and finely chiseled in an erotic register that the two of them play through in the electric moments at their disposal as they pass by each other. A kind of innocent infidelity unfolds according to strict rules that border at times on ritual. Kierkegaard portrays the meetings with a degree of detail that comes close to being painful; he fixes the time, the distance, the variations of route, wind direction, the weather in general. It is as if he would ensure that the meetings be

1. "Uncle Søren has also moved half-out into the open country," Carl Lund could inform Peter Christian Kierkegaard in a letter dated May the 20th 1851. "He has taken up residence here in a large new place on the second floor with access to, and a view over, a lovely garden and the lake." The photograph has preserved for posterity the stately villa on a summer day, when some of its occupants have settled in the garden that stretched to the east as far as the eye could see from the garden-room terrace. That is not, however, Kierkegaard who is looking out from the open second-floor window under one of the awnings, but it was in this apartment with its six rooms that he lived from April 1851 until October 1852. The villa was torn down in 1897 to give way to the twin buildings with corner towers and copper-sheathed spires that now form the entrance to Willemoesgade.

each time repeated so that the two silent figures should, in all eternity, walk slowly and soundlessly toward each other on the same narrow lane along the lake—and then disappear, each in their own direction, without looking back.

The silence helps to sustain the relationship and renew its aura. It is as if, by not saying anything, Regine lets their youthful love remain untouched by time; the wordlessness acts as a shield against everyday badgering, the endless trifles, all those accounts we humans constantly keep with one another, everything that so often drains the passion, the devotion, and the pride from a marriage. Regine comes to meet her Søren as the one she is, but perhaps even more so as the one she was, the only one he really loved. If the fact that she is married to another could be bracketed just for a careless moment, then, in that meeting's very fragile seconds, everything is in a way altogether unchanged.

Tuning In

It is only when Regine is out of Kierkegaard's sight that she reverts to being Mrs. Schlegel.

That the two formerly betrothed meet each other on a path that is rather pointedly called Marriage Path is an irony that Kierkegaard should be the first to remark and interpret as a moral reminder; but the thoughts of the Magister, whose dissertation was on that very topic, have evidently been quite elsewhere. And when looking through his journals from these years, one may with some amazement substantiate just *how* frequent these meetings with Regine have been. For instance, in an entry from January 1850, Kierkegaard writes that he and Regine have for over a month "seen each other almost every blessed day, or at least twice every other day."[1] Kierkegaard's entries from this time have the character of plain and at times almost raw reporting, something that scotches the suspicion of fictionalizing that can inescapably intrude in other contexts. "During the latter part of 1851 she encountered me every day," Kierkegaard reports in May 1852. "It was during the period when I would walk home by way of Langelinie at ten o'clock in the morning. The timing was exact and the place merely shifted farther and farther up the road to the limekiln. She came walking as if from the limekiln. . . . That was how it went, day after day."[2] One cannot help noting the altogether non-accidental nature of these meetings, the punctuality and precision, even the synchronizing, with the point of encounter shifting as if to divert attention away from it—as much for the bashful lovers themselves as for outsiders.

Little by little, Kierkegaard has become "so frightfully well known" that these meetings with a "lady," who "walks that route alone" out of town in the early morning hours, might be read as rather striking and cause gossip. He has noticed that another couple—also meeting regularly and who "knew us both"— have begun to pay just a little too much attention. What departmental head Schlegel might think if he finds out that his lawfully wedded wife is up and dressed and out walking so early seems to bother Kierkegaard less; but he has noticed, all the same, that these rendezvous have long since lost their innocence and cannot with the least probability be put down to the open account of chance: "So I had to make a change," he writes in his journal. The first day in the New Year he chooses another route, almost as a New Year's resolution.

> This resolution was kept. On January 1, 1852, my route was changed; I went home by way of Nørreport.
>
> Some time passed in this fashion, and we did not see each other. One morning she encountered me on the path by the lake, where I was now in the habit of walking. The next day I also took this path, which was my usual one. She was not there. As a precaution, however, I

2. Østerbro had, at the time, an almost rural character and, with its nursery and kitchen gardens, formed a peaceful contrast to the hectic bustle inside the ramparts. Above the dense treetops can be seen the windmill at Kastellet, and at the point where Østerbrogade turns sharply to the left one finds the gateway into Holmen's churchyard. Reflected in Sortedam Lake's calm water, the trees on the right border the path on which Søren and Regine frequently met one another at a certain period.

nonetheless changed my future route and went down Farimags-Veien, and finally I varied my homeward route.

Varying the route home seems to have worked for while—

But what happened? Some time had passed. Then she meets me one morning at 8 o'clock on the avenue outside Østerport, the route I walk to Copenhagen every morning.

The next day she was not there, however. I continued walking to town by this same route, which I cannot very well alter. So she met me here quite often, sometimes also on the ramparts, the path I take to town. Perhaps it was coincidence, perhaps. I could not understand what she was doing on that route at that hour there, but as I notice everything, I noticed that she came that way especially if there was an east wind. So indeed, it could be because she could not bear the east wind on Langelinie. But—she did also come when there was a west wind.

Regine remains a riddle, she comes walking like a goddess out of nothing, turns up in places it seems by chance—though hardly so, fails to show up, appears once again and chooses wind directions that bring confusion to the philosopher's conclusions.

On his birthday Kierkegaard usually travels to North Zealand for the day, spending the night at a guesthouse there before returning to the city. But when, on May the 5th 1852, he turned thirty-nine, he felt slightly ill and stayed at home.

> Then came my birthday. As a rule, I am always away on my birthday, but I was not feeling quite well. So I stayed at home; as usual, I walked into town to talk with the doctor because I had considered celebrating my birthday with something new, something I had never tasted before, castor oil. Right outside my door, on the sidewalk in front of the avenue, she meets me. As so often happens of late, I cannot keep from smiling when I see her—ah, how much she has come to mean to me!—she smiled in return and nodded. I took a step past her, then raised my hat and walked on.

Reading these lines can also cause a smile; one can imagine it, the birthday genius with the sluggish stomach, smiling at his beloved muse who returns the smile. A step forward, the hat doffed, then off and away.

* * *

The reason why these meetings were so poignant is not only the deep, unresolved feelings that bind these two persons together in spite of time, speech, and morals. It is due also to Regine being indissolubly linked to Kierkegaard's authorship, for which she became in his eyes the external, historical occasion. Her absolutely special status in the authorship appears already in the preface to the *Two Edifying Discourses* of 1843. Here Kierkegaard envisages how this little book will wander thoughtfully out into the world and perhaps have the good luck suddenly to meet "that single individual, who with joy and gratitude I call *my* reader, that single individual it is seeking, to whom, so to speak, it stretches out its arms, that single individual who is favorably enough disposed to allow themself to be found."[3] As the authorship developed, this appeal to the single individual acquired an almost programmatic character; "that single individual" became Kierkegaard's *trademark*. Yet, originally, "that single individual" was Regine; it was to her the edifying discourse stretched out its arms. "The preface to the *Two Edifying Discourses* was intended for her," admits Kierkegaard much later in his journal, and he adds that there "are faint hints in the book itself" regarding Regine.[4] What hints, and where they are to be found is not known, but that Regine has in fact read the book is evident from a conversation Kierkegaard had with Professor F. C. Sibbern, who has it from Regine herself. As a text for the second of these edifying discourses Kierkegaard had used James, chapter 1, verses 17–22, which was among his favorite New Testament passages. The title of the discourse is from verse 17 and reads: "All good things and all perfect gifts come from above." Without entering further into it, Kierkegaard later explains that "the first religious impression she has of me"[5] is connected with these very words, which have consequently a quite special significance for the two formerly betrothed.

On Sunday the 9th of May 1852—that is, just four days after Regine returned the birthday celebrant's smile, something happens that against all this background is totally bizarre: Kierkegaard is at morning service in Christianborg's Royal Chapel, where the king's chaplain, Just Paulli, preaches. Regine is also there and sitting quite near where Kierkegaard is standing. According to the *Ordained Altar-Book* for Denmark, the gospel for this Sunday is a text from the Gospel of St. John, but instead Paulli has chosen to preach on the text from the epistle with precisely the words that meant so much to Kierkegaard and Regine. Nor is Paulli far into the epistle's text before Regine turns and, "concealed by the person next to her," looks in the direction of Kierkegaard, who notes that she does so "very fervently," but otherwise quite consciously refrains from returning her glance. "I looked straight ahead, at nothing in particular," he explains, although this show of indifference required considerable effort:

> I confess that I, too, was somewhat shaken. Paulli finished reading the text aloud. She sank rather than sat down, so that actually I was a bit worried, as I was once before, for her emotion is so vehement.

It was to be even more shattering. For as Paulli introduces his sermon, he says to the congregation that the words of the text are "implanted in our hearts"; yes, he continues, if these words "should be torn from your heart, would not life lose all its worth for you?" Precisely because the words from James's epistle have become a symbolic sealing of the unbreakable tie between Søren and Regine, Paulli's construal of the text sounds like a direct commentary on their loving relationship, which is rooted so deeply within their hearts that life without it would have no meaning.

On looking back at these happenings it seems to Kierkegaard "inexplicable" that Paulli should have come up with that introduction to his sermon. It occurs to him that it may have been "meant" for Regine, but he feels convinced that the whole occasion had, in any case, made an enormous impression on her: "It must have been overwhelming for her. I have never exchanged a word with her, have gone my way, not hers—but here it was as though a higher power said to her what I have been unable to say."

Tuning In

It was almost like an improvised wedding ceremony, delightfully terrifying. Kierkegaard felt the very earth burning beneath him: "It was as if I were standing on glowing coals."

When "several mornings later" he again encountered Regine somewhere in the town, the tense, the spiritual eroticism that united them in the church seemed far less or as though altogether gone, so that even if Kierkegaard sensed that Regine was expecting a greeting, he refrained from giving one. It was clear to him that, in spite of all corporeal chastity, his relationship to another man's wife does in fact overstep the bounds of all decency and can only continue if Schlegel declares his acquiescence; in short, Schlegel must become the relationship's "middle term":

> I am willing to do everything, but if anything is to be done, I must have her husband in the middle. Either—Or! If I am to involve myself with her, then it must be on the grandest scale, then I want it to be known to everyone, to have her transformed into a triumphant figure who will get the most complete restitution for the stigma of my having broken with her.

Kierkegaard should have known himself well enough to realize how difficult it would be to turn these categorical remarks into reality. Besides, as will appear, he had some years earlier, in a written request to Schlegel, made an attempt to come together with Regine under more orderly circumstances. Schlegel, however, proved altogether disinclined to accede to the request, which he interpreted as an out-of-line interference in his married life, and he let Kierkegaard understand this in a letter that was in effect one big and unambiguous "no."

Although hopes of gaining Schlegel's approval of the connection were dashed, Søren and Regine continued to meet, at times daily, sometimes less often. That is how altogether simple and yet terribly complicated it had become. Regine had actually become "that single individual," who, as it goes in that preface to the edifying discourses, has shown herself to be "favorably enough disposed to allow [her]self to be found," whether in one of Copenhagen's churches or out behind the ramparts, or at one or another of those sites lovers are always so anxious to call altogether "fortuitous," precisely because that is what they are not.

Friday the 10th of September 1852 was to be a quite special day, marked by the erotic rituals of silence that had evolved between them:

> So today it is twelve years since I became engaged.
> Naturally "she" didn't fail to be on the spot and meet me; and although in the summer I take my walk earlier than usual . . . she met me both today and yesterday morning on the avenues by Østerport.

When they had met the day before and were about to exchange glances, "she suddenly glanced away," for Regine had seen a horseman approaching behind Kierkegaard, who proved to have come to inform him that his brother-in law further along the path wanted to speak with him. Fortunately the meeting on that twelfth anniversary was much more successful, even if it, too, was a trifle unresolved:

> So today she looked at me; but she didn't nod a greeting, nor speak to me. Ah, perhaps she had expected I would do so. My God, how much I'd like to do that and everything for her. But I don't dare take on the responsibility; she must insist on it herself.
>
> However, I had so much wanted it this year; and it is trying to be on the point of doing something year after year.[6]

A good month later, on the third Tuesday in October 1852, Kierkegaard moves from his villa apartment at Østerbro back to the city, where he rents a smaller apartment from Catharine Christiane Borries, a widow, at 5–6 Klædeboderne (now 38 Skindergade and 5 Dyrkøb), and in doing so acquires as his new imposing neighbor the Church of Our Lady. The move means changes in his daily routes and rhythms, but it is not long before Regine readjusts. Usually they meet on Christmas day in the Church of Our Lady, where Bishop Mynster preaches at Evensong. The same happens this year but with a change in routine because, on Kierkegaard's entering the church, Regine is standing as if waiting for him—or as if expecting someone else? At that moment Kierkegaard is quite unable to size up the situation and has to report it later in detail in his journal.

> She didn't come walking, she was standing, obviously waiting for someone whoever that was. There was no one else there. I looked at her. She then went off toward the side door through which I was about to pass. There was something odd about that meeting, so personal. As she passed by me and turned into the door, I made a movement with my body that might have been simply to make room but also a half greeting. She turned quickly and made a movement. [in the margin:] But now she had no more opportunity had she wanted to speak, for I was already standing in the church. I looked for my usual place; but it didn't escape me that, although she sat a long way off, she kept searching me with her eyes.[7]

These lines bear witness to a remarkable pantomime. The detailed choreography of the bodies' interactions, rendered in a kind of slow motion; the anxiety in case a single step be given a wrong interpretation; the awkwardness and ineptness of Kierkegaard's gestures, the repressed spontaneity—all of this imparts a painful realism to the performance in the church's porch. But it also exposes

3. With a delicate blend of light and shade over her open face, and with a lace collar held together with a sturdy brooch, Regine gazes dreamily into the photographer's lens. The year, not given, is probably 1855, and its occasion the approaching West Indian exile. The woman in the picture is the one who rushed out on the very day of departure to look for Kierkegaard somewhere in Copenhagen and, in the midst of the throng of people, blessed him after fourteen years of silence.

the fearful fascination that Regine radiates: impregnable yet so intimate, ethereal yet so impassioned, officially another's yet really his.

On Saturday the 17th of March 1855, fourteen years of silence are broken. Departmental Chief Johan Frederik Schlegel has been appointed governor of the Danish West Indies for a five-year term. On the very day of their departure Regine in all haste leaves her apartment in Nybrogade and ventures out into town in the hope of meeting her old love. And, as though the final gesture of a generous Providence toward these two persons whose life histories are so uncontrollably linked, it is not long before her eyes fasten on the familiar figure with the broad-brimmed hat. As she passes him by, she says under her breath: "God bless you—may all go well with you!"[8]

For just an instant that Saturday meeting in a random Copenhagen street turned everything upside down. Regine's blessing succeeded in rendering speechless a man never otherwise at a loss for the right words and made him stand still in a more or less symbolic posture, hat in hand. Kierkegaard was here exposed to a situation of the kind one might describe with antiquated words like "dispensation" and "visited upon," words with which one fumbles to articulate the sense that the most potent things in life always come from the other, they are not at one's own beck and call or in one's own power to effect. What went through the master-thinker theologian's mind in that moment of blessing, no one knows. Perhaps, just for once, there was no thought in his mind at all, simply acceptance of this blessing from the woman in his life.

Nor does one know what went on in Regine's mind, though she was no doubt anxious to get back quickly to the empty apartment in Nybrogade and to try to appear as unconcerned as possible.

A few hours later she began to put the city behind her.

PART 1

1855

THE PAINFUL DEPARTURE

In a letter of the 10th of July 1855, Regine summarizes her journey to St. Croix:

> You have read between the lines how sad my journey was, for what depressed me most was the complete spiritual apathy, not to say death, that ruled in my heart, yes such glorious things, but I had lost all susceptibility, it was as if on the way to my grave I could already no longer see the light of day.

The letter's recipient was Cornelia, Regine's favorite sister and confidante, who clearly was able to read between the lines. For that is where the most important things are written, in a kind of invisible ink. Regine therefore feels no need to supply the details, but one understands that the long journey to the tropical destination has been taxing, not least psychologically, an experience to be described with metaphors from the silent realm of the dead.

Such an indirect form of communication was called for all the more in the present case, since Regine was not addressing herself to Cornelia alone. It was quite normal at the time for letters to be circulated between members of the family, then to friends and acquaintances wanting to keep abreast of the letter writer's latest news. Cornelia was not necessarily, in other words, the letter's only reader; nor indeed the first, for when Regine had written a letter it sometimes happened that Fritz wanted to add his personal greeting and, if in the mood, he could therefore acquaint himself with the letter's contents—it needed only a quick glance. To talk of censorship would be an exaggeration, but it goes without saying that the knowledge that Fritz might read her letters inevitably set limits to confidentiality and discouraged Regine from wholly opening her heart. Fritz might likewise read one of Cornelia's letters aloud for Regine, a practice that also discouraged the more intimate confidences. It was as if the fourth wall that might guarantee a private space within her letters always adjoined a public reading room, or as if it just wasn't there. And then there was the uncertainty about the letter's further fate, for the result could prove disastrous were it to fall into the wrong hands.

How Regine managed to come away from Copenhagen on that ice-cold Saturday in March 1855, we don't in fact know. But from the letter that she began a day later in Korsør, it seems that she and her fellow travellers covered the first part of the journey by train to Roskilde.

The further stretch of railway from Roskilde to Korsør was not inaugurated until the 26th of April 1856, so prior to that date anyone going further west had to continue by stagecoach—or "diligence" as the vehicle was called after the French prototype. With its broad, yellow body, its looking-glass window panes and imposing lamps, the diligence was both exclusive and commanding in its outward appearance; but the inside was cramped and free movement extremely limited, not least if one had not reserved an upholstered seat with leather arm-rests in one of the better sections. The foremost seats on the right side in the driving direction were reckoned the most attractive, but opinions on this were divided and therefore much discussed,[1] as we can gather from the amusing judgment that Kierkegaard presents in the pen of one of his pseudonymous authors, Constantin Constantius, in *Repetition* (1843):

> There is a difference of opinion among the learned as to which seat in a stagecoach is the most comfortable. My *Ansicht* [Ger. viewpoint] is the following: they are all equally terrible. The previous time, I had one of the outer seats toward the front of the vehicle (this is considered by many to be a great coup) and was for thirty-six hours, together with those near me, so violently tossed about that when I came to Hamburg not only had I nearly lost my mind, but also my legs. The six of us who sat in this vehicle were worked together for these thirty-six hours so that we became one body, in such a way that I got the impression of what happened to the Molbos [inhabitants of the peninsula of Mols on Jutland, the butt of many Danish jokes] who, after having sat together for a long time, could no longer recognize which legs were their own.[2]

Nor was Hans Christian Andersen, who spent ten of his seventy years traveling outside Denmark's borders, any great lover of the stagecoaches, which he called "torture chambers" and described as "large, heavy omnibuses with an entrance only on one side, so when it overturned on that side one couldn't escape, and one always overturned."[3]

However, much more personal reasons were to blame for the nature of Regine's journey over Zealand, which she later summarized in the sentence: "my heart was near breaking-point." It had been sad as well as disturbingly final to take leave of her seventy-seven-year-old mother Regine Frederikke, now six years a widow, infirm, and not altogether herself after the loss of her husband Terkild, who had been chief of the Main- and Pass-Book Office under the Department of Finance, and for whom Kierkegaard harbored strong feelings of respect.

And it had been difficult saying goodbye to Maria, the eldest of Regine's sisters, now forty-five and still a spinster. She had for several years been housekeeper for the Soldenfeldt brothers, Ferdinand Vilhelm and Joseph Carl, who had lived together for most of their lives and also belonged to Regine's circle of acquaintances. Maria had a small house just to the north in Tårbæk, where the family and friends often met in the summer; Regine loved it, and would miss it terribly in her exile.

Worst of all, indeed just about impossible, had been taking leave of Cornelia, Regine's closest not only in age but also in temperament. She was thirty-seven, five years older than Regine, and had been married to Emil Winning since the 6th of November 1849, when they had joined hands in the Garrison Church and promised to live together in good times and bad, for better or for worse— and since then had been splendidly occupied with multiplying. By the close of 1852, Laura, Frederikke Mathilde, and Olivia had come into the world, followed, after a brief pause in production, by Paul Thorkild, who sadly proved to be of a more delicate nature and died at five days old. The best remedy for such sorrow is love, as Emil knew, for when Cornelia now kissed Regine farewell she was once more pregnant, again with a daughter, Johanne Marie, who saw the light of day on the 25th of September 1855.

Cornelia was one of those rare and radiant female figures, animated, with great presence of mind, endowed with a noble heart, graced with sensitivity, and accordingly quite simply lovable, *amabile*. At the time when everyone condemned Kierkegaard's break with Regine, she had said what several others no doubt thought in their hearts: "I do not understand Magister Kierkegaard, but I nonetheless believe that he is a good person!" It is said that when this reached Kierkegaard's ear, he was "touched, indeed impressed."[4] That both the respect and the sympathy were reciprocated on Kierkegaard's part is evident from an 1844 entry in his journal, where he cites Cornelia as the living model of a female figure that he anticipates one day portraying:

> Under the title "Private Studies," and to be kept as delicate as possible, I would like to depict a female character who was great by virtue of her lovably modest and bashful resignation (e.g., a somewhat idealized Cornelia Olsen, the most excellent female character I have known and the only one who has compelled my admiration).[5]

As it happens, Kierkegaard never got around to depicting a character so delightfully modest and bashful; but with just a single change of consonant Cornelia turns up in "The Seducer's Diary" as Cordelia, one of the most intense, sensuous and seductive female characters not only in Kierkegaard's portrait gallery, but perhaps in Denmark's Golden Age literature altogether. The fact that literature's Cordelia might have seized an opportunity to roam further as reality's Cornelia can be amusingly substantiated in one of Kierkegaard's entries from January 1851.

There, describing his regular meetings with Regine on the ramparts, he commits in this connection a divine slip of the pen: "She comes then either accompanied by Cordelia or alone, and then she always goes back the same way, alone; consequently, she encounters me both times. . . . This is certainly not entirely accidental."[6] Hardly, but scarcely less accidental is the psychologically significant slip of the pen: presumably Cornelia and Cordelia were equally delightful.

Cornelia lived with Emil and their three girls at 28 Vestergade, which runs past Gammeltorv, where the Schlegel family lived at number five, in a small, classic apartment building which had been ready for occupation in 1801. The landlord at that time had been a master tailor, Johan Jacob Schlegel, whose son, Wilhelm August, lived on the first floor of the property, which he later took over and administered until his death in 1871. Wilhelm August, who rose to the title of Chamber Councillor, was married to Dorothea Maria, a woman of similar age, who in 1815 gave birth to a girl, Emma, and in 1817 to a boy, Johan Frederik (Fritz), who in turn was followed in 1818 by Clara and she, in 1830, by the late-born Augusta.

Little is known of Fritz's childhood and youth. After matriculating as a student in 1833 at the Metropolitan School, which lies on the corner by Frue Plads, he began to study law and graduated in 1838. It was during these years that he acted as tutor in the Olsen home and developed warm feelings for the family's youngest daughter. She then suddenly took it into her head to become engaged to Kierkegaard, which landed Fritz in a state of combined astonishment and embarrassment.

"YOU MY HEART'S SOVEREIGN MISTRESS"

Some twenty lines into his notebook, Kierkegaard tells how it all began:

> On Septbr 8 I left home with the firm intention of deciding the whole matter. We met on the street just outside their house. She said that there was no one at home. I was foolhardy enough to understand these words as just the invitation I needed. I went in with her. There we stood, the two us, alone, in the parlor. She was a little uneasy. I asked her to play a little for me [on the piano] as she usu. did. She did so, but it didn't help me. Then I suddenly took the music book, closed it, not without a certain vehemence, threw it off the piano and said: Oh, what do I care about music? It's you I am searching for, you I've been seeking for two years. She remained silent.

Miss Olsen remained silent—yes, "essentially silent" as he goes on to say—as one might easily understand, and Kierkegaard himself has nothing more to tell her.

After throwing away the music book with the aforementioned vehemence, he hastily leaves the apartment and, "frightfully anxious," goes to call on Regine's father, Minister of State Olsen, who is evidently just as dumbfounded as his daughter over all this commotion. Kierkegaard presents his case to him. That leads to further silence: "The father said neither Yes nor No, but was nonetheless quite willing, as I readily understood. I asked if we could speak together; I was granted this for Saturday the 10th of Septemb. afternoon. I said not one single word to charm her—she said, yes."[7]

The scene in the apartment that Tuesday afternoon by the piano in itself shows how little the two really knew each other. And even though ritual in connection with an engagement differed a great deal then from what is customary today, the tremulous anxiety with which Kierkegaard broke in on the minister was absolutely in a class of its own.

Kierkegaard had presumably first met the girl who was now his fiancée in May 1837, at Frederiksberg where he was visiting his theologian friend Peter Rørdam, who lived with his mother Cathrine Georgia. She was the widow of Dean Thomas Schatt Rørdam and, in addition to the son, had three pretty daughters of marriageable age, Elisabeth, Emma, and Bolette. So it wasn't at all a bad place for a young man to include in his itinerary. On that day in May, Elisabeth, Emma, and Bolette had in addition a visit from their fifteen-year-old friend Regine, who later recalled how this Kierkegaard had presented himself without warning and made a "very strong impression" on her. He "spoke unceasingly," indeed his speech "practically poured forth and was extremely captivating."[8] The visit to the Rørdams also left its impression on Kierkegaard, who confides to his journal:

> Today too (8 May) I was trying to forget myself, though not with any noisy to-do—that substitute doesn't help, but by going out to Rørdam's to talk with Bolette, and by trying (if possible) to make that devil-wit stay at home, that angel who with blazing sword, as I deserve, interposes himself between me and every innocent girlish heart—when you caught up with me, O God, I thank you for not letting me instantly lose my mind—never have I been more afraid of that; so be thanked for once more bending your ear to me.[9]

The mood is tense and the tone dramatic, but it is not quite clear what really happened. Later Kierkegaard crossed out the words "Rørdam's to talk with Bolette," a fact that the editor, H. P. Barfod, omitted to mention in his 1869 edition. So that when Regine later read the entry, she assumed that it referred to the occasion on which Kierkegaard had been first captivated by her. In this she was evidently mistaken. The aim of Kierkegaard's journey on foot to Frederiksberg

4. This was approximately the view that met Poul Martin Møller, to whom Kierkegaard dedicated his main psychological work, *The Concept of Anxiety*, when looking out on Nytorv and Gammeltorv (New Market and Old Market). With the towers of Saint Peter's and the Church of Our Lady in the background, the market place is ringed by classic

middle-class houses, whose owners and tenants have done well and are not ashamed to show it. At the far left, the property of hosier Kierkegaard's neighbor can be seen. The narrow house at the far end with the two attics belonged to W. A. Schlegel, whose son Johan Frederik was married to Regine.

that day was to see twenty-two-year-old Bolette, "a very beautiful and sensible girl"—or so her brother Peter called her in a letter of 23rd February 1836.[10] Age-wise, Bolette would have been a far more suitable match than Regine, who had only just had her confirmation. Kierkegaard much later acknowledged that he and Bolette had made in fact an "impression" on each other, and that he therefore felt a certain "responsibility" toward her—"even if in all innocence and purely intellectually."[11] It appears from an entry dated May 1837 that his fascination for the Frederiksberg young lady, and the conflicts bound up with this, proved quite persistent:

> Today, again, the same performance—Still, I managed to get out to R[ørdams]—my God, why should this tendency awaken just now—O, how alone I feel!—O, damn that arrogance of being content to stand on my own—everyone will now despise me—O, but you, my God, do not let go of me—let me live and make myself better—[12]

Nor was this entry one that Kierkegaard wanted to come to the knowledge of posterity, and he therefore later tried to make it illegible with repeated crossings out. The next time the name Rørdam appears in the journal is Sunday the 9th of July 1837, when on the way back to town he stopped off in the Frederiksberg Gardens and noted with an almost prophetic self-understanding:

> I stand like a *solitary* spruce, egoistically self-enclosed and pointing toward what is higher, casting no shadow, and only the wood dove builds its nest in my branches. . . . Sunday (9 July 37) in Frederiksberg Gardens after calling at the Rørdam place.[13]

With the passing of old hosier Kierkegaard on August the 8th 1838, the son, Søren, not only becomes a wealthy man, he also feels duty-bound to complete his theological studies. He appeals in his journal to the image of the Guadalquivir river, whose name no doubt only natives can pronounce but with which he loves to compare himself: "I shall now for a season, for some miles in time, plunge underground like the Guadalquivir,—to be sure, I shall come up again!"[14] Kierkegaard vanishes from the earth's surface and with an almost supernatural energy assimilates the theological curriculum. The isolation is near to driving him mad, but that he manages to come through it is due to a young girl's having become entwined in his thoughts. From February the 2nd 1839 we have the celebration, translated now into numberless languages, of the woman so prosaically surnamed Olsen, but whose first name was by contrast thankfully so poetic.

> You, Sovereign mistress of my heart [Regina], hidden in the deepest privacy of my breast, in my most brimming thoughts on life, there,

where it is just as far to heaven as to hell—unknown divinity! Oh, can I really believe the poets' tales that when one sees the beloved for the first time one believes one has seen her long before; that all love, like all knowledge, is recollection; that love too has its prophecies, its types, its myths, its Old Testament in the single individual. Everywhere, in every girl's face, I see a trace of your beauty, but it seems to me that I would have to have all girls in order to extract *your* beauty from all of theirs; that I'd have to circumnavigate the earth to find that continent which I lack, and that the deepest secrecy of my entire 'I' nevertheless points to it as its pole;—and in the next moment you are so near to me, so present, so powerfully making my spirit whole, that I am transfigured in my own eyes and feel that here is a good place to be. . . . You blind god of love! You who see in secret, will you tell me openly? Shall I find what I am seeking here in this world, shall I experience the *conclusion* of all my life's eccentric premises, shall I *enclose* you in my arms—or

Does the order say: onward?

Have you gone ahead, you my *longing*; do you summon me, transfigured, from another world? Oh, I would cast everything aside to become light enough to follow you.[15]

There is a breathless joy in these lines, but also a sorrowful mood of farewell, which appears in such finely wrought language to suggest that the order is indeed to march on, so that Regine will never be other or more than the ephemeral stuff of which immortal poetry is made. It is significant, too, for the shifting that has already taken place between the living girl and the poetically inspired figure, that the name Regine was not in the entry from the start but inserted later and in the Latinized form "Regina."

After this ode to the unknown deity, Kierkegaard's journal entries dart once more in all possible directions. On the same day, February the 2nd 1839, he composes two more texts, but neither has anything to do with Regine. On July the 3rd 1840, Kierkegaard graduated in theology as *laudabilis* (praiseworthy) and traveled in the middle of the same month to Jutland, whence he returned on August the 8th. Exactly a month later, the twenty-seven-year-old genius made his life's happiest mistake.

What happened in the period leading up to September the 8th 1840, when, on the way home from a piano lesson, Miss Olsen was overtaken by Kierkegaard who went up and proposed to her, remains for the most part buried in uncertainty. Notebook 15 renders the period in the following, cryptic sentences:

5. In this sketch of his half-cousin Søren, Niels Christian Kierkegaard has followed the aesthetic ideals of late romanticism rather than the naturalistic call of verisimilitude. The drawing was made around 1840 and thus comes from the same time as Bærentzen's captivating oil painting of Regine, with which it is often shown side by side.

Even before my father died I had decided upon her. He died. I studied for the examinations. During that entire period I permitted her existence to entwine itself with mine. . . . In the summer of 40 I took the examination for the theol. degree. Then, without further ado, I called at the house. I traveled to Jutland and perhaps even then had begun a bit of angling for her. (E.g., by lending them books during my absence, and

6. When the painter and lithographer Emil Bærentzen, a neighbor of the Olsen family in Børsgade, portrayed the eighteen-year-old Regine in 1840, he could not know that his small oil painting would bring him world fame. Regine—or "Regina" as she was baptized and signed her letters—became engaged that same year to Kierkegaard, who brought her into the wide world of history, both of literature and of philosophy.

> by inducing them to read a particular passage in a particular book). . . . I returned in Aug. Strictly speaking, the period from 9 Aug into September could be called the period during which I approached her.[16]

It is part of the story that while Kierkegaard was harboring strong feelings for Bolette Rørdam, Miss Olsen was taken up with her tutor, the correct and handsome

Johan Frederik Schlegel, who was decidedly not blind to the charms of his pro-tégé either. Several thought an engagement was just around the corner, but then there was this Kierkegaard. "You could have talked about Fritz Schlegel until Doomsday—it would not have helped at all, because I *wanted* you,"[17] Kierke-gaard assured Regine when she plucked up courage to tell him about Schlegel. Kierkegaard himself renders his reaction to the news of another with these words: ". . . when she spoke of a relationship to Schlegel I said, 'So let that rela-tionship be a parenthesis, for I, however, have prior rights.' "[18]

Fritz nevertheless took it like a man and engrossed himself in his work. After five years as an intern apprentice in the Office of Customs and Commerce, he was in 1847 appointed head clerk. Contact with Regine was resumed, and on November the 3rd 1847, they married in the Church of Our Savior at Chris-tianshavn. The following year Fritz was promoted to head of the Colonial Of-fice; in 1852, he was made Councillor of State, like his father; everything looked as if all would go well for him, but at the end of November that same year his mother died, and in 1854 it was decided that from 1855 he should occupy the post of Governor of the Danish West Indian Islands.

THE VIRGIN ISLANDS

Fritz was on his way now, to his new posting. He sat in one of those "torture chambers" with Regine by his side and clattered slowly and laboriously toward the goal, three small islands over 4,000 miles away. Since he and Regine were accustomed to a certain standard, they had brought with them their young maid, Josephine Schanshoff, who had served them for several years and was the same age as Regine. Seven-year-old Mathilde Olsen, called Thilly (some-times spelled Tilly) was also with them. She was the daughter of Regine's eldest brother, Oluf Christian Olsen, who for the last seven years had occupied the post of Controller of Customs on St. Croix.

Far out lie St. Thomas, St. John, and St. Croix. They are called the Virgin Islands and are part of the Lesser Antilles, that chain of islands separating the Atlantic Ocean from the Caribbean. The Greater Antilles include islands like Jamaica, Cuba, Puerto Rico, and Hispaniola. The Virgin Islands lie in the tropi-cal zone, 18–19° north and 65° west, and the equator sits just around the corner, so to speak.

With an area of thirty-one square miles, St. Thomas is about a third of the size of Nantucket Island. With its almost twenty square miles, St. John is about a quarter as large, while St. Croix, spreading itself over all of more than eighty square miles, would cover about three quarters of the island.

7. To reach the West Indies from Copenhagen in the mid-nineteenth century, the first twenty miles could be covered by railroad to Roskilde, after which the journey was continued by stagecoach. If there was ice on Storebælt that winter, the sound had to be crossed with so-called iceboats.

From a European perspective, these islands first entered history when, on November the 14th 1493, Christopher Columbus cast anchor off the delightful little island that he named "Santa Cruz," the Holy Cross. Entranced, he wrote in his journal, "It is a dream land which one never wants to leave once having come to know it."[19] On the following days he sailed on "paradisial" waters and charted the other islands in the chain, which he baptized the Virgin Islands in memory of holy St. Ursula and her 11,000 virgins, who according to Catholic legend suffered martyrdom in the third century. That the entire region received the name the West Indies is due, as we know, to Columbus's having assumed on his arrival at America that he had finally discovered the sea route to India, this being the aim of his second journey of discovery. By a peculiarly illogical twist, Columbus called the natives that he met on the islands "Indians."

It is close to a rule—one without too many mitigating exceptions—that the "discovery" of a culture heralds its downfall. So too in this case: pressed by the natives' attacks on Spanish sailors, by their unsuitability as slaves, and perhaps especially by their cannibalism, the Spanish King Ferdinand decided in 1512 to exterminate all of the natives in the West Indies. In the course of shockingly few decades that decision was put into effect, so that when at the beginning of the

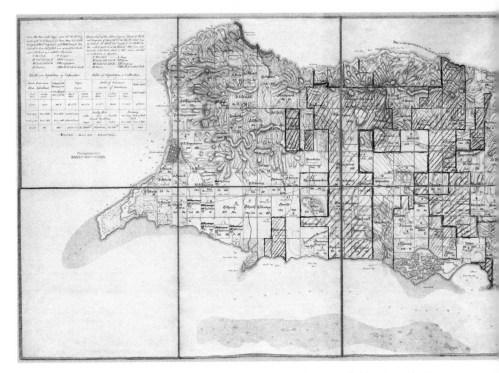

8. St. Croix is about twenty-one miles long and a good five and a half miles wide. The island's capital is Christiansted on its north coast, while Frederiksted lies furthest to the east. The square areas indicate the island's plantations. Surrounded by extensive fields with high sugarcane plants swaying in the light trade winds, the plantation owners kept house in imposing buildings that in some cases were manor houses or small palaces in

seventeenth century European sea powers such as Great Britain, France, and Holland began their colonization, the islands were almost deserted.

There were still, however, a number of smaller islands in the region that had escaped the great powers' attention, among them St. Thomas, to which the first Danish colonists came in 1666 under the command of Erik Nielsen Smed. Smed was able to take over the island in the name of the Danish king with very little difficulty. He died less than three months after his arrival, whereupon in the course of a handful of years, yellow fever and malaria, together with assaults, piracy, and a violent hurricane, convinced most of the crew to return to their mother country.

Understandably, there were such tales of the frightful conditions out there in the far-distant colonies, that a voyage to the West Indies was not normally something people longed for. In Denmark it was decided that prison inmates,

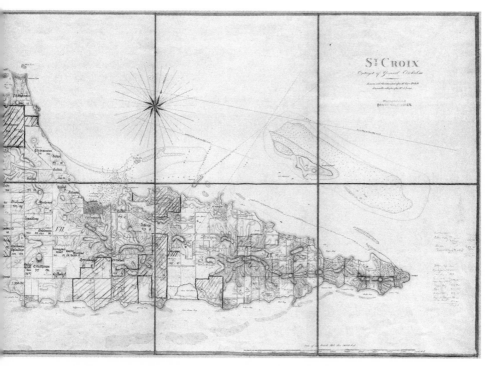

neoclassical style and bore names like Aldershvile (Rest in Age), Fredensborg (Fortress of Peace), Work and Rest, Upper Love, and Lower Love (its nearest neighbor was called Jealousy). The plantation name coming closest to reality was, plainly, Hard Labor.

superannuated prostitutes, and other proletarians with doubtful pasts would receive compulsory discharges. In 1682, when Governor Nicolai Esmit was to be replaced by the more experienced Jørgen Iversen Dyppel and the crew needed for the expedition could not be mustered, it was decided to send instead all life-term prisoners in irons, in the company of twenty ladies of easy virtue. Predictably, there were inappropriate contacts, violence erupted, and the ship had scarcely left the English Channel before the motley crew was in full mutiny. First, the Dutch captain was shot and thrown overboard, followed by Dyppel and five superiors. Dyppel's wife, who had given birth soon after leaving port, was raped in the most horrendous fashion and her blameless infant flung overboard.

The colonization and administration of this far-off region were in the early days entrusted to the Danish West India and Guinea Company, which was established by royal grant in 1671 in order to stimulate Danish involvement in

9. Sugar-mill on St. John. The sugar that Regine with touching enthusiasm sent across the Atlantic for distribution among family and friends in Copenhagen was the product of scarcely imaginable, inhuman toil, although St. Croix with its chimneys, countless cooking houses and cone-shaped sugar-mills displayed, almost pointedly, that the "white gold" required preparation and considerable sacrifice. After a period of growth lasting 14–15 months, the sugarcane was chopped up and conveyed to the plantation's sugar-mill, where a few slaves fed the canes into the rotating cylinders that pressed the juice out of the stems. Since an inattentive slave might on occasion have his hand, and even whole arm, crushed between the cylinders, there was a broad-bladed axe in the mill with which the jammed limb could be expeditiously hacked off.

the West Indies. It was organized as a stock company and had its headquarters with warehouses and shipyard in Copenhagen. The company held a national monopoly on trade with Guinea and the West Indies, and from this followed economic advantages and privileges, among them sole rights to the especially lucrative sugar refining business. In return, the company was to guarantee regular sailings to the colonies, arrange sale of a predetermined amount of Danish goods, and transport the king's goods free of charge. In 1672 the company acquired St. Thomas as its first colony in the West Indies. St. John (Danish St. Jan) became a colony in 1718, and finally in 1733 the company bought Santa Cruz, which since the middle of the seventeenth century had been in French hands and consequently was named St. Croix.

The purchase of St. Croix was the beginning of the end of the Danish West India and Guinea Company. A number of private investors and businessmen had expressed interest in taking over the company's activities and, once the State saw that the monopoly might get in the way of development, the shareholders were bought out and the company dissolved in 1754. The administration of the colonies then came under Frederik V, who in 1755, to the profit and joy of his better-heeled subjects, took the controls off trade and sea transport.

To travel at this time was less a normal part of life than an ordeal of survival, but as long as money was to be made, risks were taken and consciences were not too closely examined. A huge generator of profit was the so-called triangle trade, an arrangement as brilliantly conceived as it was inhumane. A ship was loaded in Copenhagen with various easily sold goods, such as mirrors, canvas, spirits, iron, copper, flintlock pistols, and ammunition, whereupon it sped southward with the help of the northerly winds and, when the ship had passed Madeira, the northwest trade winds blew it further toward Africa's west coast, where anchor was cast and the holds emptied and filled with black men, women, and children. Course was then set for the West Indies, where the black cargo was put on land and sold to the owners of sugar plantations. The empty ship was then filled with raw sugar to be refined in Copenhagen, though space was also found for colonial wares such as rum, tobacco, ginger, cinnamon, cotton, and mahogany from the rain forests. Once these goods had reached Denmark, the voyage was repeated as quickly as possible.

GOVERNOR J. F. SCHLEGEL AND HIS WIFE

Fritz and Regine were not totally ignorant of conditions awaiting them on the far away islands. Leaving Southampton they knew they faced a perilous voyage. Certainly no one feared sailing into the abyss, as when Columbus had weighed anchor, but there were other and far more real dangers to worry about: hurricanes, shipwreck, and tropical disease.

That an expedition to the Danish West Indies could be fatal and change things forever was a fact that now only seven-year-old Thilly called to mind for both of them and, most painfully, for herself. Three years before Thilly was born, her father Oluf, Regine's eldest brother and now Controller of Customs on the islands, then thirty years old, had married seven-years-younger Laura Isidora Winning. In 1846, with their son and first child Regnar, and Laura again pregnant, they had set out for St. Croix. On arrival Oluf was sufficiently pleased with the new surroundings and with the island's attractions, to which the local Danish court evidently saw in Laura an addition, to call it a "paradise." But sickness as well as the distance from home soon changed the picture. Laura gave birth to Thilly but died not long after of a weakened heart, aged just twenty-six. On learning this, Regine's father, Terkild Olsen, decided to send out his second eldest daughter to keep house for Oluf and take care of his children. Olivia, then thirty-seven years old and unmarried, carried out these functions for only two years before she too succumbed.

Only two years had passed since these events when Fritz, Regine, Thilly, and Josephine arrived at Christiansted. The harbor into which they sailed was well sheltered, but the narrow opening through the coral reef was not to be trifled with, so a pilot had been stationed in the middle of the harbor basin on a tiny island with the odd name of Protestant's Quay. The name is said to be due to the Catholic French not wanting Protestants to be buried on St. Croix and thus having the Protestant dead transported to that small island.

Christiansted lies on the north coast of St. Croix, Frederiksted on the west coast. Frederiksted was therefore often called Westenden (the West End), while in ordinary parlance Christiansted was often referred to as Basinet (the Basin), or—as Oluf stresses in one of his letters—"Bassenden (that is how it is spelled and not Bassinet)." Christiansted, the capital of the three islands, bore the clear stamp of the Norwegian Frederik Moth who, in 1734, was sent out by the West India and Guinea Company to take a closer look at the newly acquired colonies. Accompanied by his men, Moth "marched" into St. Croix and reached the plantation of La Grange, whose buildings were so far intact that, according to Moth, a new city could be established there "when the country is sufficiently civilized." Thus Frederiksted was founded. Moth then sailed on to the north where he picked out a fort, built by the French, to form the heart of the city of Christiansted. With his model of a city derived from the Norwegian capital, Christiania, Moth worked out a city plan with streets laid out by a draughtsman's ruler. He presumably used the same tool for measuring out the plantations, whose standard area became 140 acres.[20]

Moth was no great friend of variety, so all the houses in Christiansted came to be roughly of the same height. Their lower floors, which according to local fire regulations were to be built in stone, were as a rule broken by a vaulted gallery, so that walkways underneath became shady arcades. According to 1747 building codes, the houses' living room floors were to be built of brick, which was transported to the West Indies from Flensborg as ballast in Danish ships. Considering the islands' violent history, it is no surprise that several buildings are the work of military architects, but well-known civilian architects are also represented, such as C. F. Hansen, J. Wiedewelt, and H. C. Freund, who designed and decorated the classic houses which, with their faded shingle roofs, small balconies, and pastel-colored elegance, seem to have been well suited to the tropical climate.

When Fritz and Regine moved up through the town to find their sumptuous new address, not only did the architecture seem familiar to them, but the street signs also held echoes of home with names like Strand Gaden (Beach Street), Torve Gaden (Market Street), Kirke Gaden (Church Street), Fisker Gaden (Fisher Street), Hospitals Gade (Hospital Street), and Dronningens Tværgate (Queen's Cross Street). Fritz and his small entourage came to a halt at Government House in Kongens Gade (King's Street). This house was by far the city's largest and had been built in 1747 by John William Schopen, who had been sent out as a government official for the West Indian and Guinea Company but was also an enterprising and well-to-do plantation owner in his own right. Following his death in 1771, his widow sold the property to the government, which undertook a comprehensive rebuilding program so that it could be used as a government residence. After yet another rebuilding in 1818, when the property received a new roof and was scraped and painted, it was connected to the neighboring house belonging to prominent merchant and ship-owner Johannes Søbøtker, who functioned periodically as Governor-General when Peter von Scholten was engaged elsewhere.

It was to Peter von Scholten that the house owed its imposing exterior. He had it rebuilt in neoclassical style with a new façade and a majestically turned flight of steps in the gabled entrance, which Scholten furnished with Frederik VI's monogram and the year 1830.[21] The stairway led up to an open vestibule on the first floor, which then gave into a stylish banqueting hall, all in gold and white, that stretched almost the entire length of the building. Along each side of the banqueting hall was an outer loggia, or gallery. On the columns along the banqueting hall's side walls were gold-framed mirrors, under which stood tabourets borne by gilded griffins and covered in red leather. It was not surprising that Peter von Scholten's mansion had for generations held the reputation of being the most magnificent in the entire West Indies.[22]

It was in more than one sense an entirely new world into which Governor Johan Frederik Schlegel and his wife entered. Their furniture from the Nybrogade apartment still had not reached them, so it took some time to become properly established. It was not until the beginning of June that what Regine refers to as "our things" arrived from Copenhagen aboard the *Flora*. They had survived the voyage moderately well—"small repairs we won't discuss, I have already become quite West Indian"—but Regine's new writing table and chair arrived in a sorry state, the legs broken, and the woodwork otherwise "so completely stained with all the print from the newspapers they had been wrapped in that I never thought they could look good again." To pack the things together for sending, Fritz had obtained the assistance of a Mr. Schmidt, who was "sheer zeal from top to toe," but regrettably the energetic man had by a "stroke of genius" managed either to "forget" all the keys or to "hide" them so well that "we have never found them since, but had to break up all the locks."

10. Frederik VI's crowned signature with the year 1830 in the gable is due to Peter von Scholten, who in that year completed the rebuilding of Government House in late neo-classical style. The marble bust is thought to be by Bertel Thorvaldsen and turns wistfully toward Denmark. The stair leads up to the second floor into an open vestibule from which the Schlegels could usher their guests into a stylish banqueting hall stretching almost the entire length of the building and painted in gold and white. When the black soldier standing guard in the sentry box in the street outside proudly presented arms at Regine's arrival, she was sometimes unable to suppress a smile.

The repairs were an added burden to Schlegel's already less than optimal economy. "Fritz is being constantly pressed by his creditors and so he borrows from Oluf," explains a concerned Regine, who also tells us that Oluf had "a large bill for us for what he had bought, and our expenses from home were even bigger." As "bigwigs" they had to pay for everything so "the chances of putting anything aside seem pitiful."

New purchases were a long way off, so it was with some palpitations that Regine examined the contents of the cases. The heating elements for her flat-iron had arrived but not the iron itself. She had asked Cornelia to see to it that Fritz's and Regine's pillows shipped on board the *Flora*, since their pillowcases were suitable for just these pillows, but the pillows themselves had either vanished from the packing cases or had never been there at all. She had expressly asked that some yellow curtains from Fritz's room be packed, but they might just as well give up looking for them, which was especially frustrating since they would have been perfectly suited to covering some "old tattered sofas." Regine resented the exorbitant local prices, so she decided to embark on an import business of her own, of which she informed Cornelia in a letter dated Wednesday the 26th of September:

> I have a commission I would beg Maria to undertake, ask her to buy me a form for a sponge cake tart (as I think they are called) for 1 pound; it is high with a pipe in the middle and the stripes go diagonally, tin-plate. It pains me that you send me all your curry, but it is just like your usual kindness to take from yourself to give to others. I am eternally grateful for the jam you send, we have such good need of it that we should now begin thinking of doing something in return.

Adjusting to the new economic and social conditions was much more difficult than Regine had hoped, but she refused to let petty concerns for her own comfort get in the way of the longer-range objectives of their exile: "We came out here because it had to be, not from a vain desire for honor; we are grateful to God because we are on the whole better satisfied than we had expected." Nonetheless Fritz found it so hard to adjust that, in a letter dated Thursday the 28th of June, Regine could inform Cornelia in plain words: "Fritz said yesterday he would have had nothing against going home again with the *Flora*." For her part, Regine could not see herself returning so quickly, "not at all because I am charmed by the pleasantness of a stay out here, but the last year's struggles have been so much for me that they must have been fought for something." What struggles Regine had in mind she does not divulge, but had she returned home after such a short while, "I believe I would feel unhappy, my life without meaning, like a young girl who plays truant from school."

THE ATTACK ON THE CHURCH

While Regine was fussing about the non-arrival of her flatiron and yellow curtains, on the other side of the world Kierkegaard was in the midst of an attack
on the Church. With needle-sharp irony, he painted the frocked men as bourgeois welfare theologians, their minds filled with idyllic parsonages, a childish
and noncommittal Christianity, and lucrative promotions rather than with the
radical content in Jesus's teaching and the judgment that awaits everyone in
eternity. He called the priests cannibals, liars, monkeys, among other disre-
spectful epithets, and the Church an institution of trumpery that should be
closed down as soon as possible and dismantled. For Kierkegaard, baptism was
a drop of water, confirmation an embarrassing farce, and the wedding ceremony a seamy erotic show. What the ultimate aim may have been of what has
been called history's most spectacular one-man revolution has been the object
of exhaustive discussion. Kierkegaard himself indicates that what he wanted
was "honesty" and that he held otherwise only one "thesis," that Christianity
simply did not exist. If no meaning was any longer ascribed to God and the
world was approached with a single-minded self-sufficiency, *as if* God simply
did not exist, then Christianity was an out-of-place and leaky antique and the
church a silent museum for a mummified deity. A number of years later Nietzsche channeled the quintessence of Kierkegaard's attack into a sentence that
went on to become common property: "God is dead."

The public occasion for Kierkegaard's protest was a memorial speech held by
Professor H. L. Martensen on February 5th, 1854, at the funeral of the Danish pri-
mate Bishop J. P. Mynster, whom Martensen installed in the holy ranks of those
"witnesses for the truth" stretching throughout history and back to the days of
the apostles. Kierkegaard found the presentation objectionable, but he withheld
his protest for almost a year. He first came out with it in the newspaper *Fædrelandet* (The Fatherland) on the 20th of December 1854, calling Mynster "weak,
addicted to pleasure, and great only as a declaimer." He then gave the newspaper's
readers his own version of what a true "witness for the truth" should be:

> A witness for the truth is a man whose life from first to last is unac-
> quainted with everything called enjoyment. . . . A witness for the truth
> is a man who witnesses for the truth in poverty—in poverty, in lowli-
> ness and abasement, so unappreciated, hated, detested, so mocked,
> insulted, laughed to scorn. . . . A witness for the truth, one of the au-
> thentic witnesses for the truth, is a man who is scourged, maltreated,
> dragged from one prison to another . . . and then at last . . . cruci-
> fied, or beheaded, or burned, or broiled on a grill, his lifeless body

thrown away by the assistant executioner into a remote place, unburied—this is how a witness for the truth is buried![23]

It was with this cannonade that Kierkegaard had launched an attack in which, first in twenty-two articles, and then in nine issues of his own pamphlet *Øieblikket* (The Instant, also translated as The Moment), he polemicized with wit and without restraint against the Church and its secularized priesthood. One of his catchphrases had it that Christianity had been abolished in proportion to its dissemination, something that in the name of honesty the Church's highest authorities ought to admit. When, not unexpectedly, this admission failed to materialize, Kierkegaard felt bound to repeat his protest. This he did on January the 29th 1855, once more in *Fædrelandet*, where he stated:

> Not mitigated but intensified, I hereby repeat my objection: I would rather gamble, booze, wench, steal, and murder than take part in making a fool of God, would rather spend my days in the bowling alley, in the billiard parlor, my nights in games of chance or at masquerades than participate in the kind of earnestness Bishop Martensen calls Christian earnestness.[24]

At what point Kierkegaard came to know of the Schlegel couple's travel plans is unknown, but it is not altogether unthinkable that his very late *public* reaction to Martensen's talk of witnessing to the truth could be out of a consideration for Regine. And perhaps the reason why the attack grows in contempt and indignation in the time after her departure in mid-March is that, in worldly terms, Kierkegaard has lost the only one he has seriously loved. It may be a coincidence, but it is still worth a thought, for there is a sharp increase in the frequency of Kierkegaard's articles in *Fædrelandet* around the time of Regine's departure, more than half of them appearing within just twelve days. While Regine was sitting in an overcrowded boat negotiating the ice out on Storebælt, Kierkegaard was presenting his proposal for sweeping changes to Martensen, who on the 15th of April 1854, had been appointed as Mynster's successor. He had only just got himself installed in the episcopal see when Kierkegaard, on the 22nd of March 1855, presented him with the following altogether irrefutable agenda:

> First and foremost and on the greatest possible scale an end must be put to the entire official—well-intentioned—untruth that—well-meaningly—conjures up and sustains the appearance that it is Christianity that is being proclaimed, the Christianity of the New Testament. . . . This is how the matter must be turned: away, away, away with all optical illusions, forward with the truth, say forthrightly: we are not fit to be Christians in the New Testament sense.[25]

Two days later, Regine having now reached Altona, Kierkegaard proclaims: "Christianity simply doesn't exist, as almost anyone must be able to see as well as I."[26] And another two days later, on the 28th of March, while Regine is rattling through England on the way to Southampton, he continues his denunciation of cultural Protestantism:

> The Christianity of the New Testament simply doesn't exist. There is nothing here to reform; what counts is throwing light on a continued Christian crime perpetrated over the centuries by millions (more or less guilty), whereby, in the name of Christianity's perfection, little by little people have tried shrewdly to trick God out of Christianity, have got Christianity to be the exact opposite of what it is in the New Testament.[27]

In the following weeks, while the Schlegels are still aboard their "steamer," accusations flooded out over the "Clerical Swindler Guild," also dubbed the "Priest Company," which consisted of all those small, mediocre men who would do all they could to safeguard their comfortable positions even if the State were to "hit upon the idea of introducing, e.g., the religion that the moon is made of green cheese." With a peculiarly merciless precision, barbs are aimed at: "The priest—that incarnation of nonsense wrapped in long clothes!"[28]

After several years of public silence, Kierkegaard was again placing himself before the public consciousness and with a force he had not displayed since his debut with *Either/Or*. The compactness, the satire, parody, and irony of Kierkegaard's late texts remind us of the aphorisms with which the co-called aesthete diverts his readers in the first pages of *Either/Or*. A small cluster of aphorisms in the sixth issue of *Øieblikket* bear the heading "Brief and to the Point" and offer among other things a wonderfully absurd dialogue that betrays an unmistakable kinship between the theologian Kierkegaard and his aphoristic aesthete:

> "Did the Apostle Paul have any official position?" No, Paul had no official position. "Did he, then, earn a lot of money in another way?" No, he did not earn money in any way. "Was he, then, at least married?" No, he was not married. "But then Paul is certainly not a serious man!" No, Paul is not a serious man.[29]

To explain the difference between original Christianity and present-day welfare theology, Kierkegaard uses a long series of images, among them one of a modern traveler who, with the help of an old guidebook, tries to find his way around in a country where everything has been completely changed. The guidebook in question proves to be the New Testament, which once served as an existential "guide for the Christian" but now functions most often as a form of light reading. The consequences of the general confusion are quite amusing:

> While one is comfortably riding along in the train, one reads in the guidebook, "Here there is the frightful Wolf Ravine, where one plunges 70,000 fathoms down into the earth"; while one is sitting and smoking a cigar in the cozy dining car, one reads in the handbook, "Here is the hideout of a robber band that attacks and beats up travelers"—here it is, that is, here it was, since now (how amusing to imagine how it was), now it is not the Wolf Ravine but a railroad, and not a robber band but a cozy dining car.[30]

"THE FLIES ARE TO SUCH A DEGREE IMPERTINENT OUT HERE"

Kierkegaard's baroque travel story could be read in the second issue of *Øieblikket*, which appeared on June the 4th 1855, when Regine and Fritz had arrived at St. Croix and were gradually beginning to settle in. Some "embroidered wicker stools give me great joy," she says of her new home, noting also that "two white tigers I acquired are resplendent on a marble table in front of a beautifully gilded mirror and look delightful." Most important for Regine, however, was the private room she arranged for herself with its indispensable writing table and the pictures of the people and motifs she most loved.

Among the most perceptible changes was the tropical climate, which seemed to her an everlasting summer, for the temperature remained more or less unchanging throughout the year. In winter the average temperature was seventy-five degrees, in the summer eighty. The sun is in the sky three thousand hours a year, almost twice as many as Regine is used to. Out on the coast there is usually a salutary breeze, and the many trade winds, which with their cool caress sweep over the islands from the east and northeast, manage to keep the humidity at a tolerable level. It is also thanks to these winds that the temperature rarely exceeds eighty-five degrees.

The heat was nevertheless oppressive. On Tuesday July the 10th Regine reports that it was simply too warm to do anything sensible at all: "Yesterday I changed clothes 4 times, and each time the water could be wrung off everything I had on, and yet everyone says it will be even warmer. You can imagine what became of my silk dresses; the first day I had on the yellow one I got a big stain on the back." Later Regine complains that her "skin has become so sensitive from the perpetual perspiration."

The difference between summer and winter lies especially in the humidity that drops in step with the temperature. The rainy season begins in May or June and lasts until October or November. Rain falls especially at night. One Sunday in mid-August there was a dinner party at the governor's house. When the last guests had gone, the bad weather began. It was, says Regine, "as though everything should dissolve in water." Thunder rolled in the distance the whole night long, "which wasn't the most pleasant accompaniment to our sleep," but it was only in the morning that "the real thunderstorm" came. Thilly woke and cried so heartrendingly that Regine felt she must go in and console the frightened girl, but her courage failed her and she all but fell down, hurting her knee.

> And then the rain out here is so unpleasant, it rains everywhere, so
> that one uses thick boots and galoshes in one's own rooms, everything
> one touches is damp, yes, one is also damp oneself, so it will be a damp
> letter you receive today.

Nor is it only the cooling trade winds that sweep over the islands. High and low pressures can force their way eastward to the Virgin Islands from the South American mainland, and when a cold front gets heated by the warm ocean, it gives rise to a keen north wind and heavy rain and makes for an unruly sea. Late summer and fall are the season for hurricanes, which occur on an average every tenth year and whose merciless devastation is a phenomenon feared throughout the islands. We are in "the hurricane time," declares Regine in mid-August. A few weeks earlier the churches had held services in which the congregations prayed to God to be spared the destructive forces of nature.

For Regine the tropical temperature called for special everyday precautions: "I play blind-man's bluff," she reports on the 27th of September. The game was not inspired by Thilly or other childish souls but was due to a boil that for several days had caused her pain and gradually had "become so large and hard that I must have oatmeal on it, and it isn't a good place to put oatmeal." The boil was in the middle of her forehead and the oatmeal ran down into Regine's eyes so that she could only "open my eyes enough to be able to see and write." When, the following year, she and Fritz left the residence for an estate in the countryside, flies became insufferable teachers in the art of patience:

> The flies are to such a degree impertinent out here as one has no con-
> ception of at home; on poor me they always know how to find the
> sores from the boils in which to settle themselves; today I have taken
> the plaster off a boil on my arm, and now that I am moving the hand
> to write I cannot continually chase them away, they encamp there as
> though I were already carrion; if I sit at the clavichord, they settle in

my eyes, indeed, they can be plague enough to make one shake all over one's body; and when they rest there come lots of mosquitoes and their sting is painful; but all such torments are greater out in the country, so if one is well off in one way, one must pay for it in another.

Regine had to cover the confounded boils with plaster of a suitable size suitable for keeping off the flies. "I don't count the boils," she declared bravely; what was especially annoying were the "rather tiresome plasters." But, as she reasoned, "if one is not patient down here, then it is something one will never be." Little by little, she also taught herself the necessary amount of resignation. When, at the beginning of October 1856, she and Fritz dined "at Newton's at Castel," she managed to last out the evening "in spite of sitting in pain the whole time for, presumably from the heat in town, I have another small boil under the lip which made my whole face sore." In mid-May that same year, Regine ships off a longer sigh over the absence of the seasons that bring those congenial changes of temperature and mood back at home:

> Here it is really everlasting summer, which is probably what in particular contributes a lot to making life uniform, for the very torments that the winter causes us at home make the summer doubly dear to us, and how much we look forward to its coming, and how the first spring sunshine fills us with joy . . . out here one misses these transitions, but still, I have nevertheless been glad these days to observe that here, too, there are transitions, so that dear nature pays its silent observer with the pleasure of newness. In our so-called winter months we have constant sunshine and warmth and everything is constantly green, but if one looks closer there is no lushness in the green, and finally the drought makes all the leaves fall, and when the dry wind then blows dust up into the eyes, it can acquire a sad autumnal aspect despite the burning sun; now we have had good and bountiful rain, and it is now so clear that this everlasting summer has come out of the shower-bath rejuvenated, the earth is so green, and all bushes and trees are resplendent with the most luxuriant leaves but now also bear flowers, as mostly they do in the spring, and there is a fragrance in everything that is indescribable; yes, our estate with its many orange trees smells so good that sometimes one has the feeling of having inadvertently dropped into a scent-box with the lid closed, so that one comes close to being choked by sheer fragrance.

Getting acclimatized also meant having to treat the new residence as a public place where it appeared anyone could just turn up. It was almost like the wind that often whistled right through the numerous rooms "where everything is a door or window so that the wind comes right in and keeps house in a way one has no conception of at home." In line with Regine's new social status as First Lady of the Danish West Indian islands, her own everyday differed vastly from what it had been in Copenhagen. When she wanted to go out walking with Thilly, she had to have a bodyguard. It troubled her, moreover, "that everyone looks at me, yes I can hear them running to the window to look at me, I who have always been so happy to be so small and able to go through life unnoticed, it's almost too much for me." It was a little amusing though "that all the Negroes greet me, it is true the white population do the same too, but when the sentries present arms just for me, I come close to laughing out loud."

To all that was new and unaccustomed was added the circumstance of taking their meals surrounded by black ministering spirits. When Oluf and Thilly joined them it might be taken for a party, but since Oluf was often ill and had his food brought up to him, and Thilly had to go to bed early, it often happened that Fritz and Regine sat opposite each other in the long dining room and found it hard to find a suitable facial expression. But if the twosome at the big table could be involuntarily comical, the official arrangements required of their position were often predictably unamusing, tiresome, and also demanding in terms of what food was expected and how much. In a letter of June the 9th, Regine tells Clara and Cornelia how Pastor Brandt and his wife had come to dinner together with the sheriff from St. John. She describes her concern over the "frugality" of a menu that to our ears sounds like the height of excess:

> . . . and now you shall hear what they got, which I was very worried about owing to its frugality: soup, curry, ox tongue, roast duck, ptarmigan, together with and all kinds of vegetable, etc., cake, fruit, my Danish preserves that I have just received, (I thank everyone for their contribution, it kept excellently), candy and then port wine, Madeira, and champagne.

The parties were usually "Monday soirées" with anywhere between a dozen and twenty present. Regine writes on Thursday the 28th of June of yet another less than inspiring evening: "Here they were mostly English and I conversed as best I could, letting them laugh at my poor language." But she "nearly had a fit" when in leaving, the English priest, surrounded by his fragrant ladies, praised his hostess for the most pleasant and amusing evening in a long time! "Had we both been Danish and at home in Denmark, where I was not so up in the world, I would have asked him quite seriously not to make a fool of me; but now I answered him politely and put the blame on him for the interesting evening." Not the honor but the blame—what a beautiful slip of the pen!

As for the dinner guests, they were sometimes boorishness incarnate, or "asses" as Regine somewhere calls them. At the end of November she tells Cornelia cheerfully how the captain and four officers from a newly arrived naval brig had practically invaded their home and in no time at all were displaying their bad manners—"I almost think our Madeira was too good for them, since many of them took too much." The women were for that matter often even worse, gossiping incessantly and slandering to a degree. In their company Regine felt insecure and ignored, even though she had dressed in her finest gown: "they were all so blatantly West Indianly arrogant that they could scarcely wait to step outside our door before looking down on us."

PATIENT NO. 2067

On Saturday the 10th of November 1855, Regine wrote to her seventy-seven-year-old mother, who was increasingly dependent on care and therefore reliant on Mr. Schmidt's effective presence. Slightly piqued, Cornelia had reported that their mother had developed so much of a "little weakness for him" that she had on her own initiative presented him not only with some of the Schlegels' knives and forks, but also their dining table. The mother had clearly always had a "certain tendency to give away other people's things." A lamp belonging to her son Jonas had been on the point of changing ownership, which Cornelia managed to prevent only at the last moment. However, this rampant generosity on behalf of others now worried Regine less.

> My own blessed mother! I was very thankful to read your letter, and although I know well what it cost you to write it, I also know that if you had seen the pleasure it brought me, you would be richly repaid. It also put my mind at rest that, writing as you always do, your health is as of old, oh I do hope that with God's help we may still meet in this world. I firmly believe [that] if you had come along, you would have stood up well to the climate, but do you know, my lively old mother, it would be decidedly too quiet for you here, since except for the parties we hold, as now so frequently, we had one yesterday for 14 persons with American oysters and fruit we had received as a present from the Danish ice-merchant Kofod in St. Thomas.

Regine's sentence doesn't quite end; it grows too long and falls as it were out of her hands. And then she writes on, as one does when one has nothing in particular to write about but loves the person one is writing to. Regine tells of the quiet and rather lonely life she and Fritz lead, that they are rarely invited out, that she enjoys riding, that it will be delightful when Regnar comes to town at Christmas, so that, in company with his grandfather and cousins, he can walk on the ramparts.

In the course of that same day, as Regine sat in Christiansted writing these lines, life took its leave of Kierkegaard in Frederik's Hospital in Copenhagen. His final appeal to the public had its costs, psychological as well as economic. What the theological deficit was is impossible to estimate unequivocally, but the fact that the teasing, the generosity, and the edification of Kierkegaard's earlier writing had to make way for a gloomy theology of a pietistic cut, is something he himself bore witness to on Thursday the 25th of September 1855, when, in his last ever journal entry, he wrote: "This life's destiny is: to be brought to the highest pitch of world-weariness. The person who is brought to that point can insist . . . that it is God who, out of love, has brought him to that point: in the Christian way he has passed life's examination and is ripe for eternity."[31]

The day Kierkegaard put ink to these bleak thoughts, Cornelia gave birth to the vigorous Johanne Marie—only a few hundred yards from Kierkegaard's residence at 5 Dyrkøb. On that same day Regnar celebrated his ninth birthday, and on the following day, Wednesday the 26th of September, Regine wrote from her light green, tropical island, asking Cornelia to have Maria purchase a "form for a sponge cake tart" that she could probably buy "at the corner of Læderstræde and Høibroplads." Contemporaneity can be a curious phenomenon!

Kierkegaard's own physical state had given him optimal reason to promote world-weariness as the highest goal and meaning of a Christian life, for in September he was a man marked for death with but a few months to live. In the middle of the month, while sitting on his sofa, he had leaned a little to the side, then slid to the floor, and was hardly able to raise himself up again. On the next day, while putting on his trousers, he fell once more. He suffered neither dizziness nor cramps, nor headache, but when out walking he could not hold direction, as though his stride was too short. At the same time there was a tingling in his legs that stretched all the way down from the loins. His old difficulty passing water returned; either he couldn't at all or it happened involuntarily. It was embarrassing, humiliating. And his stomach was causing trouble as well, although strangely there was nothing wrong with his appetite. He had been coughing for some time and, when the cough was particularly violent, it was accompanied by a creamy secretion, especially in the beginning when there was pain in his chest; but now the mucous was serous and clear with yellow clots. Late in September, while out walking, his legs had failed him. A carriage was called and drove him back to Dyrkøb. But his condition failed to improve. Four days later, on Thursday the 2nd of October, he presented himself at the Royal Frederik's Hospital in Norgesgade (Norway Street; or Bredgaden as it was then commonly called, today Bredgade) and asked to be examined. The young physician on duty noted:

> He cannot offer any specific reason for his present sickness. However, he does associate it with drinking cold seltzer water last summer, with a dark dwelling, together with the exhausting intellectual work that he believes is too taxing for his frail physique. He considers the sickness fatal. His death is necessary for the cause that he has devoted all his intellectual strength to resolving, for which he has worked alone, and for which alone he believes that he has been intended; hence the penetrating thought in conjunction with so frail a physique. If he is to go on living, he must continue his religious battle; but in that case it will peter out, while, on the contrary, by his death it will maintain its strength and, he believes, its victory.[32]

Kierkegaard was directed to the hospital superintendent's office, where he registered as a paying patient with the number 2067. From there he went to Medical Department A, where for thirteen years Seligmann Meyer Trier had been the director. In the front building, facing Norgesgade, Kierkegaard was assigned a single room, appropriately enough, the "single individual" having now become his trademark. The hospital had fourteen such rooms, which unlike the common wards, were equipped with good, soft carpets, a single bed, a wardrobe, mirror, chair and table, together with a corner cupboard with a tea-set in fine porcelain. There were double-paned windows that could handle the worst drafts and the noise from Norgesgade. It was in these surroundings that the forty-two-year-old genius was to spend the last forty-one days of his enigmatic life.

Kierkegaard was on "1/2 best care," which did not mean that he ate more poorly than the other paying patients, but simply that the portions were half as large. Each day of the week, breakfast consisted of thirty-two grams of wheat bread, eight grams of butter, and half a deciliter of milk. Like the other patients, Kierkegaard had a food scale in his room so that he could ensure that the hospital's personnel had not helped themselves to anything on their way down the corridors. It isn't known whether Kierkegaard made use of the scale, but its very presence stood in grotesque contrast to the opulent dinners in the governor's house where Regine's ravenous guests gorged themselves on ox tongue, roast duck, ptarmigan, cakes, candy, red wine, Madeira, port wine, and champagne.

To begin with, only Kierkegaard's nearest family were aware of his admission to the hospital. But on the 6th of October the news reached the poet and author

Carsten Hauch, who wrote to his friend and colleague B. S. Ingemann about their shared favorite aversion.

> Søren Kierkegaard is said to have been stricken with an attack of apoplexy, for which death is the likely consequence. Most likely illness, nervous stress, and a sort of convulsive irritability have played a large role in his bitter and negative activities, during which he displayed to the entire world his face, marked as it was by hatred of humanity.[33]

Hauch on the same occasion calls Kierkegaard an "acute but ice-cold spirit whose words are as sharp as icicles." He is a "false prophet," who no doubt "comes forth like this with great gifts but with a heart so hollow that he plainly says it really makes no difference to him whether the world is Christian or not," while he "loudly proclaims that he is more or less the only person who can see what true Christianity is, and bluntly declares that God hates people."

Over the course of the following weeks, Kierkegaard's condition worsens. His ability to stand diminishes, with his left leg gradually becoming paralyzed. In addition, he suffers from increasing back pain, for which the doctors administer turpentine as a topical treatment. *Essensia valeriana officinalis* was prescribed as a means of soothing the nerves: twenty-five drops five times a day. Not quite so clinical was the prescription of a "half bottle of Bayer Ale," which Kierkegaard asked to be spared—according to his journal for "religious" reasons. The dying man received a special tea instead, made of dried clover, chamomile flowers, and arnica, of which he was to drink a cup in the morning and evening. "He keeps insisting on his near death," noted the physician on Friday the 12th of October. A few days earlier Hans Christian Andersen told Henriette Wulff of the situation: "Kierkegaard is very sick. They say the entire lower part of his body is paralyzed, and he is in the hospital."[34]

When a long-time friend from his youth, Emil Boesen, heard of Kierkegaard's admission, he traveled from his parsonage in Horsens in East Jutland to the hospital in Copenhagen where, in mid-October, he had the first of several conversations that later came to public knowledge with the publication in 1881 of the last volume of *Af Søren Kierkegaards Efterladte Papirer* (From Søren Kierkegaard's Posthumous Papers). In the very first of their conversations Kierkegaard touched on his relationship to Regine, whose new status as the governor's wife gave occasion for a little play on words, doubtless his last. It comes in reply to Boesen's asking him, "How is it going?"

> Badly. It's death. Pray for me that it comes quickly and easily. I am depressed. . . . I have my thorn in the flesh, as did St. Paul. . . . And that was also what was wrong with my relationship to R; I had thought

11. The rather somber looking Emil Boesen, who sticks his right arm into his jacket like another Napoleon, had known Kierkegaard from the time of their childhood and was his only lifetime confidant. During his first stay in Berlin, Kierkegaard sent him candid letters concerning his break with Regine and the genesis of *Either/Or*. In 1849 Boesen became resident chaplain in Horsens, where, in 1856, Cornelia and Emil Winning had established themselves and ran a steam-mill. Boesen traveled to Copenhagen when Kierkegaard lay on his deathbed and later recorded their touching final conversations.

that it could be changed, but it couldn't, so I dissolved the relationship. How strange. The husband became Governor. I don't like that.
It would have been better if it had happened quietly. It was the right
thing that she got S [i.e., Schlegel], that had been the earlier understanding, and then I came in and disturbed things. She suffered a great
deal because of me (and he spoke about her lovingly and sadly). I was
afraid she would become a governess. She didn't, but now she is governess in the West Indies.[35]

It is not known, and is still much discussed, what Kierkegaard alludes to when
talking of his "thorn in the flesh," which he professes to share with the Apostle
Paul. The suffering in question was, allegedly, the real reason for the break with
Regine. Marrying Schlegel was something to which Kierkegaard could give his
blessing, though he would rather that the man had not become governor, seeing that it was thereby he who brought Regine into the public domain, something that, all things considered, as one reads between the lines, should have
happened through Kierkegaard's renown. No less interesting is the parenthesis
just as hastily closed as opened around Regine. Boesen records that Kierkegaard mentioned her "lovingly and sadly," but why Kierkegaard's last words on
his life's love should be given so summarily and penned within parentheses
remains unclear. If it is a matter of discretion, then Boesen has achieved quite
the opposite, for parentheses of this kind invite all sorts of guesswork, which is
essentially what happened.

That Thursday, when the two touched on Regine in their conversation, was
a fine autumn day. So Boesen proposed that they go for a walk in the Copenhagen streets, just as in the old days. Kierkegaard liked the idea, but that was all.

Yes, there is only one thing wrong. I am unable to walk. But there is another method of transport, however. I can be lifted up. I have had the
feeling of becoming an angel, of getting wings, and that is of course
what will happen: to straddle a cloud and sing Hallelujah, Hallelujah,
Hallelujah.[36]

Sick and in good humor Kierkegaard seems ready to respond in kind when Boesen, on the brink of a pastoral cliché, asks him a little later whether he, too, will
now resort to God's mercy in Jesus. "Yes, of course, what else?" came the laconic
reply. Boesen began to sense that he was close to overstepping Kierkegaard's
comfort zone and so hastily left the question of Magister Kierkegaard's relationship to eternity in order to call attention to the things closest at hand. Was
there something Kierkegaard had not yet managed to say? The answer came
promptly: "No, yes, greet everyone for me. I have liked them all very much, and

tell them that my life is a great suffering, unknown and inexplicable to other people. Everything looked like pride and vanity, but it wasn't."[37]

Kierkegaard's elder brother Peter Christian, a priest in the parishes of Kindertofte and Pedersborg at Sorø (a municipality on Zealand about fifty miles from Copenhagen), had learned from guests who had traveled from Copenhagen of his younger brother's illness and that he had collapsed sometime "between the 27th and 29th." In a letter of October 7, the physician Michael Lund, Peter Christian's nephew, put his uncle in the picture and added that it was in all probability an "infection of the spinal cord, with paralysis of both legs." Some days later, Michael's father, wholesaler J. C. Lund, wrote to Peter Christian that his brother's condition was "only so-so." Like his two doctor sons, Henrik and Michael, who visited him "every day," he was decidedly not optimistic and therefore urged Peter Christian to go to Copenhagen, the quicker the better.[38]

It is understandable that Peter Christian should have hesitated. For years the relationship between the Kierkegaard brothers had been cool, among other reasons because Peter Christian, who was a Grundtvigian, had at some conventions spoken ironically of his younger brother's passionate temperament and had contrasted him with H. L. Martensen, who according to Peter Christian represented "sobriety" compared with his younger brother who was an "ecstatic monastery monk."[39] It might have seemed at first a mere tempest in a teapot, but in no time at all the aggrieved younger brother had whipped it up into a veritable typhoon. "A fuddy-duddy," "devoid of ideas," "a vapid gadabout," "nonsensical mediator" are just a modest sampling of the abuse that his journals pour out over the presumptuous brother, who is further accused of "whimpering," "driveling," "pusillanimity," "superficiality," "chattiness," "crime," "garrulity," "waste," "literary theft," "false sincerity," "characterless gadding," and in the end is appointed "the figurehead of mediocrity."[40]

Blood being always thicker than water, Peter Christian nonetheless pulled himself together and drove the long distance from Pedersborg to Frederik's Hospital, where he arrived on October the 19th to bid his younger brother a last farewell. But to no avail. He was forbidden access by hospital personnel, who made it clear that the dying brother had expressly let it be known that, in the event of Peter's coming, he would not receive him. And so, mission unaccomplished, Peter Christian could only trundle back over Zealand to his cold parsonage.

When Boesen visited Kierkegaard on Saturday the 20th of October, two sick-nurses were moving the now totally helpless man from one chair to another. Kierkegaard asked Boesen to support his head, and soon Boesen was holding it between his hands. When he looked in the next day, Kierkegaard let him understand that it was inconvenient. On the Monday, too, the visit was short. And what after all does one say to someone who is dying? Boesen tentatively suggested that Kierkegaard might prefer a better view, so that he could look out onto the hospital's lovely gardens, but Kierkegaard dismissed the idea; it didn't matter any more, his hip hurt, his pulse-rate was 100, the water left him involuntarily, especially at night. His cough still troubled him. His journal attests: "The expectoration consists of purulent clots, a few of which are closely mixed with light red blood."[41]

Just under a week later, on Saturday the 27th of October, Kierkegaard felt "weighed down." There were larger than usual crowds on the street that day and the sounds of their bustle penetrated into the hospital corridors, "Yes, that was what used to agree with me so much," Kierkegaard remarked.[42] Some time later—when is not known—Boesen came in for the last time. Kierkegaard was almost incapable of speech. Nor did Boesen write anything down. He returned soon after to his wife and little son in Horsens, where he had a priesthood to look after.

In the beginning of November, soon after dark, an attempt was made to stimulate Kierkegaard's lower extremities with electrical treatment. The effect on his failing body was very slight; his legs quivered a little, but that was all. His general condition remained unchanged and his mental faculties were still intact. He was probably able to follow the decline in his physical strength day by day, its unwinding hour by hour. Perhaps that is why the doctors moved to replace his daily dose of a hundred drops of valerian with the more aggressive *infusium tonico nervina*, a strong sedative and anxiety-relieving mixture. Kierkegaard received 50 grams daily.

The last week he lay wordless. There were bedsores, wet dressings were applied, bedclothes were changed daily, and the electrical treatment continued with some small effect on his deteriorating leg muscles. On Friday the 9th of November, it could be established that Kierkegaard was semicomatose; he didn't speak, he ate nothing. His bedsores looked cleaner, but they were not healing. His pulse was irregular. Lopsidedness appeared in his face, the left corner of his mouth a little drawn up. The following day the other corner followed suit. Patient 2067 now sat with a facial paresis, a paralysis that left him looking forward with a stiff smile. Like an ironist turned to stone. The sickness having now progressed to the upper part of his spinal cord, he could no longer communicate with the surrounding world, however much he may have wished to do so. If his arms were lifted and let go, they fell. He was still able to open his eyelids and also drew in his breath quickly, soundlessly. His ability to cough was gone. Fast breathing and a high pulse-rate indicated that he was now feverish, probably due to double pneumonia resulting from the accumulation of secretions in his lungs. Patient 2067 was still conscious but incapable of speech or movement.

The Sunday of November the 11th was Kierkegaard's last. He was totally unconscious, his pulse low, the breathing heavy and short. He was slowly asphyxiating—like his great model Socrates when the hemlock reached the region of his heart. Kierkegaard expired in the evening at about nine o'clock. Twelve hours later, when the pale winter sun made the city's tiled roofs blaze briefly, his soul-bereft body was transferred to the hospital's mortuary. One week later, on the 18th of November, a month to the day since his roguish remark about ascension astride a cloud, Kierkegaard was buried after a funeral service at the Church of Our Lady.

"The doctors do not understand my illness. It is psychical, and now they want to treat it in the usual medical manner."[43] Kierkegaard had made this comment in one of his first conversations with Boesen. The present case was not, however, handled quite in the usual medical manner; there was no autopsy, presumably because Kierkegaard was against it. Some of the medical students were unsatisfied with the decision, for they would have liked to get their fingers on his brain and dissect it into slices for the good of science. Others, too, pointed to that brilliant organ. The day after Kierkegaard's death Just Paulli wrote to one of his friends, "He is said to have suffered from softness in the brain; was this the cause of the writing or was the writing itself to blame?"[44]

Paulli's question is almost as far-reaching as the brain was brilliant, but seeing that no pathological data exist, the question can hardly be answered. We have only Kierkegaard's hospital journal of his illness, which is bound together with the papers from sixty-nine other patients who from varying causes left Ward A in the course of November 1855. As a proposed diagnosis, someone has written on the preface to Kierkegaard's journal "hemiplegia" (paralysis on only one side of the lower extremities), but that word is crossed out. The final notation is "paraplegia," but this only describes the symptoms rather than offering a proper diagnosis, and an abbreviation for tuberculosis has therefore been added in parentheses but with a question mark, leaving the cause of death a doubtful "tubercul?"[45]

The question mark acknowledges that it was a sickness that certainly looked like tuberculosis but was just as certainly something else, for there were in Seligmann Meyer Trier's ward people excellently qualified to assess tuberculosis. In the course of 1855 alone, no fewer than twenty-eight patients had been admitted with that diagnosis. And besides, Trier had written the first Danish textbook in stethoscopy, so it seems unlikely that he could have failed to uncover an ordinary case of tuberculosis. More recent investigations conclude that Kierkegaard probably suffered from a neurological ailment called "ascending spinal paralysis" or "acute polyradiculitis" or "Guillain-Barré syndrome," the causes of which are still unknown.

In *The Point of View for My Activity as an Author*, Kierkegaard had announced that he would die of a "longing for eternity," which in clinical respects is obviously no match for ascending spinal paralysis.[46]

Since both diagnoses can nonetheless have an unmistakably ascending character, maybe Kierkegaard's "longing for eternity" was not so far from the truth.

1856

❧

HIS LAST WILL AND TESTAMENT

In the year's first letter, Regine makes what by her own admission is a "quite characteristic" slip of the pen.

> ~~Copenhagen~~ *St. Croix the 10th of January 1856*
>
> Dear beloved Cornelia! Look at what I began to write over my letter; I have wondered that I haven't done so before, especially to begin with, but today it is quite typical, since all my thoughts are in the dear city with you.

That in a moment of distraction Regine addressed her letter from "Copenhagen" should not be surprising. A letter that had reached St. Croix on Thursday the 1st of January, was causing her and her husband to consider their response to a range of delicate matters in Copenhagen calling for their attention. The letter had been composed by Peter Christian Kierkegaard and conveyed the news that his younger brother, Søren, had died on Sunday the 11th of November 1855.

The background to Peter Christian's appeal was, in outline, that on Monday the 19th of November, the day after the funeral, he had been in the deceased's rooms at 5 Dyrkøb and found there, in a desk, two small sealed envelopes bearing the identical inscription: "To Mr. Pastor Dr. Kierkegaard. To be opened after my death." The envelopes were almost identical, only the sealing wax differed, one being black, the other red. When Peter Christian broke the black seal, he found the deceased's testamentary requests:

> *Dear Brother,*
>
> It is naturally my will that my former fiancée, Mrs. Regine Schlegel, should inherit unconditionally what little I leave behind. If she herself refuses to accept it, it is offered to her on the condition that she act as trustee for its distribution to the poor.
>
> What I wish to express is that for me an engagement was and is just as binding as a *marriage,* and that therefore my estate is to revert to her in exactly the same manner as if I had been married to her.
>
> *Your brother,*
> *S. Kierkegaard.*[1]

The letter bore neither date nor year, but it could have been drafted sometime in November 1849, when Kierkegaard, as we shall see, had made an unsuccessful attempt to approach the married couple. The other letter, with the red seal, was dated August 1851 and read:

"The unnamed person—whose name will one day be named," to whom the entire authorship is dedicated, is my former fiancée: Mrs. Regine Schlegel.[2]

Israel Levin, who had for long periods been Kierkegaard's secretary but was not present in the apartment on that day, recounted later that the elder brother, when he had finished reading, had to sit down on a chair and collect himself for a few minutes.[3] The relationship between the two brothers had long been wretched, and, as mentioned, remained unresolved at Frederik's Hospital, where through the duty nurse Søren let Peter Christian understand that his visit was unwanted. If he had hoped for some posthumous reconciliation, that hope was now finally dashed. The contents of the envelopes were solely about Regine, whom the man she had been engaged to almost fifteen years before evidently looked upon as his lawful wife and had appointed as his residuary legatee. Consequently, Peter Christian's dubious pleasure was to inform the governor on St. Croix that he was married to a bigamist!

Prompted by his energetic brother-in-law J. C. Lund, Peter Christian had his letter ready to send on Friday the 23rd of November 1855.[4] It went off together with a document from Attorney Maag, whom Lund had informed of the deceased's testamentary requests shortly after the funeral, asking him to look after the legal side. It was this letter that reached the unsuspecting married couple on St. Croix on the first day of the year, and to which Fritz replied with the following lines dated Sunday the 14th of January 1856:

The Reverend Mr. Parish Priest Dr. Kierkegaard,

On New Year's Day I received Your Reverence's honored letter of November 23 of last year, and I am using the first departing steamship in order to send you my reply.

First and foremost, on behalf of my wife and myself, I wish to thank you and your honorable relatives for the discretion you have observed in a matter which, for many reasons, we do not wish to become an object of public discussion.

Next, with respect to the surprising information contained in your honorable letter, I have the following to say to Your Reverence:

My wife was to begin with in some doubt as to whether the declaration of the deceased's will that you have brought to our notice might not contain a wish that she could regard as an obligation to fulfill in the direction of what is intimated in the declaration's second passage. She has let go of this doubt, however, in part because of the great difficulties occasioned by our absence from home, and in part because of a consideration that both of us view as decisive: namely, that she absolutely does not dare consider herself justified in accepting an offer that, according to what has been said, she finds totally unacceptable.

Fritz writes with a civil servant's punctiliousness and behind the polished syntax of officialdom manages on the whole to hide his feelings. One understands, however, that the "surprising information" has put him and his wife in a quandary. How far would Regine be defaulting on a duty if she were to ignore the "declaration of the deceased's will"? According to Fritz, however, she had reached a clarification. On the one hand there was the geographical distance to take into account, and on the other, and not least, a mental and symbolic distance that neither Fritz nor Regine was in a position to overcome. Understandably in psychological terms, the officialese comes to a head in Fritz's response to Kierkegaard's remark that for him an engagement is as binding as a marriage, a view—again according to Fritz—that Regine found "totally unacceptable." Fritz could therefore conclude:

> She therefore has asked me to request that you and your co-heirs proceed entirely as if the above-mentioned will did not exist; the only wish she has expressed is that she retain some letters and several small items found among the property of the deceased, which she assumes formerly belonged to her, concerning which she has written to Dr. Henrik Lund.
> I have directly informed Attorney Maag of my wife's decision.
>
> *With the greatest of esteem, I remain Your Reverence's*
> *Most respectful*
>
> *F. Schlegel*[5]

Such conversations as Fritz had with Regine before answering that letter with the "surprising information" live only in the shimmering haze of the past, but a marital compromise is not out of the question, with Regine being allowed to "keep some letters and several small items found among the property of the deceased," so as to be able to decline the rest. If it had been up to Fritz, those letters would no doubt have stayed in Copenhagen. He must have been deeply irritated that the past should overtake him in this way, no doubt sensing that the self-same past would follow him for the rest of time. All he could do now was wait for Regine, once the package had arrived, to get down to re-reading those old glowing love letters. It is not known whether Fritz looked on the message about Regine's status as her ex-sweetheart's residuary legatee as a gesture of generosity or instead as a last-ditch provocation on the part of his old rival, but the latter reaction would surely be the more human.

When and what Regine had written to Henrik Lund remains unknown; the letter has gone astray. Nor is it known when Fritz's letter came into Attorney Maag's hands. But on Wednesday the 27th of February 1856, Henrik Lund wrote to Peter Christian Kierkegaard:

> Dear Uncle! As you no doubt already know, when you were here last a letter and orders had come from Mrs. Schlegel in the West Indies concerning the inheritance. She wished some small things to be taken out—and they have been taken out and sent to her with the most recently departing ship. Now that we have freer hands over the effects, I shall allow myself to inform you of what we have found to be most correct in this connection—and we would hope that it also wins your support. There are some other items, mostly women's jewelry that belonged to her and which were included in a catalogue that had been drawn up of the things in the estate; but since we thought it not worth letting these items go to auction, we have taken them out and I have appropriated them for the time being with a view to adding their value to the estate.[6]

"*Inventory of some good furniture and effects*" is noted in the small auction catalog that was useful to have in hand for those with thoughts of acquiring some of Søren Kierkegaard's worldly belongings, which came under the hammer at a furniture auction on the 2nd and 3rd of April 1856. According to the catalog the jewelry that Henrik Lund mentions in his letter and later shipped off to St. Croix must be the "1 gold brooch, 1 ditto bracelet, 1 ditto ring, some small ditto trimmings," which were valued at ten rix-dollars.[7]

It is as curious as it is characteristic that Regine wrote not so much as a single line about all of this to Cornelia. The only indication of the oppressive presence of the past in these weeks is her slip of the pen at the letter's top right-hand corner, where St. Croix has become Copenhagen to become again St. Croix. When, on Monday the 28th of January, she wrote once more to Cornelia, she repeated the slip, St. Croix again briefly becoming Copenhagen. It begins to look a little like a thought, and, with an almost astonishing will to suppress the inheritance affair, Regine begins as follows: "Dear beloved Cornelia! Seeing as this time I have really nothing at all to tell you, I shall simply burden you with a line or two, and especially to say thank you for the exquisite Christmas letter from the whole family." The letter had made them both feel "so much at home" and had contributed in so salutary a way to wiping out the "memory of the tiresome Christmas we've had." The latter was doubtless true, but in the light of the inheritance affair, there is something jarring in Regine's having "nothing at all to tell." She writes that on the previous day Fritz had been taken over to St. Thomas in a day-long pouring rain. The intricate matter of the inheritance no doubt did little to make the expedition more enjoyable for him. In St. Croix, Regine felt "a little more lonely than usual," but she consoled herself with the thought that the trip would do Fritz good, and she hoped it would divert him enough for him to be able to recover his strength. She missed him and would really rather have gone along with him, but it wasn't to be:

> There was no talk this time of my going along; since it was a business trip that he wanted to conclude quickly, it would only be to his and my own inconvenience if I also went along; I enjoyed myself very well when I was there last, but I would just as soon stay at home and look forward to him coming back presently.

Fritz was on St. Thomas for eight days. The solitude left Regine restless. She felt as though "sorcery had a hand in the days not coming to an end," and she imagined Fritz being ill over there, which in fact he was. Indeed he was "so ill one night that he thought he was going to die (these disgusting dinner parties), so that he had to call the physician the next day." He was, thank heavens, already well on the way to recovery, but had to cancel a more important engagement that same evening, and after he had returned he went about feeling unwell for more than a week. One might suppose there were physical causes for the complaints, but perhaps not only those. And while Fritz lies ill, the letters from the old rival are on their way to St. Croix.

"MY REGINE! . . . YOUR K."

The history of the engagement can be followed first and foremost in the approximately thirty letters that Kierkegaard wrote to Regine, between September 1840 and October 1841. Of these, five are simply small notes giving the time and place for a meeting, or accompanying a gift: flowers, perfume (Regine loved "Extrait double de Muguet"), a music stand, a handkerchief, a copy of the New Testament, and for Regine's nineteenth birthday a pair of candelabra, together with something so very state-of-the-art as a "painting set." The letters begin "My Regine!" and in most cases conclude with "Your S. K.," alternating with "Yours eternally S. K.," and—toward the end of the relationship—"Your K."

As we read through this small pile of correspondence, a curious duplicity gradually emerges. In their language, the letters are among Kierkegaard's most outstanding achievements so far as a writer. The pen no longer pauses with the ink bleeding onto the paper; the creaky Latin syntax that once could force Kierkegaard's language into lackluster constructions is here replaced by a beguiling suppleness that lifts the lines from the page. They steal gently around their subject and draw on well-known Danish writers, such as Johannes Ewald, Jens Baggesen, Adam Oehlenschläger, Christian Winter, and Poul Martin Møller. Far from being ordinary communication, these letters are art.

Therein lies the triumph and the tragedy. For the letters, by virtue of their undeniably aesthetic quality, almost cry out to the writer that a husband is not at all what he is to become, but an author. This makes them in effect letters of farewell that try, with great discretion and an ingenious indirectness, to make the recipient understand that the man who celebrates her up and down the page has long ago vanished from her life because he has lost himself in recollection of her. His love is bound in artifice and imagination, and he has to accept the truth of the situation, that he is in real life unsuited to the married state. From the recollection that gives life to imagination there spreads also the death that parts the lovers.

"I instantly entered into a relationship with the whole family. I especially employed my virtuosity with respect to the father, whom, incidentally I have always liked so very much," wrote Kierkegaard triumphantly in 1849, but he continued in another, more subdued tone: "But within [myself], the next day I saw that I had made a mistake. Penitent that I was, my *vita ante acta* [previous life], my melancholia, that was enough."[8] The fact that this switch from enchantment to regret had come about early sadly agrees all too well with what Regine later related, namely, that one day "not long after the engagement [she] met him in the arched passageway [of the palace riding ring], where he was as if "completely changed—absent and cold!""[9] Nonetheless, or rather for that very reason, Kierkegaard had, already in one of his first letters, bound Regine fast quite literally to the *writing*, which is, if anything is, the medium of recollection.

My Regine!

To

<u>Our own little Regine</u>

A line like this under the words serves to direct the typesetter to space out that particular word. To space out means to pull the words apart from one another. Therefore, when I space out the words above, I intend to pull them s o v e r y f a r a p a r t that a typesetter presumably would lose his patience and very likely never set type again in his life.

Your S. K.[10]

Regine is not only spaced to such a degree that she stretches over time and place and into the entire history of literature, she has also been given a kind of *official* status from the very start. She is referred to as "our own little Regine" and is lifted thereby out of the more intimate space in which lovers' exchanges usually occur. Regine has become ours, posterity's, the *reader's*.

Some time later, Kierkegaard sends an ink drawing of his own, depicting a little man standing on Knippelsbro and gazing through a huge telescope to the right, in the direction of the words "Tre Kroner" (three crowns)—the military battery in the harbor fairway outside Copenhagen. The letter begins:

> *My Regine!*
>
> This is Knippelsbro. I am that person with the spyglass. As you know, figures appearing in the landscape are apt to look somewhat curious. You may take comfort, therefore, in the fact that I do not look quite so ugly and that every artistic conception always retains something of the ideal, even in caricature.

So far so good. But then come symbolic hints of the future. Kierkegaard pretends that his sketch has been judged by some "art experts," who have asked why he failed to provide any background. Some think it due to the artist's weak grasp of perspective, while others incline to what one is led to understand is the correct theory, that this must be "an allusion to a folktale about a man who so completely lost himself in the enjoyment of the view from Knippelsbro that at last he saw nothing but the picture produced by his own soul, and which he could just as well have been looking at in a darkened room."

There is of course no such folktale; Kierkegaard simply makes it up. But the poetizing is bleak, since it tells Regine that she is about to vanish before his eyes. Yes, he stands there sure enough on Knippel's Bridge and gazes into his telescope, but *in reality* he is gazing at a self-created image, woman as ideal, myth perhaps, but in any case not the eighteen-year-old Regine Olsen of flesh and blood and desire. Kierkegaard then comments on the telescope's special construction:

> [T]he outermost lens is of mirror glass so that when one trains it on *Trekroner* and stands on the left side of the bridge at an angle of 5° off Copenhagen, one sees something quite different from what is seen by

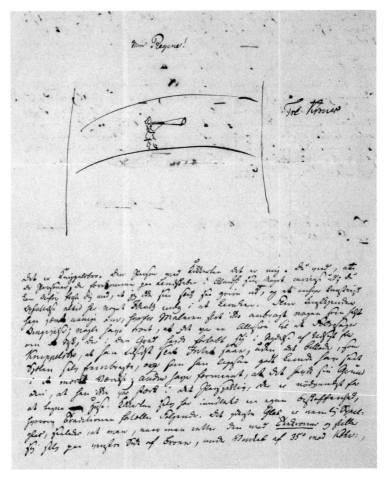

12. Several of the self-drawn ink sketches that Kierkegaard enclosed in his letters to Regine are lost, but when writing to his fiancée on the 23rd of September 1840, he included this sketch in the letter itself. The accompanying text tells us that it is the artist himself whom we see standing in the middle of Knippelsbro, armed with a huge telescope directed at the sea fortress, the Three Crowns, but which, thanks to some cleverly angled mirrors, manages to capture Regine in 66 Børsgade.

> all the other people about one. . . . Only in the proper hands and for the proper eye is it a divine telegram; for everybody else it is a useless contrivance.[11]

The telescope is thus a kind of periscope that with its angled mirror sends reality around in its own dark interior, so as to satisfy the curious eye with pictures that no one else can see: the actual Regine has been replaced by the "Regine" of reflection. And it is in all essentials to this Regine that these letters are addressed—not to "Miss R. Olsen," as is written so prosaically on the face of the envelope.

Nor is it only the immediate future that fills in the perspective in Kierkegaard's epistles, but on the contrary, studies in atmosphere and light, meditations on eternity and the moment, presence, and memory, as though becoming lost in lyricism about nature, the changing seasons, or suddenly plunging all the way back to Greek myths, only to linger soon afterward on Regine as seen in a certain setting, usually indoors with the window wide open to romantic scenes:

> It is Indian summer, towards evening. —The little window is open, the moon swells, outdoing itself in splendor so as to eclipse the mirror image in the sea, which seems to outshine it, almost audibly—it is that wonderful. The moon flushes with rage and conceals itself in the clouds, the sea shivers. —You sit on the sofa, the thoughts float far afield, your eye is fixed on nothing, infinite thoughts fade away only in the infinity of the wide heavens, everything in between is gone, it is as though you sailed in the air. And you summon the fleeting thoughts that show you an object, and if a sigh had propulsive power, if a human being was so light, so ethereal that the compressed air released by a sigh could carry him away, and indeed the more quickly the deeper the sigh—then you would be with me in that very instant.[12]

It is an almost Chagallian scenario: the sigh lifts the ethereal lovers up toward each other in a gentle arc into a bluish airspace over the city roofs. It is erotically effective, but a trifle abstract. In the letter of December the 9th, this distancing from the world and the everyday is repeated, but in the other direction: in a sketch (now lost) Regine has been able to find her way around in a subaqueous home that her betrothed has envisaged for her and has described in these words: "There are many small but cozy rooms down there, where one may safely sit while the ocean storms outside. In some, one can faintly hear the din of the world, not anxiously clamoring but quietly dying away and really irrelevant to those who inhabit the rooms."[13]

How Regine reacted to this persistent isolation from the world can be seen indirectly in four small lines in her own hand containing a protest against the, at one moment ethereal and in the next subaqueous, form of existence imputed to her. In a letter of November or December, Kierkegaard had enclosed a colored picture presenting an oriental landscape with unmistakably erotic symbolism in the form of towers, arched gateway openings, and a heaven-striving minaret in the background. On a bench in the foreground is a young man with a stringed instrument on his lap, no doubt a lute, while just over his head a smiling, bare-armed woman offers him a rose from an open window, from which a large, green-colored curtain flaps invitingly. It is all very daring. Kierkegaard himself, however, is not so daring—on the contrary, his comments cause every erotic possibility in the picture to vanish in a cloud of dialectic.

> She holds a flower in her hand. Is it she who gives it to him, or has she received it from him only to return it to him in order to receive it once more? No outsider knows. The wide world lies behind him; he has turned his back upon it. Stillness prevails throughout as in eternity, to which such a moment belongs. Perhaps he has sat like this for centuries; perhaps the happy moment was only a brief one and yet sufficient for an eternity.[14]

And so it continues. On the reverse of the picture Kierkegaard has written a small verse in German from *Des Knaben Wunderhorn*, again in all propriety; but then, just under the German verse, there follow the only lines Regine has left from the time of their engagement.

> And if my arm doth give such pleasure,
> Such comfort and such ease;
> Then, handsome merman, hasten; Come take
> them both—oh, please!

Regine could thus also quote. Indeed, the small quotation from Johannes Ewald's novel *Fiskerne* (The Fishermen) shows that she could do so with an erotic accent. She will not be deterred, will not be content with clever observations or be put off by strange metaphors but embraced by her merman, will venture out on 70,000 agitated fathoms. Not for nothing was Joan of Arc said to be her heroine and greatest inspiration.

Kierkegaard in his melancholy went in the opposite direction. He tried in the early days of the relationship to temper Regine's erotic passion by "read[ing] Bishop Mynster's sermons aloud to her once a week,"[15] but as has occurred in history earlier—just think of Abelard and Heloïse—eroticism found its way deep into religion, causing tremors: "The greatest possible misunderstanding betw. one hum. being and another with respect to the religious is when one takes a man and a woman, and then the man who is to instill in her the re⁻ ligious . . . then becomes the object of her love."[16] One may surmise that an exchange like this, a "transference," may have occurred in the present case too. In an undated letter, Kierkegaard declares that when, earlier in the day, he had to say some serious things to Regine, it had not been his intention that she should "think for a moment that I feel myself superior at such times." Far from it; as a form of evidence that he also "chastise[s]" himself, he sends Regine a copy of the New Testament "as a remembrance of this morning."[17] Between these lines with their authoritative, correctional tone, we sense that Regine has on that morning been much too direct, sensuous, desirous, and for this, although he too was not unaffected, her betrothed has resolutely reproved her. It was in his view inappropriate.

With a peculiarly ritual precision, Kierkegaard took care that, to begin with, Regine received a letter on Wednesdays;[18] but gradually, as the relationship neared its end, he allowed a longer interval to lapse between letters. So it was that, on Wednesday the 11th of November 1840, Regine sat waiting for a letter that never came. She had invited Kierkegaard to dinner in the evening with her parents, but he had left town in a coach for Fredensborg and only arrived at the home of these people, who with the greatest good will had adjusted themselves to the idea of being his in-laws, at eight o'clock—much too late and extremely embarrassing. What went on in his mind as the coach rattled through the twilight on its way back to town is revealed in a thoughtful entry in the journal: "On the bottom of the empty wagon lay 5 or 6 oats; the vibrations made them dance and they formed the most curious patterns—I lost myself in contemplating them."[19]

Nor was there a letter the following Wednesday, but Kierkegaard's servant suddenly arrives to deliver a package with Carl Bernhard's just published novel, *Gamle Minder* (Old Memories). That the title could be read as hinting symbolically at the approaching shelving of their engagement into history's open-ended archive of ended relationships, is something Kierkegaard gives Regine to understand on the Wednesday the following week, the 25th of November, when the erotic barometer plunges dramatically: "My Regine! Perhaps you were also expecting to receive, along with *Old Memories*, a potential memory in the form of a letter. It did not turn out that way, so please accept these lines which may— who knows—soon become tokens of a time gone by." It sounds as ominous as it is. With brusque sarcasm, he continues:

> It is fine that you should be expecting a letter from me, and especially when your expectation does not take the form of an intense disquiet that needs to be calmed, but is a devoted, quiet longing. . . . [F]reedom is love's element. And I am convinced that you honor me too much to want to see in me a diligent lord-in-waiting who carries out love's bureaucratic responsibilities with the conscientiousness of an accountant, or to want me to compete for a medal for perseverance in oriental handicrafts. And I am convinced that, when a letter does not arrive, *my* Regine is too much of a poet to see it as a lack of "dutiful attention," to use an official expression, and even if a letter were never to arrive, too much of a poet to long to return to the fleshpots of Egypt, or wish

13. The three adjoining gabled houses between the Exchange and Knippelsbro were built in Dutch Renaissance style and called the "Six Sisters." Their prominent gables faced Slotsholm's Canal, while at the rear a row of storehouses faced Børsgraven, where goods were carried to and from the Exchange. The Olsen family lived on the second floor in 66 Børsgade. The "Six Sisters" were demolished in 1901 after a series of insensitive extensions.

to be continually surrounded by the enamored churnings of a senti-mental lover.[20]

There was no impending danger of the latter outcome. After a dubious "Your S.K." there follows a short postscript: "At this moment I walk past your window. I look at my watch, and that signifies that I have seen you. If I do not look at my watch I have not seen you."[21]

The actual circumstances behind these cryptic words can be more or less re-constructed. Accompanied by his servant, Kierkegaard walked from his apart-ment at 38 Nørregade, across the plaza opposite the Church of Our Lady, and presumably along Strøget, then over Højbro Plads to his fiancée's residence at 66 Børsgade. While the servant delivers the letter, Kierkegaard has calculated the moment when, having read that cryptic postscript, Regine will go over to the window from which she sees her fiancé, who then signals that he sees her by taking out his watch, or indicates the opposite by letting it remain in his pocket.[22] Odd behavior, enigmatic and baroque, but not boring. Quite the con-trary. Fritz Schlegel would never have thought of such a thing.

Just before Christmas, Kierkegaard's letters sound more conciliatory. It is as if he wants to make it known that November's hurtful episodes and missing letters were meant as a test of Regine's faithfulness: "I try thee no longer, now I know thy mood," so it goes in December, along with a quotation from the poet Christian Winther. A lengthy New Year's letter that arrives on Wednesday the 30th of December is affectionate, down to earth, and uncomplicated: "I felt so unspeakably light-hearted. I drove to Lyngbye, not as I usually do, somber and dejected, carelessly flung in a corner of the carriage-seat. I sat in the middle of the seat, uncommonly straight, not with my head bent low, but looked about me happily and confidently. I was immensely pleased to see everybody." And the letter ends in a kind of submission: ". . . I came, I saw, *she* conquered."[23]

Kierkegaard had more than enough to keep him busy in the new year. In mid-November 1840 he began at the Pastoral Seminary, where he was to pre-pare sermons and assist in the evaluation of the efforts of his fellow seminar-ians. On Tuesday the 12th of January 1841, in Holmens Church, he preached his first ever sermon. The text was the passage from the letter to the Philippians (1:19–25), where Paul speaks of his being split between the earthly and the heavenly, that for him Christ is life and so dying is a gain. Parallel with his par-ticipation in the seminary's instruction, Kierkegaard made a first serious start on his magister's dissertation "On the Concept of Irony." All this stole costly time from Regine, who has clearly complained that her fiancée was using dis-sertations and pastoral seminaries as excuses not to see her. When, on the 9th of March, he had put the final period to an evaluation of one of his contempo-raries' sermons, Kierkegaard writes to her that truly it was not "because I hap-pen to have a pen in my hand that I take this occasion, as it were, to write *on occasion*," something she surely must have reproached him for.[24]

Regine had to while away the time in other ways, with the result that when her betrothed turned twenty-eight on the 5th of May 1841, he received a pearl-embroidered letter case that his nimble-fingered sweetheart had manufactured

14. "Enclosed herewith a picture, which I do not want hanging unheeded in an un-
inhabited room," Kierkegaard wrote in an instructive accompaniment to the portrayal
of an oriental couple who, flanked by pillars and with a mountain landscape in the background, are giving themselves tenderly to each other. "Your eternal S. K." or—as here—
"Your S. K." is the most intimate signature in the engagement letters, which toward the
end of the relationship shrinks to "Your K." The undated letter is presumed to be from
some time in January 1841.

on her own. The birthday celebrant sent his thanks on the same day, along with
a rose. But not just any rose:

> I am sending you a rose with this. Unlike your present, it has not blos-
> somed in my hands in all its splendor but has withered in my hands;
> unlike you, I have not been the happy witness to all its unfolding; I
> have been the sad witness to its gradual fading; I have seen it suffer;
> it lost its fragrance, it hung its head, its leaves drooped in the struggle
> with death; its blush faded and its fresh stem dried. It forgot its magnif-

icence, thought itself forgotten, and did not know that you preserved its remembrance, it did not know that I constantly brought it to mind, it did not know that we both preserved its memory.[25]

The unmistakable symbolism here and in a following lacuna in the exchange of letters speak in their own ill-fated language, which is converted into action when, on the 11th of August, Kierkegaard returns his betrothed's engagement ring together with a letter of farewell, which in his eyes was so felicitous that it was later inserted *word for word* in the publication "'Guilty?'/'Not Guilty.'" The actual letter to Regine has been lost, but in the publication it reads:

> So as not to have to rehearse yet again something which must, in the end, be done; something which, when it is has been done, will surely give the strength that is needed; let it be done, then. Above all, forget the person who writes this; forgive a person who, whatever he might have been capable of, was incapable of making a girl happy.
>
> In the Orient, to send a silken cord was a death sentence for the recipient; here, to send a ring will likely be a death sentence for the person who sends it.[26]

Regine, on reading these lines, was beside herself and ran immediately to Nør-regade to speak with Kierkegaard. Since he was not at home, she went into his room and left what Kierkegaard later described as a "note of utter despair," in which she implored him for "Christ's sake and the memory of my late father, not to leave her." Regine certainly knew how to touch her beloved's nerve. "Then," continued Kierkegaard, "there was nothing else to do but to dare to the utmost to support her, if possible, through deception, to do everything to repel her from me in order to rekindle her pride."[27]

Thus began "the reign of terror"[28] during which Kierkegaard was, according to himself, compelled to appear as a "first class scoundrel" in order to break off the connection, behavior which he himself viewed as the most "exquisite gallantry."[29] Professor F. C. Sibbern could recall: "When he wanted to break off with her—but by compelling her to break off with him—he behaved in such a way that Miss O. said he had mistreated her soul; she used that expression, and she felt deep indignation about it."

The scoundrel strategy seems nevertheless to have been effective, since many years later Regine declared that it was *she* who broke off with *him*. Sibbern tried moreover to console Regine by pointing out that it was just as well that she "did not become K.'s," since his "spirit was continually preoccupied with itself, and this man, confined as he was in self-reflection, would either have tormented her with jealousy or have lived with her as if he were totally unconcerned with her." The same Sibbern later refused to voice an opinion on the cause of the break, even though he could have told "things that only a very few people know besides myself," were it not that, as he put it, "I dare not confide the most important of these things to paper."[30]

Among Kierkegaard's contributions to the deception is a letter written late in September or at the beginning of October, which seems shamelessly harsh. A box containing a bottle of "Extrait double de Muguet" was accompanied with the words: "You may remember that about a year ago I sent you a bottle of this essence." After a short meditation on the blessings of recollection, Kierkegaard turns again to the bottle and in particular to the way it had been so carefully packaged:

> I send you then a bottle of it enveloped in an abundance of leafy wrappings. But these leaves are not the kind one tears off hastily or throws aside with annoyance in order to get to the contents. On the contrary, they are precisely of the kind that gives pleasure, and I see with how much care and solicitude you will unfold every single leaf and thereby recollect that I recollect you, my Regine, and you will yourself recollect.
>
> *Your S.K.*[31]

What could these "leafy wrappings" be that served as packing paper and were apparently of such a "nature" that Regine would have to carefully unfold them, one by one, all the while remembering everything or re-experiencing it? It isn't known, but the thought is not remote that the "leafy wrappings" that Regine had her hands full of before reaching the fine little bottle deep within, could have been—her own letters. What else could "leafy wrappings" have been? Kierkegaard himself offers no enlightenment on the actual episode, but in 1849 summarizes the whole period in these words:

> It was a frightfully agonizing time—to have to be so cruel, and then to love as I did. She fought like a lioness; had I not believed that I possessed [the power of] divine resistance, she would have won.
> Then it broke, about two months later. She was in despair. For the first time in my life I scolded. It was the only thing to do.[32]

From the Olsen home in Børsgade Kierkegaard went directly to the Royal Theater, since he wanted to speak to Emil Boesen. "This is the basis for the story that was told around town at the time, to the effect that I supposedly took out my watch and said to the family that if they had anything more to say, they had better hurry because I had to be at the theater." When the act was over and Kierkegaard left his seat in an upper box, Regine's father Terkild Olsen appeared from the lower boxes and went over to Kierkegaard to ask to talk with him, whereupon the two men walked back to Børsgade together:

> He said: It will be the death of her; she is in total despair. I said: I will try to calm her down, but the matter is settled. He said: I am a proud man; it is hard, but I beg you not to break with her. He was truly grand, I was jolted by him. But I stood my ground. I had supper with the family that evening. Spoke with her when I left.[33]

The next morning Kierkegaard received a letter from Terkild Olsen, saying that Regine had not slept at all the previous night and asked Kierkegaard to come and visit her. He did so:

> I went there and made her see reason. She asked me: Will you never marry? I answered: Well, yes, in ten years, when I have begun to simmer down and need a lusty young miss to rejuvenate me. A necessary cruelty. Then she said: Forgive me for what I have done to you. I replied: It is really I who ought to ask that. She said: Promise to think of me. I did so. She said: Kiss me. I did so—but without passion. Merciful God . . . So we parted. I spent the nights crying in my bed. But by day I was my usual self, wittier and more flippant than ever; it was necessary.[34]

In the margin of the journal, opposite where Kierkegaard had exclaimed "Merciful God," he adds that Regine was accustomed to carrying in her "bosom" a "little note on which were some words from me." What those words were no one knows, for according to K, at one point Regine drew the note out and quietly tore it into tiny pieces and, staring straight ahead, said: ". . . so you have also played a terrible game with me."[35] The gesture is decisive: Regine frees herself from the writing, gives up being a paper and ink Regine and returns to reality. She herself recalls that at their final parting, she said: "Now I can bear it no longer; kiss me one last time and then have your freedom!"[36]

From then on the break was a reality. Søren and Regine later exchanged the letters they had sent to each other, though when this was done is not known. One understands that Kierkegaard also received "all my things, etc." from the Olsen family, while a letter he had written to Regine's father "was returned unopened." The letter no longer exists.[37]

In his journal for October 1841, Peter Christian writes: "On the 10th(?) after a long period of struggle and dejection, Søren broke off his connection with Miss Olsen (Regina)." The question mark indicates an error, for the break had actually occurred on the 12th of October. Not even Søren Aabye, whose

15. "You are mine, joined with me even if a continent has separated us," assures Kierkegaard toward the end of this undated letter, which was accompanied by a picture in vivid colors where a bare-armed woman holds out a rose to a lute-playing youth, while gateway openings, minarets, and other erotic symbols tower in the background. "And when it storms and roars in the workshop of ideas, then I listen for your voice; and when I stand in the midst of need . . . then I see the window open, and you stand in summer clothing as once at Schlegel's," Kierkegaard writes, as though connivingly, midway through the letter. The episode in question "at Schlegel's" is not known.

dealings with dates otherwise bore a peculiarly ritual stamp, could recall it; and with the help of his journal entries and old newspapers, he later tried to reconstruct the course of events up to that point in time, but in vain.

The broken engagement was soon known in town and had people talking. Rumor had it that Regine had been invited one evening to attend *Don Giovanni*, but no sooner was the overture over than Kierkegaard got up and said, "Now we are leaving. You have had the best of it, the pleasure of expectation!" When, many years later, Julius Clausen cautiously presented Regine with this story, she said, "Yes, I remember that evening well, but it was after the first act that we went, and

16. "Truly you are your father's daughter," exclaimed Cornelia in a letter to Regine, who had used a certain manner of speech that their father was also prone to employ. But the similarity between father and daughter seems clearly to have extended appreciably further. The profile under the heavy locks of hair gives us regular and determined features, but it reveals also something feminine and tender to be found again in Regine's physiognomy. The drawing from which the lithograph is reproduced dates to 1825.

we left because he had a bad headache."[38] Henrik Hertz joins the mixed choir of outraged voices and is able to contribute to the story of "the young, delightful Miss Olsen," whom "he practically tortured to death with his peculiarities":

> One day he fetched her in a landau for a ride in the country, about which she was indescribably happy. But at the circle in Vesterbro he turned around and drove her home again, so that she could become accustomed to denying herself pleasures.[39]

Naturally, the dismay in the Olsen family was also enormous. Regine's elder brother, Jonas, straightaway declared his burning hatred of Kierkegaard, but when Peter Christian told his brother that he would try to explain to the family that this Søren was not the "scoundrel" he seemed to be, the protest came promptly: "I said: if you do that, I'll put a bullet through your head. The best proof of how deeply the matter engaged me."[40]

"SHE NODDED TWICE. I SHOOK MY HEAD."

Two years later, on the 16th of April 1843, Regine was sitting in the Church of Our Lady. It was the first day of Easter and she was there for Evensong, as the afternoon service between one and two o'clock was called. Kierkegaard was also sitting in the church. He had been in Berlin for almost five months and had taken home in his suitcase the greater part of the manuscript for *Either/Or*, his 838-page debut book, which came out on the 20th of February 1843 and left Copenhagen's reading public wide-eyed and dumb-struck. The two former sweethearts had without prearrangement been meeting each other, wordlessly, between nine and ten o'clock in the morning, somewhere on a short stretch where their trips through town crossed. But on this Sunday, during Evensong, their ritualized meeting took a dramatic turn, as Kierkegaard confirmed in his journal:

> On the first day of Easter at Evensong in the Church of Our Lady (during Mynster's sermon) she nodded to me. I do not know whether pleadingly or forgivingly, but in any case affectionately. I had taken a seat at a remote spot but she discovered me. Would to God she hadn't. Now a year and a half of suffering are wasted and all the enormous pains I took, she does not believe I was a deceiver, she trusts me. What ordeals now lie ahead of her. The next will be that I am a hypocrite. The higher we go the more dreadful it is. That a person of my inwardness, of my religiousness, could behave in such a way![41]

The whole entry, which midway touches on the Monday morning meetings and was apparently too private to share with posterity, is crossed out with tight wavy lines of ink. Later, Kierkegaard returns to Regine's nod in more detail. "She nodded twice. I shook my head. It meant: You must give me up. Then she nodded again, and I nodded in as friendly a way as possible, it meant: You keep my love." They meet again on the street some time later. Regine gives him a "friendly" and "ingratiating" greeting, but Kierkegaard is at a loss, looks at her "inquiringly" and shakes his head again.[42]

REPETITION AND THE REPETITION

Indirect communication can be a dangerous undertaking; you send off a message to which the recipient may attach a quite different meaning from the one you have in mind. If the communication is also a wordless gesture, things can go altogether wrong. Presumably that is what happened in the church when Regine nodded for the third time and Kierkegaard gave a friendly nod in return. He wanted her to know that she could count on his love, but most likely signaled to her that she had his blessing to resume her relationship with Johan Frederik Schlegel. Everything suggests that it was this relationship that lay behind Regine's wordless appeal that day in church, a matter of which Kierkegaard had not the faintest idea.

Three weeks later, on Monday the 8th of May 1843, he set out on a second journey to Berlin. As previously, he sailed on the *Konigen Elisabeth* and came via Ystad to Stralsund. From there he continued the next day by coach to Stettin (now Szczecin), where there was a railroad connection via Angermünde to Berlin, which meant that this part of the journey took only ten hours.[43] After arriving in Berlin and installing himself at the Hotel Saxen—at the corner of Jägerstrasse and Charlottenstrasse an der Ecke—he wrote to Emil Boesen:

> Yesterday I arrived, today I am at work, and the veins in my forehead are bulging. . . . At this moment the busy thoughts are at work again, and the pen flourishes in my hand. . . . I have recommenced my old promenades up and down Unter Linden—as always when I travel—a mute letter nobody can pronounce and which does not say anything to anyone either.[44]

Kierkegaard didn't manage to send his letter to Boesen, but four days later began another in which he could announce:

> In a certain sense, I have already achieved what I might wish for, something I had not known would take an hour, a minute, or half a year—an idea—a hint. . . . As far as that is goes, I could just as well return home at once, but I will not do so, although it is not likely that I will travel any farther than Berlin.[45]

Kierkegaard had actually thought of staying away for "a year and a half," so what he managed to achieve in less than a week after his arrival, and to such effect that he could return to Copenhagen, is not immediately clear. From the letter that he sent to Boesen ten days later, on the 25th of May, it appears that his homeward plans remained in place.

Again a little while and you will see me. I have finished a work of some importance to me, am hard at work on another, and my library is indispensable to me, as is also a printer. In the beginning I was ill, but now I am well, that is to say, insofar as my spirit grows within me and probably will kill my body. I have never worked as hard as now. I go for a brief walk in the morning. Then I come home and sit in my room without interruption until about three o'clock. My eyes can barely see. Then with my walking stick in hand I sneak off to the restaurant, but am so weak that I believe if anyone were to call out my name, I would keel over and die. Then I go home and begin again. In my indolence during the past months I had pumped up a veritable shower bath, and now I have pulled the string and the ideas are cascading down upon me: healthy, happy, merry, gay, blessed children born with ease and yet all of them with the birthmark of my personality. Otherwise I am weak, as I said, my legs shake, my knees ache, etc.[46]

A week earlier, on the 17th of May, Kierkegaard had inserted some lines in his journal with none of the same exhilaration, but certainly not dispassionately. "Had I had faith I would have stayed with Regine. Praise and thanks be to God. I have now understood it. I have been on the point of losing my mind these days."[47] Kierkegaard chose to cross out the words with tight loops of ink, but they can be deciphered and among other things they make known that: "In an aesthetic and chivalrous sense, I loved her far more than she loved me, for otherwise she would neither have acted proudly toward me nor alarmed me later with her scream."[48] One is led to understand that he had wanted to protect Regine from unnecessary pain, and so "in a purely aesthetic sense I have acted with great humanity." Indeed he believed that he had not spoken to any young girl since breaking with Regine. So little was he the "scoundrel" he was taken to be, "for in truth it was certainly a rather f . . ."

Certainly what? We will never know. The handwriting after this point is illegible and then disappears, for here Kierkegaard has torn out pages 52 and 53 in his journal, presumably because the words had become too private, too personal, so that on re-reading the entry he opted for a complete redaction to protect himself against posterity's prurient reader.

The top of the next page in the journal opens abruptly, as follows:

> . . . it would certainly have happened. But with marriage it isn't the case that everything is sold "as is" when the hammer falls; here it is a matter of a little honesty toward the past. Here again my chivalry is obvious. . . . But if I were to explain myself, I would have had to initiate her into terrible things, my relationship to Father, his melancholy, the

eternal night brooding deep inside me, my going astray, my desires and excesses, which in the eyes of God are nevertheless not so glaring, since it was, after all, anxiety that let me go astray, and where was I to find a roof when I knew or suspected that the only man I had admired for his strength and power wavered?[49]

The relationship to Regine could not be reconciled with that to a father who had crippled his *eros* and inhibited his capacity for devotion, this being something he had been unable to tell Regine, since she for her part lacked what it took to understand it, while he lacked the necessary courage, strength, faith—and all of this had at last become clear to him during that stay in Berlin. The next entry retains this insight: "Faith therefore has hopes for this life, but, be it noted, on the strength of the absurd, not on the strength of human understanding, otherwise it is only good sense, not faith."[50] Surely it is this recognition that has now restored his hopes of being able to resume the relationship with Regine in a more platonic form to be realized within Copenhagen's ramparts, which like a kind of monastery wall would encircle their chaste meetings, making them the modern age's answer to the monk and the nun.

To help in realizing this erotic utopia, Kierkegaard brought with him the manuscript which in his letter of the 25th of May he had told Boesen he is now "finished with." The manuscript in question is that of *Repetition*, in literary terms unquestionably the most eccentric of all Kierkegaard's works, but which from a biographical perspective betrays an absolutely hybrid anatomy. *Repetition* is something so outlandish as a piece of pseudonymously signed literary confessional that apportions his own experience of his engagement between two fictional figures, Constantin Constantius and "The Young Person." The former is in equal measure the possessor of psychological competency and a principled pessimism, the latter someone who has been so irrational as to fall in love, a circumstance that has aroused in him an irrepressible passion for poetizing. This does not prevent him from hoping to the very last—or nearly very last—for a repetition of the relationship to his beloved. In looking back at himself in the guise of the Young Person through the eyes of Constantin Constantius, Kierkegaard is able to present in full public view his own crisis of love, which is in itself self-sufficient and lacks only the poetic stimulant of love:

This young person was constituted in such a way, and by nature so gifted, that I would have wagered he would never be caught in the net of romantic love. There are, of course, exceptions in this respect that cannot be inflected according to the normal case rules. He had an exceptional intellect, especially in terms of the size of his imagination. As soon as his creativity was awakened, he had enough for his whole life, especially if he understood himself correctly and restricted himself to that cozy domestic diversion of following the activities of the intellect and the pastimes of the imagination; which is the most perfect compensation for romantic love, does not involve love's difficulties and fatalities, and which can be described as equal to the most beautiful aspects of romantic bliss.[51]

As one would expect, the young lover shares his author's melancholy and has therefore begun to *recollect* his love, which places him at a fateful distance from the girl who was the love's original object. For reasons hardly requiring comment, Constantin Constantius is able to make his diagnosis with quite special empathy.

He was deeply and passionately in love, this was clear, and yet he was already, in the earliest days, in a position to recollect his love. He was basically finished with the whole relationship. . . . And yet she was the beloved, the only one he had ever loved, the only one he would ever love. . . . All this was accompanied by a strange change in him. A poetic productivity awakened in him, to an extent that I would not have thought possible. Now I understood everything. The young girl was not his beloved, she was simply the cause that awakened the poetic in him and thus transformed him into a poet. This was why he could love only her, never forget her, never wish to love anyone else, and yet still merely long for her. She had permeated every aspect of his being. She had made him into a poet, and with this signed her own death-sentence.[52]

Kierkegaard's pseudonymous writings often allow a far more open insight into matters that one is forbidden to access in Kierkegaard's journals, owing to imagined future readers that he sees looking over his shoulder as he writes. Thanks to its pseudonymous signature, a work like *Repetition* enables him to take up and refigure intimate autobiographical material that is normally restricted to the journal's secretive soliloquist. His indignant reaction to critical reviews of his pseudonymous books is due, therefore, not *only* to hurt vanity as a writer but *also* to the fact that these books have the self-compromising character of confessional literature and have to be defended by the man whose life they lay bare. Let the third person give place to the first person, and it is as though Kierkegaard himself takes the floor when he has Constantin Constantius write:

As time passed, his relationship became an increasing torment. —His depression increased and he decided to continue with the deception. All his poetic talents were now used to amuse and entertain her. What could have provided amusement for many was used exclusively on her. She was and remained the beloved, the adored, even though he was near to losing his mind as a result of the lie that served only to enthrall her more and more profoundly. Her existence or non-existence, in a certain sense, actually meant nothing to him, though his depression found joy only through bringing enchantment to her life. . . . There is nothing so seductive to a girl as to be loved by a poetic-depressive type.[53]

The Young Person in *Repetition* is of course not just a Kierkegaard clone, mirroring the original in every particular. But, given the love conflict's cause and tragic background, it is not the differences but the similarities that are so immediately striking: the melancholy, the early-recognized mistake, the woman who is first the object of eroticism but soon becomes the occasion for passionate poetic creativity, the asymmetrical incurring of guilt, the desire to charm the beloved in painful awareness of the relationship's imminent doom, the deceptive and hypocritical behavior culminating in the role of true villain. For when the erotically confused youth was unable to persuade himself to explain to the girl "the confusion," to make her see that she was "just the visible form, whereas his thoughts, his soul, sought something else that he had attributed to her,"[54] Constantin Constantius urged him to resort to a radical strategy:

> . . . lay waste to everything. Transform yourself into a contemptible person whose only pleasure is in tricking and deceiving. . . . Try at first, if possible, just to be a little annoying to her. Do not tease her, that will only excite her. No, be changeable, nonsensical. Do one thing one day, and another thing the next, but all without passion, blunderingly. . . . Instead of romantic ecstasy, constantly produce a mawkish quasi-love that is neither indifference nor genuine desire. Allow your whole manner to be as unpleasant as it is to see a man drool.[55]

Although Constantin Constantius frankly admits that he finds it "indelicate," he nonetheless engages a young seamstress with whom the Young Person is to be seen in public, so that rumors of their dubious connection can spread in town and come to the young girl's ear and, with bitterness but sympathy on her side, she can then free herself from the relationship, during which time the Young Person is "in addition, if possible to work on his transformation into a poet."[56] By his own account, Constantin Constantius was "unusually anxious concerning the outcome,"[57] but although preparations for the performance were brought to completion, the Young Person's courage failed him and he took refuge in Stockholm from where, some time later, he sends Constantin

Constantius the first of a series of letters disclosing in black and white that his state remains more than critical. The letters gradually fill with reflections on the Book of Job. The Young Person sings paeans of an unusual uninhibitedness to the hard-tried main character of that book, with whom he begins to identify. This identification is problematic in several ways, but it makes clear how, by having oneself written into *the big narrative*, it is possible to get along in the world, safe in the knowledge that others have previously found themselves in the same situation. That Kierkegaard chose the title he did for the work is due, not least, to the comfort drawn from this particular form of repetition.

Kierkegaard left Berlin with the manuscript for *Repetition*, which according to his own confident words he was "finished with." It is, however, unclear how far this manuscript actually resembled the book that appeared in Copenhagen on the 16th of October 1843. The existing text does not make possible a confident reconstruction of the work's genesis, but what is clear is that, after his homecoming, Kierkegaard saw a need to revise and develop it, especially the work's second part, and to drastically revise the concept of repetition itself. The most significant changes relate to the Young Person, who in the first version of the manuscript ended by committing suicide, owing to a failure of the repetition to materialize. It was presumably in this lifeless state that he was conveyed from Berlin to Copenhagen in Kierkegaard's suitcase. The suicide was a more or less indirect message to Regine that if there should be any repetition of their relationship, then a miracle was needed, a divine intervention, which the book put more pointedly by saying it would have to be by virtue of the absurd—as happened in the case of Job who got everything back twofold.

In the summer months of 1843, Kierkegaard was busily occupied in bringing the Young Person back to life through several maneuvers partly traceable at manuscript level. A parenthesis, for instance, is omitted in the following declaration: "He confided to me with an endearing candor (which I do not misuse since he is dead), that the reason he had come to me was that he needed a confidant."[58] Similarly, "Memory of his death" becomes "Memory of his disappearance."[59] And the still-living Young Person's opposition to Constantin Constantius's indelicate strategy with the seamstress was in the orginal due *not* to his lacking the necessary "strength to complete the thing"[60] but to the more straightforward circumstance that he was no longer alive—"he shot himself," as can be read in the manuscript.[61] Where and when in *Repetition* this suicide occurred cannot be determined for, after The Young Person's penultimate letter to Constantin Constantius, Kierkegaard simply clipped out five pages, four of them certainly containing text.

Putting a bullet through one's head was no original solution to crises of the soul in late romantic literature, but considerations of originality were not uppermost in Kierkegaard's mind when he decided that the Young Person had to be brought back to life. The explanation is to be found instead in a certain event that, in its harsh reality, shattered the author's own hopes of a repetition. On the 28th of August 1843, Regine Olsen became engaged to Johan Frederik Schlegel. Period. That day is known from the date engraved on Regine's engagement ring, but how long Regine and Fritz had been seeing each other before becoming engaged remains unknown. That the connection must have been a fact before Regine's nod in the Church of Our Lady in mid-April seems more than likely. On the other hand, no one knows when or from whom Kierkegaard learned that Regine had resumed contact with Fritz. But whereas the Young Person in *Repetition* confined himself to losing the newspaper when he read of his beloved's marriage, Kierkegaard lost faith in *Repetition* as an indirect communication to Regine. The Young Person had accordingly to be brought back to life, so that the book could pretend that the repetition in question was *not* that of the relationship with the woman but, on the contrary, a religious repetition that made it possible to take repossession of one's self. Among his very last words the Young Person, characteristically enough, is able to write the following:

> She is married, to whom I do not know, because when I read it in the newspaper I felt as if I had been struck and I dropped the paper. Since then I have not been able to bring myself to any closer inspection. . . .
> Is there then no repetition? Have I not received everything doubled? Have I not got myself again, precisely so that I might doubly appreciate what this means?[62]

Although the questions are clearly rhetorical, the reader is left in no doubt that the person asking them is himself in doubt. What the Young Person received again was not his loved one, but himself, which is not owing to any inner consistency in the work, but to a constellation in the world that looks astonishingly like the reunion between Regine and Fritz. Kierkegaard tries to ease the tension in the work's construction that these enforced rearrangements caused by composing a lengthy postscript in which Constantin Constantius goes to great pains to come by both a religious and a moral restoration of the Young Person, and in which the work's actual author takes back his original message to Regine. The same author's genuine reaction to the historical facts that awaited his homecoming can be observed in his manuscript, where additions and deletions are smudged over into each other in bitterness and aggression. Kierkegaard has, for instance, deleted with a mighty loop of ink the suggestion that the girl who he tried to ensnare erotically by religious means should not only "be recognizable by a black tooth but be green all over her face. But that's too much to ask. There would be a lot of green girls."[63] In another passage later deleted, the reader is familiarized with how best to deal with one's girl when about to leave her. One must, he tells us, "get her to scream herself empty, incite her into screaming, the quicker she forgets" in that this makes the transition to a new lover so much the easier:

> If you have done that done that, then you have only to make sure to strike while the iron is hot. There is no moment when a girl is more inclined to grab a new love than when she escapes one who will cost her her life. You must then make sure to put a man on her arm; she takes him even if it was a man you bought in the hardware store.[64]

In his journal, too, Kierkegaard tried to give himself air space by, among other means, portraying Regine's love crisis as a trifle that could be dispatched cheaply by cash in hand. With unmistakable allusions to the invocation "for Christ's sake and the memory of my late father!" that Regine had once resorted to in order to keep her betrothed, the journal from 1843 reads under the heading *"Exchange"*:

> An individual with a sense of humor meets a girl who had once assured him that she would die if he left her. When he now meets her she is engaged. He greets her and says, "May I thank you for the kindness you have shown me. Perhaps you will permit me to show my appreciation." (He takes 2 marks and 8 shillings out of his vest pocket and hands it to her. She is speechless with rage but remains standing there, hoping to intimidate him with her gaze. He continues): "It's nothing. It's to help out with your trousseau, and on the day you get married and put the finishing touches on your act of kindness, I promise by all that is holy—by God and by your eternal salvation—to send you another 2 marks and 8 shillings."[65]

Regine's invocation, which was a final attempt to fend off Kierkegaard's decision to leave her, has here become the target of a mean-minded restaging and parodying that makes her actions as perfidious as possible. Nor is it any accident that the two marks and eight shillings are the exact price of a copy of the New Testament that Regine might acquire to her advantage and study a little more closely before starting on her emotional incantations. It is obvious enough that the violence in Kierkegaard's entry is due to the emotional chaos into which news of Regine's engagement to Fritz has brought him. But contributing to the vehemence there is also his frustration over the fact that the repetition that *Repetition* had set its hope on was being fulfilled by Regine, who now found herself together with Fritz and beginning over again. And this, be it noted, on the strength of the absurd—not in any philosophical or religious sense, but be-

17. Emil Bærentzen's oil painting of Johan Frederik Schlegel is taken to date from 1847, when the energetic jurist with the kindly features and diplomatic disposition married Regine.

cause of the absurd circumstance that Kierkegaard, in the Church of Our Lady, had returned Regine's nod on false premises and thereby quite involuntarily sanctioned her relationship to Fritz. Kierkegaard must have agreed to a fault with Constantin Constantius when he says that "existence" is infinitely deep, because "its controlling power constructs intrigues that are entirely different from any constructed by all the poets *in uno*"[66]—and also by that poet called Kierkegaard.

The day the banns for Regine and Fritz were announced in the Church of Our Savior at Christianshavn, he, Kierkegaard the castoff, sat in the church. But when, on Wednesday the 3rd of November 1847, they were declared man and wife, he chose to take a carriage up to Lyngby to get away from it all, anguished and miserable as he was. Some time later his journal noted: "I can with a certain freemasonry use these words by the poet as a motto for part of my life's suffering . . . *infandum me jubes Regina renovare dolorem*." Kierkegaard quotes Virgil who, in the *Aeneid*, has the Trojan Aeneas utter these words in response to Queen Dido's demand that he recount the fall of Troy. Kierkegaard cleverly exploits the fact that "queen" in Latin is *regina*, so the sentence reads: "You bid me, Regine, renew a grief too great to be told." More directly, and noticeably disappointed, he writes further in his journal:

> That girl has given me enough trouble. Now she is—not dead—but happily and well married. I said that on the same day 6 years ago—and was declared the basest of all base villains. Curious![67]

REGINE FREDERIKKE OLSEN'S DEATH

It must have been no less curious for Regine to go about in quite another world with these dramatic episodes as indelible chapters in the story of her life. Although her new life in St. Croix had settled into daily rhythms and routines, her thoughts often revolved around the situation at home and how the loved ones were, especially her mother: "Say to her I long most of all for her."

Cornelia tried to put her own and her exiled little sister's minds at rest by citing the family physician Trier who, after paying a home visit to the ageing Mrs. Olsen, had said, "You are a strong old woman whose heart beats so powerfully that you put others to shame, but then neither must you complain but take walks and enjoy yourself."

In Regine's mind, Cornelia's descriptions took on lives of their own. One night her mother appeared in "a bad dream," and Regine woke up in tears. But there was also a dream where Regine "looked at rooms for her out in Bredgaden, yes, I was so West Indianly snobbish as to think of buying a whole house for her." When, in the early spring, she heard that her mother had suffered an attack of influenza, or "Lagribe" as it was then called, she was seriously alarmed: "Can you recall that Father never really recovered after he had an attack of that bad illness while still out at the Exchange, soon after my wedding." Regine's misgivings were to prove justified, for on Saturday the 26th of April, Cornelia wrote:

> Dear, precious Regine! The last time you received from me no more than the notification and an expression of hope that our dear old mother's sickness was a temporary ill; God would have it otherwise, this time I have tidings to you both of her death.

The illness had shown its true "face" on that very same evening when Cornelia had included Trier's consoling remarks in her letter to Regine. Trier was called back and found a virulent pneumonia that raged for three days, "but then it was over and she got peace." There was no greeting for Cornelia to send to the bereaved, for their mother was "not properly conscious in the 3 days." It was a great consolation that Jonas came immediately to Copenhagen, for as Cornelia explained, "one feels so lonesome with a death." Their mother had communicated her last will to Maria, who had been taking care of her at night, so the inheritance matter was clear. The mother left a government bond of 200 rix-dollars, which among other things would pay for the funeral, but to Fritz and Regine she had also bequeathed various items that she evidently presumed they lacked in their tropical exile.

> It was mother's wish that both Fritz and Oluf should have these umbrellas at the first opportunity, and you a parasol; we have only changed the color for you; she loved Fritz as her own child; he was the calm, sensible one . . . we others have so much of this unrest and fire that consume us!

Jonas officiated at the funeral. Since he had not prepared a script there was no eulogy for Cornelia to send to Regine. Jonas had, up to the last minute, been of several minds about taking part—"Even on the morning of the burial he hadn't yet made up his mind about making the speech." But as his brother-in-law Emil had deliberately omitted to contact any other priest, there was no going back. Jonas did, however, according to Cornelia, pass the test, managing among other things to bring out how the deceased had, "through the usual human struggles and conflicts, reached a lovable, meek, and mild old age." Great was her surprise, then, when after the funeral she heard that people had found Jonas's speech altogether too theological—"he is no doubt a genuine orthodox," several had whispered. This reaction made Cornelia quite angry for, in her eyes, it showed how nowadays everything was "so criticized and discussed as to drive one mad with all the theologizing (this is a new word that Fritz will no doubt add to his catalogue over my stupidities)." When the complaint reached Jonas's ears, he was so furious that he threatened to preach a second sermon in the Church of Our Lady before retiring to his country parish; but Cornelia managed to talk him out of it, because, as she confided to Regine, it should suffice for him "to throw contempt on this Sodom" before returning to "his own Hell."

More felicitous was Jonas's choice of words for his parents' gravestone, which consisted in lines from the prophet Isaiah (43:5–6), where the prophet describes a diaspora that the Olsen family, too, has experienced, but expressing the hope that the expatriate sons and daughters will one day return safely home. The inscription on the gravestone at Assistens Cemetery reads:

> Here rest: Terkild Olsen, Councillor of State, Knight of the Order of the Dannebrog. Born the 7th of February 1784, died on the 26th of June 1849, and his wife Regine Frederikke Malling, born the 7th of August 1778, died on the 15th of April 1856. Thus says the Lord: Do not fear, for I am with you; I will bring your offspring from the east and from the west I will gather you; I will say to the north, "Give them up," and from the south, "Do not withhold! Bring my sons from far away and my daughters from the end of the earth."

Regine gave the text her "most unconditional support" and returns several times in her letters to the words that are to her "like a comforting and a hope that we could truly make our own." And "when, now, you visit the grave and read these words, it is as if the same stone covered also the dear ones who lie out here, so powerfully does hope speak through them." But it was not long before this heavenly hope had to give way to self-reproach. Cornelia felt that she had shown her mother too little care, had not sufficiently spared her from the demands of the grandchildren, while Regine accused herself of letting her mother go the whole winter without "a little jam or the like from me." But she was well able to sense the absurdity in such self-reproach, whose real cause she could identify, from her own experience, as a peculiar psychological transference:

> For if one isn't quite blind in fancying one's own infallibility, it is surely the most natural outbreak of one's sorrow over a departed that one finds something to reproach oneself for, something one has done or omitted to do for them.

And in the case of their beloved mother, she consoled herself by reflecting "how indulgent she had been, particularly in her last years, so we could be so sure of her forgiveness."

CANE GARDEN'S BLESSINGS

The Colonial Council gave Fritz far too much to attend to. The long meetings, lasting as a rule from eleven in the morning until four or five in the afternoon, often in melting heat, clearly wore him out. Since he was also—according to Regine—"served up with much pure rubbish," his patience was put to a serious test, so much the more as it was he who in the final instance could be called to account for the outcome of the meetings. Now—on Tuesday the 13th of May—

they were assembled again, while Regine was writing to Cornelia and doing her best to lose track of time: "but you understand me when I tell you it gnaws at my heart every time the clock strikes, I know that the longer they are together, the more it saps his energy."

Eventually, Regine began to see Fritz only at mealtimes and in the late evenings, but he was then "usually so dead beat that I had more sorrow than joy from seeing him."

The governor pair had also for some time wanted to leave Christiansted and move out into the country. The previous year they were both so drained after the journey, and by "the long restless time [they] had been through," that nothing came of it. Now, it was not the will that they lacked, but a suitable location. A letter to Maria written in April indicates that things were beginning to brighten just a little.

> We have now almost rented a house in the country, but first it has to be repaired and servants' quarters built; we should be paying between 35 and 40 dollars a month; but it is not furnished, so it is certainly going to be both difficult and expensive before we come to rights out there; but since, once the Colonial Council has concluded, being there could do Fritz some good, the rest doesn't matter.

A few weeks later we learn that the house is still "undergoing repairs," but the restoration must have been completed within the next few months, for when Regine writes to Cornelia on Saturday the 9th of August, her letter is headed "Cane Garden."

Regine loved the new surroundings. At the beginning of December she could report that they had "acquired 2 more horses" and a "charming little carriage," so the governor could go off with the governor's lady in suitable style— "and Mathilde sits between us on a footstool." They surely presented a proud sight. Fritz commuted daily between Cane Garden and Christiansted. Regine rode with him when social and representational duties required, but without question she and Fritz preferred country life: "We feel our loneliness much less out there than in town, surrounded by people who require us to spend our table allowances on them." Keeping the carriage was not cheap either: "All this conveyance business costs a tremendous amount of money, but it isn't for luxury alone, because since we so much want to stay in the country it can sooner be reckoned a necessity." It took time to get settled, but gradually their contentment grew. From Copenhagen there came

> . . . a specially nice carpet to lie in the middle of the floor, 2 delightful small sofas covered with red velvet with a gilded marble table for

18. Cane Garden is in the southern part of St. Croix, about four miles from Christiansted. Certain parts of the building go back to the 1650s, when Jesuit monks built a small cloister on the grounds. The Cane Garden plantation dates from 1784, and the villa was extensively rebuilt in the 1820s, with classical columns on both the south and north facades. After a devastating fire at the beginning of the twentieth century, which spared only the solid outer wall, the house remained for almost five decades little more than an overgrown ruin. Based on the original drawings and a number of photographs of the ruins, Richard H. Jenrette, who acquired the property in 1985, carried out a comprehensive reconstruction, so that today Estate Cane Garden again resembles the building occupied by the Schlegels.

each, 2 curtains to hang before 2 hideous doors going into the dining room, and it has all been so well looked after that it does great honor to Schmidt. It has cost several 100, but we are particularly happy with it just now since the weather is windy and unpleasant, so that one needs to be comfortable in one's house. You see we are grand in the West Indian way.

Regine spent most weekdays at Cane Garden alone—that is to say, together with Thilly and Josephine and surrounded by their servants. She was "well satisfied" with Josephine, who had been employed in both Bredgade and Nybrogade. After Cane Garden became the residence, Josephine too seemed happier, which Regine attributed to her not living "as isolated here as in town." She was now "together with us more because her room is close beside ours, whereas in town they were in the other wing of the house." Furthermore, Anny, the black serving maid, had been fired on the spot "since this one sowed much dissension in the house." The other members of "our large staff" were really "well behaved and able," some of them being downright devoted to Regine. "I have not taken another girl in her stead; I am not brought up to use chambermaids, except in the shape of my beloved sisters when they coddled me in the old days; since that can no longer happen, I would rather help myself." There is a special sensuousness in these words.

Thilly's thoughts dwelt frequently on her Danish cousins whom she so much longed for: "Sometimes when she speaks of them she ends by saying, 'Why did you take me away from Regnar and the cousins? You can be sure it makes me feel bad.'" There had been talk of Cornelia and Emil sending their Laura out to St. Croix to keep her lonely cousin company, but it was to remain no more than a thought, as Regine could well understand, although she could not refrain from promoting the blessings of the West Indian Islands just a little. The lines that are the closest to a regular snapshot of an idyllic day at Cane Garden read:

> . . . I will not speak of how pleasant it would be for her, out driving every day, a beautiful large estate where, with Tilly, she could play under the shade of the orange trees with a lovely little white dog that Tilly has, which for old memories we have called Fido, and also a lovely roe deer that eats its dinner from a plate with me, and if I let them, they could come and join me every day.

Thilly caused many headaches. She had not been slow to exploit the privilege of being the Governor's wife's foster daughter and, with "half of the household under her rule, namely the servants, [she] had to be kept in order once in a while by the father, Fritz and me." "[T]he very lively child that she is, she is certainly not always the most polite," nor as "sweet" as she was back home: "She

19. The foundation of a former bathing house in Cane Garden's back garden offers a magnificent view over the Caribbean Sea. On Wednesday the 9th of August 1856, Regine writes to Cornelia: "Let me . . . describe to you the delightful view I have from my writing desk, through the windows that I can have open here. . . . After gazing at it now for a long time I have to say with Bolette [Rørdam] that I cannot describe it! I hope that even this gives you an impression of how we enjoy it out here in the country."

has grown too much for that" and in fact she had turned into a "lanky lass." Nevertheless we are told on the 12th of May 1857 that Thilly has "so many of the mother's characteristics that I'm certain she will also be very captivating." Since the local schools could in no circumstances teach Thilly more of anything except "impoliteness," of which "she already possesses not a little," Regine had undertaken to be her tutor.

She was often in doubt about her teaching plan and her own qualifications, not least when Oluf once in a while examined Thilly, who "stood there with such an indescribably uncomprehending expression on her face that I quite naturally was afraid and asked myself whether it was mine or the child's fault." Since the teaching called for textbooks and other materials unavailable in the West Indies, Regine asked her brother-in-law Emil for help in acquiring these. She also had use for a map, and she looked forward to the arrival of her clavichord, so that she could teach Thilly to play and also keep her own abilities intact, thereby sweetening some of the "sourness of the long spare time."

The difficulties with Thilly grew roughly in step with the young girl herself. "Thilly is well, since laziness after all is not really a sickness," declares her

20. It was due to Peter von Scholten that the slaves' children began to receive literacy instruction in the schools he had instituted in the first half of the 1840s. Schlegel and his wife continued his practice of supervising the examinations at the islands' seventeen schools. In Regine's case what began as purely a matter of duty ended by being one of her "best diversions." The practice had been initiated by the Scot, David Stow, whose experience with so-called underprivileged big-city children had convinced him that the pupils should not only be stimulated intellectually and developed morally, but would also benefit from activity, so that between every hour they were sent out to the playground for ten minutes and in the middle of the day were able to run around for an entire hour. The schools were solidly built brick buildings designed by the Danish architect and businessman Albert Løvmand, who cultivated the neoclassical style with symmetrical facades, emphatic portals, and strong outlines. With the school up on the little hill, and the Danish flag waving picturesquely in the background, the teacher and pupils are here shown lined up on a stone pier in Cruz Bay on St. John.

exacting aunt late in February 1859. Oluf had long since given up reading with her, having neither the patience nor the will to employ the approved means to which Regine "with great effect" sometimes had to resort, namely "reprimanding her a little." Oluf himself never administered corporeal punishment, but he was all in favor of Regine and Fritz being strict with her and providing the necessary counterbalance to her irresponsibility, which would become one of her greatest faults—"and everything here contrives to encourage such a fault, the whole population's exaggeratedly insipid coddling of children out here." But Regine was afraid that the strictness might put it into Thilly's head "that we were unfair." No, there is nothing new under the pedagogical sun.

"You cannot believe how I can sometimes raise my voice to her, for which I then so heartily reproach myself, since there is nothing worse than being severe to a child, but sometimes she can be so contrary." Thilly made known her sense of injustice in a quite special way—with an expression she could create with her eyes, which may be quite characteristic of girls prior to puberty, but in this case could also have had some genetic origin. One day, Oluf had drily confided to Regine that he now understood better why their father could come to beat him even though Oluf had *done* nothing but just *looked* at him: "She can give you a pair of eyes just like that, as though to say: how dare you violate me." If Regine was over-compliant she risked giving Thilly "that idiotic blind motherly love that sees nothing but angels in their children" and which generally leads to the children becoming little devils. Unfortunately, bringing them up too strictly was no better, nor was just leaving them to themselves. Regine was really at a loss and groaned in her pedagogical agony—"Ugh, it is hard to be a tutoress!"—but she comforted herself at not, thank heavens, being solely responsible for Thilly's further fate: "Well, we will strive to do our duty and otherwise rely more on the upbringing our Lord provides through life than on what we ourselves can provide." All in all, Regine was therefore

> . . . happy that I got her to come along, the labor she gives me does me good seeing that my position prevents me involving myself in house-work. Without her, how should I have put up with Oluf's melancholy gaze; when he pines away she comes along and literally kisses the clouds from his brow.

"FOOD FOR WORMS AND THAT'S THE END OF IT"

From time to time items from Copenhagen's fashion world made their way to St. Croix: "The hat is delightful, its only fault is that it doesn't sit on the *head*, but it is no doubt fashionable." The hat was black and necessary, for it was to mark her mother's death. But Regine looked forward doubly to laying aside her grief so that she could use "old fashioned hats" that had the advantage that she could "put them on." Far from being an empty-headed follower of fashion, she was a thoughtful woman who often wrestled with existential and religious questions. True enough, her former betrothed voiced the opinion that she was not "religiously inclined,"[68] a remark to which she did not take kindly. But then, next to Kierkegaard who would not fall short in this area?

The thought of Providence's unfathomable justice was always on Regine's mind, and she found comfort in the conviction that there had to be a meaning in the meaninglessness *in spite of everything*. Her faith in Providence was nourished deep down within that very simplicity that Kierkegaard throughout his life extolled as the ideal religious state. But it meant that Regine could come to doubt all the more and be put off by the wretchedness and misery around her, the narrow-mindedness, vanity, and shabbiness—in short by the revelation of humanity's least humane side. She could all of a sudden feel in her heart that people were in actual fact not God's marvelous creatures, made in his image and with the promise of eternal life, but simply coarse and clumsy beings whose meaning was to "become food for worms and that's the end of it."

One needed neither professors of theology nor weighty dogmatists to open one's eyes to the glaring reality of *original sin*. Regine needed only to observe others around her closely or to look honestly within herself. Or if in serious want of edification, one could turn one's glance outward to the splendor and glory of nature, for "according to my belief one is many times nearer God" out of doors than inside a church, where "either one comes to hear a bad sermon, or our own frivolous nature otherwise gets the better of us." Regine felt uplifted also by music, paintings, and poetry. When just before Christmas she received "the delightful Exner picture," presumably a lithograph by Julius Exner, she exclaimed in her letter to Cornelia:

> . . . you should have just seen me these days, standing in front of it and enjoying it, yes I enjoyed it so long that I ended up being really glad. So ask Jonas whether the enjoyment of art also deserves to be called affectation, when here in our aloneness, and especially in our spiritual aloneness, it can gladden and lighten the mind. No, every spiritual gift comes from God is my faith, and the effects it has are therefore justified; whether it is music, painting or poetry, and we need not denigrate them or our pleasure in them by calling them, in what it seems to me is an almost ungodly way, affectation.

It is more than likely that brother Jonas had been reading Poul Martin Møller's little treatise on affectation, in which Møller, as one of the first and best psychologists of the time, laid bare dissimulation in its manifold forms. Møller had a keen eye for phenomena such as self-deception and hypocrisy and made no bones about pointing out to his reader "how many lies can be found in a scene from everyday life." Affectation is at its root not just an artificial way of speaking, but covers a deep-set disposition or defect in every human life. "Affectation always has its basis in a person's being corrupted by one or another inclination without knowing it," explained Møller. So anyone is affected who "imagines himself to have certain opinions, interests or inclinations because he wants for one or another external reason to have them," and, for instance, from sheer vanity "falsely ascribes to himself love of one or another art form for which he has no sense." Affectation is related to snobbism, prejudice, and arbitrary judgment, everything that has no strings attached and is artificial, the superficiality that feigns depth.

Maybe Jonas, the theologian, has pointed out to Regine that, since God as spirit was invisible, he neither could nor should be depicted. God, moreover, had nothing to do with the sense of well-being that music, pictorial art, and poetry can bring about. Christianity's God had chosen to reveal himself *exclusively* in his son, Jesus of Nazareth, to whose word and deeds God gave his divine sanction. To lose oneself in a beautiful picture by Exner was mere rhapsodizing and sentimental aestheticism. Contrary to Jonas, Regine held that it would be ungodly *not* to allow oneself to be edified by a work of art *just because* some wise heads in their out-of-touch wisdom had adopted the view that enjoyment of art belonged to the category of "affectation" and therefore had nothing to do with religion. Of course art and Christianity had to do with each other, and naturally the impression made by beauty evoked the sense of the true. To think anything else would be just as blasé, just as affected.

That she felt "more edified by seeing God's blue sky and luxuriant nature" than by the priest's sermon was also due to nature's ability to liberate her imagination and to vent some of the great longings within her:

> How often I follow along with the lovely white-edged clouds on their long journey to my loved ones at home, and think of how God has blessed me by bestowing on me the love of so many wonderful people, and especially the abounding sisterly love I have always received; then once in a while I also let the clouds dazzle my eyes so that it is as though they draw me up to those whom God in his merciful love has already taken from this life's sorrows and burdens, so that there surely is love hidden there for me too. Just imagine, it is supposed to be sin, but force me to read godly books all day long when there is no heart in need; no, I will confess then that my nature is so despicable that, however much I delight in occasionally reading the godly books I have, I believe I would read myself into being bad if I did it in that way.

Regine longed to initiate Cornelia into the miraculous certainty that life stretched far beyond death and straight into the heart of God's love. Cornelia was thus not to think that Regine went around being perpetually sad because she said that her thoughts dwelt so often on death, or rather on life after death. On the contrary, such thoughts gave fullness to earthly existence, gave hope and great open-heartedness. But at the same time they gave rise to a strange transference between the dead and the living, as Regine illustrates when she writes:

How many of those I have loved are not separated from me in death's leave-taking, and how many of those I still love am I separated from, as we say, for some few years, but none of them do I see.

Those out of sight but still living somehow step into the ranks of the dead while, as if in return, the dead live again. Since she sees *neither* those living far away *nor* the dead in heaven, the distance between them in her mind gradually disappears, so that *all* those absent actually appear before her with equal presence when she thinks of them. It was in this way that God, too, embraced with his love both the still living and the long dead, thought Regine, who would like to give herself altogether trustingly to a faith in our Lord's wise guidance, so much so that she need never more worry about Cornelia's and Emil's temporal states of health:

> If I could now properly acquire devotion in God's loving will, then I would say: whether I first join them in the hereafter or here, what is best is what God lets happen, and then I would never be plagued by unrest about how things are with you, etc. But we are human beings, and very weak at that, and I often feel that the stone I cannot lift I must leave lying.

Regine longs ardently to be able to talk to Cornelia about these most sublime of all things. Only two or three times since coming to St. Croix has she gone out to Olivia's and Laura's graves, but when she did, it took real self-mastery. "A ride on horseback for a couple of hours is for me associated with less inconvenience than the short way over there." Her thoughts focus on where the dead now are, while their graves, "which the lush nature here so quickly lets weeds so overgrow," made no impression on her. But there were of course exceptions. It would be quite different and touching were she and Cornelia "to walk in confidential conversation to our lovely graveyard at home." It may be altogether unconscious, but nevertheless comes close to being a thought, that in rounding off her observations about meeting again with the dear departed, Regine just manages to get in the word for graveyard—*kirkegaard*.

". . . FOR YOU KNOW HOW LITTLE FUSS THERE IS WITH FRITZ AND ME"

"I was also very ungrateful toward our Lord for not admitting to enjoying life," confessed Regine on Tuesday the 12th of February. However, the days were too uneventful for that. Not even the recurring dinner parties offered any real diversion. And although she and Fritz toiled "bravely on such days on the treadmill of conversation," neither the soirées nor the dinners ever became a matter of routine; each time they caused inconveniences. First of all there was the question of who to invite among the "up to 130 qualified invitees we have to take turns between." Then came the composition of the dinner, which normally was Regine's to decide and was often complicated by difficulties in securing the necessary provisions. Finally the day would come and Regine would have to put on her finery, "but I am now so used to that that I no longer take much account of it."

The dinner parties nevertheless helped to broaden Regine's knowledge of human life's many curiosities and in this way helped to increase her own self-understanding. When at one point Cornelia was troubled over all the social life from which she herself could not be excused, Regine fully understood, but at the same time told her conscientious sister that she must not reproach herself too much on this account—"Remember there is something called character and when, like the two of us, one has reached the age of discretion, I think we can say, in fact it is a duty to say it: this is something I will do or avoid doing in accordance with my character. It is our inheritance from Father that we find emptiness in the throng, contentment in solitude." One may well understand that Magister Kierkegaard and Councillor Olsen found each other—and then went each his own way.

Regine was well aware of the temptations of dissemblance. One evening she had as her table companion Councillor Ludvig Birch. He was a courteous and correct gentleman, dependable enough in that respect, even if he talked at inordinate length about his petty physical ailments and was absolutely no kind of party pyrotechnics. He nevertheless won Regine's total sympathy from the moment when he began extravagantly praising Cornelia; indeed, he went on at such length that Regine almost "had difficulty keeping the tears from [her] eyes, where they had no right to be at a fine dinner." Besides, it was not even his own personal opinion of Cornelia to which Birch was giving expression, but that of his brother Frederik Christian Carl Birch, headmaster in Horsens and therefore someone who knew Cornelia well. In the face of such sympathy Regine did not lose all her composure, for as she soberly reasoned:

> How corruptible we humans are! That headmaster, in whom I had decidedly no further interest, has so much won approval in my eyes through these remarks by way of his brother, that I could be tempted to send him the friendliest greetings through you; but I do not do so, since he would think I was mad.

The dinner parties also developed Regine's skills in language. She spoke English almost without effort and had received several "compliments" in that connection. In trying to collect her thoughts for a letter, she would catch herself formulating the sentences in her head in English. Regine could also get along in French, so it was more than appropriate when her gentleman table companion was an "ex-President of San Domingo." At other times it would have been an advantage *not* to be able to understand what people said:

> Another woman who has now taken up residence out here, and who you know, is Mrs. Banneberg, but you can have no idea how her Copenhagen chatter embarrasses me . . . this half-snuffling tone that pronounces "a" as "æ." [e.g., "cat" as "cet"]

Mrs. Banneberg—or Bahneberg, as it is properly spelled—was Dorothe Sophie, wife of Anthon Bahneberg, and with a degree of affectation that almost equaled her *amour-propre* spoke "the worst drivel." But not even in this case could Regine free herself altogether from the temptations of dissemblance—"As for this good woman, we are the best of friends," Regine confides; indeed, "I am fairly sure that her judgment of me is: by God, Mrs. Schlegel is a fine wife." Regine frets over the awful and partly mutual hypocrisy—"but still, this praise is well deserved, for no one knows better than myself what it costs me"—a not un-Kierkegaardian display of dialectic on Regine's part.

At table, she had also to keep wondering whether the kitchen staff had done their job, but the serving too required a watchful eye. The guests left the table with their stomachs very far from empty. "Just for fun, I shall tell you what we had for the big party," so it goes in a letter to Maria—and one suspects that when the fun really gets going, Josephine and her black assistant troops are having quite a hectic time in the kitchen regions:

> Real turtle soup, then lamb with capers, fish with tomato sauce, poulardes stuffed with truffles and ditto sauce, chicken in rice, ham with green peas, cabbage, etc., then comes asparagus between the boiled and the fried, roast beef, steak of turtle meat, hare with gooseberry purée, etc. Plum pudding, which she [Josephine] was very successful with and which burned the whole time it was sliced, 2 wine gelatin puddings with cream sauce, a mille-feuille gateau, a pound cake, every possible small cake, candy and fruit and then 9 kinds of wine.

All the dishes including the cakes, "yes, even the bread," were prepared in "our kitchen, since what can be bought is bad." In periods without rain, the meat becomes so poor as to be almost inedible "for the cattle get only grass and there is none in the fields, yes, so they starve, and then one is still supposed to eat the meat."

The culinary exertions in the governor's kitchen were, besides, often in grotesque disproportion to the invited guests' qualifications for appreciating the splendors with which they stuffed themselves. Customs administrator C. F. Ohsten was one of these mindless and uncultured gluttons who not only gorged himself but might blurt out anything at all, including, Regine feared, spreading the rumor, on returning to Copenhagen, that she was "pock marked." In which case "he lies outrageously, for nearly all the scars are gone," assured a wounded Regine, whose skin took unkindly to the tropical temperatures. Another reason for all but hating this Ohsten was that he had behaved so poorly toward Olivia. "The first time I saw him, I was so icily polite to him that it felt as though I were all the time drinking ice water." Nor did it mollify her any that he was "tactless enough to be a whole week on the island before calling on Fritz." Yet she could hardly avoid inviting him to dinner and, when he turned up, "I got the better of myself and was friendly toward him, true to my principle never purposely to get on bad terms, least of all in a backwater like this." In the course of the conversation he offered Fritz an apology, "so now that's all right."

At times it seems that way out there in the small islands there was simply no end to the possible embarrassments. Regine can at least join in: "Now a ditto," she warns Cornelia, upon which there follows a long and complicated story of misunderstanding, vanity, and disappointed expectation, which it seems Cornelia could not altogether sort out. The bitter moral of it all came to the following, which also includes one of Regine's few crossings out:

> We pour out our money on such people, bore ourselves to death with their conversation, waste our valuable time and patience, so there's gratitude for you . . . so let anyone reproach me that ǂ we isolate ourselves, we give them good food and drink, and the finest civility, but as for cordiality, as the saying goes: 3 steps from life.

Keeping the necessary distance was, however, complicated for a public person who could not allow herself to be isolated for too long at a time. Regine wondered at how people could be bothered to interest themselves in the governor and his wife, "for you know how little fuss there is with Fritz and me." But, inversely, the lack of fuss might mean that "in the long run we win." The same evening that Regine wrote these lines to Cornelia she had received a morning visit from Emilie de Pontavice—

> . . . but I assure you no one should believe so much evil and slander could come out of one mouth; I have cultivated a short laugh, like the one Bolette used, for what should I say? To enter into any kind of dispute with a woman like her from feelings of injustice is, as you can well understand, unthinkable; no, I get more satisfaction from the laughter.

21. Merchant Jean de Pontavice's house. "If we were the worst beggars, we could not be treated more meanly," writes Regine in her letter to Cornelia on the 28th of February 1856, after dining with the merchant Pontavice and his wife Emilie, who was their neighbor over the way in Kongensgade (King Street). Regine's indignation was prompted by Jean de Pontavice's not having proposed first the "governor's toast," but instead a toast to an inferior captain and his hunchbacked sister, together with the American flag.

That had been true of her former betrothed as well, laughter giving satisfaction, and if everything had gone differently perhaps the two of them could have laughed together at the world's follies. But now Regine laughed alone and with a short laugh like Bolette Rørdam's, her old friend for whom Kierkegaard had swooned at Frederiksberg before he met Regine. That was now the past, so long past as almost to bring pain. But Bolette's laughter, which Kierkegaard also knew, resonated in Regine when, over the damask table cloth and the cut-glass port wine goblets, she chose to be amiably dismissive of a poisonous tropical snake like Emilie de Pontavice.

HENRIK LUND AND "UNCLE SØREN"

Whitsuntide on St. Croix was quiet that year. It rained on Whitsunday from morning until evening. Thilly had been invited out:

... and then Oluf, Fritz and I went all day from his room to ours and chatted so cheerfully and nicely together; that day Oluf reminded me very much of Father when on a Sunday he was really pleased to be together with his family; on days like that I think he is grateful for our company; if only we could be a little for *him*, we owe him so much for what he has been for us.

At some point Regine withdrew to her room, despite the intimacy and the poetic Whitsun rain, and sat at her writing table to collect her thoughts for a letter to Henrik Sigvard Lund, Kierkegaard's nephew. Henrik, as he was simply called, was the son of Nicoline Christine, who in 1824 had married the silk mercer and draper Johan Christian Lund. In 1828, as an early example of families being united, his four-years-younger brother, Henrik Ferdinand, a clerk at the National Bank, married Nicoline Christine's two-years-younger sister, Petrea Severine. And while little freckled-faced Søren Aabye was showing his mettle at the School of Civic Virtue, his two sisters were employing their time in ensuring the kin's future. Fortune smiled long on the passionate couple, but then for Nicoline Christine things went suddenly wrong. On the 30th of August 1832 she gave birth to a stillborn son and soon after fell into a high fever. All but a week later her condition was so critical that one morning a message had to be sent to Peter Christian. When he reached the home Nicoline Christine was more restful, but she soon became delirious. The doctors had to bleed her, applying leeches, and throughout the day they lay ice cubes on her throbbing temples. The next day there was some improvement, but on Monday the 10th of September, in the evening, death took its inexorable hold on the fevered woman.

When hosier Kierkegaard turned seventy-eight on the 12th of December 1834, nine-months-pregnant Petrea Severine, she of the lively red-blonde hair, was at his home to offer her congratulations, though there was little cause for congratulation. Apart from his wife Ane, the hard-tried old man had lost four of his seven children, most recently Niels Andreas, who died in Paterson, New Jersey, on the 21st of September 1833. Petrea Severine, Søren Aabye's favorite sister, was the only daughter left to Kierkegaard senior. She gave birth the following day to a sound and healthy boy but became ill three days later. Although she was able to nurse, it was feared that the milk would run up into her brain, causing insanity. A boil on one leg suggested that the emetic that the physicians had prescribed to drive the milk down again had begun to take effect. But it was not so, for two days before the old year ran out, Petrea Severine died suffering severe cramps. Like her sister Nicoline Christine, she was thirty-three. And just like his brother, the widower Henrik Ferdinand would now have to try to create some reasonable framework for his children, five-year-old Henriette,

22. On graduating in medicine in 1849, Kierkegaard's nephew, Henrik Sigvard Lund, served as an assistant physician in the army. After a brief appointment at Frederik's Hospital and a period abroad, he set himself up in medical practice in Copenhagen. Lund shared his uncle's criticism of the National Church and protested loudly at Kierkegaard's funeral. He began the registering of Kierkegaard's posthumous papers but did not complete the work and applied for a position on St. John, where he worked as physician from November 1856 until May 1860.

three-year-old Vilhelm Nicolai, one-year-old Peter Christian, and a sixteen-day-old infant boy, who in memory of the mother he would never know was named Peter Severin.

As uncle to so many motherless children, Kierkegaard felt a special responsibility, which he tried to fulfill by taking care of birthday presents or arranging an unforgettable coach ride. Henriette recalls in particular how "Uncle Søren" had surprised them all by becoming engaged to a "delightful young girl of eighteen," who was "affectionate in the extreme to us children and eager to win our love in return." The Lund children paid visits to the Olsen home, "where they all, and not least Uncle Søren himself, did their utmost to delight us." Later Henriette also visited Regine alone and recalled how one day, standing and waving goodbye to Regine, she had a sudden sense of the fragility of the newly engaged couple's happiness and of its perhaps being about to fall apart. Her fears proved well-founded when, immediately before his departure for Berlin on the 25th of October 1841, Kierkegaard summoned his nephews and nieces to an evening party in the childhood home at 2 Nytorv, where he was now once more staying with his recently remarried brother. On that evening he was "much moved" and quite beside himself, recalls Henriette. Kierkegaard suddenly broke into "a violent fit of weeping" that gradually spread to the children, though without anyone really knowing why, or what it was they were weeping over. However, "Uncle Søren quickly pulled himself together and told us that one day soon he would be leaving for Berlin, perhaps to be away for quite a while. So we had to promise to write to him often, because he was anxious to hear how each of us was doing. With many tears, we promised."[69]

The children's little missives no longer exist, but Kierkegaard's replies do. In them we note that the nephews and nieces had no real idea what they should tell the Magister in exile, and he had obviously so much recovered his composure as to not only quote at them in German and Latin, but to also coolly correct spelling mistakes in the letters he received. He nevertheless concluded one letter to Carl with the words: "Just write away, whatever occurs to you, don't be bashful, your letters are always welcome." That there lay a hidden motive behind so open-hearted an exhortation is evident from a letter that Kierkegaard wrote to Emil Boesen several weeks before the first of his letters to the cousins:

> Among all the things you write about, there is only one that worries me a little, and that is that she has invited Henrich, Michael, etc., to visit her. She is clever, and one year under my auspices has not exactly made her more naïve; among other things it has taught her that I notice the most trivial triviality. My procedure with respect to the children must be altered. I regret to say it, but I trust nobody.[70]

What the "procedure" was is not quite clear, but the nephews seem unwittingly to have operated as six small spies in the service of a higher cause. Their efforts seem evidently not to have been particularly commendable, but so important were they as a connecting link between the now also geographically separated lovers that they could be used, if need be, as emissaries of reunion. Kierkegaard, in the penultimate letter to Boesen, could then make this announcement:

If I should return to her, then I would wish to include those few creatures whom she has learned to love through me, my four nephews and
two nieces. To that end I have kept up, often at a sacrifice of time, a
steady correspondence with them. Naturally, in order to divert attention, I have given this the appearance of something bizarre on my part.[71]

So the exchange of letters with the nephews and nieces was occasioned by
Kierkegaard's interest in Regine, about whose state of health, and whatever else
she got up to, he hoped to be able to form an adequate impression through this
correspondence, something of which the nephews themselves can scarcely have
had the least inkling. Like Henriette, her cousin Henrik harbored a deep and
undiminished admiration for their famous uncle. It was also Henrik who, in a
letter of the 27th of February 1843, could inform his uncle, the naturalist Peter
Wilhelm Lund, then living in the Brazilian town of Lagoa Santa, of the latest
news from the Copenhagen book world: "At my first opportunity I will send off
to you a book that has made a great stir and is read 'by nearly every cultivated
person.' The title of the book is *Either/Or* and it is assumed that Søren is the
author." The need to "assume" was due to Kierkegaard having written under the
pseudonym "Victor Eremita," which, however, was quickly seen through. And
with those words *Either/Or* was on its way to Lagoa Santa!

During the so-called Three Years' War, or the "First Schleswig War," Henrik
was a physician with the permanent field hospital in Odense and made use of
his free hours to correspond with Kierkegaard. Although there is an asymme-
try in what has been preserved, with only a single, undated letter from "Uncle
Søren" preserved while all of Henrik's still exist, it is clear that it was a matter
here of mutual devotion. In a birthday greeting dated the 3rd of May 1849, Henrik signed himself "Your never forgetful-of-you nephew, Henrik," which "Uncle Søren" repaid by signing himself "Your wholly devoted-to-you Uncle." But
where "Uncle Søren" was a master at getting much out of practically nothing
when he wrote, Henrik was a master of the opposite, getting almost nothing out
of a lot. Life as a field hospital physician exiled on Funen did not at any rate offer events of a kind he would like to be known to bore others with, especially
not a master writer like Kierkegaard.

Luckily Kierkegaard had at some point made it known that he would like to
be kept informed of "the bird world" in those parts, thereby giving the young
field doctor an excellent motive for roaming the fields and forests and filling
his letters with ornithological observations. As the birds disappeared with
the approach of cold weather, so did the epistolary connection between uncle
and nephew. Hostilities came to a halt, and Henrik returned to his work in

Copenhagen. Addressed to "Mr. Graduate H. Lund/ Frederiks Hospital" was the following message dated no more specifically than "Tuesday": "Dear Henrich! Can't you meet me this evening at the usual time and place? If not, then come out to me tomorrow morning 11–12 / Your Uncle. / S. K." One might have hoped for more information, but we understand that the two men met so regularly at this time that it made sense to speak of meeting at "the usual time," and that the meeting was so important that moving it to the following morning was imperative should Henrik be prevented. It has recently been established that Henrik helped his uncle with the transcribing of some lengthy footnotes in the draft of "On My Activity as an Author," which was published on the 6th of August 1851,[72] and it seems likely that Lund had been working on the draft during that summer, so we may presume the preserved message with its time indication "Tuesday" to date from this period. To what extent the devotion shown in Henrik's letters from Funen had been converted into greater confidentiality can only be surmised, but it is a historical fact that the nephew's sympathy with his uncle's theological concerns increased with time. It is known, moreover, that Henrik together with his physician brother, Michael, attended the dying Kierkegaard at Frederik's Hospital, that he bid tenaciously for books from Kierkegaard's collection when it came under the hammer; and that on the same occasion he secured some bookcases that had possibly belonged to the admired uncle.

Henrik's first appearance in Regine's correspondence is on Tuesday the 27th of November 1855, when she begs Cornelia to take care of a bundle of greetings to friends and acquaintances at home, among them Henrik. By the willing hand of fate, Regine had received a small sign of life from him:

> On Sunday I got a visiting card with a friendly greeting from Henrik Lund, it made me so happy, for since I have made no new friends out here I am so grateful to keep the old ones, tell him that if you can meet him.

For good geographical reasons, Regine had at this time no knowledge of the events whereby Henrik Lund had nine days previously inscribed himself in history as the man who caused a scandal at Søren Kierkegaard's funeral. That course of events had a rather undramatic beginning. When the ceremony in the Church of Our Lady was over, the hearse carrying Kierkegaard's body drove out to Assistens Cemetery, where archdeacon E. C. Tryde was to conduct the graveside ceremony. But no sooner had the last spade of earth been thrown onto the small coffin than Henrik stepped forward, removed his hat, and made as if to give a speech. This was forbidden by the rules, but Lund stood his ground against both Tryde and Klein, the police officer seconded for the occasion, and shouted: "In the name of God. / One moment, gentlemen, if you will permit me!" Since they did not do so, the silence grew. "Who is that?" could be heard in the crowd. "I am Lund, a medical graduate," answered the tall, pale young man in black. "Hear, hear!" someone shouted, while another was able to assure them "He's pretty good! Just let him speak!"[73]

Henrik then protested against the Christian burial of Kierkegaard, who despite his loud denunciation of the church and clergy had been "brought here against his repeatedly expressed will," and had "in a way been violated." As evidence, Lund referred to Kierkegaard's articles in *Fædrelandet* and to *The Moment* and quoted from the third chapter of the Revelation of St. John on the judgment awaiting everyone who is neither cold nor hot but something so unpardonable as lukewarm. After reading the short text "We All Are Christians" from the second issue of *The Moment*, where Kierkegaard fumes over the fact that not even "a free thinker" who "in the strongest terms declared all Christianity to be a lie"[74] is able to escape a Christian burial, Lund turned to the gathering and asked:

> Isn't this description of the situation correct? Is not what we are witnessing today—namely, that this poor man, despite all his energetic protests in thought, word and deed, in life and death, is being buried by "the Official Church" as a beloved member of same. . . . It would never have happened in a Jewish society, and never among the Turks and Mohammedans. . . . It was something left for "official Christianity" to perpetrate. Can this, then, be "God's true Church"? No![75]

When the speech was over, no one felt prompted to reply, but some scattered applause could be heard. People stood and waited to see what would happen next, for it was as though something *had* to happen. But nothing did. Henrik Lund vanished as suddenly as he had appeared. It caused a little merriment when a slightly tipsy fellow called out to one of his comrades: "Let's go home, Chrisshiian!" Which they did; Christian and the others went home. There was nothing more to be had that day at the cemetery, so why stand there and freeze?

The matter itself was, however, far from over. Indeed it had only just begun. Less than a day later, the story of the young physician's protest was in nearly all the Copenhagen newspapers. It was, after all, a *good* story that like most stories of the kind had *bad* consequences. In its morning edition, *Berlingske Tidende* described the events point by point, and in its afternoon edition carried a summary of the funeral oration that Peter Christian had given in the church. Early that same Monday, *Flyve-Posten* and *Fædrelandet* both left their busy printers early in the day with coverage and contributions to a debate on the possibility of negligence on the part of those really responsible.

As head of the Church, Bishop H. L. Martensen did not sit watching the confusion with folded hands. He did not wish to comment publicly, for that would be too risky. But in virtue of his office, he was deeply disturbed and demanded of Tryde a written report of what had taken place. Tryde, a moderate man, advised against taking the matter further, but Martensen totally disagreed and urged the Minister of Culture, who had jurisdiction over church affairs, to pursue the matter.

Meanwhile Lund had written out his speech from memory, and it was printed on Thursday the 22nd of November 1855 in *Fædrelandet*, under the heading "My Protest; What I Have Said and Not Said." Two days later there was a second installment, "In the next instant—What Then?" His exalted mood gave way at the same time to a deep despair, which in December led to an attempted suicide, averted at the last moment by his father Johan Christian Lund, who appealed soon afterward to the Minister of Culture, C. C. Hall, with a plea to temper justice with mercy: the son was neither morally nor criminally accountable. Martensen, however, was inflexible and began talking up his concerns for the future of the established church and for common decency, and other clichés pulled out of the same musty clerical drawer.

The affair therefore ended up in Copenhagen's fifth criminal court, in the old City Hall and Court House next door to Kierkegaard's home and birthplace, the house where, visiting as a child one evening long ago, Henrik had seen his uncle cry heartrendingly just prior to departing for Berlin. The prosecutor wanted to send Henrik to prison; the defense counsel asked for acquittal; the witnesses fell to quarreling among themselves and the case dragged on, so that judgment was not pronounceduntil the 5th of July 1856. Henrik was sentenced to a fine of a hundred rix-dollars to be paid to Copenhagen's system for poor relief. He accepted the sentence without moving a muscle. "I see now," he had written to Peter Christian two days beforehand, "that for me the only proper thing is to abandon this whole struggle that I have got myself involved in, uninvited, and seek shelter in Christ's church."[76] No doubt contributing to his wholesale resignation is the fact that Henrik had some time earlier been placed in Oringe Mental Hospital, where he had been subjected to medical treatment for an unspecified "nervous complaint."

REGINE'S FIRST LETTER TO HENRIK LUND

The letter Regine wrote to Henrik to the Whitsun rain's gentle accompaniment was studiously dated "2nd day of Whitsun, the 12th of May 1856" and was therefore written while Henrik was still awaiting the outcome of the suit brought against him. The letter begins:

Dear Henrik! By him who was the occasion for us 2 ever coming to know each other, and who is again the occasion for us 2 having any correspondence with each other, you were once attributed the very fine characteristic of being faithful. That is many years ago! Apart from whatever else these years have brought, they have taught me that these words were truly said about you. I was very young then, and had very [crossed out] only little confidence in myself; I remember clearly I thought to myself "if only that word could be used about you."[77]

In writing to Henrik, Regine's language loses its directness and she seems stiff in a way that she is not in her letters to Cornelia. It is symptomatic of the unresolved feelings she nurtures that, even if the letter is in a sense solely about Kierkegaard, his name is at no time mentioned. Regine is worried lest it should sound like "self praise," or might be so misunderstood, when she assures Henrik that in her "friendship" with him and his siblings and cousins she has shown true faithfulness, but she hopes really that it is only "your thoughts of me that I may have expressed." She recalls with much warmth Henrik's visit to her and Fritz in Bredgade, when he had reported how well things had gone with his degree and that he was now going to travel abroad. The visit occurred presumably sometime in 1849, that being the year Henrik graduated in medicine. His travel plans were abandoned because the now-deceased uncle had, one might say, other plans for him. We understand that she and Henrik have exchanged some letters (now lost), and Regine then directs her glance to the present and comments on the jewelry that Henrik took out of the auction and has sent to her:

I thank you many times for the way you have fulfilled my requests, the 2 brooches have been mine, and I was looking forward to receiving them, the 3rd I haven't seen before, but you are right in saying there can be no question of sending it back such a long way, so I'll probably keep it. The rings were right, the one with the clear stone was altered into the shape of a cross, no doubt not without meaning; but it pains me that in getting them all I may be depriving one of you of a dear memory.[78]

The two brooches were hers, but the third must have belonged to someone else. Could it have been Kierkegaard's mother's, or one of his prematurely dead sisters', perhaps even Henrik's own mother's? The engagement rings however "were right." At first Regine had some difficulty in recognizing Kierkegaard's own, "the one with the clear stone," since it had been altered "into the form of a cross no doubt not without meaning." Regine was correct in this. After the break, Kierkegaard had a silversmith convert the ring so that its four gems formed a cross to show that he belonged eternally to God—which in reality he always had. "It sometimes happens," he wrote in his journal in 1849, "that a child in the cradle becomes engaged to be married to the one who will one day be his wife or her husband; religiously speaking, I was already, in early childhood—previously engaged. Ah! I paid dearly for once misunderstanding my life and forgetting—that I was betrothed!"[79] The ring's cross was to be a daily reminder that with his earthly betrothal the owner of the ring had committed a crime against the heavenly.

The letters dating to the period of the engagement that Henrik sent to Regine have, of course, quite another value. She acknowledges their receipt with the following remarks:

> I believe with God's help it was also right that you sent me all the let-
> ters, both what should be burnt and the others, since it was his will
> that after his death I should receive everything so that he could be sure
> that precisely that part of his papers would be subject to my inspec-
> tion; and seeing I have now received them with a humble prayer to
> God for his blessing in my doing so, I hope it will do me good rather
> than harm. Also in this firm belief, I pray still that you keep *nothing*
> back from me, whatever you may have for me in the form of words
> or writing; I thought I understood that some of his writings kept in
> a Brazilian rosewood cupboard were intended for me; but perhaps I
> have been mistaken.

Regine has thus received not only "all the letters" from the time of the engage-ment, but also those that Kierkegaard had sent to his friend Emil Boesen during his first stay in Berlin. In these Kierkegaard touched frequently on the relation-ship to Regine, for which reason he later decided that, after his death, they should be burnt—though such a conclusion would seem, paradoxically, an excellent way of guaranteeing their survival for posterity. Regine reckoned, with psychological astuteness, that if Kierkegaard had indeed wished that these letters should not come to her knowledge, or anyone else's, he would have burnt them himself. For he must have known that it was this portion of his papers that Regine would read with special interest. She begs Henrik so earnestly in this connection to keep nothing back, neither written material nor whatever else he might know of.

Regine had further heard rumors of Kierkegaard's having laid aside some of his writings in a "Brazilian rosewood cupboard" with her in mind—"but perhaps I have been mistaken." She was not mistaken. In fact she was quite well informed, which might well be because she had already begun reading Kierkegaard's jour-nals, where mention is made of the rosewood cabinet, which was literally built around a dramatic line from the time of the engagement. Regine had been so bent on staying with Kierkegaard that in one of their exchanges she had offered to be content with living in a little cupboard. With this in mind, Kierkegaard had a carpenter produce a stately column-shaped cabinet, an instructive account of which is given in his journal:

> When I was living in Nørregade. On the second floor, I had a cabinet made in Brazilian rosewood. It is according to my own design, and this in turn was occasioned by words from her, the lovable, in her anguish. She said she would thank me her whole life long if she were permitted to remain with me, even if she had to live in a little cupboard! Taking this into account, it was built without shelves. —In it, carefully preserved, is everything that might remind her of me. There are also copies for her of [the writings by] the pseudonyms; there were also two vellum copies printed, one for her and one for me.[80]

Within this odd Regine-mausoleum *Either/Or* had been lying in an attractive edition, printed on that smooth, parchment-like paper called vellum, and bound in an exclusive light gossamer silk-moiré, with floral ornamentation in gold and gilded edging. The flyleaf was of Turkish silk paper, which gave an ethereal and dreamlike feel to the work's preamble. The cabinet also contained such works as *Repetition* and *Prefaces*, treated with similar care and prepared in the same fetish-like way, and a copy of *Concluding Unscientific Postscript* as well, bound in brown velvet, which must have been expensive but also leaves an impression of gravity.

Toward the end of the letter, Regine gives her approval to Henrik's sending her "the posthumous note," which probably refers to the small envelope that Peter Christian had found with his brother's testamentary request appointing Regine as residuary legatee. And just as her husband had, in his stiffly official letter to Peter Christian, expressed his astonishment at this decision, Regine now acknowledges that the chosen "form" had taken her somewhat aback.

> That "following orders" you have sent me the posthumous note was surely perfectly correct, God tempts no man; if it were not his will that I should come to know what I now know, then it would not have happened; although there has been no clarification between us since he said farewell to me (following my conscience's best conviction I agreed with my husband that an unopened letter be returned), I no doubt expected one after his death, though I must admit not quite in the form I received it.[81]

Although never having received a "clarification" from Kierkegaard, she has now got something that looks like one in the form of the letter that he had once sent to her and Fritz and had been returned to him "unopened." Regine rounds off her letter to Henrik with some general remarks on her present situation:

> Life out here is very monotonous; but God be praised we both stand up well to the climate. Schlegel has far too much to do and I almost nothing at all; just see, you well know that too little and too much corrupts everything in this world, so now it is a question of coming out of it unscathed. Who knows whether these many serious thoughts that have recently gone through my head are destined to save me from the perdition in pettinesses that accompanies life in a market town, which is what life out here should really be called. It is at least my judgment upon myself that after what I have already experienced, and perhaps through my husband's capability can still come to experience, I am permitted less than any other woman to lose myself in pettiness.

How much Henrik took from his uncle's cabinet and sent off to St. Croix is uncertain, but when in following Regine's own wishes, the librarian, philologist, and literary expert Raphael Meyer published the engagement story's most important documents in 1904, he remarked in the introduction:

> After S. K.'s death, Henrik Lund, who was the first to look after Kierkegaard's estate, sent most of the papers published in the present volume to Mrs. Schlegel in the West Indies in two sealed packages. These packages also contained Mrs. Schlegel's letters to S. K.[82]

Meyer informs us that he had also included in his edition "4 passages in the journals which S. K. himself refers to, and his testament also with Schlegel's reply and two letters from Mrs. Schlegel to Henrik Lund."[83] If this material is put aside in a bundle by itself, then the "two sealed packages" that Regine received contained the following texts by Kierkegaard:

- the letter to Regine from the time of the engagement;
- the letters to Emil Boesen from the first stay in Berlin immediately after the break with Regine—it was these that according to Kierkegaard should be burnt after his death;
- the long entry "My Relationship to 'Her'" in Notebook 15 from 1849;
- sketches and a draft in connection with the letter that Kierkegaard sent to the Schlegels in November 1849 but which had been returned to him unopened; and
- the two envelopes with Kierkegaard's testamentary requests.

This material, which except for the love letters had been unknown to Regine, must have given her ample opportunity to freshen up the old love story—and to reread her own letters to Kierkegaard. But whereas *he* left it to others to burn certain letters, *she* chose to adopt a quite different stance as regarded any possible interest posterity might have in her letters to him. "Luckily . . . I burned them," she told Raphael Meyer, a piece of information she also repeated in a kind of documentary interview with Hanne Mourier, who placed the action on record with shocking sobriety: "You received your own few letters, which you burnt."[84] How, when, and where the incineration of these invaluable documents was carried out belongs to the secrets with which the story continues to tease its historians. But that the little collection of letters was ignited somewhere on St. Croix seems most likely.

The day after finishing her letter to Henrik, on the 13th of May, Regine wrote to Cornelia: "Now Whitsuntide is over, yesterday was Whit Monday." Not a word is said about her letter to Henrik, let alone the occasion for writing it. The only possible hint is in the following remark: ". . . I believe you must admit I am right when I say that we cousins, separated as we are, could never keep what the world calls a happy Whitsun, all too many memories from the time of our youth work against it."

THE SEALED LETTER TO MR. AND MRS. SCHLEGEL

Somewhere in "The Seducer's Diary," and with a peculiarly lascivious elegance, Johannes the Seducer remarks that "to poetize oneself into a girl is an art, to poetize oneself out of her a masterpiece."[85] Kierkegaard knew the art but the masterpiece proved harder. Regine continued to be delightfully dismaying and dizzyingly forbidden; she could activate hot springs so seductively that Kierkegaard followed his nature and let himself be swept away—on paper.

The story of Søren and Regine is, however, not just a story of two people who for intellectual and psychological reasons misunderstand each other. Thanks to the actor who plays the male lead, it ranks as a grand-scale drama poised between extremes in the history of Western culture: immediacy and reflection, desire and self-control, presence and absence. "[T]o her and to my late father," Kierkegaard decreed in 1849, "all the books . . . are to be dedicated: an old man's noble wisdom and a woman's lovable lack of understanding."[86] In the year of his death he returned in more refined terms to that formulation when, under the heading "My Qualifications," he referred to his father and Regine as "the persons I love most of all, to whom I owe what I may have become as an author: an old man, his melancholic errors of judgment in love; a quite young girl, almost a child, her lovable tears of incomprehension."[87]

The peculiar prudishness about naming names that one notices in Regine, who in her letters never mentions Kierkegaard by name, is also to be found in Kierkegaard. In his journals he refers to Regine: once as "R" and three times as "Regina," while the name "Regine" occurs seven times. But otherwise she is consistently anonymous, hiding 677 times behind "She"/"she" and 802 times behind "Her"/"her"/"Her's"/"her's."[88] In the authorship itself, this prudishness is as pronounced as Kierkegaard could possibly make it, for he never mentions Regine by her civil name at all. Yet she is conspicuously present in the writings as a longing, an erotic arabesque, and she bodies forth unmistakably in those conflicts of love that the authorship plays through again and again, just as she can make an appearance where the reader least expects it, as for instance in *Philosophical Crumbs*: "The unhappiness . . . does not lie in the fact that the lovers cannot be united, but in that they cannot understand each other."[89] Nor could they, that is, understand each other. He was far too impassionedly reflective for that and she far too downright passionate.

That love in its pure form should be able to surmount every crisis of communication is no doubt somewhat too romantic an optimism. But Kierkegaard cannot be denied his *modern* attitude, insofar as it is precisely in their mutual *understanding* that he bases the relationship between the sexes. And in this requirement he was quite uncompromising, seeing that it was this understanding that was presupposed by the *confidentiality* that is the alpha and omega of marriage. "*But marriage is impossible without confidentiality*" declares a passage categorically in one of the sketches for *Either/Or*. In a later, crossed out journal entry, Kierkegaard explains that entering into a marriage is not a matter of "everything [being] sold 'as is' when the hammer falls." On the contrary, it is a matter of "honesty toward the past." He then continues in the first person singular:

> Had I not honored her more than myself as my future wife, had I not been prouder of her honor than of my own, I would have held my tongue and fulfilled her wish and mine, let myself be married to her—so many a marriage conceals little stories. I didn't want that, she would have been my concubine, and then I would rather have murdered her.[90]

So unyielding a demand for *absolute* confidentiality undeniably assists in making most relationships impossible before they even start, but clearly it was important for Kierkegaard that, as his betrothed, Regine should have full right of access to his problem-filled and guilt-ridden past—whatever that may have involved.

No less insistent was the need he felt to make himself understood to Regine in the years following the broken engagement, when she lived on in the world as Mrs. Schlegel but had yet received no clarification as to why her time as the potential Mrs. Kierkegaard had come to so sudden an end. For this same reason Kierkegaard felt obliged to direct a written appeal to Johan Frederik Schlegel, asking for a conversation with his wife. He was only waiting for the right opportunity.

This arose when Regine's father departed this life on the night of the 25th/26th of June 1849. "It made a strong impression on me," confessed Kierkegaard, who had always been attached to the authoritative and sensitive councillor, to whom he would also no doubt have liked to explain himself. But that was not easy and their last meeting ended in near tragicomedy. On the 26th of August 1848 Kierkegaard had on an impulse driven to Fredensborg, where he took a room at innkeeper Ole Kold's Hotel Store Kro in Slotsgade. Once there, he was overtaken by an "inexplicable presentiment," becoming suddenly so "happy and almost certain" that he would meet the Olsen family, since they often came up to Fredensborg in the late summer. On arriving he took his usual walk down Skipper Allé, the long straight road that begins just before Fredensborg Castle and slopes down toward Esrum Lake, ending at the shipmaster's board and lodging house. There Kierkegaard exchanged a few words with a sailor by the name of Thomas, who observed correctly that this was surely the first time the Magister had been in these parts this year. Kierkegaard asked him in passing if Councillor Olsen had been there much this year. Thomas replied that he had been there just once, on Easter Monday. Kierkegaard then walked up again to Kold's Kro and ordered his meal. Just as he was about to begin, a man passing by the window caught his eye: it was Councillor of State Olsen.

Kierkegaard very much wanted to speak with the councillor and if possible to settle with him, but not with food in his mouth. Before he could finish chewing and put aside his serviette the councillor had vanished. Kierkegaard looked for him and, since he had to return soon to Copenhagen, began to feel impatient. He decided to go down by Skipper Allé in hopes that he might bump into him, promising himself there would be just this single attempt. And, what do you know, there he stood, the ageing councillor for whom Kierkegaard harbored so many feelings:

> I go over to him and say, Good day, Councillor of State Olsen. Let us talk together for once. He took off his hat in greeting, but then he brushed me aside with his hand and said, I do not wish to speak with you. Alas, there were tears in his eyes, and he spoke these words with stifled emotion. Then I walked toward him, but the man began to run

so fast that it would have been impossible for me to catch up with him even had I wanted. I did, however, manage to say this much and he heard it. Now I hold you responsible for not listening to me.[91]

Kierkegaard was thirty-five, the councillor sixty-four, but all the same Kierkegaard could not catch up with him. Olsen was dead a year later. Kierkegaard was therefore never able to say what he wanted to say to the man whose daughter he had in his melancholy love so shamefully wronged.

On the 1st of July 1849—it was the Sunday following the councillor's death—Regine was in the Church of the Holy Spirit together with all of her family. Kierkegaard had also put in an appearance. Usually he rose and left the church immediately after the sermon while, as a rule, Regine remained seated in order to sing still another hymn. But this Sunday she and Fritz also left after Pastor Ernst Vilhelm Kolthoff's Amen:

> And indeed, she almost contrived things so that we more or less met as I passed her on the way down from the gallery. Perhaps she even expected me to greet her. I kept my eyes to myself. . . . God knows how much I myself feel the need to be gentle to her—humanly speaking—but I dare not. And yet in many ways it is as though Governance wants to prevent it—perhaps in the knowledge of what would follow.[92]

The next time Kolthoff preached at the Church of the Holy Spirit, on the 22nd of July, Kierkegaard looked out for Regine, but in vain. A good month later, on the 24th of August, he began Notebook 15, making its first entry a title page, "My Relationship to 'Her', Aug. 24th 49. / somewhat poetical." This stage direction notwithstanding, the events that Kierkegaard inscribed in the notebook were rendered with a reporter's matter-of-factness, almost telegram-like in its conciseness, so that being "poetical" hardly indicates that the reality was an invention, but rather that parts of what happened have been omitted or retouched. Or perhaps the presentation is so close to reality that Kierkegaard feared it would be too private and has therefore encrypted the text by describing it as "somewhat poetical." Whatever the case, the looking back seems to have strengthened his need to talk to Regine, whose *voice* he had not heard for now getting on eight years. He would no longer content himself with passing her on the street, with merely letting his glance lose itself affectionately in hers; he wanted to explain himself, wanted to try something so complicated as speaking out.

And so some months later, on the 19th of November, Johan Frederik Schlegel received one of his life's most remarkable letters. Or rather two: for Kierkegaard had inserted in the letter to Schlegel another, smaller letter in a sealed envelope, which Schlegel was asked to convey to his wife, "that single individual," who then alone, altogether alone, was to acquaint herself with the letter's content. The exact wording in the letter to Schlegel is not known, but in a series of continually shorter drafts the last goes:

Most Esteemed Sir,

The enclosed letter is from me (S. Kierkegaard) to—your wife. You yourself must now decide whether or not to give it to her. I cannot, after all, very well defend approaching her, least of all now when she is yours, and for that reason I have never availed myself of the opportunity that has presented itself or perhaps has been presented for a number of years.

It is my belief that a small item of information about her relationship with me [*in the draft:* concerning my relationship with her] might now be of use to her. If you disagree, may I ask you to return the letter to me unopened: but also inform her of this.

I have wanted to take this step, to which I felt myself religiously obligated, and in writing, because I fear that my pronounced personality, which probably had too strong an effect at one time, might once again have too strong an effect and thus in either one way or another be disturbing.

I have the honor, etc.,

S.K.[93]

Schlegel clearly thought the information about the letter-writer's relationship to his wife could serve no purpose whatsoever and returned the letter unopened, for which one can hardly blame him. Not only did he act according to Kierkegaard's express wish, he also had every reason to be somewhat piqued by the quite dialectically turned but still unmistakable remark about his wife having, for a number of years, been on offer to her former betrothed, whose marked personality had once already had so strongly disturbing an effect. Indeed! And besides, what did that dash in the first line before "your wife" mean? As if there could be any shadow of doubt in the matter.

That Fritz was not tempted to enlist in the service of indirect communication was the more understandable as the arrangement that Kierkegaard waved before his eyes seems, at first glance, exceedingly curious. One of the draft letters goes:

If you answer yes, then I must make some prior conditions in case you should not find occasion for it. If the exchange between us should take place *in writing*, then I require that no letter from me comes into her hands without being read by you; just as I shall read no letter from her without your endorsement that it has been read by you. If the exchange is to take place *verbally*, then I require that you are present at every conversation.[94]

One has to ask what Kierkegaard really had in mind. Had he seriously imagined that Schlegel would sit and censor his letters and—correspondingly—sign those that Regine might write to him? And it must have seemed hardly less nonsensical to Schlegel that, like a member of some higher court, he should attend conversations between Kierkegaard and his own wife. What on earth were they to talk about in that case? The weather, prices in the market place, the Schleswig question? They could never touch on what it was supposedly all about, the enigmatic aspect of their love, the unfathomable element in their togetherness, the inexplicable forces at work in their mutual bondage—for then the one angel after the other would soon steal in painful silence through the quieted rooms. That Fritz declined the proposal to open their doors to his former rival was anything but incomprehensible.

Kierkegaard however failed to comprehend it. And when, two days later, the sealed letter to Regine came in return, he noted in his journal that "the most esteemed gentleman" had enclosed a "moralizing and indignant epistle,"[95] which he hardly managed to read to the end before letting it be consumed by the flames from a candle lighter. In a later entry, Schlegel is said to have been "furious and would in no way 'tolerate interference by another in the relationship between him and his wife.'"[96] Of what the "moralizing" in Fritz's letter consisted nothing is known beyond what Kierkegaard cites. Nor is it known what information Regine was spared or, perhaps more to the point, what the material was of which she was cheated. In the first, many-paged draft Kierkegaard had written:

> Thank you, oh thank you! *Thank you for everything I owe you; thank you for that time you were mine*; oh thank you for being childlike, which taught me so much, you, my enchanting teacher, you, my lovely teacher. You lovely lily, you, my teacher, you nimble bird, you my teacher.
>
> Thank you for being childlike, which was to be my enoblement and education. Thank you for being childlike, which was to be my instruction; thank you for being childlike, through which with God's help I was in the most beautiful sense ennobled and educated.[97]

Since Kierkegaard claims elsewhere to have two teachers, namely Christ and Socrates, Regine would have no need to feel short-changed. But Kierkegaard may have sensed that he was on the verge of over-dramatizing, that he should write in a more sober tone. In the last of the drafts, whose wording safely follows that of the sealed letter, he wrote:

> Cruel I was, that is true. Why? Indeed, *you* do not know that.
>
> Silent I have been, that is certain. Only God knows what I have suffered—may God grant that I do not, even now, speak too soon after all!
>
> Marry I could not. Even if you were still free, I could not.
>
> However, you have loved me, as I have you. I owe you much—and now you are married. Well, I offer you for the second time what I can and dare and ought to offer you: reconciliation.

Just here, that is just after the colon in the last line, Kierkegaard had first written "my love, that is to say a friendship's," with "reconciliation" implied, but this evidently was too strong. So he shortened the expression to: "my friendship"— but it still seemed too emotional and was therefore altered to the contractual "reconciliation." And he continues:

> I do this in writing in order not to surprise or overwhelm you. Perhaps my personality did once have too strong an effect; that must not happen again. But for the sake of God in Heaven, please give serious consideration to whether you dare become involved in this, and if so, whether you prefer to speak with me at once or would rather exchange some letters first.
>
> If your answer is "No"—would you then please remember for the sake of a better world that I took this step as well.
>
> *In any case, as in the beginning so until now, sincerely, and completely devoted,*
>
> S.K.[98]

The long drawn out signature was no doubt crafted with much consideration and hardly by accident echoes, quite literally, the greeting with which Kierkegaard's father, Michael Pedersen Kierkegaard, ended his letter to the son Søren when as a restless young student the latter had gone to Gilleleie in the summer of 1835 to try to find himself and had pined for an "idea" that he would be "willing to live and die for."[99]

These many years later Kierkegaard had tried to find himself in a relation to a married woman, of whom he found himself unable to let go. In his various drafts one can see him systematically trying to cleanse his letters of the devotion and sensuality that, whenever he thinks of Regine, flows almost organically

from his pen. And although one may perhaps smile at his desperate epistolary contrivances and assurances, it cannot be denied that there lies in these
attempts to explain himself a genuine desire to limit the grief he had caused
Regine.

The sealed letter shows us more clearly why Fritz wanted to come to
St. Croix, why he needed to put due distance between himself and the enervat-
ing obsession with which his wife had fought ever since, when barely mature
sexually, she had met the man who was in several respects Fritz's superior. But
one can also well understand Regine's being shaken when now she relives the old
love story with its attendant documents. What were her thoughts, one wonders,
when she broke open the sealed letter and read at last what she, and no doubt
particularly Fritz, had decided in 1849 they should *not* read? Could she imagine Kierkegaard speaking to her now as he might have spoken if on the narrow
path by the lake they had not passed by each other in silence but had stopped
and talked together, opened their hearts to each other, while there was time?

THE SECRET PLACE IN REGINE'S HEART

Regine wrote her letters with remarkably few corrections. She might go over a
letter again to add a comma or, with a small loop, insert a word or two that had
slipped out in her haste, just as she might add a greeting from Fritz or Josephine
down the side of the letter or in a fold; but otherwise the letters were written
as though in a continuous movement, with rarely a crossed or inked-out line.
What Regine wrote, she wrote. The letters therefore acquire an immediacy: one
can almost hear Regine's voice, sense her gestures, a woman's body in movement over the written ciphers, vivacious, anxious, thoughtful, longing.

With few exceptions, the letters of 1856 are written on a large piece of
parchment-thin paper, bluish or greyish, folded in the middle and written on
until space ran out at the bottom of the fourth page. The letter of Thursday the
26th of August, which was composed at Cane Garden, is an exception. It is written on really sturdy paper and is modest in format. But despite its physical slight-
ness, it is perhaps the greatest of them all. It touches on something about which
the others remain silent. That it was written *after* Kierkegaard's letters were received makes that fact no less interesting.

The first part proceeds fairly conventionally. It takes the form of a response
to Cornelia's latest communication, which describes how she and Emil have
moved from Copenhagen and had now come to Horsens, but with the moving things are still a mess, the children are impossible, and outside the Danish

summer is at its blustery, grey, and leaden worst. Regine was both ashamed and grateful to Cornelia for having nevertheless taken the time to write to her "little Regine," who scruples at repaying her in this way with a microscopic letter: "Look, there's gratitude for you in this world! To your blessed long letter that we received last . . . I reply by looking out my smallest paper so as to get a letter off to you as quickly as possible today." However, Regine according to herself was "lawfully excused" in that she couldn't stand the warmest time of day—"yesterday I was in quite a good way, but today I have been sitting again all morning and moping in a rocking chair."

She felt better during the afternoon and was sitting now at her writing table trying to give signs of life. And just a few lines down the first page Regine managed to pen some of the most open-hearted sentences in her correspondence with Cornelia:

> To you, who know my nature so well, I can quickly explain how it goes with me. You know I am not among the strong, but you also know that at home I always fought in a very respectable way against my nature; here there is no fight, the heat overwhelms my nerves, which were perhaps already a little strained beforehand through struggling with a grief that I would not let overwhelm me, for I say what I believe, I am not suffering from homesickness; but there is a place in my heart that I seldom open up, for I am afraid it will prove stronger than myself, and what is it that lies hidden there? You know without me mentioning it.

With these last sentences it is as though the letter expands violently, so that it becomes a subtext to Regine's other letters, though one that is disconcertingly enigmatic. For, just as Regine comes to the crucial point, she disappears into a silence, giving Cornelia to understand that she knows very well what Regine *would* say *if* the two sisters were not each at their own end of the world but able to walk arm-in-arm in the Deer Park, down one of those small paths that lead sooner or later to a glade.

To us, this understanding can sound almost like teasing, or else it can bring to mind a secret note in the best, which is to say worst, Kierkegaardian style. By closing just *this door* in her heart to all others but Cornelia, Regine opens up a long series of other *doors* into an extensive gallery of guesswork, which is soon echoing with importunate questions: To what is Regine's heart being hospitable? What forces does she fear? What would happen in her heart if she were to defy reason and open that door wide? And has she confided in Fritz? How much does he really know about what lies behind the door to that secret place of hers? Is it reserved for Kierkegaard, and is this why he is never mentioned

23. With their blood-red seal, numerous postmarks, and other decorations, Regine's letters already had a history before reaching the flowery "Copenhagen" that Fritz's own hand gives as their destination.

in her letters? Was it simply that he filled all too much of that inner space? Was there a connection between these qualms of hers and the reading of Kierkegaard's letters and journals?

While the answers wait, several more questions come rushing in, for how are the surrounding sentences to be understood? Regine first refers to the evidently very respectable way in which she struggled with her "nature" back home—to what does this refer? One wonders what scenes and situations, in all their pain, have taken hold on her memory? But such struggle is no longer possible; one understands that the heat is too intense and her nervous system too burdened; yet clearly her psyche had been burdened beforehand, for Regine has had to use her energy grappling with a grief whose "power" she refused to give in to, and to which she still will not submit. What grief was that? Not homesickness, yet something like it. It is as if simply writing down the word "homesickness" brings such intractable memories to life that she has to force all that is unresolved and inexplicable far into the confessional's innermost room and quickly turn the key. Is her "homesickness" a yearning for lost youth, a quiet despair over the indifferently running sand in the time glass, that unnerving slipping away of time—and is it thus actually an existential or metaphysical longing for a meaning that reaches beyond not only material needs, affluence, and social position, but also beyond Fritz and the love the two nourish for each other? Or is it all perhaps in reality something quite different, down to earth and tied much more closely to the flesh and to sex and biological inexorability? Is Regine pining over the fact that she and Fritz have never succeeded in having children, that her hopes month after month, year in and year out, have been cruelly disappointed?

We never come to know. The two sisters share a secret that they will not share with others, not in their time or in any other. Indeed, what remains of the little letter offers no great help, at any rate not straightaway. For Regine continues along quite other lines:

> How much I have been thinking of you recently now that you are situated like me; even if you are nearer the capital than I, you are still excluded from the pleasures we were accustomed to from the time we were quite young, seeking comfort for tiresome and sad thoughts; and our pleasure was twofold, when either at the art collection or on the way to Father's grave (which, as you say, is so beautiful) we unburdened our hearts in a quiet conversation.

As we see, Regine's thoughts stray toward Copenhagen, to Assistens Cemetery, where the two men she once loved lie buried, her father and "that single individual," whose name must not be mentioned but whose unusual being or "existence" has presumably been touched on quite frequently in a "quiet conversation" between the two sisters. Almost as a quick correction in proof of her own associative boldness, and altogether typical of her bashfulness, Regine avoids pursuing this direction in her feelings and chooses instead to pass it off as nothing, as an untimely egotism, a whim, a singular sign in an unmanageable picture puzzle: "Yet what I have said must sound in your ears like words to the melody that the storm howls in the mill and then, for you, it is a familiar song." Little by little, Regine feels she has managed to write her way to the very brink from which one stares deep into one's own dizzying unfathomability. To stare like that arouses anxiety in a life, but it can also have a beneficial effect:

> So now I feel the advantage of having so little paper to write on, for I have now written myself so healthy that I could go on for a long time, and then I would have to pay for it afterward.

These last lines are about the process of writing, the physical act with pen on paper, but perhaps Regine is also thinking of the enormous psychical energy that continued development of the letter's innermost theme would demand. That she lacks this energy she knows only too well. So she finishes in a nook far away from its wayward theme:

> By the bye, so that you shouldn't come to believe that I suffer only from imaginary illnesses, I will now mention for you here some real boils, small and large, and painful, and diarrhea, etc.

With this abrupt turnaround, the unmanageable pains are trivialized, becoming "imaginary illnesses," and with matters so banal as boils and diarrhea Regine has reached page four, which true to form is devoted to brief reports and greetings to loved ones at home. But there is no greeting from Fritz, who may not have had any knowledge of the letter's contents.

THE PLAGUE'S PARADISE

An erotic fever can be so virulent that it courses in the bloodstream to the last. A quite different fever lurked in the West Indies, however, yellow fever, and an acquaintance with it could prove deadly. One reads in Regine's letter to Cornelia at the end of June 1855: "We have all been very healthy of late but had the sadness of losing our coachman, a soldier who kept our things so tidy." The fatal illness began as just a moderate fever, but since the coachman was afraid of letting himself be examined in the hospital, because he thought it was there that one became sick, he remained at the governor's house. "[B]ut although I believe he received all the care he could get, he got worse and worse, and when it proved definitely to be yellow fever, the doctor demanded he be moved up to the Hospital and he died the next morning."

Yellow fever, or in Latin *febris flava*, though widespread in tropical and subtropical Africa and America, is thought to have its origin in the West Indian islands. St. Thomas was especially vulnerable and was known among seamen as

24. On a good day, a schooner like the Vigilant could cover the forty-three miles (thirty-eight nautical miles) separating St. Croix to the south and St. Thomas to the north; but, in variable winds and changing currents, the voyage could take several days. Vigilant served as the government's postal schooner, and it was in its holds that the letters to and from Regine traveled. When the governor and his wife went to St. Thomas, they, too, sailed on board Vigilant, where the best seating was in a few small wicker bowers lashed to the guardrail on each side of the ship, though they gave no shelter from the unrelenting sun or the humid and chilly wind that blew when darkness fell. Below them was a deep, dark blue sea filled with a rich but voracious variety of sea-life that made it unsafe to fall too far out of one's basket cage. The Vigilant was hit by hurricanes both in September 1876 and in October 1916. She sank on both occasions but was raised and repaired, after which she did service as a trading schooner sometimes chartered to tourists. When, during a serious hurricane, Vigilant sank once again, there was nothing that could be done. But the schooner had by then sailed the Caribbean seas for all of one hundred and thirty-eight years.

the plague's paradise. In the years that Fritz and Regine resided in the West Indies, however, the fever raged far less violently than in Olivia's day, and Regine writes several times to those at home that they should not be concerned about her and Fritz.

Doctor Aagaard had given assurances that Regine and Fritz were not "susceptible to paroxysms of fever," which was comforting—but only up to a point, since Regine could supplement Aagaard's opinion with an irrefutable observation of her own: ". . . one can of course be expedited out of this world without

25. St. Thomas is a both rugged and charming island of cliffs. With its hilly terrain and fjords cutting deep into the land, it does not lend itself to agriculture in the same way as did St. Croix. The island's hills, rising to almost 1,500 feet, thrust out stubbornly from the coast and afford only a modest ridge of earth on which to settle. St. Thomas has the advantage, on the other hand, of a perfect natural harbor, which for generations has functioned as a warehousing and loading/unloading station for goods traveling between the Old and the New Worlds and bringing with them considerable prosperity.

fever." The truth of these words was something she would herself experience six months later on one of her usual morning rides:

> My illness comes from my being so unlucky as to have my horse fall with me, I was lucky though that [I] got off with limbs intact, but the fall was so sudden and right on my nose, so that my face was quite badly battered, I had to go into a house to have blood and sand washed from my face.

The fall having occurred some way out of town, the horses were led back to Christiansted and yoked to a carriage, which was then sent to fetch Regine, who took the fall bravely:

> . . . when I drove home, in spite of being in quite some pain I had to laugh, for the rumor, which in such a small town is a veritable wildfire, was that I had been killed, so that the Traffer Gallery and the street itself were filled with people out to see my funeral procession. When I

came home I had 4 leeches under my heart, because I had some very severe internal pains, presumably caused by the fear.

Josephine reacted to Regine's fall with one of her fever attacks, which were short but violent—"she said that it was the fear on seeing the rider-less horses coming home that had gone to her head and later broke out in fever." In the days following the accident Regine was sore all over and could not sleep, but a week later she had somewhat recuperated, though she was still black and blue all over. She had happily not lost her sense of humor:

> Look, there you see what comes of being refined and aping royal personages. . . . Now I take walks in the morning with Mathilde, I have overcome my aversion to going on the street, one does what one can, so they say, at least in such bagatelles there is truth.

More than a year after the fall there were still mental effects, and Regine feared the worst every time she sat on horseback. The trauma manifested itself in a most humiliating way—"when I rode out with a servant alone, I always came home on foot since he didn't embarrass me, and so I gave way to my fear, but with Fritz I didn't dare." She blankly admits that her behavior is irrational and refers to it several times as her "fixed idea," but to give up riding would be terrible, seeing that the hours on horseback have always been her "best if not to say only pleasure."

The physical fall in this case had psychological consequences; usually it was the other way around, since most often Regine's psychical conflicts brought on accompanying physical pains, and mental anxieties would cause her to fall into periods of poor physical health. In the period following the broken engagement, Kierkegaard had been much concerned for her health. On the 6th of February 1843, he wrote from Berlin to Emil Boesen and begged for information about Regine's condition, since he had heard it said that she was "sickly." Kierkegaard had reason to be unquiet, for it appears from the conversation Hanne Mourier had later with Regine that there was some fear of Regine's lungs being "affected."[100] They weren't. The impression of illness was due first and foremost to "tension and sorrow."

Regine's psychosomatic sensitivity comes frequently to expression in her letters to Cornelia. On a day late in June 1855 she had seen that Mrs. Pontavice, their awful neighbor, had received a visit from Mrs. Forsberg, who had stood crying because her son William was to go to Denmark—"and then I began to cry too, I thought of our many bitter farewells." Regine did everything possible to pull herself together, and she knew all too well that soul and body were perilously united. "Yet, sweet Cornelia, you must know that it is rarely I think

26. The designation of Charlotte Amalie in 1764 as a free port, where all ships regardless of nationality could make use of the excellent harbor facilities, was the start of the city's age of greatest glory. Around the turn of the century, Charlotte Amalie was visited annually by nearly 1,300 ships and had a population of about 3,000. Contributing significantly to the marked rise in commerce were the revolutions in Central and South America, which forced the Spanish and Portuguese colonies to reopen their harbors

about it; no, our Lord is good to me and gives me strength to show those dark thoughts the door, for no sooner am I in a bad humor than I am straightaway ill."

Fritz, too, was attentive to Regine's labile condition. One day when she was suffering a "slight headache," he sent instantly for Doctor Aagaard, who ordered quiet and told her in the strictest terms not to write letters—"now today there is almost nothing wrong with me, and so I hasten to write before I see anyone. But strange how little it takes out here to affect one." Though the headaches were a recurring problem, Aagaard believed that Regine had gradually become sufficiently acclimatized, as she could confirm: ". . . I have received almost no

for the international exchange of goods, thus making Charlotte Amalie the center of an explosive transit trade. A ready proof of its rising prosperity was the establishment of "St Thomas Bank" in 1837 as the first Danish private bank. A year later, A. H. Riise opened a well-stocked pharmacy in Charlotte Amalie, which, with its 11,000 inhabitants, was Denmark's second largest city after Copenhagen, a status that Charlotte Amalie retained right up to 1850.

medicine, a little *Kinderpulver* and bottle of the red mixture that Maria got from Trier." *Kinderpulver* (Children's Powder) was an emetic and sedative prescribed especially for infants, but also given to adults, including some of the geniuses of the species. One gray day in February 1873, Hans Christian Andersen was concerned about some pains "in the abdomen on the right side."[101] His physician, Theodor Collin, was of the opinion that Andersen was surely suffering from "wind in the large intestine," which usually went away on its own. Emil Hornemann, a colleague of Collin, prescribed "Children's Powder and chamomile tea," but these remedies had no real effect, and understandably so, for Andersen's "stitch in the stomach," as he himself called the persistent pains, proved to be due to cancer of the liver, from which he died two years later.

When letters arrived with news of something untoward at home, the distance between St. Croix and Denmark provided conditions nearly ideal for a self-reinforcing anxiety. So a letter about Emil's illness caused the heavens to fall on Regine:

> Dear sweet Cornelia! I can't describe how deeply sad I became on receiving your last letter! My own dear Emil has been ill, yes even dangerously ill, and my beloved sister has cared for him alone, I wasn't there, no, I had no inkling of it!

The latter was not quite true. Regine immediately corrected herself. For even the day before the mail ship called at St. Croix on the 7th of October she had been in a strangely restless state. While everyone was preparing themselves for "the great big bang" in connection with the King's birthday, Regine's thoughts were quite elsewhere; yes, in fact she had wished heartily that the mail ship would stay away just one more day, for she had such a premonition of its bringing bad news:

> When Fritz read your letter for me the next day, he said I was right in thinking it a good thing I hadn't received it the day before. Would to God that the danger is now over, then there usually comes a little restitution after you have come through the grief, precisely in the sense of being released from a great danger. . . . Would that we now had an opportunity to send him some good Madeira to strengthen himself with.

Two weeks later, on Friday the 24th of October, Regine had another ill-omened bout of infallible womanly intuition. She told Cornelia that she had in this way very well *known* that Emil had suffered a relapse for "that is what I dreamt"! The "outcome" of the dream, however, had been "the worst" imaginable; "yes, the dream made me so anxious that on waking I was ill," for the most dreadful thing had happened: in the dream Emil had died! Regine wished fervently that she could travel immediately to Horsens, and had now to admit, in all seriousness, how naïve she had been in imagining that over the course of the years she had "acquired more calm and power" over her "restless mind." She had become "so anguished" on receiving Cornelia's letter "that it went right down to my legs; yes I almost believe the unrest contributed something to the fever I got." This time the psychosomatic reaction didn't wait: "On Friday, when I got your letter in the morning, I felt bad all day, but I thought it was the usual nervous complaint that I suffer constantly but in honesty struggle against." To divert herself, she lured Fritz out for a horseback ride, but when they had ridden some time she noticed that she had overestimated her strength, "for never have I suffered so getting home, presumably I already had the fever in my body then."

On Saturday she was again wretched, without appetite, and could only just creep out of bed to take her medicine. Fritz had got Doctor Aagaard to drive out from Christiansted to Cane Garden to tend to her, but when he arrived she was asleep and recovering, so Aagaard contented himself with recommending that she eat sensibly. No sooner had he gone than Regine's condition worsened, and when Oluf and Fritz came home for dinner she could hardly hold herself uptight—"my head burned, and I went to bed with a real fever." All through Sunday she continued feverish. Fritz stayed at home to look after her, together with Oluf and Josephine—"so I had surely to give them the pleasure of getting better quite so quickly."

On Monday she had regained enough strength to be able to take the beneficial "quinine," with which she continued the following three days, after which her condition became more or less stable—"except that I had to fight the languor and listlessness somewhat." For other reasons, too, she had to be cautious, "for we have chilly weather now, you laugh when you hear 70 degrees, but I assure you that my sensitive nature can easily feel the difference." "Now I don't dare write more, Fritz is at the West End for a school exam, so I have stolen myself these few lines, otherwise I would scarcely be allowed."

On Thursday the 27th of November, Regine could at last draw an almost audible sigh of relief over the latest news from home. Emil was alive and, under the circumstances, fine. As a kind of "payment for the 3 last certainly very dismal letters you have received," Cornelia had, on the 9th of November, drawn a "picture" of "our dear precious Emil" sitting in the pleasant living room by the window in his armchair, wrapped in some woolen blankets; outside it was freezing, but the sun shone and made the landscape shine brightly and—

> just opposite him sits your sister Cornelia looking on him as a treasure she has snatched from death, but she has also battled for this these 10 weeks in much anxiety and trembling, though in deep gratitude I recognize that the mercy and deliverance were undeserved [compared] with so many others whose heads the blow struck, but then I also know that I shall still dare and struggle, but he has promised me and has already begun to take 2 tablespoons of cod liver oil.

Cornelia's letter had an immediate effect on Regine who, on seeing "the nice picture of Emil in the living room," teased him by suggesting that he had laid up just to "put us to the test to see how much we cared for you!" Not for a second did she doubt that her own illness was a matter of a psychosomatic reaction:

> . . . because it was due alone to grief over you that I got the fever, and before we received the last letter, which gave us hope of a lasting

improvement, I went around in such unrest that as always with me, it hit me at my weakest point, namely the stomach, yes I was so exhausted and weak that I seriously had a horror of hearing the orderly come trotting with the mail, since I didn't know from where I could collect the strength to endure the suspense while the mail and then the letter were opened; but my dear Fritz saved me from this, since he had in all secrecy had the mail sent to him, and so it was he who read the letter first and with one word brought me relief. Oh! How happy I was, how I have thanked God!

THE FIRST LOVE

On Thursday the 11th of December Regine gravely assured Cornelia that she no longer wanted to remind herself of the sad time when Emil was ill: "[I]t makes me feel bad enough, now that Emil is recovered and you yourself should rest a little after all the turmoil you have been through, that I should plague you in so many mail deliveries with my letters full of anxiety and fear." Regine was able to make just a little fun of her own concern and the whole situation:

> In your last letter you exclaimed, "how differently run the currents of our lives, will they ever be able to run together again"; this could apply also to our letter currents in particular, for what confusion they really caused: I die of anxiety about Emil, even long after his poorliness is all over; and when he now sits there, and all he needs is enough peace to eat so that he can regain some of the lost strength with solid food, he is then to be plagued by my feverish letters in which, however much I try to hide it, I believe him to be both dead and buried; so I will hope you don't let him see them, it could almost make him sick again.

But also no doubt slightly amused. The episode had once again convinced Regine that, as a letter writer on St. Croix, she had been left in an absurd position:

> Really one shouldn't correspond at such a distance; it wasn't all that mad to do what the lovers did in *The First Love*, "to look at the moon and think of each other"; you at home would then be well placed, for out here we have an altogether different opportunity to reminisce in moonlight than you; for it is just about the most delightful thing we have, the long lovely moonlit evenings, and since we never have fog, we are seldom cheated of a moonlit evening, as you are at home when you have to make do with the magistracy's moonlight.

The many moons put into circulation here call for some comment. Beginning at the end, the reference to the magistracy is to the then often-criticized authority responsible for Copenhagen's street lighting, which refrained from lighting the city's two thousand oil lamps when the moon was full, with the result that when the sky was overcast the townspeople had to grope about in darkened streets.[102] Not without interest also is the reference to the French dramatist Augustin Eugène Scribe's mirthful one-act play *The First Love*, which in J. L. Heiberg's translation had its opening night at the Royal Theater on the 10th of June 1831, and was later performed all of 139 times in the capital city. The remark about moonlight that Regine refers to occurs in the first scene, where Emmeline tells her father that she and her cousin Charles have sworn to be true to each other forever. When the father asks how they have been able to keep up their connection, Emmeline answers with sweet naivety: "Yes indeed, every time it was full moon; when the clock struck ten I went out and looked up at the moon; he did the same at the same hour, it was an agreement between us."[103]

It is hardly likely that Kierkegaard and Regine ever attended a performance of *The First Love* together, although the piece was played five times in the period of their engagement. We know, on the other hand, that on the 14th of December 1841, Kierkegaard sent a letter to Emil Boesen from Berlin to which he appended the following note: "—send me as soon as you can: *The First Love* translated by Heiberg, it is in the theater repertoire and can be got at Schubothe, but don't let anyone suspect it is for me." The cautionary last sentence is due to Kierkegaard's being at work in secrecy on the manuscript of *Either/Or*, in which he was to include an analysis of *The First Love*. Boesen was to go down and discreetly request a copy of the script from bookseller J. H. Schubothe at 17 Badstuestræde and send it off to the writing machine in Berlin. In his analysis, Kierkegaard gives the pen and word to the so-called aesthete A, but if Regine had read his introduction to the analysis, she would probably not only have been carried away by the magic of the theater but also have felt herself targeted in an especially personal way. Aesthete A writes:

> The day had come when the piece was to be performed, I had acquired a ticket, my soul was in festive mood and in a way restless, happy and expectant, I hastened to the theater. As I step inside through the door I cast my eyes up on the second circle, what do I see? My loved one, my heart's sovereign mistress, my ideal, she is sitting there. Involuntarily I took a step back into the darkness of the orchestra stalls to observe her without being seen.[104]

If Regine ever read these lines they must surely have given her a jolt, for "my heart's sovereign mistress" was the very expression Kierkegaard used of her in

1839, when he composed his first rather extensive entry about his life's love. We don't know if she did read them, however, for in her letter Regine leaves it as an allusion to Scribe's moon and returns to the news of Emil's health, which has so relieved her that she gives in to a piece of dialectical coquetry:

> All that I have lost through being happy is that I no more dream about you, little Emil; there went hardly a single night without you disturbing my sleep, for after dreaming about you I usually woke up and couldn't fall asleep again, because I strained to make out my own dreams!

One may wonder, in projecting beyond these lines, how Regine reacted to the news of Kierkegaard's death. Did she dream about him, too, when she lay in the mahogany four-poster behind the light, billowing mosquito net with Fritz sleeping heavily by her side, exhausted after yet another administrative marathon? Regine never touches on the subject, but her letter to Henrik Lund tells us that news of Kierkegaard's death provoked in her a "grief" and occasioned "regret"—so why not also dreams, those unruly and unlawful dreams that are so private that it takes an enormous effort to distance oneself from them?

"... IT'S EXACTLY A MATTER I'D LIKE TO TAKE UP A LITTLE: BLIND LOVE!"

Rather than letting her eye skim restlessly over the island to snatch at interesting events with which to fill her letter to Cornelia, on Sunday the 28th of December Regine turned her glance inwards:

> I have nothing to tell because I have a distinct feeling (so objective am I still) that life round here is so petty that there is hardly matter enough for a conversation, let alone a letter. So with my customary egotism I will speak about myself, and with whom more easily than with you, you of whose love I am so certain that I know that you go along with everything I do. Well, there you are, it's exactly a matter I'd like to take up a little: blind love! I have had great faith in it in my life, in its justification that is, and since out here I generally have enough calm to think things over (if only I also had intellect enough to come to a result), it has recently been a frequent object of my thoughts.

One draws a deep breath at the thought of a retrospective look at blind love in Regine's life, but—steady now!—Regine knows how to control herself and she has no intention of pouring out her innermost feelings on to paper. How much her reflections on the nature and ill-nature of blind love owe to her reading of Kierkegaard's letters and journals can only be surmised. The fragile, capricious happiness that the two shared is nevertheless fresh in memory and must therefore be ushered with special resoluteness into historical limbo:

> I will not turn back now to the past; I shall not put your patience to such a hard test; I shall take life from yesterday and from today. Here, accordingly, there are not many that I love in that way, for if my love for Tilly, so help me God, were blind, I would be a bad governess.

So the first living picture in Regine's gallery is Thilly, for whom her love dare not be blind, since the governess must have "an eye on every finger." Oluf is the next name on Regine's list, and she embraces him with a love that has to do especially with "his inner life, which I always think of as rich and good, although he spares no effort in trying to convince me . . . that it is impoverished and bad, but I assure you that I know him better than he does, and this is also my honest opinion." Neither here is it a matter of unconditional love; Oluf is simply too evasive for that, headstrong, obstinate, and taciturn. After these blood relations, it is the turn of Fritz. Regine declares her unqualified respect for "his outward work," that is to say his "work, duties and responsibility," which in her eyes he conducts with unquestionable skill. "You see, I believe now so unshakably that he always does and chooses the right thing; I believe either he is perfect or else that I have also not a speck of criticism in me."

It is, as we see, Schlegel the civil servant who gets top grades, not Fritz the husband—for in that capacity Regine makes no mention of him at all. And if her reflections can seem second-hand and subservient in debating how far Fritz *is* in fact perfect, or whether perfection is simply something *she* ascribes to him, this is not due to her being his uncritical puppet. Quite the opposite, it is because she is in the throes of freeing herself from the role of a governor's wedded dependent. She makes a factual appraisal of Fritz, judges him, takes a good look at him, and is increasingly aware that the lawfully wedded also owe it to each other to be critical. Not that they should be at each other's throats all the time, but they should be lovingly critical, converting love's wild electricity into a deep current-conducting layer beneath lives that are lived together, so that small corrections and adjustments are tolerated: yes, if Fritz had "a wife with more and better criticism, he would doubtless be better served in many respects."

In her desire not *always* to agree with Fritz, Regine was well able to detect an underlying urge for liberation of the bad kind; and she shivered a moment, because no doubt it was "a little devil in me that whispers in order to seduce me into self-confidence." And that wouldn't do. If emancipation's "little devil" kept on, she would be quickly carried away from her unqualified trust in Fritz—and then where would she be?—and where Fritz? There was no telling. And Regine stumbles straight into a question of unfathomable depth:

> Am I not right in thinking it is the voice of evil, for if I place it clearly in front of me, what will it mean that an old wife like me speaks about enthusiasm or blind faith in my beloved's infallibility; how can I be allowed to do that? Yes, when I was eighteen years old it might still have suited me; but have I now not seen so much of life, and should I not therefore be so experienced that I could be an advisor instead of now being at the very most an attentive auditress whose only advice consists in total approbation.

Regine's will to honesty is strong, but just as she is about to make her dialectical way in a decisive existential passage, it is as though she gets the perspective out of focus because her own thoughts terrify her. So she subjects herself to notions of her inferiority, her egotism and stupidity. She is, on the one hand, well and tired of being a subservient "auditress," one who always thinks the same as Fritz and thus has no opinion that is *hers*. On the other hand, the role of experienced "advisoress" presupposes a liberation that she characterizes with diabolic terms like "devil" and "evil." Her dilemma can, in a way, call to mind her age; she calls herself "old," but with her thirty-four years she is in an indeterminate area between being a younger older person and an older younger person. Yes, but is a person old just on account of becoming a little older than when she was a little younger? And who is one, really, when one is not yet wholly oneself but on the way to becoming oneself? Regine doesn't know which way to turn, and she has to resort to a dash in order to distance herself from this intricate theme.

> —but now I will follow my old habit of breaking off in the middle of saying what I mean, because I can see that I have come into something that belongs to my gift of the gab, and not to my writing ditto, to come out of; but I still hope for as much sympathy from you as, with its help, you will manage to get out of it.

"BUT I AM CONSTANTLY AFRAID OF HER PASSION"

Regine's final sentence is a trifle cryptic, but it probably plays on a many-stringed meaning of the word "sympathy"—both fellow feeling and compassion—and begs Cornelia to mobilize something of both in sorting out the interrupted reflections. The words "when I was eighteen years old" would help Cornelia quite a lot of the way. At that time Regine's "enthusiasm" was quite otherwise unreserved, almost ungovernable, as confirmed by several of Kierkegaard's modes of expression in his journals, where his betrothed is described as a passionately out-going creature whose inflamed sensuality he tried hard to suppress or to point in new directions. When it became too heated he would read aloud one of Bishop Mynster's sermons to get her to think of something else. One of his drafts of the sealed letter intended for Regine quite typically reads, "You were the beloved, the only beloved, you were most beloved when I had to leave you, even though you rather saddened me with your vehemence, which could not and would not understand anything."[105] Again that vehemence, the passion, the will to come together, and later in yet another draft, he writes: "For that reason I intend, if you wish to talk with me, also quite seriously to rebuke you, for with your ardor you did overstep a certain boundary."[106] What boundary, one is tempted to ask, what is it that Regine has on her conscience? And what experience lies behind the following declaration?

> With respect to "her," I am, as always, ready and willing—though even more fervently—to do everything that could make her happy or cheer her. But I am constantly afraid of her passion. I am the guarantor of her marriage. If she understands my true situation, perhaps she will suddenly lose her taste for marriage—alas I know her only all too well.[107]

All of nine years after their time together, and two years after her marriage with Schlegel, Kierkegaard fears that, were she to gain insight into how things really were with him, Regine would "lose her taste for marriage." The more specific circumstances are not known, but his comments on the uncompromising nature of Regine's passion recur so regularly in Kierkegaard's journals that some fearful experiences must lie behind them, as in this entry, likewise dating to 1849:

> Perhaps even the entire marriage is a mask, and she is attached to me even more passionately than before. In that case, everything would be lost. I know very well what she can do once she gets hold of me.[108]

It is no seducer who writes in this way, but rather the seduced, who fears the seduction will repeat itself and be more untamed the second time than the first. "'The Seducer's Diary' is written for her sake, to repel her," declares Kierkegaard, but when one reads entries like this the question instinctively arises as to whether, among his many motives for writing the aforesaid journal, there was not also a need to convince those who were skeptical that it was he, Kierkegaard, who had seduced Regine rather than the reverse. Regine seems to have been as desirous as a second Don Juan, while Kierkegaard has been evasive in his passion, as though he were a Zerlina who will but then won't. He winces at the thought of what Regine could have up her sleeve, or elsewhere:

> Then assume that the passion is ignited once more and that we have the old story, raised to a higher intensity. Assume that she bursts the bonds of marriage, that she kicks over the traces and casts herself upon me in desperation, that she wants a separation, wants me to marry her—not to mention what is even more frightful.[109]

Unless Kierkegaard's concerns are interpreted either as expressions of an erotic megalomania or else reduced to neurotic, unworldly phantasms, they point to an almost titanic intensity in Regine's passion, which has been unconditional, bordering on the unaccountable, and perhaps strong enough to drive her into leaving Fritz and exacting from her former fiancé a renewed promise of marriage—"not to mention what is even more frightful." Since, in Regine, passion's thinker had found his better, Kierkegaard had to consolidate himself in the suspect role of scoundrel that he had devised in the final phase of the engagement period and had tried to sustain until his death. "She would go absolutely wild if she found out how things actually were," goes an entry from the end of August 1848, where he "again turned to her situation" and declared it to be basically unchanged—for the worse.[110]

It was now Regine's turn to revisit the situation, which she did by quite matter-of-factly unpacking the forwarded letters from their cases and acquainting herself with Kierkegaard's presentation of the case and his confidences. The offer of a "settlement" was in the nature of the case long gone, but Regine's passion may have been no less for that. Perhaps that was why she took blind love as her topic in the letter to Cornelia. And perhaps it was also why she had to make do with judging Fritz as a dutiful civil servant, expending not so much as a single drop of ink on the husband of the same name.

". . . SO SHE EGGS THE MERMAN ON"

How unconditional devotion is able to occasion something like equal portions of rapture and horror is something Kierkegaard developed in several places in *Fear and Trembling* (1843), where, under the pseudonymous cloak of Johannes *de silentio*, he not only reconstructs the Old Testament tale of how the Lord God asked Abraham to sacrifice his son Isaac, but also subjects the ballad of Agnete and the Merman to a series of new psychological interpretations. Johannes *de silentio* writes himself well beyond bland romanticism and diagnoses the merman's demonic nature as the real reason for things going as they did, or rather *not* going for him and Agnete.

> I now want to follow this by a sketch along the lines of the demonic. . . . The merman was a seducer. He has called out to Agnete, which his smooth talk has coaxed from her secret thoughts. She has found in the merman what she was seeking, what she gazed down to find in the depths of the sea. Agnete is willing to follow him down. The merman has taken her into his arms. Agnete twines hers about his neck trustingly and with all her soul she abandons herself to the stronger one. He is already at the sea's edge, bending over the water to dive down with his prey. Then Agnete looks at him, not fearfully, not questioningly, not proud of her good luck, not intoxicated with desire, but in absolute faith, with absolute humility, like the humble flower she deemed herself to be; with absolute confidence she entrusts to him her entire fate— And look! The ocean roars no more, its wild voice is stilled, nature's passion—which is the merman's strength— deserts him, the sea becomes dead calm. And still Agnete is looking at him in this way. Then the merman collapses, he is unable to resist the power of innocence, his element becomes unfaithful to him, he cannot seduce Agnete. He leads her home again, he explains to her that he only wanted to show her how beautiful the sea is when it is calm, and Agnete believes him. Then he turns back alone, and the ocean rages, but more wildly still rages the merman's despair. He can seduce Agnete, he can seduce hundreds of Agnetes, he can charm any girl—but Agnete has triumphed and the merman has lost her.[111]

As we see, Johannes *de silentio* resorts to a series of dashes, which in the first three instances point toward the glance, vision, the eye. The dashes each time procure a small pause in the text, introducing in this way the silence that marks Agnete, for Agnete precisely *says* nothing, she just *sees*, but then manages with this look to bring about a mirror calm so as to frustrate the merman's manipulative plans. Agnete's silence accentuates her innocence, her non-participation in the seduction game. "I have allowed myself a slight modification in the merman," Johannes *de silentio* admits. "In fact I have slightly altered Agnete too. In the legend Agnete is by no means guiltless—and in general it is nonsense and sheer coquetry as well as an insult to the female sex to imagine a seduction where the girl is in no way, no way at all, to blame."[112] So Johannes *de silentio* has idealized Agnete's innocence, totalized it and thereby distanced himself both from the world of ballad and from the real world, where women never just allow themselves to be seduced unwittingly and out of the blue, but instead engage actively in the progress of the seduction and therefore share to some degree in the guilt. This presentation of Agnete as an active character in the seduction game gets Johannes *de silentio* to experiment with another casting, which he elaborates in a footnote—where, as is so typical of Kierkegaard, what is most important comes in a pile:

> There is still another way of treating this legend. The merman does not want to seduce Agnete, even though he has seduced many previously. He is no longer a merman, or is, if you will, a pitiable merman who has now already for sometime been sitting sorrowfully on the sea-bed. However, he knows (as indeed the legend has it), that he can be saved by an innocent girl's love. But he has a bad conscience about girls and dares not approach them. Then he sees Agnete. Already, many times, as he lay hidden in the reeds, he has seen her walking along the shore. Her beauty, her quiet self-possession captivate him; but his soul is filled with sadness, no wild desire rages there. And when the merman blends his sigh with the whispering of the reeds, she turns her ear toward it. Then she stands still and falls into reverie, more delectable than any woman and yet beautiful as an angel of deliverance. But Agnete was no quiet girl; she was in fact very taken with the roaring of the ocean and what pleased her about the sad sighing by the sea was that it made the roar in her breast grow stronger. She would be off and away, rush wildly out into the infinite with the merman, whom she loves—so she eggs the merman on. She scorned his humility and now pride reawakens. And the sea roars and the waves foam, and the merman embraces Agnete, and dives with her into the depths. Never had he been so wild, never so full of desire; for with this girl he had hoped for his deliverance. Before long he became tired of Agnete, but her body was never found; for she became a mermaid, who tempted men with her songs.[113]

Agnete is no longer the shy innocent but a passionate woman whose lovely exterior conceals wildness and desire. The merman, on the other hand, has virtually ceased operations as a seducer and is now sitting on the sea-bed grieving; about what one does not know, but perhaps over his *vita ante acta*, his previous life, quite like Kierkegaard, who comes up frequently with these words as a kind of collective designation for unforgiveable happenings in a wild and desperate past. As in the first version, the catastrophe is announced with a well-timed dash: Agnete is no quiet girl, but full of desire and untamable—"so she eggs the merman on." It is this shameless provocation, this laying bare of desire, this scorn of the merman's dammed-up libido that brings about the catastrophe: the merman's slighted humility switches over into an intensified pride that pledges itself to erotic wildness, symbolized archetypally by the roar and foam of the waters. Brought to breaking point by his desire, the merman plunges to the depths with Agnete, who does not die but is transformed into a mermaid, becoming thus sexually impregnable, locked up in the depths, without the ability to be fertilized and bear children.

Since childlessness was also Regine's fate, Kierkegaard's re-creation unconsciously and unintentionally acquires a horrifyingly *prophetic* quality. And as the mermaid Agnete continued to tempt men from the deep with her song, so throughout his life did Regine tempt Kierkegaard into re-interpreting the motives behind the broken engagement. The work of interpretation is carried out in the journals, but—one feels—with a kind of calculated reticence, because Kierkegaard knew well that one day his journals would become common knowledge, for which reason he either wrote around the subject, tore out the pages, or made it known that the material was to be destroyed after his death.

In the reconstructed folktale, in the freshly interpreted myth, or in the pseudonymously signed work, Kierkegaard was able to allow himself an openness and intimacy that the journals made problematic or plainly forbade. Thus, paradoxically, Kierkegaard lets some of what is most private find expression in a kind of mythical confessional writing whose primary addressee is Regine, who is qualified as no other to read the encrypted text between the lines. And precisely because in work after work Kierkegaard had *inscribed* Regine into myth, so too myth gradually became *written into* Regine, thereby endowing her with a mythical status otherwise only bestowed on goddesses, angels—and mermaids.

". . . AN UNSETTLED POINT BETWEEN US"—REGINE'S SECOND LETTER TO HENRIK LUND

Henrik too, in spite of his public penitence, failed to escape Kierkegaard's magic circle. In the letter he sent to Peter Christian on the 27th of February in connection with the coming book and furniture auction, we read somewhere in the middle:

> As for his manuscripts, he wanted me to undertake their publication, as I told you—and I hope that you will give your consent to this, whatever opinions you may entertain about the correctness and truth of his views. I realize that, for me, it will not be any pleasant task, since Father will not approve many views.[114]

Henrik based his qualifications as publisher on the fact that Kierkegaard had on his deathbed more or less indirectly—*per ironiam*—made him his literary executor. It was undeniably a very tenuous basis and one that Henrik's mental state most certainly did nothing to strengthen. In his journal, Peter Christian wrote in mid-March 1856 that Henrik suffered from "violent attacks of melancholia." Henrik's condition nevertheless improved so much in the next few months that he could take himself to Samsø to investigate possibilities for setting up a medical practice in that small Danish island community, far from the world's turmoil. But nothing came of the idea. In the early summer the physician unlocked the door to his deceased uncle's rooms in Klædeboderne, just behind the Church of Our Lady, and tried to form a preliminary overview of the manuscript scrolls and folders and notebooks and letters and bills and loose strips of paper and scraps that were distributed in boxes and cartons and cabinets awaiting posterity's acquaintance. As his registration proceeded, he conscientiously noted down where a relevant item was placed at the time it was found: "In the desk," "In the lower desk drawer." "In the box in the desk." "In the second cabinet. B. In the top drawer. To the left." He kept an exact account, correspondingly, of what sheets, notes, and strips lay together. He supplied every single item with a number, which he then entered in his "Inventory of the manuscripts of S. Kierkegaard drawn up after his death."

Henrik had taken on a job that was not merely strenuous but proved to be enormous, indeed endless. When one day in the mountains of carefully written paper he stumbled on "a big sack" filled with manuscripts, clean copies, proofs, and envelopes, together with a bag of bills, his philological passion suffered a severe blow. Henrik realized that the task should go to others, as he announced in September 1856 to Peter Christian, who before he managed to respond to Henrik's announcement received at the end of November yet another letter from his nephew laconically announcing that he had been given the post of medical officer on St. John, the neighboring island to Regine and Fritz's St. Croix. The world may be small, but not so an irony that is all-embracing!

Henrik arrived in the West Indies at the end of February 1857. Knowing nothing of Henrik's mental state or other plans, Regine had half a year earlier, on the 10th of September 1856, sent him a lengthy letter, which she introduced with the words:

Dear Henrik!

You must by no means believe that it is because I am not grateful for your letter of the 11th of June that I have let it lie unanswered so long; no, on the contrary, I have thanked you many times in my heart and today I now send you my thanks in words.

The letter Regine refers to no longer exists, so what Henrik has said can only be reconstructed indirectly and fragmentarily from Regine's words, which continue:

> It is always a rule of mine to answer each letter with the next post, but there is no rule without an exception, and so I made yours one of them, partly because we are no doubt not going to engage in any steady correspondence and a small delay therefore makes no difference, partly because I both had something I wanted to ask you about and something I would say to you that I would consider more closely.[115]

Regine then tells Henrik that she has been ailing recently because the violent heat was too much for her nerves, but that after a period when she was troubled with "some boils, which out here is quite common," she was in better shape and therefore more disposed to write letters. And then it goes on:

> Thank you for the books you are sending to me; if they are not already sent, and if it doesn't involve too much inconvenience, or even sacrifice, I would ask you for some of his theological writings, I have some [some illegible words here], and especially the last ones. . . .

Regine does not shed light on which theological works she already possesses, and then, only just, her plea for a book:

> . . . now to what I want to ask you about: You write that he has mentioned me in his illness; it was just this, I would so very sincerely like to know what he has said about me, for although I have got some information about our relationship from the posthumous papers that puts it in another light, a light in which I myself have sometimes seen it, I don't know whether you understand me when I add that my modesty, which most often prevented me from seeing it in that way . . .[116]

Regine has been—indeed she is the first woman ever to be—in possession of a judicious selection of Kierkegaard's journal entries concerning the engagement and the time that followed. Although her reading has thrown a light on their relationship that she herself has been too modest to see in it, in essence she has simply found confirmation of her own ideas about the relationship and has been strengthened in the feelings she had when she met Kierkegaard out in the town, or on receiving via Fritz the sealed letter with its offer of a "settlement": Kierkegaard's love was something she had never seriously doubted. That this love grew in its unresolved state with Kierkegaard's death was something of which she was also painfully aware:

... but what I have felt certain about was that there was an unsettled point between us that sometime had to be cleared up; short-sighted person that I am, I left it to the peaceful time of old age for, through a strange thoughtlessness, his death had never occurred to me; it came therefore all the more unexpectedly, and filled me not with grief alone but with regret, as if precisely through this procrastination I had done him a great wrong. It was this I hoped to be able to draw conclusions about, by hearing what his last words about me were, for his papers are all written, so far as I can understand, several years back; and to me the years have after all brought great changes.[117]

It was not unfamiliar to Regine's experience that death is neither peaceful nor harmonious but often comes with a jolt, usually while one is engaged in quite other things or just about to take that first step toward saying that crucial something to someone, and then, a moment later, they are no longer among the living. Regine was now hoping that Henrik could help her with information about what Kierkegaard had said about her before he passed away. There is an endearing inquisitiveness in this inquiry, but lying behind it there is surely also a hope that what was enigmatic in their relationship might cease to be so at some point. What is enigmatic, however, *remains* enigmatic and flutters off like a frightened and disturbing shadow on the other side of death.

Posterity's knowledge of Kierkegaard's last words on Regine is confined, as we learned from his conversation with Emil Boesen, to the modest information that he "spoke about her lovingly and sadly" and that he supported her marriage with Schlegel, after which, with his usual instinct for paradoxes, large and small, he had added. "I was afraid she would become a governess. She didn't, but now she is one in the West Indies." A governess is a housekeeper who takes care of the children's upbringing and development but also functions as a chaperone to forestall a premature loss of virtue. This was the double role Regine played vis à vis Thilly, but Kierkegaard can hardly have had any knowledge of that. His little joke is about Regine alone, in her capacity as a governor's wife, which made her a "governor-ess" (*guvernorinde*) and almost a "gover-ness" (*guvernante*).

"ONE UNNAMED WHOSE NAME WILL SOMETIME BE NAMED"

In her letter to Henrik, Regine admits in plain terms that she was filled with sorrow and regret by what she read about Kierkegaard's death; yes, she felt quite simply that by being reticent she had "done him a great wrong." One further understands that she has gone through the papers Henrik has sent her, but without finding anything that to her looked like a real declaration:

> Among the papers I found one sealed in which there stood *only*: It is my will that my writings are dedicated to my late father and to her. Remarkably, in a dedication to an unnamed that stands at the beginning of a smaller booklet containing 3 discourses, I have believed, from when I first saw it, that I could understand it to refer to myself. This is also something I would now also ask if you could give me any information on.[118]

Regine refers here, first, to Kierkegaard's last will and testament, which as we know lay in the envelope with the red seal and was dated 1851, and which Henrik included in the "two sealed packages" that he sent to Regine early on. Next, she refers to a dedication in "a smaller booklet containing 3 discourses." Regine, it would seem, remembers one discourse too many, since the "booklet" in question was *Two Discourses at the Communion on Fridays*, which, after much pondering, Kierkegaard had furnished with its dedication to Regine—yet without mentioning her civil name. He had originally thought of dedicating, or "consecrating," the whole of his authorship to Regine with a dedication to accompany the work *On My Activity as an Author*, and in the preserved manuscript material it is possible to follow his efforts through different versions, which are unusual in that Regine is to appear as an *unnamed* whose name would sometime be made public. Kierkegaard therefore contented himself with leaving a space for such a dedication for posterity to fill by reading in the name "Regine":

> A dedication, for which I here simply reserve the place until the moment comes when it can be filled with a name, which will inseparably follow my activity as an author, as long as it is remembered, be it for a longer or shorter time. . . .[119]

It can well be imagined that, on closer consideration, this almost audible suppression of Regine's name would have struck Kierkegaard as artificial—and one might concur. But be that as it may, he tries once more with a new and more direct version, which will prove close to the final dedication:

> An Unnamed
> whose name must still be suppressed
> but whom history shall one day name,
> and, whether this be a longer or a shorter,
> just as long as mine.
> is consecrated
> etc.

Kierkegaard obviously remained unable to let go of the thought of posterity reading "Regine" in the empty space. He therefore lets the dedication remain altogether empty, but furnished with a small star or asterisk connecting it to a "comment":

> A dedication*)
> *) *Comment.* Due to circumstances this dedication cannot yet be filled
> out with the name, but it shall already have its place now.

Kierkegaard's fourth attempt in the complicated dedicational genre is no less cryptic; it amounts simply to the following:

> One Unnamed,
> whose name shall one day be named,
>   And will—"*be named*"

The contrived result seems hardly proportional to the exertions of one usually so confident of his style. However, that one looks in vain for a dedication to Regine in *On My Activity as an Author*, which came out on the 7th of August 1851, is due not to Kierkegaard's having abandoned the project but, on the contrary, to his having decided in the meantime to move the dedication to *Two Discourses at the Communion on Fridays*, which came out on the same day as *On My Activity as an Author*. But the dedication did not come to Kierkegaard in the form of a felicitous and fully fledged conceit. In its first form it read:

> To R. S. is consecrated, with this work, an author-activity that belongs
> to a certain degree to her, by the one who belongs to her altogether.[120]

Kierkegaard, as we see, has now emboldened himself to inscribe Regine's initials and thereby has assigned the dedication a considerable intimacy, which appears provocative when we bear in mind that Regine is in fact married to Fritz. It is therefore Fritz, not Kierkegaard, "who belongs to her altogether," and perhaps it was this hint at rivalry in the dedication that led Kierkegaard to shelve that draft and formulate the following instead:

> *A Contemporary*
> Whose name must still be suppressed, but whom
> history will name,—whether this be
> longer or shorter,—as long as
> it mentions mine,
>   is consecrated,
>   along with this little work

the whole of the authorship, as it was
from the very beginning.[121]

After all of these dialectical cadences and cramped splittings of hair, Kierkegaard returns to something like his first and quite simple draft and ends with the
dedication in its final form:

To One Unnamed,
whose name shall one day be named,
is consecrated
along with this little work the whole of the
authorship as it was from the beginning.[122]

No direct reason is offered for transferring the dedication to *Two Discourses for
the Communion on Fridays*, but it was a fact that Kierkegaard noted in his journal: "When, as I have wanted to do from the beginning, I step decisively into the
character of the religious—in that instant *she* is the only thing of importance,
because I have a *God*-relationship to her."[123] That the dedication ended up in *Two
Discourses for the Communion on Fridays* was calculated to instate Regine into
the religious connection that she, according to Kierkegaard, had to him.

Although not all the documents on the matter were available to her, Regine
was nonetheless excellently informed of the place Kierkegaard had intended for
her in history; she knew too that she occupied a prominent place in his "*God*-
relationship." Having touched on the matter of the dedication, she writes in her
letter to Lund that she had always feared "all publicity," but that Kierkegaard's
death had in this respect forced her to change her attitude; yes, it seemed plain
to her that she had a *duty* to let herself be known in public. If she set aside such
a duty, she would be doing wrong:

> . . . not against him alone, but against God, to whom he sacrificed me
> even if it was (a doubt that he himself had) from an innate tendency
> to self-torment or, as I assume, that time and the results of his activi-
> ties indicated [was] from an inner call from God. The information you
> were able to give me will not for the time being make me alter my con-
> clusion, also as you can no doubt understand from a concern for my
> husband and his position, but I feel a need to have it clarified as much
> as possible for myself, I will no longer postpone it in silence, I have
> done enough of that in this life.

Regine was clearly not unfamiliar with her former fiancé's mental constitution,
and she was therefore able to construe his sacrifice of her to God as a symptom

of an "innate tendency to self-torment." Personally, she was nevertheless more inclined to believe that the sacrificing was due to "an inner call from God," with whom Kierkegaard was indeed, according to himself, "previously promised" (*for-lovet*: "engaged," literally "promised beforehand") long before he had any thought of becoming involved with Regine. One notes again that Regine is familiar with some of the deepest motives in Kierkegaard's nature, but cannot *altogether* come to terms with there being *nothing more* to impart—and the fateful contact between her and him remains accordingly a riddle, her riddle, Regine's riddle.

Her need for an explanation makes her quiz Henrik, but everything suggests that he was unable to offer her anything that she did not already know or could not already read for herself in the rich source material that he had dispatched to her. As appears from the parenthesis in her passage below, she also felt that she had laid herself bare in her letter and therefore had to assure herself of Henrik's confidence with an entreaty:

> There is still something I want to make clear to you (do you notice how unreservedly I presume your most sincere interest in myself in laying before you in this way my most secret doubt, but I know, do I not, that I can rely on you). You write that you believe you can see in my letter that I am not altogether content, you may have been partly right in coming to that conclusion from the letter you received at that time, for you no doubt know from experience how much we humans are prone to moods; but I would be very ungrateful if I did not call myself happy, yes even happy as are few others, for to be happily married is the main thing in life, as has indeed been repeated so often, and Schlegel and I mean so much to each other that we make each other mutually rich; in one way I owe him that too.

These words bring Regine's letter to a close. She has been in deep water and for a moment had lost sight of the contours of the mainland. It was a matter of urgency to have Henrik understand that he should attach no deeper meaning to the discontent he detects in her previous letter, which was due simply to her being an impulsive person. It would be most ungrateful of her not to call herself happy, seeing that being happily married is the "main thing in life." In the very last sentence she nevertheless manages to make her marital bliss waver on a problematic premise *outside* the marriage. The words "in a way I owe him this too" leave posterity in a situation of beguiling uncertainty, not knowing for sure who this "him" really is. If Fritz, to whom she owed her happy marriage, then it seems surprising that it was only "in a way"; if on the other hand it is Kierkegaard, then "in a way" says that in marrying Fritz she acted according to Kierkegaard's own melancholic intimations, and to that extent owed it to Kierkegaard that her marriage in fact proved a success.

"THEN I RETURN TO YOU . . ."

Whichever one chooses, Kierkegaard gets the last word. It is as though, once again, Fritz will forever fail to wrest Regine from the past. If the voyage to St. Croix was an attempt in that direction, then there is an almost brutal irony in the fact that they had only just settled into their new surroundings when they received news of Kierkegaard's passing, which might have meant that life in exile was hardly necessary. But then there was his will, in which Regine was appointed residual legatee because the deceased considered her his wife—regardless of Fritz's having meanwhile married her. And that was just the beginning. As we saw, letters and jewelry from the time of the engagement, together with a selection of Kierkegaard's journals, had then been carefully packed in Copenhagen and freighted the many thousand miles west to the governor's wife in Christiansted. And as though that were not already more than enough, some time later Kierkegaard's blood-relation and devoted disciple Henrik Lund took up residence on St. John—presumably because he too wanted to free himself of the palpable aftereffects of an involvement with Kierkegaard. It remained only for reality to surpass itself with the most inventive of whimsies: the priest in Horsens, from where Cornelia communicated with Regine, was—God preserve us!—the very Emil Boesen with whom Kierkegaard had conversed on his deathbed about, among other things, Regine. Had it been a novel, the arrangement would have been judged more than a little unrealistic.

It might be thought a sobering circumstance that we have no knowledge of how often Henrik and Regine exchanged memories of Kierkegaard during their exile, or even, indeed, of how often they met each other. But that the young physician's arrival was awaited with excitement is apparent from a slightly confused letter that Regine sent to Cornelia on the 28th of February, during her stay on St. Thomas:

> You have probably heard that Henrik Lund has got a medical position on St. John; he has come to St. Croix these days and is with Oluf. We are now expecting him over here before he goes to his new home, I am really looking forward to seeing and talking with him. Now I have written enough, and you can also believe I am tired, I have such a sniffle today and water pours out of my nose and eyes.

Regine says no more about her conversations with Henrik, which of course may not mean that there was nothing more to tell, but simply that Cornelia was not to be informed. After all, Regine had said nothing about Kierkegaard's testamentary requests, nor had a line been written about the love letters, nor a word about the journals, nor a single syllable about the arrival of the past in the West Indian present—in short not so much as a comma about her old love. The last hint of Henrik's presence in Regine's letters dates from more than two years later. On the 12th of October 1859, she wrote:

> On Monday a week ago Dr. Lund came from St. John and was here until Monday evening when he journeyed home again. He is tired of the West Indies and has applied for his discharge; it doesn't surprise me; it surprises me more that he came out here. Well, it was a little change for him and for us that he was over here.

Henrik had stayed with Regine and Fritz for a week before traveling back to his mother country. Talk of his visit as a "little change" may sound like an outrageous understatement. Similarly, one may wonder at Henrik's no longer being mentioned by his first name but instead oddly identified by his profession. Is this due to a need to neutralize her relationship to him, so that Cornelia or other co-readers should not begin to think obvious thoughts and draw compromising conclusions?

Henrik gave up his position with effect from the 31st of May 1860, the date on which Fritz did the same.[124] Some time in July of that year Peter Christian Kierkegaard noted in his journal: "Henrik Lund came home from the West Indies on the 18th [of July] (that is, on his birthday) via England, where J. C. Lund received him."[125] If we want to know whether Henrik and Regine managed to help each other toward a better understanding of their common relation, we are referred to one of history's blank pages. Should Regine, on the other hand, one day wish to be reminded of the love with which Kierkegaard had it in mind to enclose her for all time, she need only settle herself comfortably in her rocking chair, pick out one of the undated and thereby wonderfully eternal letters from the time of the engagement and reread a passage like this one:

Midday 1 o'clock

My Regine,

Even at this moment I am thinking of you, and when it sometimes seems to you that I keep myself away from you, then it is not because I love you less, but because it has become a necessity for me at certain moments to be alone. But that in no way means you are excluded from my thoughts, forgotten: on the contrary you are really livingly present. And when I think of your faithful soul, I become happy again, you then hover around me, and everything else then vanishes from my horizon, which expands infinitely and has only one boundary. . . . Then I turn back to you, and the hovering thought finds rest in you.

Your S.K.

1857

~~~

"THE SEDUCER'S DIARY"

Cornelia, as has been mentioned, had a near namesake in Cordelia, who has left three letters in which she interchangeably deifies and condemns her malefactor, who not only nabbed her virtue but also ran off with her happiness. The three letters in "The Seducer's Diary" are addressed to Johannes and signed: "Your Cordelia." Toward the end of the third letter, we read:

> Be patient with my love, forgive me for continuing to love you; I know my love is a burden to you, but there will be a time when you return to your Cordelia. Your Cordelia! Hear that entreaty! Your Cordelia, your Cordelia,
>
> *Your Cordelia*[1]

Noting how Cornelia ends her letter with Cordelia's concluding words to Johannes can produce a little shiver in our minds:

> You have sent me so much, my dear beloved sister, that I do not know how I shall begin to thank you; I do it with all my heart and soul. Be happy with that if I have wearied your patience.
>
> *Your, your, your faithful sister Cornelia*

We do not know for certain, but it seems unlikely that Cornelia has *not* read "The Seducer's Diary." That she should consciously allude to Cordelia's letter is, however, not very plausible; more likely it is a mere but gratifying matter of coincidence. Nor do we know whether Regine has read "The Seducer's Diary," but that she should not be interested in a work whose main female character borrows her characteristics and shares to some degree her fate, would be a breach of all elementary laws of curiosity. In view of this, we should also hope that she *has* familiarized herself with the questionable diary; for if not, it would have failed in the self-denigrating mission that Kierkegaard had assigned to it when, with her in his thoughts, he let it be known in 1849: "'The Diary of a Seducer' is written for her sake, to repel her."[2] The diary was meant to prove so shocking to Regine that she would have to dissociate herself from Kierkegaard and in this way would find it easier to overcome the grief and pain he had caused her by breaking off the engagement.

27. The wind-driven mill built over one that is driven by steam provides an almost symbolic manifestation of the meeting of old and new forms of production. The mill was activated when the wind dropped. Standing in front of the residential building are Cornelia, the children, and some servants. A head can also be seen up in one of the windows of the windmill looking down at the photographer. It was in these far from silent surroundings that Cornelia spent her life between 1856 and 1880, the year when she and Emil returned to Copenhagen.

"The Seducer's Diary" has in the course of time also repelled others, but since what one finds repellent can have a special power of attraction, several readers have in the same course of time fallen for the work's ability to fascinate, witnessing with bated breath the way in which Johannes the Seducer gains possession of the innocent Cordelia, carries out his project, and then leaves the broken woman to herself and an uncertain fate. Unaffected by Cordelia's tears, prayers, and letters, Johannes steals on toward new erotic adventures, thereby inscribing himself in posterity's moral records of those unforgiveable exponents of a crime that is in the offing whenever a taste for beauty, rhetorical virtuosity, and sexual energy are administered with amoral genius.

Upon its publication on the 20th of February 1843, *Either/Or*, the first part of which concludes with "The Seducer's Diary," aroused as much enthusiasm as dismay in (among others) Hans Christian Andersen's gifted and eloquent writer friend Signe Læssøe, who on the 7th of April informed the whimsical writer in Paris of the latest news from the Copenhagen ramparts:

> A new literary comet . . . has soared in the heavens here—a harbinger and bringer of bad fortune. It is so demonic that one reads and reads it, puts it aside in dissatisfaction, but always picks it up again, because one can neither let it go nor hold onto it. "But what is it?" I can hear you say. It is *Either/Or* by Søren Kierkegaard. You have no idea what a sensation it has caused. I think that no book has caused such a stir with the reading public since Rousseau placed his *Confessions* on the altar. After one has read it, one feels disgust for the author, but one profoundly recognizes his intelligence and his talent.[3]

Two weeks later Andersen responded with a shake of the head, motivated apparently by a certain envy: "What you have sent me about Kierkegaard's book doesn't particularly arouse my curiosity. It is so easy to appear ingenious when one disregards all considerations and tears one's own soul apart and all sacred feelings! But this kind of thing has its effect. It is reasonable to assume that Heiberg has been instantly dazzled by the philosophical illumination!"[4] In this particular assumption Andersen was thoroughly mistaken, for when Johan Ludvig Heiberg reviewed *Either/Or* on the 1st of March, he called the book a "monster" and made sport with its title, which he transferred to his own relationship to the book: "Am I *either* to read it, *or* shall I refrain?" Regarding "The Seducer's Diary" he was in no doubt: ". . . one is disgusted, revolted, offended."[5]

One should perhaps show some restraint in condemning the diary, which only deals at a most superficial level with a lustful libertine's need to deflower blameless Copenhagen innocents. From the preface with which an unnamed gentleman has furnished the diary, it also appears that, properly viewed, Johannes was "of far too spiritual a nature to be a seducer in the usual sense,"[6] which is why one should be cautious in stigmatizing him as a "criminal." The passion Johannes reveals is bound up with the realizing of the strategy itself, the tactic, the absolute victory of manipulation. What drives him is, in short, not something so biologically banal as a need for satisfaction, but on the contrary "the astuteness, the cunning with which he can insinuate himself into a girl's heart, the dominion he can acquire over it, the fascinating, systematic, progressive seduction."[7] The unnamed author of the preface is in fact not alone in thinking that Johannes is an untypical seducer and that, genre-wise, his diary is out of line; this is a claim we find in a footnote Kierkegaard himself made to a draft of *The Concept of Anxiety*, where he begged his readers to keep in mind the following:

> Anyone with a psychological interest in observations in this respect, I will refer to "The Seducer's Diary" in *Either/Or*. From a closer look it differs altogether from a novella, has quite different categories in reserve; and for anyone who knows how to use it, it can serve as preliminary to highly serious and not just superficial investigations. The seducer's secret is precisely that he knows that the woman is anxiety.[8]

For reasons unknown to us, Kierkegaard omitted this reference to the diary in his final preparation of *The Concept of Anxiety*, but whatever they were, those reasons cannot have been compelling. "The Seducer's Diary" can be viewed as an excellent prolegomenon to *The Concept of Anxiety*, just as much as the diary can itself be read as a modern version of the biblical account of the creation and fall, to which the author of *The Concept of Anxiety* gives an advanced psycho-theological interpretation.[9] As a second Lord God, Johannes forms or creates his Cordelia by way of an erotic experiment, which, in compressed phases, puts her through an evolution from innocent young girl to sexually hungry woman. The fact that the experiment succeeds in a fraction of the time that Nature itself has thought to set aside for that purpose is due to Johannes's managing to control Cordelia's emotional register and the fluctuations of her sexual excitement through a series of anxiety-provoking maneuvers.

If knowledge of a woman's anxiety is part of the seducer's manipulative repertoire, so in return is it the woman's "secret" that she can be *seductive* without wishing to be so. And this makes her a far more active and scene-setting figure than either she herself or her more or less imaginary Johannes-style seducer imagine themselves to be. It is also she, Cordelia, who puts the whole thing in motion. As Johannes struts along Langelinie with his thoughts elsewhere, his eye is caught by an unknown woman who so completely blinds him with her beauty that for a moment—as when a being from another world appears—he loses his sight and consequently fails to keep in view what he has seen:

> Have I gone blind? Has the soul's inner eye lost its power? I have seen her, but it's as if I'd seen a heavenly revelation, so completely has her image vanished from me again. Vainly do I call upon all the strength of my soul to conjure forth this image.[10]

The religious metaphors reveal almost to excess that what happened to Johannes that day on Langelinie had the quality of something "befalling" him, a present, a heavenly gift. It was not *he* who, in Cordelia, had picked out a victim, but quite the opposite: it was *she* who captured Johannes, though, note well, without wishing it, that is to say unconsciously, quite without calculation, simply by being present at that place and at that time. Cordelia is accordingly *instantaneously seductive*, something that Johannes will never be, and consequently he must, with his *delayed seduction*, try to compensate by resorting to an intellectual strategy, putting into action what the editor calls his "systematic, progressive seduction."

Traditional ideas of subject and object, ruler and ruled, male and female are thus all suddenly rendered bankrupt. "She herself will become the tempter who seduces me into going beyond the boundary of the normal,"[11] acknowledges Johannes, at a point when she will, according to his psychological calculations, cancel the engagement. Yet this very choice of words can lead the reader to ponder whether the switch from seducer to seduced might not already have occurred, and much sooner than Johannes imagines. It is hardly quite without rhyme or reason that the diary's editor comments in his preface that the seducer's "affair with Cordelia was so entangled that it was possible for him to appear as the one seduced."[12] What was planned as a portrait of the sovereign, self-staging director draws one's eyes unerringly toward the uncomfortable fact that the seducer is "entangled" in the seduction play itself, and is therefore not its director but, on the contrary, under *its* direction.

Had it not exceeded his credentials, the editor might well have added that the story of the seduction was further "entangled" with another story—Søren and Regine's. On the other hand, to be informed of such an entanglement would not be strictly necessary, either in Kierkegaard's own time or in the future, insofar as the diary had for better or worse been equipped with an unmistakably *biographical subtext*, which becomes hardly less evident when Kierkegaard remarks that he has written the diary for her sake—"in order to repel her." He thereby furnishes the diary with an unmistakably (auto)biographical subtext, though he may not have been the only one, let alone the first, to see it. In taking special aim

28. In this pencil sketch of Regine in a wide-collared dress (c. 1840), Emil Bærentzen has managed to capture something vivacious, wistful, and open-hearted, which in his painting of the same year has had to give way to the romantic, lingering gaze of someone still untouched by life.

at "The Seducer's Diary" in his discussion of *Either/Or*, J. L. Heiberg not only gave strident voice to his indignation but also tried to home in on the author's deeper motivations. He was in no doubt that there could indeed be someone like Johannes the Seducer, but he was unable to fathom how "as an author an individual can be so constituted as to find pleasure in putting himself into such a character's shoes."[13] Heiberg thus draws attention to the actual author behind the fictitious seducer. But why does he do that? Might it be through wishing to suggest that Kierkegaard, the author, could have motives altogether of his own for writing "The Seducer's Diary"? That is, that Kierkegaard had sought refuge in a "character" such as Johannes in order to create a fictional distance from the fact that, in reality itself, a woman had succeeded in seducing a man. Is Heiberg insinuating, in other words, that Kierkegaard had to write "The Seducer's Diary" in order to give his reader the impression that it was *he*, Kierkegaard, who seduced Regine, while in reality is was Regine who had signed her name to the erotic dynamic in their relationship and had to that extent seduced Kierkegaard?

It remains a hypothesis. But if this is indeed what Heiberg wished to hint at, there would be a special connection between this suggestion in full publicity and the thought-provoking ruminations that crept into the draft of *The Concept of Anxiety*, where Kierkegaard began to speculate about why in fact it was really Eve who seduced Adam:

> For that matter it has always struck me as peculiar that the story of Eve has been the exact opposite of all later analogies; for in ordinary usage the words "to seduce" used for her are generally aimed at the man.[14]

Kierkegaard tried to explain the situation through a "third power" seducing the woman, namely the serpent, it being the latter rather than Eve who seduced Adam. But the reading provides only a provisional solution, because now "there remains the serpent"[15] and Kierkegaard must "freely admit to being unable to attach any definite thought to the serpent." His interpretation merely pushes the problem further back in time—to the mythical beast whose power and meaning he has been unable to explain. But Kierkegaard may have been closer to an explanation than he imagined; indeed, he has perhaps *experienced* the explanation in person: the enigmatic Old Testament serpent symbolizes the play of seduction, which like *an alien power* draws its protagonists into its magic circle. Just as the snake was there in the garden before Adam and Eve were created, stealthily waiting for them, so too, and no less treacherously, the seduction play is waiting for other pairs in history to enter its territory where the relation between power and weakness is exposed to a range of unfathomable exchanges and unforeseen switches.

In late August 1849, Kierkegaard thought back to his time with Regine. In his journal he reflected upon "what power she really has," and continued: "Truly when Providence gave man strength and woman weakness, whom did he make the stronger?"[16] The question remains unanswered and, as for that, can be called rhetorical. But just possibly it reveals the truth that Kierkegaard's Old Testament author-colleagues chose from experience to have Eve seduce Adam—which supposedly was the first time in history though certainly not the last, nor hardly, as Kierkegaard would like to believe, "the exact opposite of all later analogies."

TROPICAL YULETIDE

The editor announces in his preface to "The Seducer's Diary" that the seducer's feet "were so formed as to retain the footprints under them," the consequence of which was that his "path through life left no trace."[17] Something similar is true of Regine. Her path through the "Seducer's Diary" has indeed "left no trace," in the sense that we do not know exactly where, or exactly how much, she has been present. All we know is that Kierkegaard could not have written the work were it not for his experience with Regine, a fact that in the reader's mind more or less imperceptibly grants her a potential presence on every page. In this way Kierkegaard brought Regine not only into history but also into fiction, with the latter, paradoxically enough, the decisive condition of the former.

Now, however, she was no longer the material out of which genius created its fictional works or reconstructed folktales and myths. She was the governor's wife, who was about to melt in the tropical heat and, moreover, had to try to get herself into some semblance of a Christmas spirit, which was quite a problem in itself. "Really, I'm a little afraid of Christmas," she had to admit, and gave way to ponderings over her pre-seasonal anxieties, which may have been due to Christmas, or Yuletide (Danish, *Juletid*), in these parts being "so colorless." Not of course the nature outside, which was always "green and delightful," but rather, as she thought, the lack of color "inside the house":

> . . . and then I am overcome by a sense of it being as though my fault; for if anyone should give it color, it is me, for my little family, Fritz, Oluf and Tilly; but what can I do, I am as stupid as a stockfish; but I grieve over this stupidity, it no doubt comes from being uncharitable.

A stockfish is a dried cod, its strange name due to its being dried on thin sticks (Danish, *stokke*). Referring to someone as a stockfish is to declare them boring or untalented. In her letters, when zeroing in on her own poor opinion of herself, or on all that she would so much like to do to make others happy but doesn't get around to, Regine uses the word several times of herself. She had plans to "have a magnificent Christmas tree," but since relations with most of the circle of acquaintances were by no means cordial, it was surely "too much to ask of me that I should bestow more time on them than they get with the regular dinners and balls." In addition, there was the very situation itself—"Don't you think it sounds ridiculous to want to be convivial with the West Indians?" But it was a pity for Thilly, as Regine was the first to admit, and when a few lines further on in her letter she came to think of Cornelia's children, further feelings of inadequacy welled up in her—"and what kind of an aunt am I to them, I who am so rich and send them not a single Christmas present; but where should I find anything in this dog-house." Not even Cornelia had been remembered with the smallest of gifts, nor had she the year before, or the year before that, which now practically causes Regine's letter to blush with shame:

> It occurs to me now that not for a single moment have I thought of giving you something, but anything I can get over here would not give you any joy, and me vexation, for in spite of our large incomes it annoys me when I am to pay four or five times as much for poor wares; besides, I hope you agree with me that we are now too old to rejoice over birthday presents, yes, perhaps you do as I do, try to erase that day from your memory. For me, it would not be difficult for, in this perpetual summer, the days, weeks, months vanish without one being aware of any difference between them, and I hope the years do the same. That's how it goes with me as far as Christmas is concerned, for although we are approaching it with steady strides, I have not in this connection sent a single greeting or New Year's wish to any of my dear ones; but it is plainly impossible for me to grasp that we should have Christmas in this light and warm summer time. Nor have I thought of any gifts to either big or small.

THE WHITE GOLD—A DARK CHAPTER

The Spaniards were the first to import slaves from Africa to the Virgin Islands—the first load arrived already in 1517—and this black workforce helped to make Spain a Great Power in the course of the sixteenth century. Spain's success caused Britain, France, and Holland to take an interest in the profitable islands and the fight for the colonies was on. Denmark's participation in this orgy of greed under far-off skies had its beginning under Christian IV at the start of the seventeenth century, but it was only when St. Croix came into Danish hands in 1733 that sugar production got properly under way. The island was measured and partitioned into plantation areas, the so-called estates, which were offered for sale on conditions so favorable that Dutch and French planters also found themselves drawn to the island. After coming under state administration in1755, sugar production rose from 700 tons to more than 20,000 tons in 1812.

An increase of that magnitude was possible only through the steadily growing number of African slaves brought over to the labor-hungry colonies. The crossing from Africa to the West Indies was a voyage of 4,000 nautical miles and took, on average, a good three months. Millions of slaves never reached the

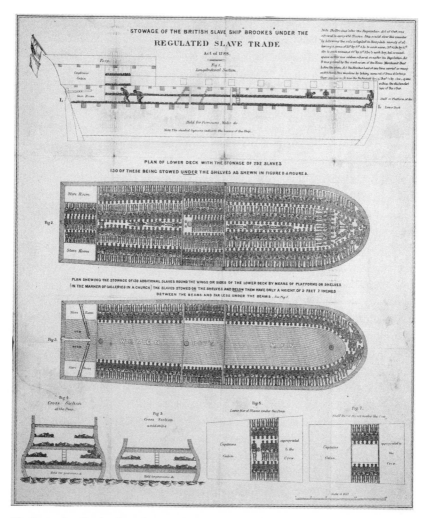

29. Cargo plan for the slave ship *Brookes* with space for 454 individuals. When the ship's cargo had been unloaded on Africa's west coast, the between deck was reconstructed and furnished with a series of shelves to allow two layers of slaves. An adult male slave had about six feet by less than one-and-a-half with two-and-a-half above, roughly the same amount of space as a coffin affords. There were two kinds of slave captain: "loose packers" who believed that more space meant lower death rates, and "tight packers," whose understanding was that, all things being equal, the more slaves on board, the greater the profits. "They lie . . . in two rows," wrote the former slave captain John Newton in his book *Thoughts upon the African Slave Trade* (published in London in 1788), "one over the other, on each side of the ship, close to each other, like books upon a shelf. I have known them so close that the shelf would not easily contain one more. . . . And almost every morning perhaps more instances than one are found of the living and the dead . . . linked together." Between 1500 and 1870, Europeans carried more than eleven million African slaves over the Atlantic.

destination but died of dysentery, yellow fever, smallpox, or trichinosis, took their own lives, were shipwrecked, or were killed during slave uprisings, which the crew feared more than the plague. Precautionary measures were therefore taken. A large wooden wall was erected in the middle of the deck across the entire ship's beam so that the white crew, who generally kept to the aft of the ship, were segregated from the slaves. The wall was furnished with small cannons, the so-called swivel guns, aimed at the part of the deck where the slaves were allowed to come up for air. The highest ranking on board got a commission for the sale of slaves, so a high death rate meant a significant loss of revenue, and for this reason peas were generally used in place of bullets in order to cause minimal harm. In serious cases, whole containers of boiling water could be emptied on the desperate insurgents.

Male and female slaves were separated on the between deck, but in good weather were aired on the main deck, where they could exercise a little, be dowsed with saltwater and make use of the primitive privies that were put up as an extension on the port side of the aft deck. Meanwhile the ships' boys had their hands full scrubbing the platforms and benches that the slaves lay on and fumigating with a mixture of tar and juniper, in order to lessen the stench below. In spite of these tested remedies, the teeming platforms always stank heavily of excrement, decomposition, and death.

The desperation of the slaves on board these floating concentration camps would seem to call for no further psychological explanation, but in fact quite irrational factors contributed to their panic. The experienced slave dealer, Ludvig Ferdinand Rømer, writes: "The slaves that come from far up in the land think that we Europeans buy them to fatten them like pigs, and that we shall eat them when they have become fat."[18] It is reckoned that the miserable lives of about twenty percent of the slaves ended on the open seas. The practice was to sew the dead inside their own hammocks, taking great care that the last stitch went through the departed's nose so as to ensure that the slave in question was actually dead and not just in appearance. Holes were then clipped in the hammock so that trapped air would escape, the flag was lowered to half mast, a hymn sung, the Lord's Prayer recited, and the corpse then heaved overboard from the gangway port on the starboard side. The rest was bubbles and gorging by sharks. The Danish ship's chaplain, H. C. Monrad, tells how "the sharks continually follow in great shoals" and that he has "seen them tear apart in a moment bodies thrown overboard from the ship, despite their being sewn in their hammocks as is customary and being provided with weights of coal, cannon balls, etc. to force them to sink."[19]

Before arrival, the survivors received special treatment. They were released from their chains, and their scanty provisions were replaced by meat and fresh vegetables, together with rice pudding and sugar. They were washed, the men shaven, and their neglected bodies were rubbed with palm-oil, so that they would appear sound and sturdy when the white buyers set eyes on them at the coming public auction on the town square. Before the auction, large quantities of brandy or rum were poured down the slaves' throats so that their traumas would be suppressed and perhaps for a moment replaced by a sales-promoting amenability. Attempts were sometimes made to give them the impression that they had arrived in Paradise.

The auction itself was a brutal humiliation. Clad in small loincloths of blue cotton, the slaves were groped in their most intimate places, examined for venereal disease, inspected in the mouth and commanded to run and jump, to show if they were worth the money. The men were sold first, then the women, the boys, and finally the girls. Children under four years old were sold together with their mothers, but those over four separately. The sick and elderly went under the dreadful rubric of "waste slaves" and were sold in groups, usually to a physician who hoped to be able to doctor them a little and then, in a later sale, do good business. Some planters required a cook or a maid, but there were other needs to be met as well, and the expression "sex slave" becomes here especially apposite. When a transaction was completed, the slave was branded and bore for all time the owner's initials on the breast or arm. As an ultimate destruction of identity, the slaves were given new names—English, mythical, biblical, or whatever the owners came up with—after which they would leave Christiansted, in great Babylonian confusion, as Andreas, Katha, Toni, Akajem, Jeppe, Caesar, Samson, Oliver, Roland, Codjo, Thomas, Takki, Simon, Cipido, Emmanuel, Loubouk, Wanico, Goliath, Cecilia, Susanne, Serfina, Aba, Aurora, Lovisa, Marianna, Fibi, or Martha.

Although a long-term investment that one would not simply do as one liked with, a slave was exposed frequently to indescribable suffering that naturally enough led to resistance and attempts at escape. When a slave ran off, it was said that the slave in question "ran maroon," and such slaves were called accordingly "maroon-Negroes" from the Spanish "cimarrón" (wild). Some were fortunate enough to reach Puerto Rico, where on the whole the Spaniards treated black people better than the Danes did, while others tried only to keep body and soul together in the readily accessible jungle areas—a mountain by the coast north of Høgensborg is called simply Maroon Ridge. There were now and then "maroon hunts," in which fully armed huntsmen backed by baying hounds chased after the frightened, naked Negroes, who were then shot in cold blood or exposed to routine torture in accordance with the nineteen-clause ordinance that the governor, Philip Gardelin, had officially declared in September 1733. Article Five of the ordinance asserts that a maroon Negro who has been absent for eight days is to be punished with 150 lashes. A maroon Negro who has enjoyed freedom for twelve weeks is to have a leg amputated, while six months of freedom would cost the slave his life, unless the slave's owner wished to impose a more lenient punishment. The most frequent form of punishment was the whip. The slave was bound and laid on the ground and then given the prescribed number of lashes, which could be from 50 to 500—the latter being so terrible as to be reckoned tantamount to a death sentence. When the whipping was over, the slave's bleeding back was rubbed with salt and pepper. In especially serious cases a slave was chained, or given a collar, and indeed even castration was practiced. The remaining clauses in Gardelin's ordinance also betray stunning inhumanity. The back-men behind runaway slaves were to be clamped with glowing iron and then hanged. The guilty in a plot were to lose one leg or, alternatively, have an ear cut off and be dealt 150 lashes. If a slave had stolen an object with a value up to four rix-dollars, the slave was to be clamped with glowing tongs and hanged. Lesser larcenies were to be punished with branding on the forehead and from 100 to 150 lashes. If a black raised a hand against a white, or answered back, he was to be clamped three times with glowing tongs and then hanged or, alternatively, have one hand chopped off. No slave could go into town carrying a stick or a knife, and if they were caught in a brawl they were sentenced to 50 lashes. If it could be proven that a slave had plans to poison someone, the slave was to be clamped three times with glowing tongs, maimed, and broken on the wheel.

"WE HAVE HAD A NEGRO-UPRISING ON ST. CROIX!"

In large parts of Europe, 1848 was a year under the sign of crisis, with revolutions in Paris and Vienna, and a whole world order on the march. "The thread of prudence broke in the year 48, there was a shriek to be heard that heralds chaos," Kierkegaard discerningly wrote in *On My Activity as an Author*.[20] The situation in the Caribbean was also tense. Rumors of slave-uprisings on Martinique and Guadeloupe spread to the other colonies. As the drop that caused the cup to spill over, Christian VIII had, in an ordinance, informed Peter von Scholten that children born to slaves were in future to be free, while their parents could acquire this right, but only twelve years later. Not surprisingly, what was thought to be a change for the better brought about violent protests among the slaves that came to a climax in the beginning of July 1848.

When all hell broke loose, Regine's brother Oluf found himself in Christiansted. From there he wrote a letter to his brother-in-law Emil, dated the 6th of July 1848, in which he gave an eyewitness account of the course of events into which he and his family were suddenly dragged. "We have had a Negro-uprising on St. Croix," he writes some lines down in his letter, and then he goes on to describe events right up to the hours before the mail boat departed from Christiansted on the 12th of July.

> On the morning of the 3rd of June, it was heard that the Governor had, at two o'clock in the morning, received news from the West End that the plantation Negroes there had left their plantation and, armed with their sugar axes and clubs, were flocking in large numbers towards Fredriksted. During the day the news became more threatening: the Negroes were 5 to 6,000 in numbers, forced their way into Fredriksted, where not the least resistance had been dared, broke into the police chief's . . . and the administrator's houses, where they destroyed everything, plundered a few merchants' shops and stores, and moreover encamped in the streets and under the fort with a racket, shouting, and threats that became more dangerous the more eagerly they intoxicated themselves with stolen liquor. Obviously the Negroes came in order to demand their freedom! They sent deputations to the general governor and demanded that he should come to them—the government, that is to say Scholten, did nothing!—absolutely nothing! . . . Finally came the last message from the Negroes: if General Scholten was not in their presence before four o'clock in the afternoon, Fredriksted would be put to flames!

When Peter von Scholten arrived at Fredriksted, he was received by a thousand-strong crowd, which enthusiastically hailed their "Massa Peter" welcome. On the square in front of the fort, he climbed out of his coach, raised his arms in the air and shouted to the crowd "You are now free. You are hereby emancipated!" The square and adjoining streets echoed to outcries of joy, the freed slaves fell on one another's necks, the impossible had happened. After von Scholten's short speech, which was accompanied by some admonishing words about restoring calm and order, the insurgents withdrew from Fredriksted and moved in groups eastward toward Christiansted, where alarm and fear were spread with their overwrought behavior and the ravaging of plantation properties and other dwellings. Oluf tells in his letter how, in Christiansted, people took precautionary measures by arming themselves and rolling out cannons. Suddenly, a man shouted down the street that the black workers of six plantations were approaching the town on Negervejen (Negro Way).

> Although I didn't put my trust in that, I hastened all the same to close everything, dowse the light, and shut ourselves in an inferno of heat and anxiety—you can imagine what pictures were conjured up in our imaginations. I sat there alone with my wife, two infants and two girls.

There were musket shots and a violent cry (so near do I live to the entrance to the town)—a few moments' silence—then the firing of a cannon and a musket salvo, now shouting and a stream of people down
on the street—straight afterwards two cannon salvoes from the fort
and the warning drums from all corners and all sides! I didn't know
whether the town was taken, whether there was fighting in the streets,
or not—but I had to go out, that is what the remainder of human in-
telligence told me. I leaped out, locked the door and ran down to the
street. The Negroes had been beaten back!—at any rate on this side of
the town. Badly armed but with sharpened axes, and a good 1,000 in
number, well-equipped with material to set fire to the town, they had
come rushing like wild animals, they had laughed at the musket shots
and stormed on until a short way off the cannon was fired, one was
killed and a number dangerously wounded—

Oluf goes on to describe how the city's women and children, with the sound
of shooting in their ears, rushed out into the night to seek refuge in the fort or
onboard the ships down in the harbor. Oluf got his wife Laura and the children,
Regnar and Thilly, out of their beds, packed the necessities, and half an hour
later was able to bring them to safety onboard Captain Hansen's ship *André*. He
himself took up station with a "good double-barreled gun" by the west entrance
to the town, where he stayed "24 hours at a stretch and later every night." But
the attack never came, a fact that Oluf attributes to "the Negroes' lack of reflection and reason," for the district would have been easy to take, poorly equipped
as it was in military respects. Oluf continues:

In the following days the Negroes have approached cautiously and one
by one, as though on reconnaissance. But in the countryside things are
all the more lively, with the exception of quite a few plantations where
the Negroes have already left their work, plundered the stores of provisions, such as sugar and rum supplies, destroyed with malicious pleasure
all furniture and the like, in so far as they haven't stolen it, let hundreds
of vats of rum and sugar run out and spread it on fields and paths.

Peter Scholten tried to pour oil on the troubled waters, but in vain. When, on the
6th of July, he rode into the harbor square in Christiansted, he was bawled out
by some planters who accused him of being the direct cause of the tumultuous
state of affairs and of their bankruptcy, which it had led to: "then Scholten lost
the last remnants of self-control, he wept, became ill, imbecilic, and withdrew
altogether, a physician's certificate that I have seen testified that he was incapable of governing or doing anything." The physician could declare that he was

30. More than anyone else, the controversial and charismatic general-governor Peter von Scholten managed to inscribe his name in the history of the Danish East Indies. Von Scholten entered his adventurous career in charge of roads on St Thomas and thereafter proved himself in increasingly more lucrative positions, which culminated with an appointment to the general-governorship of the Danish West Indies in 1827. Von Scholten had a reputation for dubious economic affairs and an extravagant lifestyle, but he was considerably more humane toward the slaves than many of his fellow countrymen. He spoke their language, Creole, and invited free colored to his parties, had colored adjutants in his service, reduced the scope of whip lashes to twelve for men and six for women, made it illegal to send pregnant women to work in the fields, and in 1839 introduced the first free public school system in the West Indies. It was not so very surprising that the freed slaves devotedly called him "Massa Peter."

"altogether destroyed" and had symptoms of apoplexy. Just eleven days after his proclamation of the slaves' freedom, the sixty-four-year-old general-governor had to resign his position. A week later, in the lee of the dark and in deepest secrecy, he left St. Croix on an American steamship—it was the 14th of July 1848, twenty-one years to the day from his accession.

Before his breakdown, Peter von Scholten had turned to the governor of Puerto Rico and asked for military assistance, which arrived on the 7th of July in the form of a British steamship with 600 Spanish soldiers, whose very presence contributed to calm and order. Although most of the insurrectionists had returned to their plantations, Oluf continued to sleep with a loaded gun by his headboard. Nor did his wife feel safe in the situation—"Laura trembles at the sight of every crumb of a sinister Negro face"—and there were rumors abroad that a "band" had assembled on Blue Mountain. A provisional balance sheet gave, according to Oluf, the following account:

> Something over 100 Negroes have been killed, according to what I hear—and a few hundred prisoners. The court marshal yesterday sentenced seven of the worst scoundrels to death and they were shot. . . . That the Negroes have become free must indeed make everyone rejoice who has a heart or is receptive to ideas—but it is damnable that these inarticulate people could not be content with that but have acquired a taste for plunder and robbery! The fundamental stupidity was without doubt committed by the wise men at home who, for more than half a century, talked to people like that about freedom without either giving it to them or preparing them to take advantage of it.

Upon arrival in Copenhagen, Peter von Scholten did not receive the hero's welcome that, seen with hindsight, he deserved. He was, on the contrary, discharged without a pension for misuse of power and of his office. In the course of the spring of 1852 he was nevertheless exonerated by the High Court. The restoration of his honor had little real meaning for Peter von Scholten, however, who died in January 1854, far from the capital, at the home of a daughter in Altona. Later, his body was conveyed to Copenhagen and buried in Assistens Cemetery in a special mausoleum, where he lies together with his wife, some hundreds of yards from where Kierkegaard and the Schlegels lie buried.

After the emancipation, the West Indies was never the same again, which is something no one today can regret. The price of freedom was, however, considerable. It introduced a period marked by economic crisis, wide-ranging changes in the relations between workers and employers, reforms in the administration of justice, poor relief, and the education authority—together, not least, with long-unanswered questions of economic compensation for the considerable loss of a workforce that the emancipation had notoriously inflicted on the slave-owners. It was this epoch of winding down and readjustment that awaited the Schlegel couple when, in the spring of 1855, the delightful islands hove in sight.

REGINE AND "THE BLACKS"

After spending the Christmas days in Christiansted, true to tradition Regine and Fritz were to arrange a tremendous New Year's ball which would include black people among its guests.

> On New Year's Day we were to have the same hullaballoo as last year, but both Fritz and I offered ourselves gladly on that day, so that the Negroes could have a little amusement; also it would be a shame if we couldn't do something once in a year for the blacks, since we have to butcher ourselves so many times for the whites.

Her consideration seems reasonable, the more so as it was the blacks who had been more or less literally butchered for the sake of the whites. Regine seems, however, not to have taken much interest in the historical and social situation and appears on the whole to have reacted as would be expected of a white and well-situated woman. The cause of the former slaves and their situation occupies little space in her letters, but a single letter—from the 27th of November 1855— marks itself out negatively from all the others. It is addressed to Cornelia, who had been feeling unwell for some time but was now improving, and who Regine wanted to cheer up with some facetious remarks. So perhaps it should not be taken all too seriously when, in a mass of subordinate clauses and long interpolations, Regine presents her view:

> But I will tell you, since the baseness of human nature is so recognized, that without being all too impudent I can take it that it will please you to hear (you see, I assume you are now quite well, since I am joking) that the blacks over here are no better, yes, I go so far as to believe and, being a high-placed person, if it were to be known it would naturally incur Mrs. Stowe's and all her party's curses, that the Lord has never created the emancipated slaves for freedom.

The Mrs. Stowe in question was Harriet Beecher Stowe, whose *Uncle Tom's Cabin* was published in 1852 and came out in Danish a year later. It became a huge success. The story tells of the honest, good-hearted, and God-fearing Negro slave Tom, who in the time leading up to the American Civil War tried to improve conditions for his fellow slaves. *Uncle Tom's Cabin* was widely influential in the

31. When Regine walked through the long gallery of Government House, running parallel to Kongensgade (King's Street), she came to the Lutheran church with its entrance just behind the small girl. Over to the left, on the other side of Kongensgade, can be seen the school, then the parsonage. The bowler hat of the gentleman in white fits in perfectly with the arch behind him.

debate about Negro rights, but we register that Beecher Stowe and her supporters could reckon with little sympathy from Regine. Evidently she was quite aware that she could acquire enemies with such a view, one that she did not air in official circles. Whether in jest or earnest, Regine then brings her letter to Cornelia to a close, in the worst possible taste, by letting it be known that, with the blacks, she finds—

> . . . such a mixture of the child's and the animal's nature, by the animal I almost think of the monkey, that I am nearly convinced that keeping them always on a leash could have worked more to their own and their master's advantage than now as free people, a freedom that is far from bringing them their true happiness.

Here Regine adopts a dictatorial tone of the kind she normally ridicules when she encounters it in her stuck-up colonial sisters. And even though she modifies it with an "almost" and a "nearly" there is obviously no way to defend her attitude—not even as a colossally miscued witticism. But if an explanation of her remarks were to be offered, it would depend, we can assume, on the provisional and at times chaotic conditions following on emancipation, when the slaves' newly won freedom was little more than an official statement of purpose and had in no way been converted into palpable reality. The fact that this, understandably enough, caused frustration among most people, black as well as white, is something that Regine was able to affirm from seeing it for herself:

> I am not judging in this way from our household alone, large though it is, but also from what I see around me; after emancipation, with the constant disruption it has caused, especially the governor's work and responsibility have become altogether more difficult than they would have been otherwise. . . . But here I will break off short, since what I am writing is doubtless stuff and nonsense of the kind Fritz perhaps finds "must not be written," and so I will begin on something more sensible that fills my heart: Thank you, so infinitely many thanks for the lovely jam, it had kept so well, there was just one jar with a little mold as if to show how good the other was.

We must give Regine credit for knowing how to change topics, from Negroes to jam in a couple of lines! One more than suspects that Fritz by no means shares Regine's views, which she labels on his behalf "stuff and nonsense," before forcing herself almost defiantly to impart banalities, so that Fritz—whose words she puts a little cheekily in quotes—is not to be reproached for having his wife sit there peddling politically incorrect views in her correspondence with the motherland.

These remarks of Regine's are presented in a letter written relatively soon after the couple's arrival at St. Croix, and if we collect the comments on black people that crop up sporadically in her letters from the following years, a rather different picture emerges. There is indeed no conspicuous turnaround, but the imported prejudices seem to give way to a more humane and sympathetic attitude that, on several occasions, led to Regine's overstepping traditional class distinctions and forgetting her status as First Lady of the West Indies. Most often, what negative comments do occur prove to be based on personal disappointments in quite close relationships, or due to differences of opinion regarding the efficient execution of the big and little tasks of every day. Regine had, for example, a bad experience with the black maid Anny, who in the end she fired because, in her eyes, Anny was "mean" and "arrogant" in her dealings, in particular with Josephine, but after a while also with Regine herself, who confides to Cornelia that she really doesn't know "how to handle slave constitutions," since "I treat them too well." She therefore chose for the umpteenth time to follow her "old principle," rather to "do the work oneself than have sloppiness."

32. The photographer has placed himself and his apparatus in the proximity of Government House and from here permanently recorded the course of Kongensgade (King's Street). The school building and the parsonage are on the right. Farthest away, where the road comes to an end, there is a glimpse of the planted area by the entry to the churchyard where Laura and Olivia were buried. As the perfectly posed black extras illustrate, the photographer is not a totally reliable portrayer of real life.

Her comment about the right way to deal with "slave constitutions" is hardly flattering, but the fact that Regine to some extent includes herself in the conflicts, enforced as they were by practical circumstances, and is not being simply ideological or expounding a principle, can be considered a mitigating factor. Not long after her arrival at Christiansted she found that "down here" one is sure enough "very lazy," but also that this same "West Indian unconcern" had already got "such a grip" on her that she could "look on all the loafing" without being particularly vexed. She assumed that the way they dragged their heels in everything they did was due to a mental attitude that they had developed in the face of what fate had handed to them. Or was it perhaps that, as a consequence of the outer pressures so long exerted on them, they had acquired a special imperturbability in their work that could be mistaken for lassitude? It was hard for Regine to form a clear picture of what was going on, but she at least understood the need to learn the rhythms and response patterns of the new surroundings. When a ship had lain hove-to along the Norwegian coast with the materials for a bazaar that Regine was to organize, she was at first impatient, but then came to terms with West Indian conditions together with what things cost, both psychologically and economically, for as she confided to Cornelia:

". . . I take it *coolly* [she uses the English word], which is the wisest thing to do here where one comes to waste money in so many ways."

How money disappeared like dew in the sun once it came into the hands of black people was something for which Regine could provide a concrete example: "The housekeeper told me this morning that in 14 days we have used 20 pots of oil, and 40 wax candles, 20 every Monday evening." The stumps from the candles lit on festive occasions were used during the rest of the week, but they were gone, those candle stumps, "so we illuminate quite a few Negro cabins, since they steal like ravens." When the theft was discovered, Oluf took it upon himself "to give a severe lecture to the whole house," but Regine had little faith in its helping and consoled herself with the thought that "we have incomes, we'll make ends meet."

That attitude is typical of Regine, who has surplus enough, both materially and mentally, that she can wink at the pilfering, which it would be unbecomingly petty to be indignant over let alone prosecute. That she was fully aware of what went on is clear also from the following episode: the cook, by agreement, slept overnight in Government House, "but in the morning when I went out riding before 6, I saw his wife and 3 naked young ones come out of his room." When Josephine heard of this, she loudly voiced her dissatisfaction at such disrespect for the prevailing rules, but Regine reminded her calmly that resentment was in the first instance a harmful state of mind and, secondly, in this actual situation, misplaced, since there was always something left over after the daily "3 to 4 courses before dessert" and thus plenty to feed some of these shrunken stomachs. Elsewhere, in a similarly conciliatory spirit, Regine is amused at the childlike innocence often displayed by the blacks—"yes, my girl tells me that the Negroes say the Governor must be a very good man, since the Lord is giving us such good weather since he came out here." When Regine told this to Fritz, he laughed too, and begged "the Lord to preserve him from the added responsibility of furnishing good weather, when he had enough responsibility as it was." Regine had to agree: "[I]t was too much for a plain mortal, even if he is Governor over all the King of Denmark's West Indian Islands."

Regine also observed the activities of black people outside Government House. At the beginning of September, she tells Cornelia that she and Fritz have been at a race meeting arranged by some of the island's well-to-do Englishmen. There wasn't much amusement to be had from the races themselves; on the other hand, it was "very amusing to see the Negroes *en masse*, how they laid bets like the other gentlemen, and then they are so enthusiastic in their movements, as if it was going to end in a fight even though they are the best friends in the world."

Regine informs us also of a small gentleman's party that included a dinner where, together with much else, a goose that Fritz had acquired from the excellent Captain Lassen was consumed. According to Regine, a piece of poultry like that is "a rarity out here, and then they tried Fritz's new weapons; he has got 2 pistols and a rifle from home, so that we should not go unprotected if the Negroes took it into their minds to make a rebellion again, of which there is however very little prospect." If it is hard to tell whether the goose provided a living target, it is at least clear that Regine did not see the black population as forming a real threat and thus judged the risk of revolt from their side differently from the administrators in the motherland.

BIRCH AND HIS BROTHER

It may help a little in restoring the balance in the story's rather confused account to note that it was not just against the blacks but also the whites that Regine, when she was in a really fine bad humor, delivered her broadsides. She could, for example, be perfectly ruthless in her judgment of Councillor of Justice Vilhelm Ludvig Birch, who was in many ways the perfect civil servant—correct, industrious, cultivated, and unmarried to a fault. The latter from Regine's point of view had very unhappy consequences; a wife might have been an invigorating corrective, an antidote to the tedium of his continual fussing, which slowly but surely sapped all of his zest for life, so that he became progressively a more and more wizened Birch. By force of circumstances, Birch was fated to realize himself solely through his work, which had consequently to compensate for all the unrequited life-demands that jostled inside this aloof and reserved civil servant, whose ungrounded smugness curiously enough grew by the day more cheerless and refractory. Birch had become a victim to the sneaking logic that seems to threaten all whose ability is directly proportional to their unappreciated pig-headedness. At any rate, the result of his petty-minded cultivation of his own excellence came close to an ingrown distrust of his so-called subordinates, who allowed themselves the luxury of a life outside the office and were consequently suspected of being shallow, incompetent, and negligent. Birch was, in Regine's eyes, like one of those madames who, driven by distrust of their girls' ability and from sheer perfectionism, end up making themselves do everything, tight-lipped and punctilious. Added to all this, Birch was a self-appointed bottleneck through which all matters, from the weightiest to the least significant, had to pass. He had in short all the leadership qualities required of a properly bad leader.

Birch, long plagued with eye trouble, had on Dr. Aagaard's advice traveled home to Copenhagen. The optician in Copenhagen evidently failed to achieve miracles, so Birch seized the opportunity for further recreation on the Rhine,

33. An incorrigible "dry stick" is what Regine called the government's secretary, Vilhelm Ludvig Birch. Birch was the governor's right hand and in 1861 was appointed as his successor. He was a fastidious and ambitious civil servant who never found time to get married and lived the life almost of an ascetic. Eye trouble caused him on several occasions to take recreational trips to Europe. After combined periods of service adding up to almost 3,921 days, Birch died on St. Thomas in 1871.

and then in Italy, and did not return to St. Croix until the spring of 1858. This meant a great deal of extra work for Fritz, since even matters that had already gone through his own hands had still to be dealt with. Regine gave vent to good old-fashioned indignation, unhesitatingly passing the following judgment: "Birch's ambition, along with [Fritz's predecessor] Feddersen's absurdity, has decidedly been much to blame for the office getting into this state: he wouldn't have any younger people out here, perhaps he was afraid of a rival."

Aside from the mud-slinging, there was an added legal problem that the civil servants at the colonial office confronted daily: however many good reasons could be adduced for the emancipation of the slaves, it had meant a real loss for the planters. They could rightly contend that, in supporting emancipation, the Danish State had set aside their property rights. In other words, the State had brought a responsibility upon itself to compensate the individual planters, who could point to colonial powers such as Great Britain, France, and Sweden, where in analogous situations a decent compensation had been provided.[21]

The Danish government thought differently. Of course, in a certain sense the State had indeed been responsible for the planters losing their workforce, but since slavery was incompatible with both religion and justice, this was a special case in which compensation claims were null and void. The planters could not accept such an argument and pointed out that the Danish State had for hundreds of years profited from slavery and thus given it its de facto approval. To this the astute lawyers responded that slavery had not been introduced by Denmark; nor had Denmark said that it should continue forever. After this abstract legalism brought further objections from the planters, the government decided to pay compensation calculated according to the number of emancipated slaves. The then governor, Peter Hansen, had reckoned that the average worth of the colony's approximately 19,000 ex-slaves amounted to one hundred dollars apiece. The government would not agree, put the price at forty dollars, and contended, moreover, that it had been generously open-handed toward unknown people in a faraway colony that was operating at a loss. Following yet another round of negotiations, in which the planters demanded seventy-five dollars, on the 23rd of July 1852, the government set the price at fifty.[22]

But the matter did not rest there. On Saturday the 7th of November 1857, Cornelia reported that "people are writing incendiary articles in *Dagbladet*" on conditions in the West Indies, including the governor. Cornelia is referring to a comprehensive, anonymous contribution that had appeared in *Dagbladet* two days earlier, under the heading "From a Letter from the West Indies." After some background remarks on rainfall and sugar cultivation and some yellow fever statistics, the writer takes the West Indian administration into his warm embrace and caustically exposes the disparity between the large number of juridical co-workers and the actual effectiveness of the government. The anonymous author is not sparing of irony or sarcasm and leaves the reader in no doubt that the islands' government is marked by bureaucratic inertia and would function far better without its expensive juridical officialdom. That government had stood while Government Secretary Birch, "our leading idea," was absent on his recreational travels. That tactless remark about Birch made Regine exclaim, "Worse luck for that leadership." Neither she nor her criticized consort had seen this issue of *Dagbladet*, so they had no "opportunity to show that we were above it all by acting indifferent to the criticism."

Cornelia believed the article to have been written by a troublemaker from St. Thomas who had earlier exposed himself as a quarrelsome sort. "How Fritz with his priceless calm will laugh at this article when he reads it," Emil had exclaimed spontaneously on refolding *Dagbladet* back home in Horsens. At first, Regine herself had been indignant at the unreasonable claims put into cackling circulation back home in the henhouse, but she managed "on a little closer reflection" to overcome her negative feelings. One trusts that her husband dealt with this rancor with similar calm, but an ambitious and pharisaical whistleblower was, in the nature of the case, a burden.

Fritz still had *Dagbladet* to look forward to, but in the meantime he could pass the time with tidings of a similar caviling kind, for as Regine says in her letter of the 27th of December:

> We have read another criticism of us in *Fædrelandet*, which includes poor me, but spare me from having to say anything more about it, I have mentioned it to both Clara and Oluf, just to put your minds at rest let me just say that we are both not guilty.

Regine is referring to a similar anonymous contribution that appeared in *Fædrelandet* on Thursday the 5th of November under the heading "From a Letter from St. Croix, the 13th of October 1857." The "letter" in question registered nowhere near as many complaints as the previous one, instead focusing on a single issue, which it presented in all the more painful detail:

> ——I assure you that instead of improving, the state of affairs is becoming steadily worse. The caste spirit goes beyond all bounds, and I believe I do not do the Governor an injustice in saying that to a high degree he encourages and strengthens it. On the 6th of October last year (on the King's Birthday) a reception was held at midday, according to custom. Some days previously the Governor sent out invitations to the dinner and some of us so-called *colored* men were invited. Altogether we were about 70 persons at table. After the meal a whole crowd of white ladies put in an appearance (to whom it had been whispered in secrecy that it would please Mrs. Schlegel to see them in the evening) and the festivity ended with a ball. Our wives were of course not present, and yet no one could say that the Governor had sent invitations to the ball and that our families had been overlooked. But we were all agreed about not being caught in the same trap again, and we waited to see what the next King's Birthday would bring. It came at last. Some days before the 6th, the Governor had an announcement printed in

the paper in which he invited the island's inhabitants to a reception at Government House. At the same time a private invitation was sent by word of mouth to all white men that Governor Schlegel and his wife would have great pleasure in seeing [them] and [their] families on the 7th in the evening, while not a word was said about our class. We then all decided that, because of this, we should not attend the reception either. Our absence has caused a whispering among those present, and some few of us have not been slow to inform these of the reason for our absence. What do you think of all this, especially from a governor who should show a good example to others? If the expenses for this party came out of his own pocket, it would be another matter, but the government pays him a sum for this purpose, and all of us who pay taxes contribute to providing these means.

Early in the New Year, on Thursday the 27th of January, Regine let Cornelia understand that the government offices are "filled with folk who are weak in mind and body; Fritz is the only strong one, in the end he gets to do all the work!" Much of the confusion was due to Fritz's predecessors having filled empty positions with a series of subordinate and incompetent officials whose responsibilities quickly outgrew their capacities, "and now they are sick and nearly all need to go home." But not Fritz: "Yes, God will keep his hand over him and give him strength; so things will no doubt be all right."

Yet, despite his incontestable diligence and diplomatic temperament, it was increasingly difficult for Fritz to make the civil servants and out-of-touch pedants back home take a serious interest in the colony's welfare. Subjected to a juridical and bureaucratic task of Sisyphean proportions, which for long periods must have struck him as totally absurd, Fritz tired visibly. He reached the point where he could stand it no longer and more than willingly tendered his resignation—as we learn from Regine's letter from the 12th of January:

> Fritz assured Oluf the other day that he would like to go home straightaway; if he says so it must be true; but I have the feeling that it wasn't right; it is work that God has given him.

"MEET HER WITHOUT BEING OBSERVED"

In one of the packets shipped out to Regine, thanks to Henrik Lund, were the letters that Kierkegaard had sent on his first stay in Berlin to his friend Emil Boesen in Copenhagen. The letters' earthly fate might have been quite different, since Kierkegaard had written on the outside of the packet: "This packet is to be destroyed unopened after my death. / This for the information of the surviving family. / It isn't worth 4 shillings." Not only Lund but later editors as well left their matches unstruck and by doing so preserved source material in which, unlike most of what Kierkegaard left for posthumous publication, we may assume that not the least comma has been censored—"[I]n conversation with you," confesses Kierkegaard, "I jump about stark naked, whereas I am always enormously calculating with other people."[23]

As a tangible expression of this confidentiality, Kierkegaard had hardly arrived at his Berlin lodgings—*Mittelstrasse 61, eine Treppe hoch*—before sending off the first of his in all seven letters to Boesen. After some comments on the journey, the lectures ahead, and the like, the letter without warning switches over into a series of imperatives:

> Provide me with news. But the deepest secrecy must prevail. Do not let anybody suspect that I want it. . . . Meet her without being observed. Your window can assist you. Mondays and Thursdays from 4 to 5 p.m., her music lessons. But do not meet her in the street except Monday afternoons at 5 or 5:30, when you might meet her as she walks from Vestervold via Vestergade to Klædeboderne, or on the same day at 7 or 7:30, when she and her sister are likely to go to the Exchange by way of the arcades. But be careful. Visit the pastry shop there, but be careful. For my sake practice the art of controlling every expression, of being master of any situation, and of being able to make up a story instantaneously without apprehension and anxiety. Oh, one can fool people as much as one wants, as I know from experience, and at least with respect to this I have unlimited recklessness. . . . I trust nobody.[24]

It must have been eerie for Regine to peruse these espionage plans worked out by her former fiancé in a hotel room in Berlin so as to steer Boesen as though by remote control—the same Boesen who was now Cornelia's parish priest in Horsens. Clearly, Kierkegaard knew of Regine's day to day movements, sometimes from hour to hour, the routes she took around town and who accompanied her, when and for how long, and now, believe it or not, has set Boesen off on a mission to find out what Regine gets up to at the coffeehouse of Johan Monigatti, who just happens to live in a ground-floor apartment at 63 Nybørs and might well have useful information about the Olsen family at Number 66.

None of Boesen's letters from this period survives, so there is no way of knowing how he reacted to these instructions that would have him sneaking around Copenhagen like a stalker. From the exiled Magister's next letter, one senses that he had been hurt by so much mistrust and had expressed some distaste for the

34. "You know that I made a small quick sketch of your brother's profile in 1838 and began another *en face* some years later, but both these sketches are very incomplete," writes Niels Christian Kierkegaard to his half-cousin Peter Christian in late January 1875. The occasion for this communication is his having repeatedly been asked to lend his sketches for "copying and publication," a request that he had up to then denied, knowing well that "Søren did not wish to leave a picture of himself." Since the alternative was to bring out the caricatures from the *Corsair*, Niels Christian now thinks his own drawings are, in spite of everything, preferable—even though he can only vaguely "refresh the memory of Søren for those who had known him personally."

Kierkegaardian setup, which was all the more unpleasant as Boesen was himself unhappily in love and had plenty to worry about on his own account. This does not unduly bother Kierkegaard, who demands bulletins about Regine and, in a later missive, recommends that Boesen pump Emil Bærentzen who, with his residence at 67 Børsgade, "must be a good source." Further:

> That the family hates me is good. That was my plan, just as it was also my plan that, if possible, she be able to hate me. She does not know how much she owes me on that score. . . . [M]y unfortunately all too inventive brain has not been able to refrain from planning this or that.

She must either love me or hate me; she knows no third way. Nor is there anything more corrupting for a young girl than the stages in between. . . . What does it matter if people believe that I am a deceiver? I am just as able to study philosophy, write poetry, smoke cigars, and ignore the whole world. After all, I have always made fun of people, and why should I not continue to do so to the last?[25]

These are plain enough words, but Kierkegaard would hardly be Kierkegaard if from first to last he had truly jumped around "stark naked" in his long letter to Boesen. Separately enclosed was a small slip on which Kierkegaard has something especially piquant to relate, prefixed by a startling announcement:

I have no time to get married. But here in Berlin there is a singer from Vienna, a *Demoiselle* Schulze. She plays the part of Elvira and bears a striking resemblance to a certain young girl. . . . When my wild mood sweeps over me, I am almost tempted to approach her and that not exactly with the "most honorable intentions." . . . It might be a small diversion when I am tired of speculation. But meanwhile I do not want you to mention to anybody that there is such a singer in Berlin, or that she is playing Elvira, or etc.[26]

Kierkegaard is referring to Hedwig Schultze, who sang the part of Donna Elvira in Mozart's *Don Giovanni*, which was performed during Kierkegaard's stay on the 3rd and 10th of December at the Berlin Opera House, with its prominent address on Unter den Linden. Kierkegaard also mentions Miss Schultze in a journal entry from the same period, but in greater detail and, again, with particular reference to Regine. This gives him an opportunity to describe the latter, though in an oddly indirect way:

Here in Berlin a Demoiselle Hedwig Schultze, a singer from Vienna, performs the part of Elvira. She is really beautiful, assured in her manner,—in the way she walks, her height, manner of dressing (black silk dress, bare neck, white gloves), she resembles strikingly a young lady I knew. A strange coincidence. I really had to make a bit of effort to banish the impression.[27]

The slip enclosed in the letter to Boesen assumedly sprang out of Kierkegaard's "all too inventive brain" and it was clearly not directed at keeping Kierkegaard's fascination for Miss Schultze secret, but designed on the contrary to tempt Boesen into putting the knowledge entrusted to him into circulation. Kierkegaard was not unaware that the broken engagement had opened the floodgates of gossip—just a short time before his departure, for example, he had heard that

Professor Sibbern had called him an "ironist in the worst sense."[28] Should news of Kierkegaard's flirtations abroad reach the gossiping Copenhageners, the scandal would soon find its way to Regine, whose indignation over her Berlin lookalike would help to liberate her from her depraved ex-sweetheart.

". . . I AM AN EXCEPTIONAL LOVER"

Dissimulation's Magister was in Berlin from the 25th of October 1841 to the 6th of March 1842, but the German capital seems not to have invited further investigation. He was not, in the ordinary sense, a tourist—"travel is foolish,"[29] he affirmed near the top of the first page of his first letter to Boesen. Impressions were few, fragmentary, and somewhat accidental. As a curiosity, he entertains his nephew Carl with tales of big dogs harnessed to small wagons that carry milk from the farms into the city, sometimes the husband and wife going along, which makes the scene even more comical. And then there is the "Thiergarten" (Zoological Garden), he notes, full of noisy squirrel monkeys and intersected by a large canal rather like the one in the Frederiksberg Gardens, but with innumerable goldfish like the ones Carl can see in the window of the grocer's in Nørregade, just opposite Kierkegaard's old residence.[30] Kierkegaard's limited radius of action is also to some extent due to the practical, or rather impractical, circumstance of there being so few public lavatories that the length of a trip in town had to be calculated according to the elasticity of one's bladder.

> At ten-o'clock precise I go to a definite nook to p[ass]—m[y]—w[ater].... In this moral city one almost has to go with a bottle in the pocket. . . . I could expand much more widely on this theme; for it has an upsetting effect in all life's situations. When two people walk together in "Thiergarten" and one says, excuse me for a moment, the tour is over; for then one has to go straight home. Nearly everyone in Berlin therefore goes on necessary errands.[31]

Getting along in a foreign country was difficult in any case. It was embarrassing when, for instance, visiting an exclusive restaurant one evening and politely greeting a group of gentlemen dressed in black with white neckerchiefs, a few minutes later the same gentlemen come hurrying over to offer themselves as waiters. In spite of an hour's language instruction every day, it was hard not to make a fool of oneself in German. "I really see how important language was to me for hiding my melancholia.—[H]ere in Berlin it's impossible for me, I can't fool people with language."[32] Even something as elementary as asking the host for a candlestick involved well-nigh superhuman effort. That the same host was also a swindler to the point of indecency didn't make things any the more tolerable—even though, as a form of recompense for increasing the room rate, he let his lodger rise in the grades from Magister to Doctor, and then to Professor. When Professor Kierkegaard could no longer afford further rises, he moved early in the New Year to a property on the corner of Jägerstrasse and Charlottenstrasse, where—once more—he was installed *ein Treppe hoch*.

In several ways the lectures, the official reason for his journey, proved from first to last a disappointment. Friedrich Schelling, who though perhaps romanticism's greatest philosopher was an unassuming man, began well. Students streamed to his lectures. Quite a few came in vain and were reduced to standing outside banging incessantly on the auditorium's windows. But it took only two months before Schelling resembled a sour "vinegar brewer," whose diction annoyed Kierkegaard beyond measure, especially when Schelling said "... *ich werde morgen fortfahren* [I shall continue tomorrow]. Unlike Berliners ... he pronounces the 'g' as a very hard 'k'."[33] After following forty-one lectures and recording them meticulously in his small notebooks, Kierkegaard could no longer stand Schelling, who from then on had to get along "*morken* after *morken*" with one listener less. For some time Kierkegaard had been *anderswo engagiert* (otherwise engaged), and in his letters to Boesen he continued to home in on the love crisis, confiding in his fourth letter:

> Just as strongly as I feel that I am an exceptional lover, I also know very well that I am a bad husband and always will remain so. It is all the more unfortunate that the former is always or usually in inverse proportion to the latter. . . . In saying this I am not underestimating myself, but my spiritual life and importance as a husband are irreconcilable entities.[34]

A writer is what Kierkegaard wanted to become, not a husband. In a letter to Boesen sometime later he admits without fuss that he would be a "lifelong torment" to her, upon which, quoting himself, he has added in a gossipy slip of the pen: "It was a godsend that I did not break the engagement for her sake." This is not what had been mailed, for "her" is crossed out and replaced by "my." Boesen has "missed the point," but then Kierkegaard's motives are not all that easy to penetrate either:

> I am born to intrigues, entanglements, peculiar relationships in life, etc. . . . The affair, which by now has been dealt with often enough, has two sides: an ethical and an aesthetic. Were she able to take the affair less to heart, or, if it might even become an impetus for her to rise higher than she otherwise would have, then the ethical factor is

cancelled—then only the aesthetic remains for me. . . . The aesthetic is above all my element. As soon as the ethical asserts itself, it easily gains too much power over me. I become a quite different person, I know no limit to what might constitute my duty, etc.[35]

Kierkegaard acknowledges here something that he later would have to resort to some inventive apologetics in order to forget: the "aesthetic" was his element and the artistic impulse so irrepressible that it forced him to abandon Regine and thereby to bring upon himself a guilt of which he would never rid himself—whether ethically or religiously. In the letter in which he begs Boesen to send him *The First Love*, he signs himself, tellingly enough, "Farinelli." True, he crosses the name out, but it stands there all the same. Farinelli was a famous castrato singer who dispelled the Spanish king Philip V's melancholy by every evening singing the same four songs for that mentally disturbed monarch. Kierkegaard more than suggests by the signature that he, too, has sacrificed his erotic passion for the sake of art. Or that art has required him as one of its selected sacrificial victims.

EITHER/OR

It was not just Schelling's metallic "k"s that led Kierkegaard to prefer his hotel room to the auditorium. In mid-December he announces to Boesen: "I am writing furiously. As of now I have written fourteen printed sheets. I have thereby completed one part of the treatise which, *volente deo* [God willing], I shall show you some day."[36] Boesen himself was struggling with a short story which was teasing him, so this bragging about fourteen sheets—corresponding to about 224 pages—aroused his curiosity: "You ask what am I working on? Answer: it would be too tedious to tell you now; only this much: further development of *Either/Or.*" Kierkegaard begs Boesen to hold his tongue about it—"Anonymity is of the utmost importance to me"—and confines himself to commenting on the work's title, that it is "indeed an excellent title," since it both is "piquant" and has at the same time a "speculative meaning."[37] In the middle of January 1842, Boesen receives another report from Berlin:

I am working hard. My body cannot stand it. So that you may see that I am the same, I shall tell you that I have again written a major section of a piece, "Either/Or." It has not gone very quickly, but that is due to its not being an expository work, but one of pure invention, which in a very special way demands that one be in the mood.[38]

In the next letter, Kierkegaard expands the list of his sufferings—"Cold, some insomnia, frayed nerves, disappointed expectations of Schelling, confusion in my philosophical ideas, no diversion, no opposition to excite me"[39]—but he also wants to return now to Copenhagen. Four days before departure he sends the last of his seven letters to Boesen:

> I am leaving Berlin and hastening to Copenhagen, but not, you under-
> stand, to be bound by a new tie, oh no, for I feel more strongly than
> ever that I need my freedom. A person with my eccentricity should
> have his freedom until he meets a force in life that, as such, can bind
> him. I am coming to Copenhagen to complete *Either/Or*. It is my fa-
> vorite idea, and in it I exist. You will see that this idea is not to be made
> light of. In no way can my life yet be considered finished. I feel I still
> have great resources within me.[40]

These big words in February were not to be put to shame. On the 6th of March 1842, when the steamship *Christian VIII* berthed in Copenhagen, the twenty-nine-year-old Kierkegaard could walk down the gangway with the better part of the manuscript of *Either/Or* in his suitcase. Just under one year later, on Monday the 20th of February 1843, the work, whose eight hundred and thirty-eight pages were printed in five hundred and twenty-five copies, lay on the counter at Reitzel for four rix-dollars, four marks, and eight shillings a copy.

It has always seemed strange that, so soon after the break with Regine, Kierkegaard should set his mind on writing one of the longest apologias for marriage in the history of literature. The defense is to be found in the first of two extensive missives that Assessor Wilhelm addresses to the aesthete in the work's first part, with the aim of convincing him to abandon his promiscuous activities and develop a sympathy for the institution of marriage, which offers a far wider range of aesthetic qualities than the aesthete presumably has the fantasy to imagine, and which Wilhelm has accordingly titled "The Aesthetic Validity of Marriage." Wilhelm is the indefatigable spokesman for harmony, for the home, and for family life, and he therefore lays great emphasis on the meaning of time for an ethical way of life, for which he provides the following refined illustration:

> As a true victor, the husband has not killed time but saved and preserved
> it in eternity. The married man is truly poetical, he solves the great rid-
> dle of how to live in eternity and yet hear the parlor clock strike in such
> a way that its striking does not shorten but prolongs his eternity—[41]

With himself as the itinerant occupant of the main role in "The Seducer's Diary," the aesthete unequivocally reports his preferences and, in the same place, ironizes unforgettably over "the domestic kiss with which married people, for want of napkins, wipe each other on the mouth while saying, 'You're welcome.' "[42] Correspondingly, in one of his later much-quoted *Diapsalmata*, he puts marriage into a pseudo-logical time machine whose elements can be exchanged according to need and inclination:

> If you marry, you will regret it; if you do not marry, you will also regret it; if you marry or if you do not marry, you will regret both. . . . If you hang yourself, you will regret it; if you do not hang yourself, you will regret it; if you hang yourself or you do not hang yourself, you will regret both; whether you hang yourself or you do not hang yourself, you will regret both. This, gentlemen, is the sum of all practical wisdom.[43]

The aforesaid life's wisdom coincided to some extent with the bittersweet recognition that Kierkegaard had reached in his Berlin reflections on marriage and art as "irreconcilable entities."[44] So it is almost an echo of his own self-description when the ethicist in *Either/Or*'s second part characterizes the first part's aesthete in the following words:

> There is an unrest in you over which your consciousness nevertheless soars light and clear. Your whole soul is gathered at that point. Your mind draws up a hundred plans, everything is prepared for the assault; it fails in one direction, instantly your well-nigh diabolical dialectic is ready to explain it away as a necessary part of the new plan of operation.[45]

Understanding *Either/Or* as an extended conversation that Kierkegaard has with himself over his incompetence as a husband would no doubt be a mischievous misrepresentation, but it cannot be altogether excluded that he is here, in the guise of an authoritative ethicist, trying to convince himself, an incorrigible aesthete, of the validity of marriage. If the attempt had succeeded, he would have been able to return to Copenhagen and take up again with Regine. Instead, he was now returning home as a writer who could give her, and the public at large, an eight-hundred and thirty-eight page reason for his plans, at times in such autobiographical terms that the work itself has forgotten that it is fiction and not confession. Following several pages in praise of marriage, Wilhelm is able (is made to) suddenly deal with a justified exception that departs significantly from the cancelation that he has earlier defended:

> I, for my part, will mention just one circumstance, which arises when the complications of the individual life are such that it is unable to reveal itself. If the history of your inner development contains something unutterable, or if your life has made you privy to secrets—in short, if

in one way or another you have gorged yourself on a secret that cannot be dragged out of you without you losing your life, then never marry.[46]

Wilhelm is discreet enough not to enlighten us as to who constitutes this tragic exception, but Kierkegaard's reader needs no further biographical information to be able to sense the direction. The Assessor's exception is the actual author's message to the work's most important reader, who in the present instance had no need to read between the lines.

"THE PRIEST PEOPLE IN HELLEVAD"

Some letters never reach their addressee, not because they have gone astray in the postal system but because they were never written. Jonas in the course of time put his name to a considerable pile of these, and by the end of March 1859 Regine was so tired of his silence that she called it an "incurable cancer sore." Her sympathy for Jonas and his wife, who is frequently referred to in the correspondence as Laura Jonas to avoid confusion with Oluf's Laura, had for a long time been wearing rather thin. On Monday the 27th of April, she wrote:

> The good dear Emil will certainly call me harsh in my judgment when I give you my opinion on the priest people in Hellevad; but so be it, he can put it down to my having sweated away so many good feelings in the heat, and among them sympathy; at least I have none for them. Is Laura mad! She complains about having too much to do! When one lives alone out there on the heath as she does, then it is, on the contrary, something she may thank God for; is it not a blessing to have work, how often have we not talked about this, my Cornelia? And if one works only for one's husband and children, is that something to complain about?

It was perhaps not so very becoming of the materially favored Lady Governor, living on her picturesque tropical island with a black servant "on every finger," to rage over her sister-in-law's lack of industriousness in a wind-blown parsonage out on the God-forsaken Jutland heath. But Regine was not in her tolerant corner that day and simply could not free her mind of images of the sister-in-law's sloppy and uncaring housekeeping, which made Jonas dispirited and forced him to entrench himself behind a mountain of theological literature at the other end of the house:

> That Jonas shuts himself in his study I find quite right: he has certainly better company there than with her; he is a priest, so closest to the

35. Kierkegaard writes in one of his first letters to Regine: "Your brother reproached me yesterday for always talking of my cobbler, my fruit dealer, my grocer, my coachman, etc., etc., etc." Jonas Olsen has evidently commented on the well-to-do Kierkegaard's extravagant habits, which the latter tries to offset by choosing another "possessive pronoun," signing himself in the letter "Yours eternally." Jonas, like his three-years-older prospective brother-in-law, had been a pupil at the School of Civic Virtue and, like him, became a theologian, working first as a priest in Sønderjylland (South Jutland). As a spokesman for the Danish side during the 1864 war, he was removed from office and imprisoned by the Prussians. Regine loved the good-hearted Jonas but was annoyed at his perpetual irresoluteness, and she could not for the life of her understand why it should have occurred to him to marry a shrew like Laura.

source from which comfort is to be found in the face of all earthly need and misery. That he doesn't participate in the children's upbringing is doubtless due to his not wanting to get involved in the 2 women's [Laura and the governess's] scolding; he has no power over them, he should grab the one to thrash the other with; at any rate that is what

Fritz would definitely advise him to do. That there is a lack of cheer and warmth in the house is something I know from experience, but these 2 people have definitely no sense of it themselves.

Regine here shows sides of herself usually kept coolly in the background. She seeks more resoluteness in Jonas; he really must make the women understand that he is the one wearing the trousers, the man in the house, and not just a good-natured mollusk to be chased about and humiliated at will. Regine was fully convinced that Jonas needed a change of air; he should get away from that depressing heath with those stern and foursquare women. An outing in the capital might do him good, but as far as that goes, Regine has little faith in changes in externals having all that much impact, as with downright caustic pessimism she makes plain:

> . . . it might be good for him to come to Copenhagen, yet I still hold strongly to my view that people create their own happiness; so if he is unhappy on the heath, then coming to town won't help him much; this life, after all, lasts but a short while, so why be so greedy in asking happiness of it!

"THE DAY IS BAD, BUT THE NIGHT IS WORSE"

The two sisters entered into a "silent agreement" that they would write to each other every other ship's departure. So on Saturday the 27th of June Regine should not have written, "but today I can't resist, I am afraid that my own sister is saddened, life is hard in its vicissitudes." In her efforts to make amends for her untimely intervention, she repeats pieces of a conversation she has had with Oluf, who said of Cornelia that she "was really the only one of all of us siblings who had become someone of character." God had placed trials before Cornelia, but she had withstood them bravely and vigorously. And perhaps life itself consisted in a series of trials, which might seem inhuman to human eyes, but seen from the point of view of eternity, and thus through God's eyes, were just about over before they began.

> You mustn't be surprised at what I have written, but Fritz is quite right when he says that I make a new eternity every day; but you see, when one is much alone and one comes together with strangers, they differ so much from oneself that even in the greatest throng one remains alone and then falls into broodings, and you can well understand that no broodings are as inexhaustible as that about eternity, so nor is it

very surprising that I fetch material from where there is always some
to be found.

Regine has taken Fritz's remark about her "broodings" to heart, but she defends
herself by insisting that the reason for her daily seeking back into eternity is that
she feels alone among the strangers, alone among people with whom she never
becomes more than superficially acquainted. Regine's eternity is filled in quite another way—with a "material" that she can retrieve and use to pass away time with
all its trivialities. Bashful as she is, she does not wish to describe the exact character of this "material," but she perhaps lifts a corner of the veil when in her letter
of the end of August she takes up the eternity theme again and confronts herself:

> . . . if you overcome the fear of death, only then have you truly gained
> life, and this thought has been so much in my mind these days that I
> have dreamt every night of nothing else than of all our dear departed.

Regine had been dreaming night after night of those now buried whom she once
loved. In those still living one may find kindred, perhaps finer, traits, certainly
more noble dispositions, but since a person is more than the sum of their qualities, the one that you miss can never be replaced by another, who can neither,
therefore, dispel the nearness of death that by their absence the dead have left
in one's life.

Still other dreams tumbled out of the tropical nights' dense darkness: bad,
somber dreams littered with impressions of young warm bodies lying around
in field and naval hospitals, with their sickly sweet smell, and reminding the
still living of the unbearable uncertainty of everything, of life's offensive brev-
ity. At the end of August, Regine writes to Cornelia: "The day is bad, but the
night is worse, I never more than half sleep, and even then am as troubled as
though delirious from fever." Luckily, the really dangerous fever had at no time
got its hold on either Regine or Fritz; if it tried it was repelled by the quinine
prescribed by the laconic Dr. Aagaard. Not everyone in Regine's proximity was
equally resistant:

> Unfortunately there has been another sad death from yellow fever,
> the cleverest of the young people who came out here to the office, an
> Olivarius, has died of it; he got the fever on Saturday, it couldn't be ar-
> rested, there was no quinine available, on Monday he had black vomit
> and on Tuesday he was dead.

At the beginning of September a report in *Departementstidenden* from the "dep-
uty medical officer on St. Thomas" told of "a strongly rampant yellow fever"[47] that
had lasted from May to July in the harbor area, but which now, thanks to lower

temperatures and the presence of fewer colliers in the harbor, was on the decrease. When the illness was at its worst "there lay daily 50 to 70 patients in the naval hospital, and at the same time 20 to 30 at various places in town. During the whole epidemic there was oppressive heat and the wind maintained more or less full strength." Of the roughly four hundred and fifty who had been admitted for treatment, one hundred and thirty-five were dead, but the majority of these had already been in such a bad state when brought on shore that medical assistance was without effect. With few exceptions, the illness had confined itself to the harbor area and, as was usual, had afflicted in particular the crews of the colliers.

In the middle of September ominous news reached the inhabitants of St. Croix. Yellow fever had been found in a "newly arrived recruit." A regular "yellow fever epidemic" gradually developed; indeed the illness, according to the head physician's report, "behaved as violently as ever, for no reason that it was possible to point to." Up to now "4 rank and file had died and 10 yellow fever patients were still undergoing treatment." It seemed as though St. Croix might once again get off more cheaply than St. Thomas, but the horror spread when in Christiansted's garrison the epidemic suddenly took on a "malignant form." By the 27th of October, there were "37 patients, of whom several got black-vomiting a few hours after admission."

The cause of the yellow fever was, as we have seen, unknown to the colonial physicians. They assumed it had something to do with "climatic conditions." But they also suggested "the soldiers' poor pay as a circumstance that had a bad effect," since with their limited means it was impossible for the rank and file to acquire "the necessities of life as these are required under present conditions for sustaining their strength and health. The commission therefore submitted unanimously that the pay be raised or else board and lodging granted."

It was not until a report issued on the 13th of November that people could begin to reassure themselves and their loved ones that "the rampant fever-epidemic in the garrison in Christiansted" had assumed a "far milder character." The total number of those affected since the start of the epidemic amounted to a hundred and one, of whom thirty-three had died and twenty-two were still in care, while the remaining forty-six were released with their lives intact—for the time being. Among the dismal death records were the names of several young persons whom Regine had known personally. On Thursday the 12th of November she wrote to Cornelia:

> The yellow fever is now slightly in abatement, but yesterday a young girl died, a daughter of Doctor Knudsen, if not exactly of yellow fever then of the climate fever that Olivia and Mrs. Feddersen died of; I don't know if you have seen from the newspapers that another of the

young men Fritz got out to the office has died of yellow fever; he was a handsome young man, I rather liked him, he was called Moltke and was a cousin of Louise's husband. It seems very ominous to the other newcomers, and it is sad that it should be so bad just this year when so many young people have come out here.

Regine, too, felt the yellow fever breathing down her own neck. And she had to steel herself. "Do you understand me now," she asks Cornelia, "why I try to make myself stronger, even if it is at the expense of the softer side of my character?" That she had again enlarged on her own condition was not "from egotism" but in order to reassure Cornelia and Emil—"and so I spoke, it is always the way I console myself and others." The family members in the motherland had their complaints too, but these were not amenable to being talked away. Maria had "blood suction therapy," Laura Jonas "a chest complaint," and Cornelia was in such constant bad health that, were Regine not to make herself "hard-hearted" but take Cornelia's infirmities to heart just half as much as she did in her younger years, then she would "lie tomorrow of a furious fever and the day after be both dead and buried, and then my poor Fritz would be left standing there! No thanks, I have become wiser than that!"

Fritz, as it happens, had not altogether escaped but had been suffering a "fairly serious attack of fever." Conscientious as he was, he went back to work too soon and so became sick again—"the only day he was in town, he came home in such a state that my heart was in my mouth from anxiety." But, God be praised, "he got medicine in time." During his illness he developed "2 large boils on his face," which according to Dr. Aagaard was a good sign: "the evil is now taking that path," explains Regine knowledgeably. The boils had, however, begun to spread. From his face they crept down by way of his neck to his back, and Fritz was for a time unable to sleep due to the boils and seeping sores. Regine, who had first-hand knowledge of the problem, took it upon herself to be his "doctor." Fritz was against her treatment at first and half in jest complained that she only "used the occasion to pinch him and pull his hair," but it was—according to Regine—"not really true, I treated him softly, as if he were made of sugar."

And that kind of treatment usually has its effect.

". . . THEN I STAND THERE SO UNTOUCHED BY IT ALL"

When on Sunday the 27th of September Regine again reported a miserable night, her irregular sleeping curve was due neither to sickness nor to "unsettled weather with wind, thunder and lightning," but rather to "the after-effects of a strenuous day yesterday" when she had been the rounds in Christiansted making "10 visits." This exhausting visiting schedule was due to the coming celebration, on the 6th of October, of Frederik VII's forty-ninth birthday. It was to be marked by, among other things, a ball hosted by Fritz and Regine.

On this side of the well-concluded events, Regine could report, with a small note of triumph, on her own busy participation: "I helped the house-keeper, can you believe it when I say it? I have no idea what Laura Jonas and her family would have said if they had seen all the salads and gelées I decorated!" The result of these gastronomic exertions might not stand up to the sister-in-law's "strict criticism," but the food was really "a great success"—Regine lent a hand from early morning to shortly before noon—

> . . . then in my finery I went on a drive with the Governor, so that people should not imagine that the Lady Governor had the least thing to do with it; and then after the dinner I dressed up first Tilly and then myself, with the house-keeper helping to hook the dress and fasten some bows, and the dress, hair decoration, and every single bow I had sewn myself. Be sure not to think I'm telling you all this so as to seem important, but you who know me so well, can't you well understand me when I tell you that it is the only way possible for me to coax a gram of interest out of this whole place; it amuses me when the ladies are gathered around me in gold and satin and everything glistens doubly in the strongly lit hall, and the servants swarm, and the pitch torches sparkle for the gaping crowd outside; then I stand untouched by the whole thing, the old Regina and the old Fritz are there so unchanged, but the Governor and the Lady Governor, they are fine gentlefolk, they fulfill their duties with all conceivable grace, as courtly hosts.

It is a grand scenario that Regine manages to unfold in these lines. To begin with, she herself and Fritz are removed to the third person so as to mark the distance between the official figures that the governor and his wife are outwardly when courteously receiving their guests, and the quite ordinary, mortal humans that they remain, especially inwardly. Regine never grows into her role as a proper and presentable Lady Governor; she disguises herself, puts on a smiling official mask, and enjoys in all innocence her small professional deceptions. It then pleases her to let the other ladies preserve their preconception of the governor's wife as this slightly blasé, always idle, and expensively dressed woman from Copenhagen. If only they knew how she had sat laboriously pottering away at every single one of her dress bows, and besides that had busied herself most of the day with pots and pans and casseroles alongside Josephine and the black domestics out in the kitchen.

And just as the West Indian ladies had no suspicion who, deep down, their lady governor really was, having never seen beyond the costume, so too, thinks Regine, would Cornelia scarcely be able to form anything like an idea of "how everything out here differs from home." Back home in Denmark, for example, balls or parties were held for a narrow circle of the specially invited, but nothing like that was ever done in the West Indies:

> The doors are open and the galleries and stairs swarm with spectators who belong of course to the plebs, but no silverware is ever stolen, though that would be easy since everything is a mess; however the eat-ables vanish quite quickly, I am certain more is eaten outside the hall than inside; and imagine what fine folk would think of me out here if they knew that I nonetheless don't begrudge it to them. But enough with all this nonsense, if someday you get to talk to Oluf about our parties you may come to know the truth, how many stupid things I am always doing, and which I naturally have not been so stupidly honest as to confess to all of you at home.

1001 NIGHTS

The day Regine drove from Cane Garden to Christiansted to celebrate the King's birthday, she sat alone in the coach and thought:

> . . . one of us is now sure to get yellow fever, for the evil visitant broke out quite violently in the barracks, but God be praised we came back alive and have all so far been fine, and that in spite of the whole month having been dreadfully hot especially at night, if I make an exception of the night after the ball when I slept like a stone since I was dead tired; I can hardly recall a night when I haven't suffered so horribly from the heat that I slept only a little.

That night the yellow fever was busily occupied elsewhere, so Regine escaped with only a fright, but at the cost of having to live with a dizzying deficit of sleep and on sheets soaked in sweat. She was now back at Cane Garden, where her days had recovered their leisurely West Indian rhythm and gave her rich oppor-tunity to reflect on life itself. But she felt, as so often before, that at one moment she had far too much and at another far too little to reflect on. And no matter whether the thoughts she entertained were large or small, they were not such as to lend themselves well to transference from the inner convolutions of the brain to the open surfaces of paper. On the 12th of November she wrote to Cornelia:

You cannot believe what a quiet life we mostly lead; generally I am very satisfied with it, yes, many times I think I have so much to think about and to consider that I never have peace enough; at other times, [and] as you well enough know, one is not always one's own master, I feel so empty that not one thought worth anything will come out of my foolish head and go down in my letter to my own Cornelia, but I know you are more indulgent than I. We read a lot out here, and as evidence I will only cite the fact that we have both read a thousand and one nights from beginning to end; now there you have a thick book. Recently I read Andersen's new novel, I don't like it, the usual gleaning from right and left, and so very little to give of himself, and I shall not deny that the folk-tale style is not suited to novels.

Regine's fearless judgment on poor Hans Christian Andersen refers almost certainly to his *At være eller ikke være* (To Be or Not to Be), which came out on the 20th of May 1857 and was the only novel Andersen put out that year. It takes up the relation, much discussed at the time, between faith and knowledge, which for the main character, Niels Bryde, are not absolute opposites but poles that modern people must learn to commute between. *At være eller ikke være* got a generally favorable reception, but the *Atheneum*'s reviewer did not care for the book and called it "dangerous," which put Andersen, then spending some months with the Dickens family in their country residence just outside London, in a black mood. On Sunday the 28th of June he noted in his journal: "Slept badly, dreaming; 'Atheneum' like a vampire on my heart; I sit still depressed this morning."[48] Dickens tried to comfort his Danish colleague by telling him that he himself never read anything in the papers that he hadn't written himself, and so in more than ten years had not read a single review of his own books. Andersen unfortunately *did* read reviews of his own books, and that summer it cost him dearly.

Two decades earlier Andersen had suffered an almost similar fate. The occasion had been a devastating critique, delivered by a young theology student, of his novel *Kun en Spillemand* (Only a Fiddler). The critic's name was Søren Kierkegaard, whose unassailable opinions on Andersen gave rise to an entire little book, which bore the cryptic title *Af en endnu Levendes Papirer. Udgivet imod hans Villie* (From the Papers of One Still Living. Published against His Will). The young Kierkegaard's will to browbeat the socially awkward Andersen, however, lacked for nothing, and his words affected Andersen so deeply that, according to the notes in his almanac, he stumbled about "as if in a daze" and had to take "cooling powders"[49] to regain his normal mental temperature. Kierkegaard, in contrast to Regine, thought not that Andersen gave too "little" of himself in his novels but that he gave far too much. Indeed Andersen's novels stood in "so physical a relation to him that their genesis is to be regarded more as an amputation than as a production."[50]

If the choice were between *Kun en Spillemand* and *One Thousand and One Nights*, Kierkegaard, like Regine, would unconditionally prefer the Arabian folktale collection to which he kept returning throughout his life. The external frame for the adventures in what is also known as the *Arabian Nights*, is the macabre tale of King Shahriyar who has his vizier bring him every night a virgin with whom he diverts himself and who is then killed at the light of dawn. Among the beautiful innocents is the vizier's own daughter, Scheherazade; but she saves her life by entertaining the king with a new adventure every night for a thousand and one nights. When, after the last adventure, she presents the king with the children to whom, in miraculous obscurity, she has succeeded in giving birth, he abandons his murderous plans and marries her.

In his journals, Kierkegaard can compare himself with Scheherazade, placing his own unconquerable need to write on an equal footing with Scheherazade's fantastic will to tell stories. As in Scheherazade's case, his innumerable words are due to a need to keep something at a distance: melancholia, yearnings, misunderstandings, humiliations. In an entry from 1849 we read:

> Ah, what a weight! As I've often said about myself, like the princess in *1001 Nights*, I save my life by telling stories, that is, by producing. Producing was my life. I was able to conquer it all, all of it—prodigious melancholia, inner sufferings of a sympathetic kind—when I was able to produce. Then the world stormed in on me; mistreatment that would have rendered others unproductive only made me more productive; and everything, all of it, was forgotten, it had no power over me when I was able to create.

Earlier than most others, Kierkegaard recognized the beneficial effects of writing on mental crises, the therapeutic character of the process itself. He found that through his writing he was able to alleviate his suffering; writing was an exercise in the demanding art of self-forgetfulness; it was to be euphorically present in something other than oneself. Besides being infinitely more, his writing was *also* a vitally necessary skipping from peak to peak over mountains of paper, a monumental abstraction from rummaging among the demons within. In a journal entry made some time in 1847, we read:

> There you see, Andersen can tell the fairy tale about the "Galoshes of Good Fortune," but I can tell the fairy tale about the shoe that pinches. Or rather, it is something I could tell, though precisely because I will

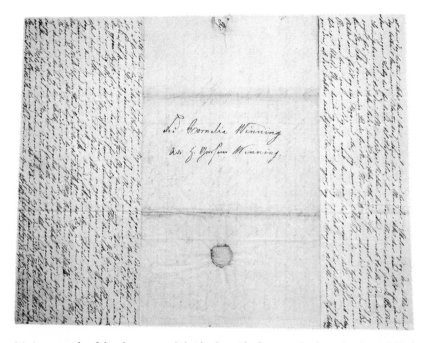

36. An example of the elegance and thrift of vanished times. The letter has been folded in on itself to make an envelope on which, with a flourish, Fritz has given Cornelia as its addressee. The red seal, when broken, took a piece of the paper with it, leaving a hole in the text.

not tell it, but conceal it in profound silence, I am able to tell quite a few other things.[51]

The entry has several layers: first there is the delightful comparison between two items of footwear that serves to mark the essential difference between Andersen and Kierkegaard, the one a child of fortune, the other pain's thinker; but there then follows the notion of Kierkegaard's authorship being one long hushing up of what, for Kierkegaard, was the reality of his life, all that he could well have imparted to his reader if only he had wanted to. Kierkegaard wrote, it seems, not to reveal but to conceal himself. How far such a project can be carried through remains an open question, but as we saw, Regine also was unwilling to provide Cornelia with full documentary access. When writing to her sister in Horsens, she acted in somewhat the same way as when in the alias of the governor's wife, she went the rounds cordially greeting her evening guests while her thoughts were quite elsewhere. In her letters, Regine persistently concealed something of the very greatest importance—though of the concealment itself she made no secret. That here too she had something in common with Kierkegaard comes out a little coquettishly when, in a letter on the 27th of April, as one of her concluding confidences to Cornelia, she writes:

> There you see, the 4 statutory pages are now full and so I stop; nor have I anything more to say, and my thoughts! yes, it will certainly do them good to be forgotten.

Like Kierkegaard, Regine begins her letter with "There you see," but the similarity in their modes of expression goes substantially further. Regine fills the four pages as she should, with neither more nor less; and then adds that she does not have anything more to tell. But then she lets it slip that the four pages have in the best Kierkegaardian manner only been a conscious omission, inasmuch as what she has written has no genuine connection with her innermost thoughts, for these she intends to keep to herself. Where exactly the shoe pinches she does not tell—and for precisely that reason she is able, like Kierkegaard, to "tell quite a few other things." On Saturday the 12th of December, she writes to Cornelia:

> There you see, it was a long chat about nothing; but as dear as your last letter was, and so infinitely much there that I would so much have talked with you about, then this same thing just doesn't lend itself to writing; we must hope we can get together sometime and unburden ourselves a little once again by talking a little together; and as Emil and Fritz spitefully suggested, and perhaps rightly, best that talk about this and that took place on the stairs.

Leaving talk of this and that on the stairs is just about as inventive as putting joy's galoshes alongside the shoe that pinches. But besides that, there is here again this hushing up, almost aloud, this flickering or masked communicativeness between the lines; Regine will and she will not—and absolutely not in a letter. And then, all the same, just perhaps; but only after a rather long run up:

> There you see, it is 5 and the sun is beginning to go down; at this time of year it sets early out here too; but it is quickly down behind the horizon, and yet this short moment, with the shadows becoming longer, is the only one where the light reminds me of home; in the middle of the day the sun is too bright for that; I become quite sorrowful, for the love of my home is still preserved in my heart, it will never be forgotten, but I rarely give in to my feelings; so, I think, however much I love those I have left there, if God will call me to my true home before seeing them again, then one time an hour will strike for our meeting there too. On

the other hand, should such a joy still be reserved for me and Fritz here on earth such as you have recently experienced at home, oh I do so hope that neither God nor Man should find me ungrateful for the gift of love.

Regine is still an enigma, but after commenting on how the setting sun carries her thoughts eastward toward her Copenhagen home, she refers to the "joy" that has "recently" befallen Cornelia and Emil. That joy could conceivably be little Johanne Marie, except that she had come to the world not all that recently, but as long ago as the 25th of September 1855 to be precise. Still, Regine's last sentence may be read in that way, and so perhaps she and Fritz were hoping in those days for a similar joy. Had she perhaps "gone over the time," as it is so metaphysically put? Would she be like Sarah who, against all biological reckoning, gave birth to Isaac in great old age and so became doubly blessed? But if this was indeed the "gift of love" Regine had in mind, she was content to touch on the matter in a most indirect way and moved on quickly to talk of jam and other things much easier to put a lid on.

Scheherazade related tale after tale to keep death at bay, but she also let herself be impregnated and bore children who became her salvation. Kierkegaard wrote and wrote to hold off a symbolic death, his depression. He called his own thoughts and ideas his "healthy, happy, merry, gay, blessed children," who all bore his "personal birthmark." His books were his children. Regine, for her part, wrote letter after letter, but child came there none, even if with Fritz she might have tried for one thousand and one nights. Never did she approach this topic nearer than in this letter, perhaps because the pain of childlessness filled her so much that she simply could not endure giving it shape in writing. And so she had consciously to omit to write of it, and filled her letters with something that might easily be mistaken for nothing.

1858

"YOU IMAGINED IT WAS CORNELIA"

At the beginning of 1858 Regine, Fritz, Thilly, and an unspecified number of servants moved back from Cane Garden to Government House in Christiansted. Breaking camp left a "little wound" in Regine's heart, but it was not long before she could note that the "emptiness and disconsolateness" that used to overcome her when living in town was now much less evident. Nor did people's curious glances trouble her as before, and if nothing else, the diversion offered by town life was badly needed. If her humor was not equally good every day, being in town had the "invaluable advantage" that she could "look forward to coming out into the country again." Happiness lies, as we know, where we are not. Also, Josephine's humor had considerably improved: "The loneliness in the country often made her almost muddleheaded; you may be sure I went through a lot with her."

On Saturday the 13th of February, Regine was sitting in her room with a "lovely view over the East End hills" and writing to Cornelia. She began her letter with assurances that her love was unchanged even though some time had passed since she had last shown signs of life. As so often before, she homes in on the "separation," but that was how it had to be—"and it is both good and wise to come to terms with the inevitable." True to form, she placed everything in the hands of higher powers, although in this case her faith in Providence was accompanied by a reflection of surprising scope. Recently, she had often been thinking how foxy "humankind is, after all, in following its inclinations, yes even without being altogether clear about why it does this or that, precisely because what drives one is a kind of repressed feeling."

The problem Regine touches on here rightly concerns the extent of the unconscious's activity, that strangely disquieting fact that we are controlled by obscure forces and have at times hidden motives for our actions that may connect with what Regine calls a "repressed feeling." She herself had just had an experience that fully confirmed her impression in this regard. A certain Mrs. Schwartz had arrived in St. Croix with several letters of recommendation provided by Councillor Feddersen, Fritz's predecessor, one of them to Regine. Mrs. Schwartz was an extremely cultivated but visibly rheumatic woman, partly paralyzed in hand and foot, for which reason the physicians had recommended that she take recreation in these tropical climes. Together with a Mrs. Meineke, Regine had taken care of Mrs. Schwartz, inviting her to tea at Government House and arranging drives out into the countryside. During all this she "had come on quite good terms with Mrs. Meineke" and had at one point been plainly "incautious." She would not tire Cornelia with the details, "for fortunately it is a trifle," but when one day she had confided the matter to Fritz, he promptly remarked, "You imagined it was Cornelia you'd made an arrangement with." Regine was struck by the remark and felt convinced that Fritz was right. Her concern for Mrs. Schwartz was a kind of transference of her love for Cornelia, which for good geographical reasons it was impossible for her to express directly. Cornelia was irreplaceable, but for that very reason others must, paradoxically enough, step in momentarily in her stead.

But nor can the possibility be excluded that Regine's love for Cornelia was also a morally redirected love for quite another. Did Fritz the psychologist perhaps have a similar thought when in the late night hours, after a hot day of tiresome West Indian bureaucracy, he sat in his favorite rocking chair and to the impatient chirping of the crickets tried to size things up? He was supposedly well qualified to interpret his wife's complex feelings and, in one of those moments we call "weak" because their effect is so strong, could hardly have avoided asking himself whether the love that Regine confided in letter after letter to Cornelia was not only for a women in an East Jutland province but embraced also a man, beyond doubt dead and buried, but whose physical presence he could almost sense when he came upon his wife, bowed down over her desk, concentrated in her writing in the room with the lovely view over the East End hills.

"WHAT DOES THIS SILENCE MEAN?"

In one of her many letters, Regine might well have told Cornelia about the materials that had come into her hands after Kierkegaard's death, but she never found the opportunity to do so. She said nothing, therefore, of how Fritz reacted to the epistolary ghost from Copenhagen who had quite unexpectedly turned up in their West Indian exile. His reaction is something about which one can therefore only surmise, duly assisted by empathy and imagination in equal measure—together with a small text of Kierkegaard's. In about the middle of *For Self-Examination*, which was to be his second but last publication before he cocooned himself in what is known as his "silent" period, because in it he published nothing at all, he captured and held a situation in some odd way extricated from the Letter of St. James, chapter 1, verses 22 to 27, which forms the text over which the first of the book's three parts is built. The situation could have occurred at the dining table or out on the terrace, or anywhere where people talk but do not really talk to one another.

> You are sitting and speaking with her; and just as you are sitting there you say to yourself: She is silent—what does this silence mean? She tends to the house, is completely attentive . . . she is joyful, at times full of jest and jollity—and just as you are sitting and looking at her you say to yourself: She is silent—what does this silence mean? And if the very person who stands closest to her, to whom she is bound with indissoluble bonds, whom she loves with her whole soul and who has a claim upon her confidence—if it could be imagined that he would straightforwardly say to her, "What does this silence mean, what are you thinking of, for there is something behind all this, something you always seem to have in mind—tell me what it is!"—she does not say it directly. At most she may say evasively, "Are you coming to church with me on Sunday?"—and then speaks of other things. . . . What does this silence mean?[1]

Has not Fritz also asked himself this question when his wife was not there, remote, or in her study with her thoughts markedly elsewhere? Has he really never inquired about the contents of the letters that were sent to his wife from Kierkegaard's estate, not asked about the nature of the material in the diaries that accompanied them, never urged her to tell him about the feelings and impressions imparted to her by these posthumous confidences and confessions? Has the governor just taken things as they were, leaving the two formerly betrothed to each other's intense company in the room next door? Or, disgusted at his own curiosity, has he sneaked into Regine's quarters to seek some documentary insight, peeked into the boxes while she was out riding in the early hours of the morning, or swimming, or a little later in the day reluctantly killing time with Emilie de Pontavice over the way. Guesswork, but it is indisputable that in those boxes there were several sketches of letters and drafts of the missive that Kierkegaard had sent along with his sealed letter to Regine. The sketches were addressed directly to Schlegel, which now forced his wife to face the moral dilemma of whether to confront the addressee with these drafts or, in the interests of their marriage, to keep their existence secret, consigning them resolutely to the bottom of the pile of correspondence. One would well understand if she chose the latter course, since several of the sketches are quite harsh reading. Kierkegaard announced, for example, the following:

> Remarkable, in a sense, what in a way I experience with this girl. When we parted at that time I was, as unchanged I still am, the only one who

held and holds the explanation of my relationship; I was the only one who could appreciate the girl's worth; I was the only one who took stock of the relationship; the only one who suspected that what has now happened would happen, as I intimated often enough. And yet at that time I was "a villain, a low-down villain," etc.—"our parting would be the death of her"! And now, now she has long been happily married—and I altogether unchanged.[2]

The exultant detail in which Kierkegaard protests to being the "only one" with the definitive explanation of the relationship, and that he was "the only one" who knew how to appreciate Regine, would hardly cheer Fritz. Kierkegaard's quotations would have to have been painful; the first sounds like an echo of the indignant judgment of the people, the second repeats the words with which Terkild Olsen tried to get Kierkegaard to reverse his decision and not abandon the proud councillor's youngest daughter. The historical document is accompanied as though by a kind of jubilation that would have to be terrible for Fritz, because it bore unequivocal witness to the definitive passion with which Regine had at that time embraced Kierkegaard, who these many years later is able, with an especially tightlipped primness, to stress the irony inherent in Regine's having ended up "happily married," while Kierkegaard has remained "altogether unchanged," which more than suggests that his own love for Regine remained undiminished.

Apart from being a mental and erotic turf war, the draft letter is a rendering of accounts to Schlegel for the guilt Kierkegaard had incurred at the time. Thus he admits a little further down that he is "in a sense totally in the wrong and guilty" toward Regine, who "perfectly innocent" had to suffer "a great deal, a very great deal," but that he wishes for that very reason—"only with your consent of course"—to give Regine "an explanation of her relationship to me."[3] The formulation looks as if it were the wrong way around, for it would be more natural for Kierkegaard to initiate Regine into his relationship to her and then leave it to Regine to provide an explanation of her relationship to him. But clearly the explanation that counts is Kierkegaard's, the more so as it could decisively "enhance" her marriage and give her an idea of the significance that was in wait for her. Kierkegaard continues:

> For that matter a young girl can be lovableness itself and highly gifted as well—and still lose her foothold when she is led out into such terrible decisions as those, alas, into which she had to be guided by my hand. Her relationship to me in the latter days of the engagement was such a mistake, without her losing essentially anything of her lovableness although without realizing it she was working on that.—Now, when so

much time has passed and the same girl has had time to collect herself, she can show, through what she then does (by becoming engaged,
then married, with this or that one) that she is not just the lovable and
gifted one, but an extremely sensible girl as well; and then she can, in
the same step, assure herself of the other party's lasting gratitude. This
is the case with "her" case in relation to me by being united with you.[4]

The rivalry exercised in the letter in so cultivated a manner toward its recipient
is counterbalanced by the corrective it administers to its unnamed feminine object, of whom we are to understand it became touch and go whether she would
lose her "lovableness" as the engagement came gradually to its end. Having recovered her senses, however, she knew she should behave sensibly and marry
"this or that one," as it is put with such impolite anonymity, thus tendentiously
making Fritz dispensable, exchangeable with any "this or that one." Consonant
with this is the strong stress on Regine as a "sensible girl," who following her
much-publicized youthful infatuation, chose to enter a marriage of convenience.

In the draft to Fritz it is not, however, the unforgettable first lover alone who
guides the pen, but also the experienced psychologist who can explain that when
such a marriage "has had time to consolidate itself," it can be "one's duty" to "let
the girl" be acquainted with the fame that the "villain" had "honestly saved up"
for her in compensation for his guilt-incurring behavior.[5] His offer to ensure
Regine's literary immortality while she still lived is presented in the following
metaphor:

> In the ordinary course of events, a wife is in such a position that it is
> only in a marriage that a distinction can be made between the everyday
> dress worn for everyday use and her festive gown worn on a few festive
> occasions; but this extraordinary girl will differ from the ordinary in
> that, besides the everyday dress of her marriage, she owns a more pre-
> cious ornament, the festive gown of fame and historical significance,
> which I have already prepared for her for after her death, unless the
> girl's heart, perhaps as a little restitution for so many violations, wishes
> to put it on at once; for it can be done at once.[6]

Within the "wife" whom Fritz had married there still lives the "girl" who had
been engaged to Søren. In her marriage, Regine went around in her everyday dress. But she owned another, fame's much lovelier dress, which, although
lodged for the time being with her former betrothed, she could put on "straightaway" if that should be her wish. We can easily understand that Fritz would
think there was little hurry for that festive change of costume, the less so as it
would inevitably secure for himself much less heroic apparel, the fool's motley,

the costume of a clown, the badge of the one who always comes second, or just the cuckold's up-raised horn in the middle of his forehead.

With its explicit wish to bring Søren and Regine together, the draft begins to look like a letter of separation between Regine and Fritz who, although they have each other in time, will be separated in eternity, where Fritz must cede place to his old rival. Until this eternity begins, Regine is still his. Kierkegaard further declares that when Regine receives the message about her future "significance," he will remind her in all seriousness to forget him, so that she can belong wholly to her husband. This again is a dubious guarantee. Behind the suggestion that such urging makes any sense at all is the admission that Regine has failed to relegate Kierkegaard to a parenthesis from the days of her youth. She is still obsessed by him, continues to love him, and so must be helped to keep her passion current inside her marriage with Fritz. She must learn moderation, sublimate, so that an uncorrupted passion can be reserved for eternity. The difficulty facing Regine when she is asked to forget Kierkegaard will not be lessened by Kierkegaard's assuring her husband that "the opportunity of seeing me will be as good as altogether denied." Yes, as good as—and just how often will that be?, Fritz might rightly wonder. The separation letter then approaches its conclusion:

> God bless her! In this life she will belong only to you; in history she will stand by my side; in eternity, after all, it cannot disturb you that she also loves me, who was already an old man on the day I became engaged to her and a thousand years to be able truly to love any girl, as I ought to have realized and as I now realize only all too well, now that the matter has long ago made me another couple of thousand years older.[7]

Stressing his "abnormal" old age allows the thirty-six-year-old Kierkegaard to transform himself into a mythological *Übermensch* who breaks with the normal categories of space and time. The same maneuver allows him to limit his share in the calamities of the engagement and to furnish a basis for the privileges he takes upon himself. Thanks to the "thousand years" he is practically already in eternity, where he patiently awaits Regine's planned arrival. But Kierkegaard will not be unreasonable and therefore explains, diplomatically, that his reason for addressing himself in writing and not by word of mouth is to ensure the necessary "calm and insusceptibility" for the married couple to think through his offer.

> My unfortunately all-too-distinctive personal presence might possibly disturb you both in one way or another, persuading you of something

undesirable, or causing you to refrain from something that might be desirable after all. That is why I have not exploited the opportunity, either, for a personal approach that has frequently presented itself or perhaps has been presented.[8]

The content of this passage was transferred to the final letter, in which Kierkegaard warned against his "distinctive personal presence" as having already on an earlier occasion had "far too strong an effect," which it would be better not to repeat. Also in the final letter we find the remark that Regine had for a number of years *offered herself* to her former betrothed, a remark that was the result not of a sudden whim but of a minutely worked out teasing that, typically enough, was promptly countered by a formal politeness:

> Perhaps—who knows!—this will be the first and the last time I shall have the pleasure of your company. Therefore I take this opportunity to testify to you my very high esteem. . . . The good fortune that united you with a girl who *poetice* deserves to be called *Regina*, this good fortune of yours was a true act of kindness to me. How lovely also for her! And besides what more can a girl ask? You make her happy in this life—I shall see to her immortality.
>
> Not at any cost must she read this letter. If she should insist, tell her that if she reads it she will for the first time in her life really sadden me.

With exceedingly high esteem,
Your respectful
S.K.[9]

It is highly unlikely that Fritz foresaw any particular "pleasure" in the prospect of sharing Kierkegaard's "company," for his demands and conditions clearly contradict the "exceedingly high esteem" with which he signs off. There also follows a "P.S.," whose two lines make it clear that the thousand-year-old Kierkegaard is now back from eternity and is impatiently stamping his foot in the busy present: "As it is possible that I shall go abroad for a little while, I should like to have a speedy reply."[10]

As we know, it took Schlegel only two days to comply with Kierkegaard's wish. The sealed letter to Regine came back unopened, accompanied by a "moralizing letter of indignation," which Kierkegaard immediately destroyed, after which he filed away his draft letters in the Regine mausoleum that had been made to his own specifications: "Everything is found in a packet in her cabinet, in a white envelope with the inscription: 'About Her.'"[11] Some months earlier, Kierkegaard had also placed in the cabinet his Notebook 15 with its lengthy entry titled "My Relationship to 'her' Aug. 24th 49. somewhat poetical."[12] He admits, with uncommon fragility, that he had hoped for a "sisterly relationship" with Regine, one that "would certainly delight her." And then comes his settlement: "My collision was a religious one. The deception about being a villain was done for her sake. But she let herself be carried away by her despairing declaration of love and about wanting to die, her religious entreaties, etc.: she who is now married—and I unmarried."[13] Kierkegaard consoled himself with the thought that he had, in spite of everything, tried an approach to Schlegel, but the man had obviously no sense at all for the "gift" that Kierkegaard's assurance of Regine's fame really was: "If he had understood me, I would almost have been a servant in his hand—but now the matter is really decided."

> *And never have I felt so light and happy and free with respect to this matter, so entirely myself again, as just now, after having taken this sacrificial step; for now I understand that I have God's consent to let her go and spare myself by complying only with her last request: "to think of her now and then."*[14]

". . . I SHALL THE SECOND TIME WITH GOD'S HELP BECOME MORE CRUEL"

It was from this Regine mausoleum that the nervously impaired Henrik Lund extracted the materials that he then shipped off to Regine, who would have ample opportunity in Christiansted to come to grips with both Kierkegaard's various preliminary drafts for the accompanying letter and the sealed letter. In his longest draft Kierkegaard acknowledges that he has been "cruel," but explains that his conduct was motivated by love and religiously founded. Although he is clear that Regine has "suffered indescribably," he thinks that it is he who will "suffer more," but he will beg Regine for forgiveness all the same. In other words, she has *mistakenly* interpreted the situation in such a way that Kierkegaard becomes simply a "lowdown villain" who out of sheer self-love has "cruelly deceived[ed] a lovable young girl," who gave herself to him with "the righteousness of innocence on her side." If this is an accurate picture of Regine's own interpretation, Kierkegaard comes "as a suffering penitent and beg[s] forgiveness."[15]

But there is, thinks Kierkegaard, another possible interpretation that puts the matter in quite another light. It will of course be eternally his fault "that I snatched [her] out into the current," but if Regine has seen that the "villain" was simply a "fraud," a necessary deception, then Kierkegaard's part is to offer "thanks" because Regine has fulfilled the "only wish . . . at which all my cruelty was aimed: . . . [that she should] marry and marry Schlegel in particular."

Kierkegaard would have Regine further understand that he will not be content to express his gratitude in a letter, but has it in mind to express it "on a different scale." He will not disclose further details to her yet, but after reproving her for her desperate attempt at the time to "obligate" him by calling on Christ and the memory of his late father, he continues in a milder tone, assuring her that he has kept "beyond measure" his promise to "remember you now and then":

> Be assured that in Denmark there lives not one girl, without reservation not one, of whom it will be said as it will of you: "Her life had *extraordinary* significance." . . . all my fame—that is our will—shall be owing to you, "our own dear little Regine," you, whose grace once enchanted and whose grief forever moved him whom neither the world's flattery nor its opposition has moved. There are only two people who affect me thus: my dead father and our own dear little Regine, who in a manner of speaking is dead.[16]

Kierkegaard might have chosen—some will think appropriately—to close his letter with this tribute, but he does not do so; he is intent on adding a "word of admonition," and to that end he makes the following somewhat elaborate attempt:

> You yourself have no doubt understood your task profoundly and clearly and devotedly: after suffering what you have suffered with me, the worthy capable and admirable Schlegel is the very man you can make happy, with whom you can be happy, and you will be; there shall not be so much as a fleeting tremor of mood. . . . You are in an awkward position with respect to me; but honest willing is capable of much. . . . It is a heavy burden to be that cruel one who is forced to be cruel out of solicitude and love, but beware, if it should become necessary—God forbid—if it should become necessary, I shall the second time with God's help be more cruel, more callous than the first time. Yet there will be no need for that, of that I am sure. So live well; may it delight you again, for your own good, to hear it repeated once more, then hear it now: "Yes, you were the beloved, the only beloved, you were loved most when I had to leave you, even though you saddened me with your vehemence, which could and would not understand anything, so that cruelty became necessary."[17]

Kierkegaard never goes into the exact nature of this oft-mentioned cruelty; whatever episode it refers to remains known only to him and Regine. His fear that he will have to be "more cruel" a second time is due to his anxiety that once

Regine sees that the "scoundrel" she felt forced to abandon was not at all identical with the Kierkegaard she continued to love, she may want to resume their relationship. We note how Kierkegaard's anxious imagination can here envisage Regine's "los[ing] her taste for marriage" as nothing but a provisional "mask," just as we saw how horrified he could become at the prospect of "fire" reentering "the passion" and pressing Regine into demanding a separation from Fritz and wanting to marry her former betrothed—"not to mention what was more frightful."

It is a well-attested psychological fact that a feared and forbidden sensuousness can give rise not only to trauma and an aggressive reaction, but in the worst case also to cruel action. On this background, it is as logical as it is painful that Kierkegaard should juxtapose the strict inquisitorial father with the animated woman, who would with her sensuality subconsciously bring paternal admonishment and prohibition to her former betrothed's conscious mind so vividly that he found it necessary to be cruel. One wonders at Kierkegaard never questioning whether the cruelty he practiced was indeed out of consideration for Regine, and did not stem rather from frustration at having to honor the paternal demand for sexual continence. In connection with a draft to a letter in which he seeks Schlegel's acceptance of a planned dedication to Regine, she is again brought into apposition with the father as "dead" and transferred thereby to that silent emptiness that is the legacy of suppressed sexuality:

> That is my will, and that is what you have deserved, you our own dear
> little R., you who once with your grace enchanted and with your grief
> forever moved him who neither the world's flattery nor its opposition
> has up to now moved. Only two persons affect me in that way: my
> dead father and then—someone else who is also dead: our own dear
> little R.[18]

The plural "our" is a logical and provocative extension of his remarks about the double ownership to which Regine is subjected, as a wife to Schlegel in time and as Kierkegaard's companion in fame in eternity. In anticipation of the bewilderment that this alleged bigamy would surely occasion in Regine, he advises her not to ponder too much over the strangeness in this constellation, for it isn't worth it; the aforementioned bigamy will last and thus continue to be Regine's riddle:

> For you there will always be something inexplicable in this whole affair; accept it, do not brood over it, you will not get to the bottom
> of it anyway. It seems to me a girl cannot ask for more than a happy
> marriage—and then mean so much to another.[19]

1858

". . . MY BESETTING SIN, MAKING ETERNITIES!"

It can cause no surprise that Regine had difficulty in getting her suddenly so vividly revived past into clear perspective, which may have contributed also to her failing so miserably at forming new connections. When, in a letter of the 12th of May, she explains her few friendships by pointing out that "since my childhood my sisters have occupied my heart so exclusively that no other women could find a place," we would naturally be inclined to believe her, but we would also understand should this to be less than the *whole* truth. To be fair, Regine considered possible exceptions outside her flock of sisters, but the only potential candidate was Laura, Oluf's Laura, who with her winning ways and luminous sweetness had been welcomed into the Olsen girls' circle. "But who could also take hearts by storm like her?" Regine lets her thoughts run freely back to her childhood home and vanished youth—"Oh my God, can you recall how at the Exchange we and Laura had such a good time together?"—but she pulls herself together with the words:

> But quiet, that time will never come again; not at least in this world, those two are already dead! Will eternity unite us, and how? Not indeed as foolish young girls, as we were then; but that which had eternity's stamp in us, namely our heartfelt love, will that not survive and overcome death? But now look where I have come, my besetting sin, making eternities! Therefore it is best to cut off short, for I never get out of this in a sensible way.

It was Fritz who invented this expression about Regine's "making eternities" so that she could slip away from the present and bathe in the delicious flowing springs of memory. And, of course, in those days they were only young and confused Copenhagen maidens in light summer dresses, tremblingly sensuous and with naïve notions of fortune's openhandedness; yes, of course. But would the feelings they nurtured at that time, especially their heartfelt love, which possessed precisely "eternity's stamp," not reach out beyond death in an eternal confirmation of life? Or was it all just nothing, emotional trivialities, sweet nothings of the past, deceptive eruptions of an accidental vitality in the hustle of a world history that has no other thought than to move on? Regine did not know the answer. What she did know was how difficult it was to remind herself that certain things in this world were best forgotten. In the letter of the 13th of November, which proved to be the year's last, she nevertheless resumed the topic of recollection, but now in a more subdued tone:

> It's not my view that one should altogether forget how it was possible when, after the course of years, one returns to the town where memories

are as numberless as the cobblestones in the streets; but one must master the sorrow of recollection in thanking God for the joy that is left.

Recollections cannot be deleted, but one should try to limit the sorrow to which vanished times instinctively give rise, lest one become a victim of one's own sentimentality or of the cloying self-pity that, as a kind of secular consolation in spite of everything, is always waiting to envelop the despondent. Regine continues:

> It may certainly be strange to come once more to Copenhagen! To see the old familiar faces changed by time in the oddest way! If I live, no doubt I will come to experience that; but I am afraid I may be unable to take it in a sensible way; I myself have become old in many ways (I still feel young in some) and also antiquated under a burning sun.

The woman who wrote these lines was only thirty-six years old, but in some ways she felt old, although as appears in the touching parenthesis, there were still areas unaffected by age. Her anxious looking back and fearful thoughts about what it would be like to see again old familiars back home in a beloved city teeming with memories, had made Regine ponder over the inventiveness of a hard-hearted fate that brought people together in unpredictable constellations, defying the plans they had drawn up in their earliest youth. "I have so completely given myself up, and all of the human race," she confesses with a resignation that has grown, she says, from her experiences of people's "paltriness" and their lack of "strength even just to overcome one of our small sins." When it came to grading her own sinfulness and owning up only to small infringements, trivialities, puppet sins, she was not for a moment in doubt about the true state of affairs:

> . . . for it is as clear as ink that if we were unable to put right the small ones, we would not be able to correct the big ones either. Accordingly, we are just as big sinners all of us, whether it is a matter of our not treating our servants well, or higher up, our subordinates, whether we torment a fly to death or the Creator's masterpiece: "a human being." I say with Adam Homo, we all stand and fall together, for either none are saved, or all.

The Olsen sisters had always had a weakness for Frederik Paludan-Müller's *Adam Homo*, in which they could certainly recognize essential elements of their own view of life, among them reliance on Providence's all-wise dispositions, a religious *amor fati*, if you will. Paludan-Müller's eleventh song develops the view on which his work rests: When the aged Adam lies on his death bed, he is cared for by a night nurse who proves to be his youth's sweetheart, Alma

37. From Government House in Christiansted, on the 13th of November 1858, Regine writes to her sister in Horsens: "Dear beloved Cornelia! This is now the 4th letter I am starting on today, and you will therefore forgive me for it turning out as it does. Really I shouldn't write to you at all now, for I am tired in both spirit and fingers. . . ."

Stjerne. He had given her up in preference for a refined but superficial and empty-headed baroness. Alma dies a few days after Adam, but she manages to secure him a grandiose posthumous reputation in a speech that doubts the reality of hell and sings the praises of a comprehensive interdependence between this world's peoples. The fellowship extends beyond death and is borne by a "general conscience" that expresses itself in the individual's life and reveals a common fate, the formula for which was:

> That with each other we must stand and fall,
> That the palm reaches none or all!

These were in all probability the lines that Regine quoted from memory in her letter to Cornelia. Whether she was especially taken by the circumstance of Adam's having been saved by the girl he had so disgracefully betrayed remains an open question. But Regine's own life story could well support that assumption. Whatever the case, Regine would have neither herself nor Cornelia imagine that she understood every scrap of her emotional life. All too often she had been exposed to the capricious laws of nature, or turned upside down by big passions and strong feelings that she thought she had put behind her—right up until the moment when they returned and brought that old silent heart to beat again as violently as in the days of her youth:

> Yes, it is all very well with all that talk one charms oneself with, when everyday life here is such that the heart beats so calmly that one hardly knows one still has one; one tells oneself that now one has become calm, cool, collected, etc., etc., until something happens one fine day that makes the heart beat with its old violence, just like a farewell, yes, so all reason goes by the board and the calm with it.

That, it would seem, was how things went when one was in the dark about one's own situation—and more especially when one had one's own secret reasons for being so! It was then easier to sprinkle a little conventional wisdom and pedestrian theology over the letter to Cornelia, as in Regine's insistence on the importance of "being of good cheer" seeing that a just God looked with his loving eye upon all human striving for the right; yes, in an imperfect world this striving was what life was all about: "Perfection is reached after death." So swiftly and so nimbly can personal problems be removed to a due theological distance—as Regine was also the first to remark: "But stop, this sounds like a bad sermon by a bad priest, and we can get enough of that, though I have to say, thankfully, that we don't get a lot of that, since we have a good priest."

"GOD PRESERVE ME FROM THEIR CHRISTIANITY"

The priest Regine refers to was theology graduate A. S. Ussing, who was not only good but also a "very handsome man" and reminded Regine of her own brother Jonas—"not at all in appearance, but in his views. Fritz will no doubt deny it, but for now I prefer to stay with my illusion, but at least he is also anti-Grundtvigian." And this was an antipathy that had Regine's sympathy. In a letter to Cornelia shortly after Ussing's arrival in 1857, we read:

> We have got a young priest out here, who God be praised is no Grundt-vigian but is for that reason also all the more serious and humble, al-beit he is definitely very capable; I am so pleased about him, for there is a feeling in me that says that now there is at least one person here who can understand and appreciate a character as upright as Fritz's.

At the end of September that same year Regine expanded on her "anti-Grundtvigian" views:

> You have held a big priest meeting in Denmark, I have not read much about it . . . but according to what I have read in some old *Berlingske*, this meeting might well also be called a rubbish meeting, with its old ditto head leading the way: Grundtvig. Are we to believe our Lord pays this same man in earthly fashion by letting him live long in the land, because he must be really old by now. It seems to me that the good priests operate in this world more for their own kingdom than for God's kingdom.

Further down in the letter Regine admits that these days she is "biased" and explains, quite cryptically, her partiality as due to "arrogant Catholics, bishops and priests" having for some time "got at" Fritz and causing him a mass of extra work. Her bias could also have other causes, however, since she may have ac-quainted herself with the polemical pamphlets that Kierkegaard published in the last year of his life and to which he gave the name *The Instant*. The sixth number of *The Instant*, which became available on the 23rd of August 1855, contained a crass criticism of Grundtvig and of all his works:

> Consider, then, Pastor Grundtvig. . . . The highest he has fought for is to receive permission, for himself and for those who want to join him, to express what he understands by Christianity. . . . [F]reedom for himself and for any who might agree with him, freedom to express what he and those along with him understand by Christianity, that is the most he has wanted—and then he would conduct himself calmly,

at ease in this life, belong to his family, and otherwise live like those who are essentially at home in this world. . . .[20]

For the sake of completeness, Kierkegaard added that Grundtvig's religious "enthusiasm" was only "tepid" and imbued with an "indifferentism" compared with the "passion" of "original Christianity." His testimony understandably enough aroused both astonishment and wrath in wide circles. But Grundtvig had in a way got off cheaply, for Kierkegaard could be much more savage. In his journals, he had, through the years, made a fool of Grundtvig, among other things calling him a "world historical companion in arms," "roaring blacksmith," "yodeling hail fellow well met," and "beer-drinking Nordic giant." But he also gets characterized as "rubbish" pure and simple. Already in 1851 Kierkegaard had summed up a lengthy journal entry with "Grundtvig seems to me rubbish," thus anticipating the unsuspecting Regine's remarks about the Grundtvigian "rubbish meeting" and Grundtvig himself as a "ditto head."

In 1857 Kierkegaard was not in a position to comment on the "priest meeting" referred to by Regine, but on earlier occasions he had made sport of such gatherings. Inspired by *Fædrelandet's* description of a joint Nordic student meeting that took place in late June 1845 and brought together Scandinavian enthusiasts in the Deer Park where Grundtvig made a speech, he put together a so-called Apotheosis that is wonderfully grotesque tableau:

> Grundtvig, supported by Barfoed and Povelsen, appears on an elevation in the forest background. He is artistically draped in a great cloak, has a staff in his hand, and his face is concealed by a mask with one eye (deep and profound so as to see into world history) and a mossy beard with birds' nests in it (he is very old—about 1,000 years); he has a hollow voice melodramatically accompanied by a few blasts on a conch (as at a town meeting); he speaks in a dithyrambic rhythm. When he has finished his speech (that is, when the committee in charge of the festivities says, "Enough," for otherwise he would never finish), a bell rings, a cord is pulled, the beard falls off, followed by the enormous cloak, and we see a slim young man with wings; it is Grundtvig as the spirit of the Scandinavian idea.[21]

Kierkegaard had a keen and malicious eye for all that was loud, extraverted, and obscure in Grundtvig, whom he criticized for making "the profound thoughts' profundity . . . self-evident by furrowing his brow, yodeling, rolling his eyes, staring in front of him, taking the deep F in the bass scale." Kierkegaard's displeasure was due less to Grundtvig himself than to his disciples, the Grundtvigians, whom he tastefully calls "pure drivel heads." The drivel is due, among other things, to their ceaseless "rubbish about nationality," about the excellence of Danishness, which theologically speaking was a regular "step backward to paganism," seeing as "paganism's deification of nationalities" was just what Christianity "wanted to abolish." Straying even further from the path, the Grundtvigians had a predilection for exchanging the paradoxical aspects of Christianity with cossetting ideas of Christianity as "marvelously delightful, the delightful, the matchlessly delightful and deep, etc., in short *simple* categories," all of which were just as inappropriate as their promotion of childbearing and family life, which was in conflict with Christianity's innermost nature and, deep down, merely reflected "Jewish values." We note here again a coincidence between Søren and Regine's choice of words in distancing themselves from the Grundtvigian forms of life. Regine tries to explain Grundtvig's great age satirically by our Lord's rewarding him "in the Jewish manner" by allowing him to live long in the land. The coincidence is no less remarkable when we note that Regine cannot have derived her impertinence from Kierkegaard, since his journals were first published much later. It can only be put down to what, with all possible reservations, one might call kinship of spirit.

As for her remarks on "the good priests" who were more concerned to work "for their own kingdom than for God's kingdom," Regine could well have been inspired by the seventh number of *The Instant*, in which Kierkegaard ironizes over a certain theology graduate, Ludvig From (or Louis Devout), who appears in a "kind of short story" entitled "*First* the Kingdom of God." Ludvig From is a seeker. "And when one hears that a 'theological' graduate is seeking, one does not need a lively imagination to understand what it is that he is seeking— naturally, the kingdom of God, which, of course, one is to seek *first*. But no, it is not that; what he is seeking is a royal livelihood as a pastor."[22] Before getting that far, he *first* went to grammar school, after which he *first* took the obligatory first and second (university entrance) exams, and then after four years' studying, *first* the exam for his degree. So now he is a theology graduate, but that does not mean that he can begin working for Christianity; no, no, he must *first* have a half year at the pastoral seminary, and when that is over, according to existing regulations a further eight years are to go by before he can seriously devote himself to the priestly deed.

He finally gets a position, but no sooner is the appointment a fact than he learns that his income is a hundred and fifty rix-dollars less than he had reckoned with. Whereupon From almost despairs, immediately buys more stamped paper in order to solicit the minister for exemption from the position, but is talked out of it and comes to terms with his wretched condition. "He is ordained—and the Sunday arrives when he is to be presented to the congregation. The dean, by whom this is done, is a more than ordinary man, he not only has . . . an impartial eye for earthly gain, but also a speculative eye on world history, something he cannot keep for himself but lets the congregation share to its benefit." Parodically enough, the dean has chosen as his text the words of the apostle Paul on giving up everything and following Christ; then it is From's turn and the day's text is, ironically enough, the one about *first* seeking God's kingdom. "'A very good sermon,' says the bishop, who himself was present, 'a very good sermon; and it made the proper impression, the whole part about "first" the kingdom of God, the manner in which he emphasized this *first.*'"[23]

Regine's sneers at the priests, whose self-interest pushes "God's kingdom" shamefully into the background, have an obvious commonality with Kierkegaard's short story about Ludvig From, who had come near to running his legs off to provide for himself materially. It seems probable that among the unspecified "theological writings" that Regine had asked Henrik to send out to her were numbers of *The Instant*. If not, the similarity in language between the two formerly betrothed becomes so remarkable that one must grasp at explanations of a more metaphysical nature.

Still another motive for Regine's partiality could be her mixed feelings about Bolette Rørdam. Not only was she a Grundtvigian, but she had also been the object of Kierkegaard's interest before Regine's *entrée* that spring day in 1837 at Frederiksberg. This friend of her youthful days crops up only very sporadically in Regine's letters, but it is clear that Bolette and her family have left a deep impression in Regine's mind. Indeed she frankly confesses that, in her young days, she could feel an "excessively great sinfulness" when together with members of the Rørdam family, who presented themselves in her eyes as "almost holy persons." This had changed with time: "I by no means doubt my sinfulness now, but it has seemed to me since that their holiness stank a little." After saying that much Regine forces herself into silence and takes it that neither will Cornelia be able to "make much out of what I have written, since written language is unfortunately not something over which I have so much control." If Regine were to try to convince Cornelia that "it all made very good sense" when she thought it, this would hardly help, for "the point has got lost on the way from the head to the paper."

Regine's remark about the unsavoriness of Rørdamian holiness bears an unmistakable scent of its own, of inferiority and jealousy. And when she touched on the Rørdam family in a letter of the 12th of October 1857, her words were again less than conciliatory:

How amused we were, by your and Maria's letter, to hear a little about the Rørdams! Fritz the woman expert says it is entirely as he had expected of Bolette's supercilious worldly mind; but I think it is almost too bad! There is decidedly nothing to the whole Grundtvigian party and crowd: God preserve me from their Christianity.

It is unclear what Regine refers to here, but she may have heard that Bolette was married—at last. Bolette had spent ten of her youthful years as housekeeper to her elder brother, Peter Rørdam, who had studied theology together with Kierkegaard and since 1841 had been priest in Mern just south of Præstø at the southern end of Zealand. Bolette left no memoirs to posterity, so we know regrettably little of her life, but just over six miles from Mern lay the estate Iselingen, where the Aagaard family lived until 1866. Their foster daughter Charlotte has written about those years, describing how Peter Rørdam often came by, spreading joy with his lively and straightforward ways. At times he had the company of Bolette, whom little Charlotte found "entertaining and amusing." She recalls their very first meeting clearly:

> I well remember the first time I saw her, a summer day in Mern; we small ones were in church and afterwards at the parsonage. Bolette stood and talked eagerly, leaning against a doorpost, she had on a tight white dress and a light green waistband. Her lovely thick black hair sat in a big knot on her neck, and then her large, sharp, wise, light blue eyes. I thought that this was how Queen Margrethe must have looked. . . . At Iselinge we were very fond of Bolette, but our circle of acquaintances didn't much like her and called her "Princess Rørdam." She had a rather superior manner toward those she didn't bother about.[24]

This portrait from memory undoubtedly captures a side of Bolette: of strength and an assurance bordering on arrogance and self-conceit. But we also detect in Charlotte's description a fascination with Bolette's charismatic presence, effortlessly combining physical elegance with intellectual acuteness. So we are surely not mistaken in detecting something like envy in Regine's remarks, and memories of an embarrassment that has never worn off.

". . . AS THOUGH I WERE 16 AGAIN AND NOT 36"

In mid-November Regine mentions a "dinner party for ladies from St. Thomas," but she cannot tell us anything about the gathering "since it has vanished from my memory without trace." And then: "This evening we were to have a card game here in the house, that's nothing for me." It was a small bright spot that

Mrs. Schwartz and Mrs. Meineke were invited, but, to be really honest, Regine would rather sit alone by herself:

> I surely don't need to whisper in your ear that I would rather see them
> go, and could sit in peace and remain silent, instead of now having to
> sit and converse; but one mustn't be so egotistical, and it doesn't help
> if I say that it is a family weakness from which we all suffer; I at least
> should have been cured of it, for I have had occasions enough for hav-
> ing to get the better of myself; but what help is that, nature outshines
> discipline.

Usually it was the opposite; usually it was discipline that outshone nature, or duty that triumphed over inclination. The days assumed a certain uniformity, there was nothing to fill the time, and the letters became correspondingly empty. Regine knew it herself and frequently gave voice to the trivial life she led, but at the same time she let Cornelia understand that there was much more she could report if only, yes, if only the precious sister had been within reach:

> No this paper is full of a sheer lack of content! Alas, alas, I am so empty,
> just made for the West Indies! But my love for you is just as warm, and
> if I could fill my letter with talk about that, then there would be some
> content in it.

Regine had to write about other things, and woven through the letters for 1858 are remarks about Miss Simmelkjær's engagement and a couple of lines about Miss Krebs who had now returned from Nykøbing, where on Regine's initiative she had helped an elderly spinster named Cattala with the means to acquire fuel; about the scarlet fever that had been particularly virulent in Jutland, but thank the Lord never took foothold in the Winning's family in Horsens; about the large portrait of Laura, which was to return to Denmark with the *Concordia*, so Emil Bærentzen could avoid a catastrophe "since the frame over which the canvas was stretched is so worm-eaten that, here, the painting will surely one of these days fall out like a rag"; about a new big sending of oranges and "ditto salep," along with thirty-two bottles of "punch extract" to friends and acquaintances back home; about another cargo which was to go the same way with the brig *Georg* and consisted of "the usual 6 barrels of sugar, 12 bottles of guava rum, 48 glasses of old rum, a case with 9 jars of pineapple jam"; about the many hours spent sewing her own and Thilly's dresses—"I unpick and sew like mad, so that it is a delight," which was something the "nosy sewing ladies who go around telling everything in town" are very busy shouting from the rooftops to God and everyone; and about the mornings with Thilly, who has still to be kept to the books with a hard hand, but who grew and matured and developed and could not sit still very long at a time, so when a whole "circus company" came to St. Croix at the beginning of July, she really had "a fever of longing to come out there" and "literally couldn't think of anything else."

Exposed to these West Indian trivialities, and as the more intellectual big sister, Cornelia has clearly felt emboldened to suggest that Regine could perhaps spend time catching up on the latest books and reviews, to which her little sister, hurt, replied:

> You doubt whether I read the critics of our new literature, yes indeed, I say, like you, if I can't get hold of a book to read I make do with the review, besides there is no fear here of coming to prostitute oneself, since here they read absolutely nothing.

The ignorant West Indian women had a demotivating effect; presumably they would never dream of opening a book, having more than enough to chatter about with their ceaseless gossiping. But nor did the fact that the new times had introduced women authors in any way appeal to Regine:

> Like you, I have also noted that our sex has become author-happy. God help us, as though there wasn't enough junk already in print; but let them have the joy so long as I don't have to read it, and there is no danger of that. Like you, I read much Dickens, it is a pleasure after all to have time enough that the thicker the book I begin on, the happier I am.

Regine's scornful comments on the writing-mad women could have been directed at a writer such as Mathilde Fibiger, who with her novel *Clara Raphael, Tolv Breve* (Clara Raphael, Twelve Letters) of December 1850 had made a decisive contribution to the domestic discussion of women's liberation and rights. Fibiger was in many ways a Danish equivalent of the French feminist George Sand, but in her style tended more toward Thomasine Gyllembourg's everyday stories and Hans Christian Andersen's novels and tales. The latter was very appreciative of Fibiger's style, though the book's ideological content evoked his condemnation. Shocked, he wrote to Henriette Wulff: "The style is quite admirable, but the idea in itself eccentric, untrue and unnatural."

Like Cornelia, Regine preferred the humor-spiced narratives of Dickens, who wrote those thick books that Regine nevertheless was unable to read at length, her head simply not being "strong enough." But when, in the course of the day, she sat and fussed with needle and thread, she could work up a kind of reading appetite and in the evening really devote herself to "a good book which, thanks to Fritz's foresight, is never wanting." Fritz's library contained, we can assume, a judicious selection of J. L. Heiberg's works, among them some of his vaudevilles, those light and engaging entertainments that saw the light of day in the 1820s and 30s, and were Heiberg's most successful contribution to Danish theater. In mid-May, Regine exclaimed in her letter to Cornelia:

> Do you know what I have been reading recently? Heiberg's vaudevilles! And will you believe me, I have read them so that the tears have run down my cheeks. I don't know whether it was this healthy laughter, or the scent of the vaudevilles, or youthful memories connected with them, or indeed all of them together, but I felt so young through reading them, oh so youthfully fresh as though I were 16 again and not 36.

It was certainly all of these together, the healthy laughter, the lovely scent, the innumerable youthful memories, that made the tears run so freely that Regine suddenly felt two decades younger and happily transported to times long vanished. Although vaudevilles, which usually offered sweet, simple songs, did not aim to bring the deepest of furrows to their audience's brows, this form of theater was not only sheer froth. It might, for example, contain mild satire on social situations, ironize over poor teaching in private schools, or expose the ridiculous things that were to be read in the small-talk journalism of the time.

But what Heiberg's vaudevilles offered, from first to last, were conflicts of love of the delightfully resolvable kind, and good-humored jabs at the inhumanly extended periods of betrothal to which bourgeois parents exposed their lovesick children, as Regine knew all too well, having twice tried her hand at it. Five years in all. And that was a long time to be a small, passionate, virginal Miss Olsen.

"WHAT AN ENORMOUS LOSS, THAT MRS. HEIBERG HAS LEFT THE THEATER!"

While Regine wept from happiness in the West Indian heat over youth's irresponsible situation comedies, Heiberg had quite other reasons for which he might have let fall a tear—if he had been the sort to do so, which he was decidedly not: after seven irascible years as director of the Royal Theater, he had chosen to take his leave. He was tired and his mind was made up. Since his appointment in 1849, not only had he had to take on—as he himself put it—"an unbelievable mass of inane details," but also had had to fight several battles with the theater's younger forces, the Messrs. Frederik Ludvig Høedt and Michael Wiehe in particular, both undeniably talented but with demands for scenographic innovations and a more dramatic repertory that grated with Heiberg's conservative taste.[25] When his decision to withdraw became known, the Copenhagen press, against whom Heiberg had been so bold as to take up arms, was not sparing in the malice of its good wishes. *Fædrelandet* announced on the 5th of June 1856:

> At last the event has befallen that has been anticipated with so much longing by all friends of art: Councillor Heiberg has given up his directorship. Last Saturday the curtain fell on a time that we hope will never return for Danish dramatic art.[26]

Mrs. Heiberg, who defended her husband with admirable solidarity throughout their lives together, and indeed far beyond his death, was also exposed to the conceited stupidity of the modern press. It was more than hinted, and increasingly, that she had benefited well from her close connection to the directorship, which cast her in roles for which she was really too old. At first Mrs. Heiberg tried to ignore the criticism, but after a period of leave in 1858, when she could no longer hold out, she left the Royal Theater. When the sad news reached Christiansted after the usual delay, Regine was disappointed and resentful:

> What an enormous loss, that Mrs. Heiberg has left the theater! And as far as I could understand the newspapers, she was really driven from it through bad treatment. Our little friend, Councillor Kuntzen said the other day that one lives a cud-chewing existence out here from constantly having to live off the memories one has brought from home; and it was exactly of Mrs. Heiberg that we were speaking; but that is how you must all live now at home, for, truly, a theater season without Mrs. Heiberg is poverty.

Regine's reaction to Mrs. Heiberg's exit may reasonably be said to cover a whole generation's sense that an epoch in the history of the Danish theater had come to a definite close: for more than a generation Mrs. Heiberg had been the uncontested prima donna, who thanks to her effervescent sensuousness, scenic genius, and intellectual gifts attained near divine status. She was not just a rose-perfumed incarnation of all romanticism but also her worth in gold as an icon, and as a brand name that the business world knew how to exploit by offering all sorts of bargain-priced merchandise to her innumerable fans. Her portrait could be bought as copperplate or sewn onto a handkerchief or ingeniously fastened to the crown of a hat. But it was also possible to savor a Mrs. Heiberg cigar, or use one's savings on plants, lamps, soaps, cakes, and chocolates bearing her name—and then perhaps, finally, to hum to a waltz that H. C. Lumbye himself had named after the Danish diva.

FRITZ AND HIS TORMENTORS

It was difficult for Regine to keep up with theater life in Copenhagen. The advance notices were delayed, and sometimes the reviews first became available after a show had closed. The principal roles in her daily existence were played by the weather and general issues of well-being: "As for our states of health, they are really good just now and in spite of our having such terribly dry and hot weather; we ride a little and drive a little, and so the days go." So, too, went one of the days in March. Fritz had invited Mrs. Schmidt on "a drive over the North Side Hills down to the West End," where the small party, which included Thilly, "had breakfast under a tree" and then went in "to lunch with Rahrs," a lunch which Fritz had to forgo due to official business at West End, "so as to combine business with pleasure," as Regine put it.

The pleasure was limited because it became so hot that day that the beads of sweat ran down one's body in small unstoppable rivers and made the clothes stick; yes, Thilly became directly ill "so that she didn't recover until she got to sleep in my arms on the way home." Regine, now otherwise fairly acclimatized, also suffered from the heat—"I imagine that I can feel as though the heat sucks the vitality out of me like a vampire."

Regine's report on the scorching breakfast in the greenery is readily supported by some of the statistics that Fritz and his staff perspired over for the government gazette, *Departementstidenden*. Already nine days into January, which in Denmark is usually the beginning of a severe winter, it could be announced:

> In the last half of November and until the report went out, a good deal of rain had fallen on St. Croix, which has had a fortunate effect on the sugarcane's growth, but the continuous rain for from 12 to 24 hours, or a so-called season, which is necessary for opening the springs and underground water courses, and without which even a shorter time's drought cannot be prevented, is something the island has not had.[27]

The general state of health of the man who, as the islands' highest authority, was to report month after month to *Departmentstidenden* was far from optimal. Fritz had been frail for some time and had caught a cold he could not be "quit" of. Dr. Aagaard, a man of the old school who did nothing unless "there was danger afoot" had, on her "appealing," as Regine explains, "prescribed a cup of bitter herbal tea in the evening before going to bed." It sounds unappetizing and Fritz would sooner sneak away so that Regine really had to go after him. To Oluf, who was in Copenhagen at the time, she confided:

Can you remember, Oluf, how Fritz can be poorly over long periods?
And the worst is that he loses his humor, and then it is doubly difficulty
for me to get him out driving or riding, and neither can I deny that,
for him who never cares much for getting about, it is a stiff cure to get
out *par force* in this way, when one simply feels heavy and indisposed,
but . . . I become untiring, even if one day I get dispirited and give up
when quite seriously he calls me his tormentor, so then I begin over
again, I have been lucky enough, after a whole week's stoppage, to get
him out on a riding tour today in which we managed at best a small
drive in the evening.

The bitter bedside tea was not enough to restore Fritz's humor, and Dr. Aagaard's
forbearance was no doubt due to his medicine chest not containing any effective remedies for the low spirits of which Fritz's persistent cold was presumably
but a physical consequence. A small episode in July speaks, in its own low-
key language, of the vitreous fragility that had gradually found its way into the
governor and his wife. The external occasion was a letter from Jonas, whom
they rarely heard from and whose letter therefore attracted special attention.
It was, to be sure, a "lovely letter," explains Regine bravely to Cornelia, but also
stamped with the minus "that it was rather too long to read in a tropical climate." Fritz and Regine, though, had made careful preparations and "chosen a
Sunday morning." There was no Church service, so they "could read the letter
in undisturbed peace." It went badly all the same:

> Fritz read it aloud for me, as he usually does, and I listened; but would
> you believe it, out here one is so weak that when I'd heard most of it,
> a cold sweat broke out on my brow and I felt as though about to faint;
> that Fritz became hoarse from reading was reasonable, since he has
> had a cold and has been coughing for over a month.

It was hardly the letter's length alone that caused the perspiration and hoarse-
ness; their physical reactions undoubtedly had an additional source deep down
in a repressed longing to be united with their loved ones in the far-off fatherland. Never before had Fritz been so tired of his calling, which was making ever
more demands on him while all the time fewer people appreciated his efforts.
"The situation gets constantly more difficult, Fritz's work constantly increases,
and people are becoming constantly more discontented, impossible to please."

The general displeasure grew and at the end of August Regine, as in a pained
whisper, let Cornelia understand that Fritz had for a time been considering
giving up his post in preference for "Garlieb's position." Seventy-one-year-old
Peter Johann Gottfried Garlieb wanted to resign from his position as depart-

mental head for trade and consulate matters in the foreign affairs ministry. He had given Fritz timely notice of his intention and let fall a remark that could be read "as if he would like to have him as his successor." Fritz had replied that, if that were the case, "then he was more than willing to forgo his large salary, glittering position, etc. to come home." This unqualified consent to the proposal was followed by a long and painful period, for not a word came from Garlieb. But then finally, "with the last boat," Fritz and Regine "received ease for the expectant heart."

The position had not gone to Fritz but to *Geheime-Legationsraad* Adolph Skrike, who was departmental head in the foreign affairs ministry and a Knight of the Russian Order of Saint Anna, of the Swedish Northern Star, and of the Dutch Order of the Lion, but now could add to his visiting card "Colonial Director." Skrike was recognized as an efficient and charitable man and was on innumerable committees, so Fritz could have nothing to object to the appointment, neither on a human nor a professional level. He took the defeat like a man, but the whole process pained Regine, "for he would so rather have been home, and that is not so strange, if once in a while he wants to be free of all the burdensome responsibilities heaped on his shoulders out here."

So much for Fritz according to Regine, but then we hear from Regine according to herself: "You have no doubt also now been aching to know my own feelings during this time of waiting? Well, they were very mixed." In the first place, there had been consideration for Oluf who, after several months in Denmark, was on his way back to St. Croix. Regine simply could not bear the thought of her mild and gentle elder brother sitting alone back in Christiansted if Fritz had actually taken Garlieb's position. Secondly, it had cost Regine "such unspeakable struggles" to accustom herself to West Indian conditions that she had made up her mind to put up with the remaining two years. Finally, and/or in third place, she found that Fritz was doing a lot of good in his position and felt that he should therefore stay on. "From all this you now see that I really have taken on not a little of Fritz's tenacity in my nature!" came the stoic assurance in her letter. But her heart was decidedly not made of tempered steel:

> For regardless now of everything I have written, you know the contradictions in a human heart well enough to understand me when I tell you that I nevertheless had to weep so heartily when I came to know for certain that all hope was lost.

"—AND WHEN I GREW DIZZY THROUGH GAZING DOWN INTO HER INFINITE DEVOTION"

Such contradictions in the human heart were something Kierkegaard also knew. On Monday the 26th of October 1841, he found himself in a cabin on board the royal mail steamship *Königen Elisabeth* on course for Ystad and Stralsund, whence "Mr. Magister Aaby-Kierkeyoord," as he had come to be called on the passenger list, was to be conveyed further on to Berlin. Fourteen days earlier he had broken up with Regine, inexorably and definitively. But she was intensely present in his thoughts down there in the cabin, where he tried to abstract himself from the steamship's rumbling engines and write his way into a kind of clarity. In a more or less fictitious conversation with himself, he wanted to give shape to the nature and scope of his loss in having left Regine, whose "depth" he opposes, in some staccato summarizing clauses, to his own "instability." After which he continues in a fragmented vein:

> . . . and when I grew dizzy gazing down into her infinite devotion; for nothing is as infinite as love—or when her emotions did not sink into the depths in this way—but danced away over them in the light play of love——what have I lost, the only thing I loved, in people's eyes my word as a gentleman, what have I lost, that in which I always have and, without fear of this blow, always shall place my honor, my joy, my pride——being faithful. . . . Yet my soul at the moment of writing this is as turbulent as my body——in a cabin rocked by the pitching and rolling of a steamship.[28]

It gives the feeling that the sentences have been torn thoroughly from one another and have become quite literally so disjointed that they appear to run on aimlessly. Before the *Königen Elisabeth* docked at Stralsund, Kierkegaard had managed to add a few more entries in his journal, among them this:

> You say: she was beautiful. Oh, what do you know about that; I know, for this beauty has cost me tears—I myself bought flowers to adorn her; I would have decked her out with all the ornaments in the world, only, of course, so far as they accentuated her loveliness—and then, when she stood there in her finery—I had to leave—I went out and wept bitterly.[29]

What begins here as a sensitive and almost touching celebration of Regine's beauty is given a disconsolate exit—for "wept bitterly" was what Peter did when he betrayed his lord and master and the cock crowed for the third time. The last that Kierkegaard managed in his cabin was to write three small lines that, unlike the former, which made Regine an object of his observation, allowed her to take the opposite position and to observe him:

> She did not love my shapely nose, nor my fine eyes, nor my small feet—nor my good mind—she loved only me, and yet she didn't understand me.[30]

In an unkind mood, one might allow oneself to smile at the characteristics Kierkegaard points to in himself, the nose, the eyes, the small feet, and the brilliant mind. The point, though, is that it was neither these nor any other *qualities* that Regine loved, not this or another excellence, because she loved *him*, unreservedly, unconditionally, totally, as he had never before been loved. So much the deeper, then, was the tragic element in the consequent "and yet she did not understand me," which in a way cancels Regine's devotion with a retroactive thrust. If one loves but without understanding the one who is loved, then the love obviously falls short, is inadequate and doomed to fail. But is this what love is? Is it so very much more important to be understood than to be loved? Is such a distinction at all meaningful? And how did Kierkegaard, down there in the cabin, know that Regine did not understand him? Or that he had understood her? How could he be so certain that she did not in some respects understand him better than he understood himself? Can it not be imagined that the insistence with which the other's understanding is demanded is due precisely to a *weakness* in one's *own* self-understanding? Has that person, in other words, who so unconditionally demands to be understood by another, really understood himself?

Kierkegaard complained of his "instability" and was fond, then and later, of quoting Socrates's remark that he could not definitely know to what extent he was a human being with the necessary self-knowledge and a part in the divine, or instead a being even more changeable and incalculable than the mythological Typhon, who had all of a hundred dragon heads and eyes that emitted fire. After spending some summer months up at Gilleleie with a view to coming further along with his studies and finding himself, the twenty-two-year-old Kierkegaard had noted laconically in his green-shaded diary: "What did I find? Not my I." In order to be himself he must accordingly enter on an existential grand tour with this "I" as both a compass bearing and an ultimate goal. To what extent and when in fact Kierkegaard arrived at the authentic version of his "I" remains an open question, but what is certain is that the compass with which he tried to orientate himself along the way pointed in the most varied directions and led him far into the world of fictional literature, where, uninhibitedly, he experimented undercover with potential versions of his own "I." It took on the guise of diverse pseudonymous authors and involved numberless fictional figures whom Kierkegaard either took over from the enormous fund of world literature or conjured up from the magic darkness of his own inkwell. And some of the fascination with the existential "experimentarium," which this authorship amounts to, is indeed precisely that its constructor is him*self* actively engaged in the various experiments, is him*self* on the way to *his* self and therefore passionately present—but this does not mean that we can point to Kierkegaard in this or that actual figure, for they continually relieve or succeed one another and in doing so lead their author—and the reader—further toward new figures and increased self-insight.

Kierkegaard's journey to Kierkegaard is to be followed first and foremost in the wealth of journals in which he sketches and describes the different stages on his life's way. The accounts are to be found in entries like "About Myself," or are undertaken in more graphic form, as in an entry from 1837 where Kierkegaard compares himself sadly to the Roman god Janus, who with his two faces could look both backwards and forwards in time: "I am a Janus bifrons: with one face I laugh, with the other I weep."[31] That the comparison was well chosen was confirmed as the production that was his life took shape and made clear that the categorical *either/or* for which Kierkegaard became world famous should have been *both/and*, because that came much closer to his own dialectical nature. Thus he became *both* melancholy's theologian *and* irony's Magister, *both* edifying author *and* merciless prophet, *both* rhetorical artist *and* critic of the aesthetic, *both* the paradoxical thinker *and* the teller of simple tales, *both* Copenhagen's dandy millionaire *and* modernity's martyr, *both* the epitome of anxiety *and* the fearless polemicist, *both* a self-effacing penitent *and* monumentally self-aware, *both* the refined aristocrat *and* the open-handed street preacher, *both* a classical master-thinker *and* a teasing deconstructionist, *both* the pious monk *and* the devil-may-care enjoyer of life, *both* absolutely unmarried *and* yet betrothed for all eternity to the love of his youth.

This, then, was the man Regine loved, naturally not because of his nose, eyes, feet, or mind, and scarcely either because he was this incomprehensibly rich example of humankind, but far more miraculously because he was in her eyes "that particular individual" whom she so dearly loved that she was ready to take up lodging in a modest cabinet in his elegant apartment, just to be in his vicinity. And then, for heaven's sake, he sat there and lamented that she didn't *understand* him! Understood *who*, one might ask, understood *which* Kierkegaard? Was this not an outrageously unreasonable demand from a man who throughout his life had struggled to understand himself!

In the happily breathless entry about Regine as his "sovereign mistress," Kierkegaard asked himself whether Regine might form the conclusion of his "life's eccentric premises." From a narrow historical point of view, there can be no doubt of the answer, but in a wider and more meaningful perspective the answer becomes far less unequivocal. Regine became the conclusion of Kierkegaard's eccentric premises in the sense that, through her, he learned that *the understanding* of the other means less than *the love* for the other. It came slowly, perhaps, but this recognition did come to Kierkegaard, as he let it be known once in 1853, when he had once again installed himself in a cabin, this time of a more metaphorical quality, but again with Regine in mind:

> I live now in melancholy's separate cabin—but I can take pleasure in seeing the pleasure of others. . . . To be loved by a woman, to live in a happy marriage, pleased with life—that is now denied me; but when I go out from my separate cabin, I can take pleasure in seeing the happiness of others, can strengthen them in it being well pleasing to God to be happy in life and to enjoy it. To be healthy and strong, a complete person, for whom there is hope for a long life ahead—this, now, is never to be granted me. But when, then, on coming out from my lonely pain among the happy, I believed I could have the sorrowful pleasure of strengthening them in being thus happy with life.[32]

Pleasure over the pleasure of others becomes just as enigmatic as the love out of which this pleasure springs. Correspondingly enigmatic is the love that has its origin in God, who has lodged it in our hearts, for what does that really say? No one knows, no one understands it, but perhaps one receives a hint of it when, somewhere in *Works of Love*, Kierkegaard writes so grandly:

> As the calm lake stems from the deep springs that no eye saw, so too a person's love has a still deeper ground, in God's love. If there were no gushing spring at the bottom, if God were not love, then neither would there be the little lake nor either a person's love. As the calm lake stems darkly from the deep spring, so does a person's love originate *mysteriously* in God's. As the calm lake indeed invites you to contemplate it, yet with the darkness of the reflection prevents you from seeing through it, so does love's *mysterious* origin in God's love prevent you from seeing its ground. When you think you see it, it is a reflection that deceives you, as if what only hides the deeper ground were itself the ground.[33]

1859

༺࿇༻

"THEY PLAYED MOSTLY DANCE MUSIC"

Winter had arrived in the West Indies, but as always it brought with it a salutary snugness:

> We have it pleasantly cool here now. The water we take a morning bath in is so cold that I shiver when I get into the bathtub, and on my early morning ride I have to let my horse trot away all it can to keep me warm. Now I ride alone with the coachman, since poor Fritz is so fatigued after the day's load that he really can't go without sleep in the morning, so he rides before dinner with Oluf, but I can't manage that since I simply can't eat after a ride, and without food and drink the hero is nothing, as you no doubt know.[1]

True enough, but with an excess of food and drink he is no better off, for then he becomes inactive and idle. While the slim, erect Birch rode both morning and evening and did "almost too much for his health," Fritz did "all too little, or rather, [he did] absolutely nothing," and with all due respect, had become "stout." "You know the Schlegelian immobility well enough; he always has some work or other as his excuse." She herself tried to maintain a slim figure by frequent swimming and riding, now that the trauma caused by her fall three years earlier was happily behind her. Second to the stay at Cane Garden, she wrote, these "morning tours" on warm, rhythmic horseback would be among the "finest memories I will take from here."

Among the less formal diversions in this period, there was a concert with "3 brothers from Naples," whose musical ability was not that impressive, "but what excellence can one expect here in the West Indies where the conditions are in every respect so unfortunate." This matter of being unfortunate was something the three brothers themselves had been forced to experience, for on their arrival in the West Indies they had been five and able to call themselves a quintet. One died on St. Croix and another on St. Thomas, after which the brothers had to content themselves with being a trio. When these doomed fiddlers found themselves one morning at Government House and extended an offer to Fritz to play at "our soirée," Fritz had been softhearted and engaged them—"and then word was sent out to the town and the housekeeper made cakes, etc." In the evening "people swarmed in here so that even our big rooms began to be overfilled. They played mostly dance music, and people had a wonderful time." On a quite usual Monday, yet another successful festivity had taken place, but one that was out of the ordinary in several respects. Regine had heard that the youngest of Stackemann's daughters, whom Regine could recall from some summers in Humlebæk, was unhappy at not being able to celebrate her birthday, because her mother "was still confined to bed after the birth of a little boy." Regine grabbed the chance to improvise a birthday party in Government House and saw to it that the good news was quickly circulated throughout the town:

> And then a crowd of people also came, probably 60. And there was good music here, excellent illumination, champagne, cakes, and salads, etc. People enjoyed themselves immensely, and the young girl was in bliss. What a delight.

At the end of April there was a dinner for the newly "arrived priest family, who have had a 4 month journey out here," which Regine not inappropriately described as "rather long." They were the thirty-two-year-old Daniel Christian Vater, together with his wife Camilla Marie Unna of twenty-seven summers, and a batch of unspecified "young sisters-in-law." They were due to move further west to the parsonage in Frederiksted and were definitely good and sensible people, but in the end Regine became heartily tired of being a talking, handshaking and politeness machine, all the time having to make "acquaintance with total strangers only in one way or another to lose sight of them after a short while, it makes me sick at heart when I feel a loss, or else I also grieve over my hardheartedness when I feel no loss at all, which is really most often the case!"

Seeing that the large hall was "so dilapidated" that restoration was impossible, the celebration of Frederik VII's birthday on the 6th of October had to be canceled. Although the situation in the Colonial Council was not much better, for several of the council's members could have done with a brush up, Fritz bid a new season welcome on Saturday the 19th of November and later in the day hosted the traditional dinner party, which was "elegant in the highest degree." Fritz was in full uniform and she herself in "the blue moirée" that had been hanging so long in its cupboard that it "began to be stained with damp" and was almost begging to be used. "As always I had my little *Conferentsraad* as my table partner since he is chairman in the Colonial Council, so he shall enjoy the honor every time," explained Regine, who did not wish to elaborate on the "Colonial Council's activity" since it would be much too tedious, but anything "great or good they have not accomplished."

Unusually, on Christmas Day Fritz and Regine were in the Catholic Church, their own priest having been loaned to St. Thomas. The Catholic clergy had, according to Regine, a strained relationship with the Danish government and caused Fritz a deal of "bother," so it was a well-remarked sign of courtesy that

38. At that time, too, there was lively traffic on Kongensgade, which the photographer has captured around 1900, when electricity cables had made their entrance and can be seen stretching past the school building's gallery at second-floor level. Visible behind the large treetop on the right is the four-cornered tower of the Protestant church, which was a neighbor to Government House. Before the end of Kongensgade, there is just a hint of Christiansted's harbor.

he and his wife came to *their* church. Regine was, to put it mildly, not impressed with the service and in her letter to Cornelia sighed, "Alas, how little of Christ's spirit there is in any of his churches here on earth, but to me it seems least in the Catholic." After the service, the Bishop thanked them so persistently that Fritz and Regine could find no excuse not to invite him and his colleagues to dinner:

> 3rd day of Christmas the Catholic Bishop ate here with all his priests, he was an elderly man, gentle and pleasant in his being, he was a Frenchman, born in Brittany, and he would have been very interesting to talk with, since he was very knowledgeable, if he hadn't been rather deaf.

Besides the hard-of-hearing bishop and the many priests, the guests at the dinner party were members of the Catholic congregation, who were for the most part Irish and "have been managers, and later worked their way up to being plantation owners." Excessively cultured they were not, but at least they made "good use of a dining table by eating and drinking well, so the mood became lively." When, by way of conclusion, the partially deaf bishop proposed a toast to the Governor's wife, things went less well. One of the Irishmen, who had enjoyed a drop too many, had forgotten the hostess's name and managed in a loud voice to toast "Mrs. Feddersen." Regine calls the episode a "little mistake," which must be considered a charitable understatement, the more so as the Mrs. Feddersen for whom she was mistaken had been dead these six years.

THE FRENCH OFFICER—A LITTLE WEAKNESS

"... we had always to acquire our youth's pleasures through dangers and annoyances," Regine declares, her thoughts going back to the upbringing to which she and her siblings had been subjected. The forbidden fruit tastes best, for nothing is as inviting as a boundary, nothing as tempting as an abyss, scarcely anything teases more than a taboo, of this Regine is in no doubt—"no, the perils before we came to enjoy it were after all the best seasoning." If such an upbringing, in which most enjoyments had to be taken on the sly, without the knowledge and consent of parents, might strike some as "bad upbringing," it was at least an antidote to the philistinism and staidness of later life: "... for now, for example: you and I, who now both live in a market town, I haven't a moment's fear that you shall be infected by the narrow-mindedness that always prevails in such places." Nor can Regine imagine herself ending up like one of those cut-to-size conformist market town wives, for like Cornelia she has preserved an element of rebelliousness in her nature, which prompts her to ask, half rhetorically:

> ... shouldn't we suppose the germ of that was planted in our fantastic young days? Wouldn't one or another image from that time always come and startle us when we were in utter danger of sinking right down into the fleshpots of Egypt?

Regine provides no chapter and verse to what she refers to as her "fantastic youth," but we understand that she and Cornelia have kept some well-preserved memory-images from that period, pictures that, one might say, develop themselves whenever the Olsen sisters are in danger of falling into apathetic self-satisfaction, a process that Regine sums up as a "sinking right down into the fleshpots of Egypt." A delightful aspect of that expression is that it reaches all the way back to a critical phase in the engagement, when Kierkegaard put it into Regine's letter-hungry head that she was decidedly "too poetic to long to return to the fleshpots of Egypt." Do we dare to speculate that Regine has been rereading the love letters and, with a kind of tingle of indignation, has snatched hold of that striking expression and then woven it into her letter to Cornelia? And was it perhaps Kierkegaard's scorn for the bourgeoisie's banal routines and anemic notions of love that rekindled in Regine as she sat thinking back on her "fantastic youth"? The resoluteness with which she leaves the temptations of the uncontrolled past behind her and hurries apologetically back to the eventless present would in any case render such an assumption plausible:

> There, now you can see what nonsense one can come up with in filling a letter from lack of material, indulge a poor muddle-head who only now recalls that she could have filled the whole letter with common-place Christmas and New Year's wishes!

Clearly Regine found it much more meaningful to tiptoe around like an explorer in her own enigmatic past than to put a chatty letter together with conventional Yuletide greetings. What also leaps to the eye, tentatively stowed away in the word "nonsense," is the unresolved nature of her real difficulties—the disparity between what can be written, which will have to pass through a gauntlet of censorship, and all the much else that Regine would *much rather* have imparted. We read in a letter of the 11th of February:

> Look now, I have now filled 4 pages, but I couldn't exactly have said the same in 4 words; my letter is empty! And yet I don't feel empty myself, alas no, often I have so many thoughts that they won't leave me in peace; but write them down, that I neither can nor will. Today I have longed for you, oh, like the first day I left you! Alas, as old as I am, how I so very much long at times to be caressed, by you.

Although at that time people aged significantly earlier than today, Regine's remark about being old clearly conceals a certain coquetry, as is proved both directly and indirectly in other places in her letters. That she was far from having lost a sense of the power of sex becomes clear, for example, from a piquant episode whose more detailed logistical circumstances were quite complex but which had their proper beginning when a "steam warship" from Martinique docked at St. Croix and the captain came on land with his officer—for yes, indeed, there was an officer!

> My own sister, you have the same weakness as I, so I need only tell you that there was a Frenchman and you will know that he was to my liking, and also would have been to yours; but in my own justification I will add that he really was an unusually cultivated and likeable marine officer, and I can prove it to you through Fritz and Oluf, both having thought so well of him, and the latter as you no doubt well know is very particular.

The incomparable officer had taken part in the Crimean War in 1855 and told grippingly of the bravery he and his countrymen displayed in the fight against the Russians, "but [he] never went too far." The war ended with a crushing Russian defeat at the famous battle of Sebastopol on the 11th of September, a date that has a definite tendency to attract catastrophes. "George Sand's countryman," as Regine called her officer, further proved to be of the nobility and could consequently entertain "a part of the society in Paris and the beautiful Empress, for whom he had a weakness." Perhaps the charismatic officer developed a little weakness for Regine, who seems to have so enjoyed the attention shown her that she continues her description with the following apologia:

> You mustn't wonder that he came to be spoken of so much, but he came up to us at 10 o'clock in the morning and was here until 10 in the evening . . . on Sunday he came up just to say goodbye, and then stayed a whole 2 hours and talked, so we became better acquainted with him in one and a half days than with many Englishmen in one and a half years.

On Saturday a dinner party was arranged in Government House, but it was not "agreeable." Apart from Regine herself, there were only a very few French speakers present, so the party became "unpleasantly silent, and then I mostly heard the captain's and my own voice." It is unclear whether the officer had been promoted in Regine's letter, or whether she had the ship's commander, the captain himself, as her table companion, which is the more likely. But in any event it was a painful matter that it was only he and she who spoke together, while the rest of the guests sat and clinked their knives and forks. The evening's host cannot have cared much for the situation either. First there had been the gallant and courteous officer who was openly prepared to wait on his wife in every possible way, and then this conspicuous silence at an official dinner, where he was unable to make his mark in conversation.

THE COLLECTIVELY UNUTTERABLE AND
SOME STOLEN REFLECTIONS

"Really I shouldn't be writing to you now since I am tired in both mind and fingers," writes Regine to Cornelia in mid-November 1858. "It is now the 4th letter I am starting on today and you will therefore forgive me for it being as it will." Writing was not really, for Regine, the necessity of life that it was for Kierkegaard, but neither was it merely a way of whiling away the time in the tropics. In fact, she often sat writing "most of the day," but then had to "lie fallow a bit to collect material." Usually she quickly "used up events in a letter" and toward the end "I am always quite empty." Sometimes she fantasized about being able to write as well as Olivia, who had a real "talent for letter-writing" and managed,

charmingly enough, as though to "shake different things out of an empty sack."
Maria could do something of the same sort, and though she was perhaps not
the world's greatest stylist, her letters were "in a way excellently written," since
she communicated so modestly and directly that it was almost as if what she
reported was happening before the recipient's very eyes. Cornelia, too, could
paint pictures and inject vigor into her words, writing in a way that made episodes come alive so that they became solid, full of sensations that stayed in the
memory long after the letter had been read and carefully tucked back into its
envelope. Regine found her own letters on the contrary often so dilettantish that
perhaps they should never have been written, let alone sent. She felt she had not
at all captured the reality, the smells, the sounds, the exotic folklore in these foreign surroundings that really burst with engaging topics and quirky tales that
could have gone directly into her letters to Cornelia—if only Regine had possessed the necessary knack.

She might shrewdly have brought other correspondents, besides her sisters,
into these comparative studies had the situation permitted. Kierkegaard's letters
would have lent themselves perfectly to stylistic and rhetorical analyses, profes-
sionally turned as they were, or rather *also* were. Kierkegaard was never at a loss
when it came to getting much out of nothing and could, to that extent like Olivia,
shake a variety of things out of an empty sack. Quite minor events were enough,
or hastily thrown-off remarks, a tableau in the city or a situation on the sofa, even
a shift in the weather or a change of season might provide opportunity for—
among other things, an allegory like one that according to its precise dating was
worked up on Wednesday the 28th October 1840, at 4 o'clock in the afternoon:

> *My Regine!*
>
> . . . And winter came, and the flowers withered, but some he took in
> and saved from the cold. And he sat by the window and, filled with
> yearning, held them up. But the life in them was too weak, and in order
> to preserve it if possible, he crushed them in his hand, and they died;
> but one drop remained, which, born in pain, has an immortality that
> only the fragrance of flowers have and old melodies.[2]

With overwhelming frequency Kierkegaard's letters are about the letters themselves. As we saw, the first of them all explained why Regine's name was un-
derlined ("serves to direct the typesetter to space out that particular word").
Similarly, other letters have as their topic the means of conveyance whereby they
succeeded in coming from the sender's point A to the recipient's point B. However, there are also letters that account for why they were written on certain days,
or quite to the contrary accentuate the meaning of their not having a date or

place of sending. Others, again, describe their own coming into being almost line by line, while Regine is all the time being told she is to add an erotic significance to the pen's rhythmic movements and to the ink that it empties onto the paper:

> . . . if you could then see what pains I take to write legibly, with what pleasure my hand delineates every letter, if you could see how lightly it rests upon the paper, and with what emphasis it dwells now and then, with what abandon it now and then flings out a flourish, but which does not go astray but bends back and rounds off the word—then you would know that I am thinking of you and that I read far more significant gestures into the movements of the pen.[3]

It would hardly be an excessive piece of "biographism" to transpose Kierkegaard's consciousness of his letter's eroticizing effect onto Johannes the Seducer, who in one passage in his diary confides to himself and to posterity:

> If I could stand behind Cordelia when she received a letter from me, it might be very interesting. Then I could convince myself more easily how far she had taken them in erotically in the most literal sense. On the whole, letters are and will always be an invaluable means for making an impression upon a young girl; often the dead symbol has far greater influence than the living word. A letter is a secret communication; you are master of the situation, feel no pressure from anyone's presence, and I think a young girl would really rather be quite alone with her ideal.[4]

If for a moment we ignore the ice cold cynicism that ripples beneath these lines, Johannes the Seducer betrays a nuanced psychological knowledge of the erotic fantasies that an effective letter can elicit in its recipient, who may become so thoroughly abandoned to the ideal love's most pure but also most sensual forms that the sender fades into the background or maybe even disappears altogether:

> When I am present only in a letter, she can easily stand up to me, she to some extent confuses me with a universal being who lives in her love. Also, in a letter it is easier to let oneself go; in a letter I can very well throw myself at her feet, etc., something that would very likely look nonsensical were I actually to do it, and the illusion would be destroyed. The contradiction in these movements will evoke and develop, strengthen and consolidate the love in her, in a word, tempt it.[5]

The letter opens the way to bold erotic posturing, as though it were a stage upon which Kierkegaard could do what would be impossible in real life. He could, for instance, transport Regine to far-off meadows with breath as the magical means of motion, or lead her down to the sea-bed to pleasantly furnished love cabins. But besides providing the setting for such fantastic trajectories, the letters also form a shield with which Kierkegaard can both protect himself against actual reality and safeguard an inwardness that neither can nor will reveal itself, or make itself known, say what it is—perhaps because language is the very thing that threatens to flatten, render hackneyed, or directly exhaust that inwardness. That of which one cannot speak, of which one should remain silent, was something Kierkegaard knew long before Wittgenstein.

This singular situation that Kierkegaard called "inwardness's incommensurability" was something that Regine came to know. It happened just as she sat trying to express what *really* lay in her mind. Her innermost thoughts, which had proved calamitous enough to resist transference to paper, suddenly no longer looked like themselves, since

> . . . when they are to be spun out in written language, then it looks to me as though they consist of wind and whimsy and were not sound thoughts that could be sent on in good order, yes in the end I have to declare my hand void, like Bolette in the old days, and say that I cannot express myself. And it is really hard for a governor's wife with standing, who has to express herself in several languages, not to be equal to written language.

Regine is being slightly facetious about this embarrassment of hers, but she cannot escape the fact that what is hardest to put into words is what matters most—as latter-day psychoanalysis would unhesitatingly grant her. She therefore feels a kind of solidarity with Bolette Rørdam, who also felt at times incapable of expressing herself and consequently declared that in the unregulated language-game of life, her hand was empty. But when it came to subjects other than her innermost thoughts and other quite private matters, the letters practically wrote themselves, sometimes so much so to that Regine had to remind herself to keep a level literary head.

> . . . in glancing out over the estate, which is wreathed in orange trees, where the yellow gold fruit are resplendent in the dark green leaves, and the sky is so delightfully blue that nothing competes with it but its own mirror image, the lovely sea that adds an even deeper blue shade; see when one now at least will receive this with thanks to all the giver's good gifts, so one has almost enough to compensate for the many dark hours and days, when the heart is so troubled that it seems a thick veil is drawn over all these glories, and the eye can reach no further than seeing the frightful images made by one's own imagination. But stop,

I believe God forgives me my grave sin, as Mother always said in the
old days, that I become quite poetic, but be comforted, my dear sister,
it is definitely not mine, no, I have no doubt stolen it from one or the
other bad novel I have been reading recently.

It is seldom that Regine allows herself to be so literary, and quite understandable
that she suddenly breaks it off and pushes it all aside as theft from a "bad novel."
We are nevertheless left wondering a little at the abruptness with which it occurs.
We would like to know what novel it was that Regine had "recently" been reading and which she now evidently found she was plagiarizing. She is not as a rule
communicative about her reading habits, so the book remains anonymous. And
the possibility remains that Regine had no specific novel in mind but was referring more broadly to an alien rhetoric and vocabulary that, in an unguarded
moment, has stolen its way into her letter. She never, as we have mentioned,
discusses Kierkegaard's writings in her correspondence with Cornelia; so it just
might be his poetic voice that suddenly begins to resound in her own quick,
workaday prose and makes it take a turn so conspicuously different from her
usual writing style. A series of expressions and motifs bear a clear Kierkegaardian stamp: the troubled heart, the contrast between imagination and reality, but
especially "the good giver's gifts," which occurs in several places in Kierkegaard,
first in the *Two Edifying Discourses* of 1843, whose preface introduced the description "the particular individual" used by Kierkegaard with Regine in mind.
Similarly Kierkegaardian is the picture of the sky reflecting itself in the sea. It
can be found in elegantly developed metaphorical form in several of the edifying
discourses, where the image of the sky is at one point calmly delineated in the
glassy surface of the sea, at another disturbed by the wind so that it disappears
into the deep. In his letters to his family and acquaintants, Kierkegaard also
comes up with a "mirror," but only in one single case does he use the word "mirror image," and that in the very letter to Regine, where we have read:

> . . . the moon . . . is outdoing itself in splendor, so as to eclipse the mir-
> ror image in the sea which seems to outshine it. . . .

It just might be this passage that floats into view as Regine writes to Cornelia:

> the sky is so delightfully blue that nothing competes with it but its own
> mirror image. . . .

Although Kierkegaard's train of thought departs in several ways from Regine's,
there is a near coincidence—or reflection, if you will—in the thought itself. And
Regine appears unable to let go of the water metaphor. In a letter that, according
to her calculations, should be in Cornelia's hands sometime in May, she imagines

the time having come for a "lovely cold swim," and refreshes Cornelia's memory in this connection on having "drowned our sorrows there."

> Let us do it still, my Cornelia, never drown our sorrows except in the water that is so clear and pure that it can reflect the image of the sky.

Here again there could be talk of a sly little loan from the former betrothed, who wrote in the last of his *Four Edifying Discourses* of 1844:

> When the ocean is exerting all its power, that is precisely the time when it cannot reflect the image of heaven, and even the slightest motion blurs the image; but when it becomes still and deep, then the image of heaven sinks into its nothingness.[6]

There is some coincidence of ideas here, even if Kierkegaard's train of thought is subtler. But most marked is the idea, found in both, of reproducing the image of the sky.

Kierkegaard tried to hide behind his pseudonyms. Regine tried to hide him with the help of a little white lie about her text being a theft from a "bad novel."

BIRTHDAYS—AND OTHER FATALITIES

Cornelia had thoroughly enjoyed Regine's portrait of the charming officer and at the end of September repaid with a kind greeting to "the unknown French personage of a captain." She was simply unable to put words to how much she would have liked to have been at the "dinner party," and even if her French was now a little rusty—yes, it hardly allowed her "to put two words together"—her "natural cheek" never left her at a loss for an opinion on most things in this world. The freshness in question was now unfortunately packed away like a dead chapter in Horsens, "since with the ladies one is rarely or never urged to abandon crinoline and the subject of toiletry, and with the ugly sex, crops and weather reports; so one is a little boring, like stagnant water."

Regine was afraid of sinking into the depths of the Egyptian fleshpots, Cornelia of ending like stagnant water; both had preserved their passion, their intensity, and that degree of rebelliousness required to oppose the smugness and despondency that so often accompanies an unrelieved domesticity. Cornelia's dauntlessness is shown by, among other things, the quick-wittedness she shows in connection with Emil's birthday, which for a long time looked like being a pure fiasco. Out of sheer consideration for her husband's health, she had presented him with a "beautiful saddle with all extras" so that he could divert himself during the hectic everyday; but that idea had no appeal at all to the mill-master, who day in and day out fussed and fumed and was so vociferously discontented over Cornelia's having come up with the idea of "inviting strangers to a card-party in the evening." Cornelia was at first "rather warm about the ears" but chose to think again and promised herself to "preserve amiability." Among the invited that evening was Headmaster Birch, whose fastidious and desiccated brother had on an earlier occasion confided to Cornelia that on his stay in Europe he always wore "3 pairs of woolen underwear," at which she was on the point of asking him "how much of it was Mr. Birch himself when the items went away." She managed again to control herself, but admits in the letter to Regine to having actually speculated on whether "the desiccated mummy would go overboard with the first wind and Fritz will have no use of him at all." She knew very well that such silly comments were out of place, no less so since for "2½ months" Birch "had been spitting blood," but she could not resist a little teasing. And that was something Birch's headmaster brother came to experience on Emil's birthday. Earlier in the day Cornelia had found a book that one of the young girls in the house had forgotten in the sitting room. It was *Maren Kokkepiges Drømmebog* (Maren Kitchenmaid's Dreambook) and it proved to be a "dreadfully trashy book" containing, among much else, a crude "presentation of every person's life according to the month in which they were born." No sooner had Cornelia acquainted herself with the tawdry content than she got the idea that if only Birch could be persuaded to read parts of the book aloud "then the game was won and we would surely come to enjoy ourselves." The strategy worked down to the last detail.

> . . . the amusing effect of Birch, reading with his serious undertaker's tone the great load of stuff and nonsense that the book contained, was beyond all description, people laughed and enjoyed themselves immensely, yes, I am convinced that it was one of the most amusing gatherings they have attended for a long time, and I stood there vindicated before my reluctant consort.

By way of bringing some balance to her account, Cornelia hastily adds that she was far from blind to Headmaster Birch's social virtues and humane disposition, to say nothing of her appreciation for his sound political judgment—"Birch talks well and with a clear view of situations and people, he is only boring when he talks about his vegetable garden or about the carpeting in his rooms." And that he unfortunately had a tiresome tendency to do. On the other hand, what the episode with the crazy Dr. Neukirch documented in black and white was that things could perhaps be just a shade too jolly:

> . . . I haven't experienced anything so lamentable, sinister, for a long time; the day the cholera was demonstrably over he summoned a large

meeting of priests and doctors at the town hall and told them [that] during the night he had had a revelation from God that a big epidemic was imminent in the town, and that they should now pray together so that the misfortune could be averted; in the evening he went out and practiced in his unmentionables, the next day he was raving, had a straitjacket put on him and was conveyed to Aarhus; his poor wife, who is only 25, is now sitting there in the empty home and she has confessed that, for her, it had been quite unexpected; we others have nevertheless suspected it the whole summer; she always looked up to him as far her superior and an epitome of wisdom, so I can well imagine that he could babble on for a long time before she took it to be insanity; lately they had neither eaten nor slept, just talked, yes she herself was so exalted that one feared for her too, she would only touch on it but I thought I noticed that it was mainly a matter of religious scruples, he was after all a Jew and she a Christian.

A Miss Henck, an aristocratic lady's companion with Grundtvigian sympathies, would so much like to do something for this "matter" of the confused doctor's "salvation," but when she good-heartedly visited him, she had to "pay for the pleasure with a new white silk shawl, which he tore all to pieces while threatening her and her black soul with the same treatment." Kierkegaard's old friend Pastor Boesen "hastened there, too, as a curer of souls, but he at least escaped with losing his hat and gloves," for Doctor Neukirch was not bent on being pacified—"How the chosen do always want to mix themselves up in everything," remarks Cornelia with a shake of the head.

What thoughts went through Boesen's mind as, having hastened to the recue, he returned hatless and gloveless to the safety of his parsonage, is not known; but four years earlier he had visited a dying man at Frederik's Hospital, a man whose name reminds us a little of Neukirch's and who had similarly tried to bring his contemporaries to their religious senses. That man, who on Saturday the 5th of May had spent his life's last birthday, had on the 23rd of May put out "This Must Be Said; So Let It Be Said," in which he appealed to the so-called common man:

> *Wherever you are, whatever your life is otherwise, my friend—by ceasing to participate in the public divine service as it now is . . . you have always one and a great guilt less—you are not participating in making a fool of God. . . .*[7]

Kierkegaard, unlike Neukirch, was not a physician, but nonetheless he came across as a diagnostician of the modern age's follies and had, in the second number of *The Instant,* presented his reader with what he called a "Diagnosis." While

Neukirch believed that a "big epidemic was imminent in the town" but could be averted by prayer, for Kierkegaard it was a matter of an epidemic infecting cultural Protestantism—"Christendom"—due to a powerful State Church and a corrupt clergy, something that he tried to illustrate for his reader with the image of a hospital:

> Imagine a hospital. The patients are dying like flies. The treatment is changed in this way and that: it helps not at all! What then might be the cause? It lies in the building, the whole building is toxic. . . . The same is true in the religious sphere. That the religious condition is wretched, that in a religious respect people are in a pitiable condition is undeniable. So one person thinks that if we could but have a new hymnbook; and another a new altar book; a third, a service in music, etc., etc. then that would help.
>
> In vain; for the fault lies in the building. The whole scrap heap of a state Church, which spiritually speaking has not been ventilated in time out of mind, in this scrap heap the enclosed air has turned toxic. . . . Then let this pile of rubbish tumble down, get rid of it, close all these boutiques and booths . . . and let us once again worship God in simplicity instead of making a fool of him in splendid edifices; let us be in earnest again and stop playing. . . .[8]

At the time quite a few people thought Kierkegaard totally unqualified to undertake anything like a "diagnosis," since it was he, *le sain imaginaire*, that was the patient and therefore it was he who should go for treatment as quickly as possible. On Christmas Eve 1854, *Kjøbenhavnsposten* had an article in which a gentleman, calling himself by the medical appellation "Asclepius," declared that Kierkegaard had certainly been "original" but was now deprived of this word's "assembled letters with the exception of three" and had accordingly become *gal* (mad). With variations, this madness theme recurred over the following six or so months. Kierkegaard is urged, for instance, to take a "trip for his health 25 miles out of town"—the exact distance to the St. Hans psychiatric hospital in Roskilde. The newly appointed Bishop Martensen thought Kierkegaard's conduct showed him to be "obsessed by a fixed idea," and concluded that he had now definitively "lost even his simplest wits." It was but a short distance from this to Just Paulli's remark that Kierkegaard "is said to have suffered from softness in the brain," which was presumably "the cause of the writing," unless "the writing itself was to blame."

Prophets have never been particularly well received in their hometowns, whether Bethlehem, Horsens, or Copenhagen, and their contemporaries have always kept busily occupied with getting their prophets executed, driven out, or hospitalized.

PART 2

1860–1896

"... I AM NOT LOOKING FORWARD TO COMING TO COPENHAGEN"

The party was more subdued and the rhetoric more restrained when Regine celebrated her thirty-eighth birthday on the far-off island. The previous day Fritz had turned forty-three, and the incessant congratulating had sapped the hostess's energy—"I was so tired when I was to go to bed that I could hardly take my clothes off." When she awakened the next day with an excruciating toothache, her husband was not slow in reaching a teasing diagnosis: "Fritz said it was due to my mouth not having been closed the whole previous day."

The toothache lasted "12 days and nights" and Dr. Aagaard had to be summoned. He prescribed "various drops" but these proved worthless. "In the end I got a drop of chloroform on cotton up into the tooth and I haven't had any toothache since." Regine realized that chloroform was an "excellent remedy," but for some time she hesitated to use it, nor did she even care to have such a medication in her house—"I think if I take too strong a whiff of the bottle that I have now in my cupboard, it would be death." But Regine reassures Cornelia that she mentions the danger of chloroform only as a way to underscore for herself the "needed caution."

That rather too inquisitive a nose might cause Regine's death would be the greater irony now that her time of exile would soon be over. The date for the voyage home was still not known, but Regine could inform Cornelia on Tuesday the 10th of April that they now had departmental secretary Adolph Skrike's word for it that Fritz's application for "discharge" had been passed to the King. Regine still did not know when her husband's retirement would become official; nor had they been informed of their departure date or of the appointment of Fritz's successor. The uncertain future could mean a "real loss," since furniture and other items that Fritz and Regine had bought from Feddersen could likely be resold to the new governor, which would be significantly more profitable than letting the furniture go under the hammer at a public auction.

The time of waiting was spent planning the immediate future. Although Regine knew better than anyone how such plans can be thwarted time and time again, that they often come to naught and that it is indeed quite foolish to grapple with them, she simply couldn't help doing so: "Well, now that I have mentioned it, I might as well tell you, particularly taking in mind that it is all fantasy hatched in my brain." And she then rolls out her endearing request list: "I wish I could be lucky enough to spend the holiday month with you, and that Regnar was also there for Thilly's sake." But here already Regine had to pause to stress the unreliability of her plans. If she and Fritz left St. Croix too late and they also had "to go by sailing ship," then the month of August would hardly be spent in Horsens but rather in some uncertain spot on the open sea.

This possibility was not, however, to stand in the way of initiating Cornelia into her other and no less wild plan, which was that she and Fritz should use some of the summer months in company with members of the family in Denmark and, after that, travel south together until the winter took serious hold. Cornelia was to accompany them—and Emil too, of course, if he could tear himself away from his everlasting mill. As for their own situation, no argument was needed: "Fritz has no position and I have no house!" It would not be inexpensive, but since on Regine's calculations there would be not much more than "a few thousand" rix-dollars left when she and Fritz had paid again for all new household goods, the money was not "worth saving" anyway and consequently would be used "most sensibly by far" on a trip that moreover could serve several ends: "A journey, besides the strength and enjoyment it can give us, could also serve as a transition from having lived in a refined and prominent position, with a horse and coach and servants, etc., and 20 thousand a year, to having to live on 20 hundred a year (that's about the extent of Fritz's pension)." To these practical considerations she added a psychological factor:

> . . . I am not all that concerned about coming to Copenhagen; Mother is dead, you don't live there any more, and many other things make me think that I no longer have the old love for it, so that I'd rather, if I could choose, live in the country!

Regine does not say what "other things" she has in mind. But it is not impossible that having no longer her "old love" *for* Copenhagen might be related to having no longer her "old love" *in* Copenhagen.

HOMECOMING AND THE TIME THAT FOLLOWED

Regine's last letter from St. Croix is dated the 27th of April 1860. The next is composed on the 29th of September in Copenhagen. None are to be found that tell of what happened in the meantime. So in exactly what circumstances Regine, Fritz, Thilly, Josephine, and we assume little four-legged Fido, left Christiansted, we do not know. As so often before, the distance between the motherland and her far-off possessions played tricks on Regine's reckonings and reasonings. *Departementstidenden* could announce already on the 21st of April:

> On the 10th of March the Governor of the Danish West Indian possessions J. F. Schlegel, Knight of the Order of the Dannebrog and Dannebrog's Man [honored with the Silver Cross of the Order of the Dannebrog],[1] is according to his application released from office with assurance of royal favor effectively from the 31st of May this year.[2]

Henrik Lund, as mentioned, resigned as colonial physician effective from the same date;[3] but apart from this particular coincidence, there is nothing to report about the conclusion of the Schlegel couple's five years abroad, during which Fritz had been on duty for 1,859 days.

Hardly had Fritz and Regine found firm Danish soil under their feet before they made for Horsens to see Cornelia and Emil again. We have no knowledge of how this reunion, so often dwelt on with such sweet anxiety in Regine's letters, actually turned out. History lowers its decorous veil over the sisterly tears that surely fell in those happy September days in the miller's house in Horsens, and it hides with fitting consideration the feelings the two brothers-in-law doubtless tried to suppress when, with manly emotion, they stretched out their hands to each other.

Symbolically enough, it began to rain when their time to take leave approached. A little way out in Horsens fjord the passengers had to creep down into the cabin, the wind blew up, and the waves forced most of them to lie down. Thilly was seasick and soon far too miserable to enjoy the delicacies Aunt Cornelia had given her for the journey. Regine had her sea legs and managed to get some sleep: "In the evening I undressed properly and went to bed and slept a little during the night." A little before five the next morning they docked at the Customs House in Copenhagen, but then had to wait until half past six before they could leave the ship—"in those one-and-a-half hours I froze as I have not been frozen for 5 years." When the far-travelled ones finally came ashore, there stood the ever "faithful Clara" to bid them welcome to Copenhagen. Clara was Fritz's forty-two-year-old sister who lived with the family and who, together with Schmidt from Fritz's office, had found her way to the Customs House in the early morning hours. A tour followed that took them through the old city streets to their temporary home at 59 Lille Købmagergade, where Widow A. N. Bjerring gave them a kind welcome, and "had the coffee table covered and served us herself."

It was all of a week later before Regine wrote her very first letter to Cornelia after the homecoming from the West Indies—and from Horsens. She should have written earlier, that she admitted, but had been so terribly "caught up" and only now found time for her letter, which deals for the most part with the difficulties involved in simply getting settled—once more:

> On Saturday we went out straightaway to look at rooms, and there were not many apartments to choose between. Clara gave us the advertisements for all of them, since she had seen them all but waited until we came to decide. But there was one she had not seen, since it had only just become vacant and was advertised in the paper the day we came, and strangely enough it was the one we fastened on. I wouldn't say it was anything special, for the rooms could have been a little larger, but they were the best of those there were, so we must be thankful for that. . . . It is at 32 Nørrevold, the second floor, in the big house that H. H. Lund owned in the old days, and which he bequeathed to Gammeltofte, who is now our host.

Gammeltofte was master shoemaker O. C. Gammeltofte. And the paper Clara had glanced into was in all probability *Adresseavisen*, since on page 3 of its September 21st 1860 "supplement" there is the following advertisement:

At 32 Nørrevold

> is a fine second floor, consisting of 6 rooms, with lobby, corridor and all conveniences, owing to unforeseen circumstances ready for occupancy on removal day October next. Shown from 9–1 o'clock by the house agent in the basement to the right.

An apartment was advertised on the same page that might seem more suitable for a returned governor and his wife:

> An elegant 2nd floor cons. of 6 rooms with *entré*, kitchen, maid's-, dining- and storeroom, food- and wood-cellar, with garret and water and gas, to rent from October in the tenement building No. 7 in Tornebuskegade, newly built 4 years ago, hard by the rampart; rent is 200 Rd. semiannually. Shown from 11 to 2 o'clock.

It might seem strange that the Schlegels should decide on the apartment in Nørrevold and show seemingly no interest at all in the much more elegant apartment on Tornebuskegade. But Fritz certainly had his reasons. One consideration was that an annual rent of 400 rix-dollars was a bit steep, but there was also the fact that the Nørrevold apartment could be taken over some time before the stated removal day, which could have been decisive for an impatient couple dreaming

39. On her nineteenth birthday on the 23rd of January 1841, Regine received a pair of candlesticks from her betrothed, along with something so advanced as a "paint set." In the accompanying letter Kierkegaard expressed the hope that Regine would with her paintings "rescue the modest flower from the night of death and oblivion." It is not known when she painted this *nature morte* with the inviting peaches, ready-to-burst grapes, and a fruit that resembles a colossal quince, but the strokes are sure and the talent indisputable.

of having their own floor under their feet. But on top of these factual considerations there was another that could well have had symbolic weight. The stately property at the corner of Tornebuskgade and Rosenborggade, and so just a few yards from the "newly built tenement building No. 7," was where Søren Kierkegaard once kept house. He had lived in the property's second floor for half a year since moving in on April 1848 before transferring to an even larger apartment at No. 9 Rosenborggade, where he stayed until April 1850, with moreover an annual rent of 400 rix-dollars. Returning home as the sweetheart of the genius's young days would be trial enough for Regine, but there was surely no need at any price—so Fritz may have thought—to settle in exactly this street of all streets, where his old rival had led his daily life, and from which in certain periods he had regularly wandered out to catch sight of his former fiancée, she who had now returned from her exile with a suitcase full of old love letters and a head full of memories. In any case, Regine and Fritz chose the second-floor apartment at Nørrevold and set about acquiring new furniture:

> Beds we have bought, and yesterday a saddler was put to work with the mattresses, and on Monday a seamstress begins at the Schlegels with the bedding, so you see, I haven't been altogether unemployed.

Regine had also managed to get hold of a kitchen maid on Mrs. Bjerring's recommendation. She, the kitchen maid, should have been married, Regine reports, "but her sweetheart has broken with her, so she is coming to us in November." Broken engagements can give rise to so much, so too old residences. Regine, for reasons unknown, did not want to keep Josephine in her employ, even though Josephine begged to be able to stay with the Schlegels. When Regine writes to Cornelia at the beginning of January 1861, it seems as though some irreparable catastrophes must have occurred:

> I no doubt never told you about Jospehine? In the first months of my stay here in Copenhagen she tormented me terribly, she couldn't find a place and so in the end wanted to be with us again; naturally I would not go in for that and in the end she has been lucky enough to get a very good position from New Year, namely at the rich wholesaler Hansen.

At wholesaler Hansen's, Josephine got 100 rix-dollars a year "which indeed is high pay," and in addition her chores were quite reminiscent of those she had "with us in the West Indies."

Exit Josephine Schanshoff. We are left vainly wishing that Josephine had left a diary giving her own version of the story.

REGINE'S COPENHAGEN AND ENVIRONS

On returning from the West Indies Regine had more than half her life left to live. One year had been spent with Kierkegaard, five in the West Indies, and ahead lay forty-four more years with memories, among others, of the West Indies and Kierkegaard. It ran against expectations, but was perhaps not altogether unforeseeable that things mostly went very smoothly. Everything remained, to a surprisingly extent, the same. She and Fritz could now of course go to the theater again, take in art exhibitions, renew contact with friends and acquaintances. But the obligations that came with their new social life were virtually indistinguishable from those they had put up with in their West Indian period.

Above all, and with undiminished strength, Regine missed her beloved Cornelia. Although it was no longer over 4,000 miles that separated them, but only 300, they seldom saw each other—all too seldom, according to Regine. But happily for posterity, she continued to correspond with her sister, with whom she also exchanged small parcels. From the capital to the East Jutland market town there were sent in the course of time jars of jam, wristbands for crocheted collars, and faded ribbons, to be dyed so that they would be ready for Cornelia whenever she came to Copenhagen. And from the miller's family came diverse parcels with slaughtered hare, partridges, ox-tongue, and cucumbers of various sizes and preparations, bringing joy to their Copenhagen recipients—"Regnar, Thilly and I have been outdoing one another in eating the cucumbers during the vacation"—and at the end of the year the considerate Emil sent brandy, pepper-nut cookies, and freshly milled flour for the Christmas cakes, which according to Regine were so good that they "trumped the baker's."[4]

If the emotional coordinates remained more or less unchanged, Copenhagen itself had, during Regine's absence, undergone significant alterations. Most obvious was the demolition of the high and picturesque ramparts, which had for hundreds of years surrounded the compact fortress town. These were now being carried away, load by load, so that the city could expand over the bridges, making room for modern many-storied properties to house the 11,552 new inhabitants who had arrived in the course of the five years Fritz and Regine had been away.

As the area beyond the ramparts began to be built up, the narrow town gates became obsolete, especially Nørreport and Vesterport. The Ministry of Defense insisted on the gates' military importance, but the liberal paper *Fædrelandet* had a different view and urged the inhabitants of Copenhagen to attack the ramparts from *inside*. Demolition applied in the first instance to the monumental Nørreport, which on the 18th of October 1856, and without any trace of sentimentality, *Fædrelandet* referred to as "antiquated." In the following year the same could be said of Amagerport, Vesterport, and Østerport. Copenhagen was no longer encircled by fortifications but had become an open city whose ramparts gave way to crowded boulevards bordered by elegant gas-lamps that cast a clearer and stronger light than that of the old sallow oil-lamps.

Contributing to the changing picture in the 1840s, there was also the new means of conveyance that, borrowing a democratic Latin word, was called an "omnibus" because it was available in principle to everyone. The first of these were horse-drawn wagons that attracted attention with their radiant colors and grand names, such as "The Sun," "The Red Lady," "The Lion," "The Eagle," and "The North Star." At first their route ran from Amager Square to Frederiksberg, but before long omnibuses ran all the way out to Lyngby, Charlottenlund, and Dyrehaven. A novelty for Regine and Fritz were the English-manufactured tramcars introduced in Copenhagen and environs during the autumn of 1863.

Although the wagons were still drawn by a pair of horses, they now rode on tracks and were provided with an open platform at the back, as well as a narrow outside ladder that led up to open seats on the roof. A trip cost between 4 and 8 shillings, which meant that it was generally only the well situated who could afford to use the trams.

It was to these, the well situated, that Fritz and Regine belonged, and at weekends in the summer months they stayed with Maria, who owned the dearest little house up in the fishing village of Tårbæk. The journey there was on one of the two small steamers, *William* and *Emma*, which departed daily from Klampenborg, where the military surgeon J. J. Hjaltelin had opened a spa to which *William* and *Emma* busily ferried clients. After a while several more boats were added to cater to the rising number of passengers who on warm summer days liked to go into the woods without facing the tumult on Strandveien.

Regine and Thilly had more time than Fritz, and they were usually first to get away. Fritz would come along when his various duties and his mood permitted. The Soldenfeldt brothers also looked in regularly, as did Oluf when his sensitive stomach permitted. The party also took trips out into nature with a picnic basket, or set course for a suitable restaurant whether in Klampenborg, Sorgenfri or Frederiksdal, the town that Kierkegaard had also once frequented. Regine never tired of these tours and in her letters to Cornelia she often describes North Zealand's nature—as on the 19th of June 1861:

> How much I enjoy Dyrehaugen. . . . I have veritably gorged in pleasure seeing the trees becoming so dense and full, and now the chestnut trees with their proud blossoms, but my special favorite the white briar, how it has really gladdened my heart to see it again after so many years separation. I spoke to Fritz the other day about what it was that caused the nature last summer to make really so little an impression on me. I assumed it was because I was much too concerned with people, but he remarked quite correctly that last year I came from everlasting summer, so that a little more or a little less green couldn't possibly make any real impression on me; but this year, having again experienced a winter and felt what it means, one has a better understanding of it when it returns. . . . At Friday's dinner Fritz came out with his family to drink coffee at Klampenborg. Thilly and I then went up to them there, and then we went through Dyrehaugen with them to Fortunen to drink tea there.

During the winter, either on Saturday or Sunday, dinner was served with civilized punctuality at the Schlegels' on Gammeltorv. But Regine's relationship with her in-laws seems not to have been excessively cordial—"there is no one

40. This was the view Regine saw when she looked out from her father-in-law's house toward Gammeltorv (Old Market) and its fountain, Caritasbrønden (the Caritas Well), which Christian IV had erected there at the beginning of the seventeenth century. Behind the fountain lies Nytorv (New Market), the city's great market square, where one could buy meat, fish, poultry, and vegetables. The property to the right of the picture, beside the Court House with the conspicuous columns and flagpole on the roof's ridge, belonged to the Kierkegaard family until 1847 and was demolished only in 1908. From the Schlegel's living room, Regine had thus had an unobstructed view of her Kierkegaardian past.

that attracts me, and if I except my father-in-law they don't yearn for me either." The father-in-law's yearning was of the manageable kind, for when Regine visited them he usually amused himself with a round of l'Hombre[5] in the neighboring room in the cheery company of the gentlemen Juul and Brondum. Fritz, no doubt out of filial piety, played from time to time, but the card game held no interest whatever for Regine, who became bored stiff. There was hardly more cheer when Regine and Fritz had to function as host couple and to take up half-heartedly where they had left off in the West Indies. On Sunday the 24th of March 1861, she tells Cornelia:

> We have been well trained in this respect out in the West Indies, so we were able to behave with quite a bit of decorum; but I must confess to you here in confidence that I always begin quite early in the evening

to look at my watch and think to myself, won't these people go soon? This doesn't suggest I take much interest in their company, and unfortunately that is something I do not do, since you must not believe that it is because I am sleepy and in want of some peace; alas no, Fritz never goes to bed before getting on for 1 o'clock, so I know that my prospects of peace are far off whether the people go or not. Alas, you see, I miss you. . . . Who could take your place? No one, you know all our circle of acquaintances, and many of them I can very well put up with, but none to whom it could occur to me to say what I think to say to you.

After a party earlier in the year, Regine had reported that everything in the main had gone well, "if I except a few small misfortunes," among them that their maidservant Grethe had not "filled the oyster patties enough, so we had so much filling left over that we have been eating patties every day since." Regine made every effort that evening to contribute as much gaiety as possible to the conversation— "I gave them chat for filling, unfortunately the filling was better." The menu suggests that the guests did not leave the table hungry:

> Turtle soup, oyster patties, tongues and herring with cauliflower and green peas, turkey steak, ice cake, raisins and almonds and apples, and also punch, red wine, Madeira, port wine and malmsey.

". . . A WORD OR TWO ABOUT THE DEAR FRITZ"

However demanding the arrangement of these dinners might be, the work at least put melancholic thoughts to flight—"it banishes the fanciful ideas"—but Regine, who according to herself was "burdened with duties," also liked to take on chores in her circle of acquaintance, for instance selling lottery tickets for their housekeeper, Bøttger. "You can be sure I have a lot to do with that," we read in a letter to Cornelia; indeed, had Fritz not taken it upon himself to function as the project's "secretary," the job would have grown completely over her head. Collecting for various bazaars also made worthy demands on her time, since she had to go out and press doorbells with various letters of reference, or "addresses" as they were called, of which by the end of November 1865 she had distributed one thousand.

The reason why the former governor of the Danish West Indies could give his time to acting as secretary for his wife's collections and her lotteries for pensioned spinsters was simply that on his homecoming he had found no position anywhere. This involuntary unemployment was a psychological burden and,

41. In 1863 the Schlegels went to Niels Willumsen's newly opened photography studio at 7 Holmens Kanal. Regine is in a ruffled crinoline, whose perfect roundness is due to a series of steel hoops of varying sizes that are fastened together with narrow bands. Fritz has placed himself on a chair and looks tired. The West Indian everyday has left its clear marks, but he is impeccably clad in his heavy diplomat's jacket, has a signet ring on his left forefinger, and his shoes are so highly polished that they leave strips of white on Willumsen's lightly brown-toned paper.

according to Regine, manifested itself in various forms of unspecified "indisposition," even though Fritz did his best to give meaningful content to his days. In a letter from the end of April 1862 Regine could confide to Cornelia that while Oluf, Emil, and Jonas had gone to Confirmation in Sorø, Fritz had chosen to stay at home, "*since he didn't feel quite well.* You know how he can be." There follow some lines that are more confidential than what Regine would normally dare write. Brother-in-law Emil was on a visit to Copenhagen and he would take the letter to Horsens and give it directly to Cornelia without Fritz's knowledge:

> Since I am sending this letter through Emil, I will say a word or two to you about the dear Fritz, which naturally I would not let him see, so you must not mention it in your letter. He is decidedly very gloomy

at having no definite work, he doesn't complain about it, you know, he is withdrawn, but I can tell by his mood. I do so wish that he will get something, but I know that our Lord has always taken such loving care of us, and it is still my hope that if Fritz gets no work, then it is to our advantage, so we should practice patience through having nothing, also that it is a test and thus a labor, God helps us to do what we should.

It is curious that Regine should apply to Fritz a word that Kierkegaard two decades earlier applied to himself when explaining why he could not marry Regine. Fritz is "withdrawn," she writes. One inevitably thinks that in Regine Kierkegaard would have had an empathetic wife, not only understanding of reticence and reserve, but also capable of helping someone who was withdrawn in this manner to get better. Yes, her remarks about the need for practice in patience when out of work are not unlike a little demonstration in Kierkegaardian dialectic!

"I CANNOT BE QUIT OF THIS RELATIONSHIP"

The past turned up at regular intervals and quite demonstratively. After considerable discussion back and forth, Kierkegaard's journals began to appear under the title *Af Søren Kierkegaards Efterladte Papirer* (From Søren Kierkegaard's Posthumous Papers).[6] In 1881 they were published in a nine-volume edition, but the first volume came out in 1869, on the 13th of September. It covered Kierkegaard's journals from 1833 to 1843 and included were "introductory remarks" by H. P. Barfod, whose enormous efforts were rewarded with unequivocal criticism. On the 9th of February, Frederik Meidell announced in *Fædrelandet* that he would find it particularly unfortunate if

> the gentlemen biographers, autobiographers and editors of collected correspondence and the like, in order to titillate curiosity, out of blind respect for the demands of history or for whatever other reason irrelevant to literary *art*, get themselves lured little by little onto recklessness's dangerous false path, where not many steps are needed before one stands right in the middle of the scandal.[7]

On the same day, editor Erik Bøgh announced in *Folkets Avis*, under the otherwise somewhat nonchalant title "This and That": "I can almost not imagine any author whose memory would be served by publishing his 'Posthumous Papers.'" Indeed, thinks Bøgh, "the moral health police should keep an eye on such things." On the 23rd and 24th of February *Dagbladet* took aim at Barfod, indicting his lack of tact and judgment, particularly in his treatment of the story of the engagement. He advised Barfod to show greater discernment in his treatment of this topic in the coming volumes. *Aarhus Amsttidende* could tell its readers on the 1st of March that a Kierkegaardian was usually "a person who shirks all social duty and disdains every movement that has no connection with the distressing, partly unaesthetic self-contemplation from which the master could never tear himself loose." A similar view was presented on the 30th of March in *Illustreret Tidende*, where publication of the journals was described with adjectives such as "boring" and "embarrassing," "something more considerate to living persons would have been appreciated."

Among the still living was Regine, who asked Fritz to buy the double volume but reportedly felt "uncomfortable" due to the journals' "personal relation to her" and therefore refrained from reading "the continuations."[8] Since she had become familiar with Kierkegaard's entries about her from the material she had received on St. Croix, it could hardly have been the content itself that was disturbing, but rather the airing of their relationship in public, and, we may assume, the information about her time with Kierkegaard that Fritz would now receive. The intimate intensity that stamps several of the entries must in itself have been overwhelming:

> And when the sun closes its searching eye, when the story is over, not only will I wrap my cloak around me, I will throw the night around me like a veil and I will come to you—I will listen as the savage listens— not for footsteps but for the beating of your heart.[9]

Although the man behind this entry had long since been buried, these words could easily have caused the married couple "beatings of the heart" in a mutual embarrassment of the kind that can take hours to put behind one. Not only had Fritz access now to documents that he may have preferred to do without, he also felt himself enveloped in an elegant erotic scent that was worlds away from his own more rigid abilities in the domain of fascination. It was an area in which Kierkegaard was skilled:

> As agreed, I am returning herewith the flower that for eight days now has brought me joy, has been the object of my tender loving care. But that says little; for after all it is you yourself who *nurtured it forth*— nurtured it forth, what a beautiful and rich expression, what treasures language possesses—nurtured it forth; for should not your spiritual gaze, which has rested again and again on this tender plant, should not all the warmth of your love be more than enough to make it unfold in a very short time.[10]

Between carefully chiseled praises like this, we find Kierkegaard's depiction of himself as the true power in the love relationship, which for Regine was as essential as the heavenly father was for Christ:

> R . . . and I loved her much, she was as light as a bird and as daring as a thought; I let her climb higher and higher, I stretched forth my hand and she stood upon it and beat her wings, and she called down to me: It's splendid up here; she forgot, she did not know, that it was I who made her light, I who made her daring in thought, [that it was her] belief in me that made her able to walk on water; and I paid homage to her and she received my homage. —at other times she fell down upon her knees before me, merely wanting to look up to me, wanting to forget everything.[11]

It was precisely this worship of hers, this total submission, even a deification of him that, according to Kierkegaard, multiplied the complications following upon their break. Under other circumstances things would have been far simpler: "Yes, if she hadn't abandoned herself so much to me, confided in me, given up living herself in order to live for me; yes, then the whole thing would have been a piece of cake."[12] What did Fritz think on reading these accounts of his wife kneeling in devotion before Kierkegaard, intoxicated with sensuality, euphoric with joy? And how did Regine react? Could she recognize herself in his words, or did she find them poetically exaggerated, out of proportion? Or did she, evasively, stress the latter because in fact the former was the case?

In among these tableaux of Kierkegaard's unforgettable moments with Regine, we find other entries describing the situation after the break, in which rapture and inebriation are succeeded by shame and self-reproach. In one instance, Regine revisits the tormented writer and appears before him in widely differing, imaginary guises, each struggling with the other to make the right representation:

> My thoughts continually flit between two images of her—she is young, exuberant, animated, transparent, in short as I have perhaps never seen her—she is pale, withdrawn, waiting for the lonely hours when she can weep, in short, as I perhaps have never seen her either.[13]

The woman who for a brief moment came into contact with Kierkegaard left him as a creature transformed into literature, yet at the moment after the break she was almost alarmingly real and, moreover, a moral philosophical problem from which he could not escape. In spite of his repeated attempts, she could not be removed to that distance which is required for the artistic rendering of a figure:

I cannot be quit of this relationship, for I cannot poetize it; the moment
I want to poetize it, I am immediately possessed by an anxiety, an im-
patience which wants to resort to action.[14]

These extreme versions of Regine, at one time happy as a lark and transparent,
at another weeping and pale, mark the extremes in Kierkegaard's reflections
over the relationship's possible restitution:

> . . . and this terrible unrest—as if wanting to convince myself every
> moment that it was still possible to go back to her, O God, grant that
> I might dare to do it. . . . I've always scoffed at those who talked about
> the power of woman; I do so still, but a young, beautiful, animated girl
> who loves with all her heart and mind, who is absolutely devoted, who
> pleads—how often I have been close to setting her love on fire, not to a
> sinful love, but I had only to say to her that I loved her and everything
> would be in motion.[15]

That these lines should make Regine "uncomfortable" is understandable enough,
but it is even more certain that Fritz should feel the same. We can well suppose
that he read with displeasure and bitterness this account of an enflamed love
that was, to be sure, not sinful but hardly unaffectedly platonic either. Fritz must
have recalled how miserable Regine had been long after the break-up, and how
he, the slighted one, had to begin over again with a nervous Regine and little
by little—what was the expression?—"nurture forth"—what the Magister had
managed to destroy. And the humiliation that Kierkegaard so often bewailed
when looking back on the dissolved relationship, can it have been greater than
the humiliation he, Fritz, was exposed to in this reopening? Notwithstanding
his considerable tolerance, it would have been past endurance to have to occupy
himself again with this unaccommodating and intriguing Magister who, first
having frustrated his engagement plans, then post mortem pursued him to the
ends of the earth, and now, would you believe it, was being resurrected volume
by volume in Copenhagen.

When, in the summer of 1872, the first half-volume of Kierkegaard's journals from 1844 to 1846 was published, reaction began to stir in the neighboring
countries as well. Bjørnstjerne Bjørnson, Norway's national poet and unofficial
literary ambassador, wrote in a letter to one of his coeditors of the journal *For Ide
og Virkelighed* (For Idea and Reality): "Kierkegaard's posthumous work, which
I have painstakingly read, can at times almost induce the vertiginous feeling
that accompanies the desire to throw up. I could write a book, so much has it
repelled me." Unfortunately Bjørnson never wrote such a book, but the criticism
continued in the same journal. It was felt that one had to affirm, with regret, that

in Kierkegaard's case idea and reality were not in sync: "It is the finite side of S. Kierkegaard's talent that is placed here before the public's inquisitive gaze." Throwing the papers out "to the whole world to be pawed and fiddled with" was therefore an "act of great crudity," and one had to ask oneself whether this "offensive exercise is really to continue." About Barfod, we can read that his being "granted access to all these extensive manuscripts and journals" had been "unfortunate."

In the preface to the second half-volume of Kierkegaard's journals (1844–1846), published in November 1872, Barfod tried to counter this ungracious reception by professing his objectivity and conscientiousness. But he spoke to deaf ears. It was only when the 1847 journals came out in 1877 that a gentler breeze began to blow. Thus, in the journal *Nær og Fjern* (Near and Far), Otto Borchsenius is delighted that:

> The lively antipathy to publication of the journals has given way little by little to a scarcely less lively acknowledgement of the colossal posthumous literature's value for literary history and its psychological interest. We might easily agree that it would have been better if, from the start, the journals had been given to a biographer who, in an exhaustive presentation of Kierkegaard's life and activity, could have given us all that was most valuable . . . but at this date such a biographer is not to be found.[16]

"SO CLOSE TO ME THAT IT WAS ALMOST A COLLISION"

In one of these journals a dialectically exhausted Kierkegaard sighs, "The affair has now been settled once and for all, and still I will never be through with it."[17] Ironically enough, Fritz could have said exactly the same about his own relationship to Regine's relationship to Kierkegaard. The publication of the next volumes brought more disclosures, making it suddenly clear to Fritz that his lawfully wedded wife had been regularly meeting her former betrothed in the Copenhagen streets, or along the ramparts, wordlessly, determinedly, and intensely, and had in the process substantiated the paradox that, in special cases, platonic love can be stronger than consummated passion. "We have seen each other regularly," wrote Kierkegaard in January 1850 and explained that he and Regine had for a month to a month and a half "seen each other almost every blessed day, or at least twice every other day."[18] And although he often warned against every conflation of the aesthetic and the religious, theater and church, their meetings, would you believe it, took place in the semi-darkness of Copenhagen churches, where they had apparently evolved their own more or less *erotic* rituals. They met, for instance, in the Palace Chapel—"lately more often than usual"[19]—where *he* had his regular seat and *she* sat nearby. During Christmas 1849 there occurred, however, an extraordinary scene that Kierkegaard preserved in his journal. In this entry he managed also to leave one of the few portraits of himself as seen from *outside*:

> [S]he sat right in front of me; she was alone. On other occasions, she generally sang a hymn after the sermon, which I never do. That day she refrained from doing so. Consequently we left at the same time. Outside the church door she turned and saw me. She stood in the curve of the path to the left of the church. I turned to the right as always, because I like to walk through the arcade. My head naturally inclines somewhat to the right. As I turned I tilted my head perhaps a little more markedly than usual. Then I continued on my way and she went hers. Afterwards I truly reproached myself, or rather, I worried that she might have noticed this movement and interpreted it as a nod indicating that she should walk with me.[20]

Kierkegaard didn't know whether Regine had noticed anything special and would in any case have left it to her "whether she would have spoken to me," which in this case would have required "Schlegel's consent." But if Regine had wanted to talk to him, the present situation offered "ample opportunity." He was correspondingly certain that Regine had the necessary courage to turn to him, seeing that, in the time between the break-up and her engagement to Schlegel, she has "with a little telegraphic gesture . . . searched for a hint from me, and indeed she got it." As for Schlegel, Kierkegaard was quite certain that his interests were taken care of. Without his "consent" the affair held no interest at all for Kierkegaard: "A relationship to her in which there was the least trace of *nefas*: Oh, Good Lord, in that case people just don't know me."[21]

Schlegel, however, knew Kierkegaard very well, and he probably also knew that the Latin *nefas* describes conduct in infringement of divine law, a disgrace, a sin, but that it is furthermore a concept that had been evoked in connection with the broken engagement. There was no question of such a thing, according to Kierkegaard. But a broken engagement can be a matter of degree, and that a "little telegraphic gesture" might not always be as innocent as he would like it to be was something that Kierkegaard, as the man behind "The Seducer's Diary," should know as well as anyone. Johannes the Seducer could affirm, from experience, that "my sidelong glance is not so easily forgotten."[22] Nor, no doubt, had Schlegel forgotten that special "sidelong glance" he had received less than two months earlier in the shape of Kierkegaard's sealed letter, which he had promptly returned with the remark that he did not wish "any interference of anyone else in the relationship between [himself] and his wife."[23]

Against this background, what is most surprising in Kierkegaard's entry is his massive silence about the fact that Schlegel had unequivocally and unmistakably asked to be spared any intervention in his marriage and so, naturally, had no wish to give Kierkegaard any kind of "consent." The two formerly betrothed nonetheless continued their rendezvous, which remained wordless but had at times a quite physical character, as appears in an entry from 1849, where Kierkegaard portrays a Regine who literally came close:

> Without deviating from my usual pattern, she has more than once managed to pass so close to me that it was almost a collision. Oh, but I cannot very well take the first step.[24]

If the seducer's sidelong glance had been hard to forget, then avoiding these goal-directed maneuvers that nearly ended in one kind of coming together, an embrace or a "collision," as Kierkegaard anxiously calls it, cannot have been easy either. A few lines further on in this entry he fears that Regine might perhaps not have altogether forgotten their shared past, in which case "tearing it open at this point would be dangerous." However, Kierkegaard's worry was ephemeral and belied in part by his continued meetings with Regine, in part by his frequent reporting of actual "collisions" in journals whose future publication was in no doubt. In an entry from the summer of 1849, on his "Relationship to Her," which bore the symptomatic addendum "The Final Word for Now,"[25] he again homes in on the joy it would bring him if only he could give Regine some impression of the literary immortality in store for her; and then he moves on to a characterization of her erotic disposition as evidenced by her susceptibility to 'the poetic'":

> Indeed, I see her prick up her ears—true enough, she herself is not poetic, but unless she is utterly confused, when the poetic beckons, she is *schlaget an und gebet Feuer* [German: take aim and fire], as it were. For, as to whether she understood me at the time? —Yes, indeed she did. That is, she did not understand my innermost self, she *understood* precisely that it was ἄδυτον [Greek: not to be entered upon]. But as to whether she understood her erotic relationship to me? —How could I find enough A-pluses and gold stars to add to the highest marks she deserved, both for rote learning and for inward appropriation, etc.?[26]

So Regine gets full marks for her erotic achievements, which is why Kierkegaard has to declare further down in his entry that he is now busy with plans to make her understand that "it was precisely this sisterly relationship that was the poetic," since this was a relationship that could ward off all "danger of the erotic sort." This Kierkegaard can well guarantee, "for with the poetic—and then with a little bit of help on my part—she can walk a very fine line," which we may suppose means that Regine can balance with a tightrope-dancer's lightness on these guidelines that, with his choreographic know-how, Kierkegaard is able to extend beneath her. From the continuation of the entry it appears that it would be practically a sin of omission were Regine not granted such a possibility; with a peculiarly pensive cynicism, Kierkegaard remarks:

> And it is truly sad that this girl is continually consigned to the shadows, as it were. Schlegel is surely a likable man; I really think she feels quite happy with him. But this girl was an instrument he does not know how to play. She is capable of tones that I knew how to summon forth.[27]

Kierkegaard could perhaps sense that in using these words he was on the verge of overstepping the bounds of decency, but after something like a microscopic pause in thought, he goes on doggedly:

> Good Lord, humanly speaking it is after all a rather paltry request for a renowned figure, such as indeed I am, to beg that he be permitted to assume the modest position of a sort of unhappy lover at the side of a girl who had adoringly begged to become his maidservant. . . . To walk as an unhappy lover on the left-hand side of a girl who had disdained my love: No, I was not suited for that. But to walk like this alongside a girl whose love I truly had not disdained, but which I had to give the appearance of disdaining: Yes, this is the task for me.[28]

History does not tell us what task Regine's lawfully wedded husband saw himself facing, but the belittlement that Kierkegaard so delights in, since it is simply fiction, was no doubt something that Fritz read quite straightforwardly—however devotedly and faithfully he tried in other ways to keep pace with his wife's right-hand side.[29]

". . . MY HEART IS DEEPLY GRIEVED OVER MY POOR NATIVE LAND"

When traveling back from the West Indies, the Schlegels had journeyed from the Danish Kingdom's most westerly point to its most easterly. Greenland, Iceland and the Faeroe Islands were its northernmost possessions, while the duchies of Schleswig, Holstein, and Lauenburg belonged to the most southerly. Just four years after Regine and Fritz retuned home, Denmark underwent a dramatic change as a result of the Second Schleswig War, better known as the 1864 war, a national catastrophe without parallel.

The war had several roots—in complex inheritances, royal rivalries, incompatible legal traditions, the urge for independence, and the lust for power—but, more immediately, in the political and national repercussions of the Three Years' War that lasted from 1848 until 1850 and ended in a narrow Danish victory. While democratic politicians called for reforms that would liberalize the relationship of the three duchies to the Kingdom, more conservative forces worked in the opposite direction. So-called *helstatsmænd* (supporters of the United Monarchy) wished to keep the duchies together and fought against their incorporation into the German Federation, which consisted of thirty-nine larger and smaller kingdoms, principalities, and free states. When, in 1863, the Danish government agreed to a constitution that tied Schleswig more closely to the Danish kingdom and drew a new boundary at the river Eider between Schleswig and Holstein, it provoked loud protests among the German-minded population in the duchies and reinforced the desire for revenge that followed the Three Years' War.

The Danish government would not be swayed, and so the conflict grew more heated. In mid-January 1864, Prussian Minister-President Otto von Bismarck presented the Danish government with an ultimatum. Unless the constitution was declared null and void within forty-eight hours, Schleswig would be invaded. This demand was not acceded to, and on the 1st of February fifty-seven thousand troops marched into Schleswig and, with modern breech-loading rifles and newly evolved field guns, made their first attack.

The old Dannevirke fortification system in Schleswig-Holstein soon proved less impregnable than Danish politicians and romantic patriots had liked to believe. A war council was summoned and following intense discussion of the situation, General Julius de Meza decided to abandon Dannevirke and move north toward Dybbøl near Sønderborg. Rumor of the desertion of Dannevirke spread like wildfire throughout the entire country and had people talking of the cowardice and treason of those responsible. Soon after, a telegraph from Copenhagen brought a protest to de Meza, who was called home and at the end of February suspended.

Regine's first reactions to the dramatic events can be read a month later. In a letter she began on the 29th of March, she thanks Cornelia for her matchless portrayal of the disorders. She would rather have forwarded the letter down to Jonas and his family in the war-affected area, but didn't dare, for "if the letter should be opened and read by the Germans, they might not think so well of it." She herself did not feel impending danger, but:

> . . . my heart is deeply saddened over my poor native land, I think it might sooner bring relief to suffer something for it . . . think, if one

could let oneself be killed now for one's native land, then one's death would be more useful than ever one's life was. You mustn't be astonished at my coming to talk about death today, but this morning we saw many wounded soldiers being carried past here from the railroad station to the field hospital.

While, with its faint hope of a Danish victory, Regine's letter traveled from east to west, the Prussians in the south worked energetically at annihilating every such hope. At the beginning of April, Sønderborg was exposed to a bombardment that left large parts of the town in ruins. The Danish command advised the Ministry of War by telegram to abandon the position, but the request was turned down. When some few days later it was announced to the ministry that a withdrawal was inevitable, the reply was that they had free hands, but some hours later a counter directive came ordering that the position be held "even if there should result from this a relatively significant loss."[30] When, on the 17th of April, the Prussians had completed their last trench work less than three hundred yards from Dybbøl's earthworks—from which the Danish soldiers had a view of one hundred and twenty-six field guns and mortars distributed among as many as thirty batteries—the general repeated their request to abandon Dybbøl, but the commander-in-chief pointed out to his men that an order is an order.

Monday the 18th of April 1864 was a fateful day in modern Danish history. At four o' clock in the morning the Prussians began a heavy bombardment of the earthworks at Dybbøl, which were struck by almost eight thousand shells. Six hours later ten thousand Prussian soldiers poured over the trenches and stormed the earthworks. The Danish soldiers met the enemy with gunfire, but in less than ten minutes the first earthwork had been captured, and twenty minutes later all seven were in Prussian hands and the ignominious defeat was a historical fact.

On the 12th of May a truce was declared, but negotiations had already begun at the end of April at 10 Downing Street, with delegations from Prussia, Austria, and the German Federation. A proposal to partition Schleswig could be subscribed to by all delegates except the Danes, who would only accept cession of the most southerly part of Schleswig. The final drawing of the boundary offered likewise opportunity for wide-ranging discussions, not least due to Danish insistence on a boundary at Dannevirke. Negotiations finally broke down on the 25th of June, the participants in the conference went their ways, and less than a week later twenty-five hundred Prussian soldiers occupied Als. On Wednesday the 6th of June, Regine wrote to Cornelia of the sorrow to which the occupation had given rise—but especially of the difference between men's and women's abilities to expose themselves to the beneficial effects of weeping:

I wept my brave tears so much over your letter it did me good, for one is weighed down with such deep sadness that one would rather weep all day, it isn't possible when one has to look after one's things, but when the opportunity is there, as just now with your letter, then the tears are a true relief. That is why we women are as a rule tougher in sorrow and preserve our humor better under it, while the gentlemen, to whom this alleviation is practically unknown, become peevish and glum. Can you recall how much we always laughed at Adamine because first she packed her suitcase with great calm, and then took her handkerchief in order to weep and take farewell, just as though it were a chore like any other, will you believe me that, at this time, I am behaving in just the same way.

REGINE'S BOARDING HOUSE

Regine tried to secure the diversion she needed by opening her doors to women friends and various visitors. They were sometimes so numerous that the apartment came to resemble a small boarding house. "I have my guest room occupied by the English ladies"—she reports to Cornelia with a telling choice of words—"it is indeed so odd to be able to do people a service, but . . .". The rest needs no words.

The numbers rose markedly when brother Jonas and his Laura, in the late stages of pregnancy, together with their seven children, came to Copenhagen at the beginning of September 1864, their parsonage having been taken over by the Prussians and Jonas put under "house arrest." Regine had heard that the family was in a wretched state: "Laura had become so severely ill with stomach cramps after Jonas was taken away that the children had been compelled to send for the doctor, he prescribed leeches." Due to the bad weather, the journey to the capital had been drawn out—"they had been 2 times 24 hours on board the steamship"—but the many members of the family had now got firm ground under their feet at last and had been installed at, respectively, the Soldenfeldts and the Schlegels, where beds had been made up in various guestrooms. Laura's large stomach in the summer heat, their new refugee status, and an uncertain future did not make Jonas's wife easier to get along with. Regine describes her as a "very unreasonable person with an unfortunate temperament," and she was in no doubt that it would be good for the children "to escape for some time from the mother's very strict dominion," which was leaving its unmistakable mark on the small ones:

. . . you have no idea how difficult it is to get on with her, the day the girls
come from her they are so strangely cowed, it was only on the second day
that they began to be persons, the 2 smallest are not very well endowed
and a bad upbringing has made a mess of them, so it is no easy task to
deal with them, and Thilly's constant illness doesn't make things easier,
she is so nervous and irritable that she is hard to handle, and I almost
dare say nothing to her, since she looks so bad that one just doesn't know
what it will lead to, recently she has had a severe cough, I am filling her
now with milk and rye meal gruel, which I hope will help.

While Regine was trying to raise the spirits of her intimidated nieces and feed-
ing gruel to an irritable Thilly, in the greater world negotiations toward the
peace treaty signed in Vienna on the 30th of October 1864 were nearing their
conclusion. It had been a long process and had been followed with bated breath.
"I have not wanted to write before the armistice had begun," goes a letter from
the 3rd of August, "but here in Copenhagen we still don't know which way to
turn, the ministry keeps everything so secret, alas to no good purpose since the
conditions are said to be as severe and humiliating as can be."

Regine's worst fears proved justified: the victors demanded unconditional
cession of Schleswig, Holstein, and Lauenburg, which amounted to an area
roughly a fifth of the kingdom's total size with a population of about one million.
Denmark was reduced to junior-league status with approximately 1,600,000 inhabitants. In political circles there were doubts about survival and some thought
it expedient that the remainder of the country be incorporated in the German
Federation as a naval state, or so-called admiralty state. Regine was horrified,
but saw at least one bright spot in the fact that after the war there was an acute
need for people with humanitarian and logistic qualifications of the kind Fritz
possessed.

Fritz has got so much to do that he is quite overwhelmed, and as a result he has almost become the old [Fritz], his humor is quite changed,
he has become chairman of the relief fund that has been established to
help the unhappily retired Schleswigian civil servants. You can be sure
this is something to get down to.

THE SCHLEGELS' "PLACE ON THE CORNER"

When you go over Dronning Louise's Bridge, on the right at the corner of Nørrebrogade and Sortedam Dossering you see a high, whitewashed building with

42. For more than three decades Regine and Fritz had their home on the fourth floor in the conspicuous, whitewashed building on the corner of Nørrebrogade and Sortedams Dossering. From the window in her "corner place," as she would refer to it, Regine could look out over Sortedamssøen and, on clear days, let her eye follow Gothersgade all the way to Kongens Nytorv. The heavy wagons that roll over Peblingebro are heading for Nørrebro and will not long afterward pass by Assistens Cemetery, where Kierkegaard lies buried.

a small zinc cupola that on a calm sunny day is reflected in the lake below. The building was completed in 1858 and enticed the Schlegels out of their less stately second-floor apartment at Nørrevold. "We have got rooms at the corner of Nør-rebro out at the lakes on the 3th [for us 4th] floor," writes Regine in mid-July 1864 of the new apartment at 8 Nørrebrogade. One understands that the re-moval caused complications in a class of their own, but now the earthly belong-ings, which included Fritz's many thousands of books, were all in their places, and while a ceiling was being whitewashed, Regine sat in the adjoining living room at her writing table to keep Cornelia up to date:

> Our host had promised Fritz a good usable wine cellar, but when all was said and done all he got was a little rectangular room that was under water, so Fritz had to pack the wine into cases, which are placed for the time being along with his books up in Schmidt's storehouse. . . .
> We are very pleased with the rooms, especially the lovely view and the

sun. You can be sure it was already extremely cold at Nørrevold before we moved from there, and here the sun heats so beautifully in the
morning.

At the close of November Regine returns to the view from the south-facing windows in their new apartment, which was so grand that one could well imagine
"being blown out of one's bed in a southeasterly storm." In moderate weather the
conditions were in fact excellent: "When we do not have the wind directly on
the panes they are delightfully cozy rooms, and when the sun comes up again we
have so much of it that perhaps we even have too much." But the cold also found
its way into the new apartment and, one winter at the beginning of February
1870, Regine lists some of the precautionary measures called for by the falling
temperature:

> Excuse this rough paper I am writing on today, but Fritz has gone to the
> magistracy, so I can't come up with anything else just now, and since I
> feel like writing to you today I will not put it off for that reason. I think
> the paper is suitable for writing on in this weather, for my fingers are
> so stiff that they would definitely scratch through thinner paper. You
> can bet we die of cold at this time in our place on the corner! There
> have been 3 degrees of frost in our bedroom at night, I thought yester-
> day evening, when I went to bed, of the story housekeeper Cathala told
> once about her having been governess at a place where in the winter
> they had to lie with masks on or else their noses would crack and fall
> off. These days you poor creatures at the mill are no doubt suffering, it
> is specially the nasty wind that makes it intolerable, and you on your
> hill are just as exposed as we are on our third floor, not to speak of Jut-
> land being colder than Zealand.

Regine never rid herself of the notion that Jutland was a considerably colder and
darker part of the country than all the other regions in the kingdom. The tough
conditions sent her thoughts back in time:

> Today it is Father's birthday, I would so much like to take a wreath
> out to his grave and send greetings from you all! At this time of year
> he would surely have hung curtains in front of the window out by the
> Exchange, yes we have put up with the cold before; but how we load
> ourselves down now with clothes, (and for heaven's sake be absolutely
> sure that none of you catch cold,) and Father, on the other hand, when
> he went to the office in his thin coat on winter mornings! Yes, he was
> hardy! I don't think any of us resemble him or Mother in that way;
> Thilly has a letter today from her father, in which as is reasonable, he

too complains about the cold, he calls his house an ice palace, I think that fits.

Her own domicile had so far not become an ice palace, but the lakes had long since frozen over and were serving as skating rinks for Copenhagen's youth, among them Thilly, who spent hours at a time on the ice. As co-responsible for that young person's intellectual development, Regine might well be just a little concerned at all this unconcern:

> It is no doubt a healthy form of exercise, so up to a point I have noth-ing against it, but when the whole morning passes on ice, and in the evening they are to go either to the theater or a party . . . then one may well have some scruples about how they are going to get used to a life of industry and calm. I do what I can by giving some moral lectures to them, though young people must have their fling; but my task is really not easy, you are quite right, it is especially this absence of rule in all their being that destroys everything.

No stranger to the conflict between duty and inclination herself, Regine too had been young and had enjoyed an unruly fling, so much so that it had left its deep and enduring mark, physical and mental alike. Perhaps it was for exactly this reason that she felt obliged to deliver moral lectures to the unruly young-sters. And perhaps it was also for this very same reason that she knew that such lectures seldom did any good and sometimes served just the opposite purpose. Nor could she come up with any reasonable alternative to the merry figure-of-eights and other twistings and twirlings down there on the ice:

> . . . these days it has unfortunately not been possible to get the room warm where the clavichord stands, so that practicing has also come to a halt, so I don't really know what they do; when they are at home in the evening, I read aloud to them from a good book while they work, it comforts me, for then it is as if I was doing a little for their develop-ment, and yet this may just be idle talk, it can well be that what we take to be the greatest idleness is what nonetheless helps the development of the young most.

In spite of the poor heating, the Schlegels were to live for three decades in their "place on the corner" which, in Fritz' case, was to be his last earthly residence. From Regine's point of view the apartment must have been ideally located. It was no further from the town than she could manage on foot, and if she walked in the opposite direction, she would in ten minutes be at Assistens Cemetery, where her parents and a former fiancé lay buried. And finally, the property faced

Sortedamssøen, and although the surroundings certainly had changed after the removal of the ramparts, she could yet cast a glance through her windows towards the Love Path, where at one stage of her life she and he had passed by each other in those silent, erotically vibrant seconds. If she stood in the middle of Dronning Louise's Bridge—or Peblingebroen as it was called until 1887—which joins the new part of town with the old capital, she could glimpse Kierkegaard's former residence as a small white square up at Østrebrogade. If Fritz had felt he had to drop the apartment in Tornebuskegade in favor of Nørrevold because it was too close to Kierkegaard's old residence, Regine had nonetheless acquired from her "place on the corner" something like a perfect panorama of her past.

"ALAS, I AM INDEED SOMEWHAT SPECTRAL"

Although the Schlegels neglected to acquire "the continuations" of Kierkegaard's journals, there were many others who were unable to resist the temptation and so read on in this singularly erotic serial that wound its way through innumerable pages almost to the very last. The chronicle of events had at times been recorded in a kind of dramaturgical short form, as once in 1849:

1st Section

The engagement. I, basically introverted, suffering the torments of melancholia and conscience for having "carried her out with me." In the relationship to her [I was] of course love and solicitude itself, perhaps to excess, but I was indeed already a penitent. In other respects I paid no attention at all to her, as if there were a possibility that she could be the source of some difficulty.

2nd Section

She tries her hand at an inordinate self-confidence. Instantly, my melancholia respecting this matter essentially disappears, and the pangs of conscience have no connection with it. I breathe as easily as usual.

Here I have some guilt: I ought to have made use of the moment and let her break off—then it would have been the triumph of her overweening confidence.

But the question whether I ought not be able to enter into a marriage was too serious a matter for me, and there was also something childish in her overweening confidence.

In any case, in a way I now had command of myself—and I approached the matter somewhat from her direction.

3rd Section

She yields and transfigures herself into the most lovable being.

At that same instant my initial situation returns for a second time, intensified by the responsibility, which of course has now been increased by her feminine, almost adoring devotion.

4th Section

I see that there must be a separation.

Here, behaving honestly to her and treasonably to myself, I advise her not to fight by making use of pride—for then the matter would become easier for me—but by submission.

Still, a break must be made.—I send back her ring, enclosed with a letter that is printed word for word in the psychological experiment.

5th Section

Then, instead of letting the matter be decided, she goes up to my room in my absence and writes me a note of utter despair, in which she pleads with me for Jesus Christ's sake and the memory of my late father, not to leave her.

Then there was nothing else to do but dare to the utmost, to support her, if possible, through deception, to do everything to repel her from me in order to rekindle her pride.

Then, two months later, I broke off the relationship for a second time.[31]

The reference in the "4th Section" is to " 'Guilty?'—'Not Guilty?' A Story of Passion. Psychological Experiment" in *Stages on Life's Way*, in which the work's main male character, named "Quidam," exclaims in dismay:

What happens? Great God, she has been in my room while I was out. I find a small letter composed with a desperate passion, she cannot live without me, it will be her death if I abandon her, she pleads with me for God's, for my salvation's sake, by every memory that binds me with the holy name.[32]

This passage from the fictional work bears, as we see, a similarity to the journal entry's "5th Section," which shows how open the boundaries between private and public, or between experience and art, can be for Kierkegaard. The episode in question has clearly been so horrifying for Kierkegaard that he could not free himself from it and so returns to it again and again in the hope that this time will be the last. A few years earlier he had noted the interesting psychological circumstance that certain folktales tell how "the enchanted person must play the same piece of music through backward, and every time he made the least mistake he had to begin all over again and perform the work backward."[33] The folktale contained, in other words, a therapeutic recommendation that Kierkegaard tried to follow by playing the piece about Regine backward so that it could end at the very point at which the catastrophe had begun, that is to say, the relentless pleading. In an entry dated Friday the 7th of September 1849, we read:

> She herself pleaded with tears and supplications (for the sake of Jesus Christ, by the memory of my late father) for me not to leave her—I could do anything to her, absolutely anything, she would put up with absolutely everything and would nonetheless thank me all her life for her relationship with me as the greatest act of kindness. The father, who explained my behavior as eccentricity, begged and beseeched me not to leave her: "She was willing to put up with absolutely everything." As far as he and the rest of the family were concerned, he promised me in most solemn fashion that if I wanted it, then neither he nor any of his family would ever set foot in my house, and as soon as I married her, she would be under my absolute control as if she had neither relatives nor friends.[34]

The councillor's offer to cede his youngest daughter unreservedly to the strange theologian looks like a desperate act of sacrifice, and there are sexual undertones in his repeated promises about her willingness to put up unconditionally with everything. Looking back at the situation, Kierkegaard takes exception to the councillor's dubious offer of a kind of gentleman's agreement that would have bound Regine to an eternal debt of gratitude to her husband and given him free rein to do as he liked with her, as he says, like another "tyrant": "Truly, if I had done that, I would have been a scoundrel; in the meanest, outrageously meanest fashion I would have taken advantage of a young girl's distress, which brought her to say what she never ought to or could have meant in that way."[35] Although it was obviously correct to decline the councillor's offer, Kierkegaard is unable to control his urge to imagine how things would have gone if his no had been a yes:

> Then I would have married her. Let us assume that. What then? In the course of half a year or less she would have torn herself to shreds.

There is something spectral about me—and this is both the good and the bad in me—something that makes it impossible for anyone to endure having to see me every day and thus have a real relationship with me. Of course, in the light cloak in which I generally show myself, it is another matter. But at home it would be noted that I fundamentally dwell in a spirit world. I had been engaged to her for 1 year, and she did not really know me. —So she would have been shattered. In turn, she would probably have made a mess of me, for I was constantly overstraining myself with her because in a certain sense reality was too light. I was too heavy for her, and she was too light for me, but both can truly lead to overstraining oneself.[36]

The scenes from a marriage thus imagined are marked by their realism, psychological sobriety, and clarity of vision. He and she were simply not suited to each other, he too heavy and she too light. The one gifted spirit and the other sensual sweetness, they were doomed to wear each other out. What would have been the consequence had they gone the whole way and married? Kierkegaard hesitates a little, but then brings himself to hazard a hypothesis:

Then I probably would not have amounted to anything, or perhaps I would have been developed anyway, but she would have been a plague to me, precisely because I would have seen that she had become improperly situated through having married me.—Then she would have died. And then, then everything would have been over. To take her with me into history, when she had become my wife—no, it cannot be done. She may certainly become a Madame or a Mrs., but she may no longer remain in the role of my lover; it must be presented as the story of an unhappy love affair, and for me she is to be the beloved "to whom I owe everything": look, then history must take her—that is something I will certainly teach history.[37]

From this summary account of the Kierkegaardian marriage's all-embracing *tristesse*, it is unclear whether it is due to the loving pair's incompatibility that Kierkegaard ended up as a writer, or the opposite, that it was his wanting to be a writer that brought the relationship to an end. In the former case an ethical conflict led to aesthetic practice, in the other an aesthetic ambition led to an ethical conflict. What was cause and what was effect? Kierkegaard usually portrays the break-up as the result of an ethical and religious crisis, but this passage makes it clear that the marriage is to be seen not just as a limitation, but as directly destroying Kierkegaard's possibilities of an artistic career, so that instead of becoming what, as a genius, he was fitted to be, he would have ended up as "nothing." And if, in a marriage to Regine, he had managed against all odds to make something of himself, she would have been a "plague," the more so that, as a Madame or a Mrs., she would have frustrated the master plan that required Regine ideally to remain his "lover," so that their shared history could be preserved as an "unhappy love story" from which, sooner or later, Regine would pass over into the great history of literature as *his* Regine. But the fact remained that Kierkegaard was more spirit than flesh, more ink than blood, and therefore he feared that Regine would fade away in his company:

> Alas, I am indeed somewhat spectral, and it would have been an agony for me to see all that adoring charm wasted on me . . . I don't cling particularly tightly to life but would gladly die. The day I die, her position will be enviable. She is happily married, and her life has an importance that is unusual for a wife's to have for a husband, who surely is not far from worshipping her—and thus my life expresses that she was the only beloved; my entire existence as an author is to accentuate her. And if no sooner, she will understand me in eternity.[38]

REGINE'S MYTH AND BRANDES'S BIOGRAPHY

That Fritz and Regine were especially bent on securing a suitable match for Thilly, to avoid having her fall into the hands of a gentleman with dubious intentions, was something Georg Brandes could attest to. When he paid a visit to the Schlegels, it was not simply in the hope of getting Kierkegaard's one time sweetheart to say something; there was also a second hope, as is clear from his journal where, under the date 27 April 1867, Brandes notes:

> The most singular and embarrassing confusion of infatuations. The story of L. D. Then the quite thrilling infatuation with M. O. And finally, to fill the measure, the not purely unimportant attraction to L. B. The remarkable thing is that the feeling is always mutual. And I cannot think of anything else.[39]

The woman with the initials L. B. we know nothing of, but behind L. D. lurks the twenty-year-old Louise Dorré from Brittany who taught Brandes French during his first stay in Paris, and who became almost frighteningly attached to him. The initials M. O. are those of Mathilde Olsen's, also known as Thilly, whose presence in the Schlegels' home had Brandes spellbound as if by another siren song and drove him out to Nørrebro. He himself explains his visit as follows:

> It is because of that eighteen-year-old elf, her niece, who had a face one could not help but dream about. It was not from the very features in

43. On reading *Either/Or* and *Stages on Life's Way*, Georg Brandes as a young man became almost obsessed by Kierkegaard. "Is he not Denmark's or the World's greatest man?" he wrote, entranced, after reading *Concluding Unscientific Postscript*. "And yet God save me from him, I will never come to live." Brandes wrote his critical biography with the very aim of being able to live further—in the face of Kierkegaard and in spite of him. When Brandes, on the 11th of January 1888, writes to Friedrich Nietzsche, it is to recommend to the tormented philosopher that he acquaint himself with Kierkegaard, because he is "one of the most profound psychologists that has ever lived." His own biography, however, was not something Brandes would recommend. As he explains, it was "a sort of polemical work, written to arrest his influence." Brandes pursues that aim—that is, to bring Kierkegaard's influence up short—by, in particular, portraying Kierkegaard as short on nature and weird. Kierkegaard's lack of a sense of the scope of his own radical contribution is effectively caught by Brandes's image of a spiritual Columbus who, after crossing the deep ocean, finds a new land, the America of the personality, which—and from this follow the calamities—he continues to call the India of faith. "His indisputable greatness is that he discovered this America; his incurable madness was that he stubbornly continued to call it India."

this face that the sorcery came, although its form was an irreproachable oval, the small brow high and well shaped, the chin strong. Nor was it from the personality that gleamed through the features. Psychically, the young girl seemed constituted like other young girls, was mostly silent or communicative concerning small things, without any other coquetry than those of youth's most innocent pleasures at being attractive as are required by nature itself. But still, there was a spell around her, like that around the elves. Her blond hair sparkled with light; blue-tinged flames gleamed from her blue eyes. Around her, these flames drew a magic circle. . . . She was not from Copenhagen, spent only a few winters in the city and disappeared again. Some years later, it was said to general surprise that she had become married to a widower in a provincial town—she who belonged to the world of poetry.[40]

But Brandes's devoted celebration of Thilly's Nordic delicacy and captivating innocence leaves little doubt as to the genuineness of his youthful infatuation, which supposedly was reciprocated—and it is impossible to avoid the question of how history would have turned out had Brandes married Regine's foster child and acquired Kierkegaard's youthful sweetheart as his unofficial mother-in-law. Think of what information he could have wangled out of her once the necessary confidentiality had been established, what confidences and secret thoughts, what fascinating possibilities for access to documents!

If Brandes failed to conquer Thilly, he nonetheless succeeded in writing a biography, *Søren Kierkegaard: A Critical Presentation in Outline*, which was published in a print run of twelve hundred copies in April 1877. The book came out that same year in Swedish and two years later in German. Regine thus began to take her place in history, a prospect that Kierkegaard had on several occasions held out to her. But she was also able to study a *litterateur*'s first attempt at explaining why the famous engagement neither could nor should have succeeded. Brandes writes:

On the 10th of September 1840, Søren Kierkegaard became engaged. It sounds odd as soon as one hears it. It rings a bell, as they say: in this and that year on this and that day Simeon Stylites climbed down from his pillar, offered a young lady his arm and urged her to take her place up there, however small the apartment. He became engaged to a young and pretty girl of good family, a child in mind, almost a child in years. . . . Even had there been absolutely no special circumstances, this relationship would have been a practical impossibility. He as young betrothed! He the Sphinx who, as Egypt's, had lain in the desert for some thousand years and brooded over life's riddle, engaged to a pretty young light-hearted girl. . . . Him and her! It was the old folk tale: beauty arm in arm with the beast, except that the beast was so wise, so captivating, so indescribably interesting, that the beauty could not tire of listening; for the beast was after all, as in the story, in no way any beast; the beast, it was—spirit.[41]

Whatever did Regine think on reading those lines? Did she react with a shamed nod of recognition, or was it with an offended shake of the head? Could she recognize Kierkegaard in the description of the fabled being that had suddenly, after some thoughtful centuries in the desert sand, looked in her direction and overwhelmed her with the greatness of his spirit and spellbound her with words she could never later forget? Or did she simply not wish to read what Brandes had to say in public about her youthful love? We don't know, but taking into consideration that Regine often received Brandes in her home, and that the biography caused much discussion, it seems unlikely that she would have ignored the book with its portrayals of scenes in which she herself not only played the main female role but also provided the motivational energy. Brandes underlines the engagement as the event that brought Kierkegaard's artistic powers to life, so that Regine becomes a kind of unwilling muse. But note well, a muse most effective in her absence.

> He is amazed that he longed so deeply for the young girl when she was not there, that he was really happier sitting alone and thinking about her than when she was there. He needed her not for loving her . . . yes, sometimes it was as though her presence could be disturbing for him. He also wrote to her rather than spoke. He had lived far too inwardly, far too spiritually, for this sensual nearness not to be as though too much.[42]

Brandes's apportioning of male and female characteristics may look at first glance rather traditional: Kierkegaard is the spiritual and introverted one, the brooder, who sits in melancholy recalling his love before in any physical sense it has even begun, while Regine is the one of immediacy, innocence, and quite unqualified to grasp what kind of a being she had got involved with. But Brandes is not simply rehearsing prejudices about traditional gender roles. More discerningly, he goes on:

> In this relationship he was, as odd as it sounds, the passive, the young girl the active force. He approached her; in a trice her nature fertilized his inner being. From that moment on he cannot but help it that she becomes unnecessary for his life.[43]

Brandes has grasped here an essential dimension in the relationship between Kierkegaard and the object of his love: in a metaphorical detail he inverts the gender roles so that, instead of Kierkegaard fertilizing her, it is Regine who fertilizes Kierkegaard, but in doing so she unwittingly signs her own death warrant and is left to herself with her desire unsatisfied, her deep longing for love, her aroused and ill-fated expectation of happiness. Brandes knew nothing when writing his biography of the entries in which Kierkegaard in plain words acknowledged his fear of Regine's passion and expressed horror at the thought of her breaking with Fritz, but they provide undeniable support for his suspicion that Regine was the "active force" in the relationship. This force, according to Brandes, was first and foremost sensual or erotic in nature, a bright and shining lust for life that failed to penetrate the gloom of Kierkegaard's later so world famous melancholy:

> She was not the one who could break his melancholy's silence; she even had no suspicion of what struggled within him. He could not speak; but without speaking he did not dare to possess her; so there was no other way out than a break, a break on sadly humiliating conditions.[44]

Brandes interprets the break as Kierkegaard's desperate attempt to save Regine from a fearful marriage with a demonic and speculative spirit who had in an unguarded moment let himself be seduced by his deep but totally unredeemable longing to live a quite normal bourgeois life. His genius made such a life impossible, so he had to be content with poeticizing it; but just as he also knew how to poeticize, so existence itself was resurrected in a transfigured form in his works, genuinely tragic and universally relevant. A mere fleeting snip of reality was for him stimulant enough:

> There are productive spirits who require many and great destinies or experiences in order to produce a small work. There is a kind of poet who, from a hundred pounds of rose leaves, produces one drop of attar of roses. And on the other hand there are talents whose nature is so fruitful, whose inner climate is so tropical, that from a quite plain everyday life situation, which they experience with the highest energy, they extract whole series of important works. They are like those treeless islands in the Pacific on which passengers from a passing ship leave some fruit-kernels, and which many years later are covered with mighty forests. Kierkegaard belonged to the latter kind.[45]

It is an impressive image, the more so as Regine had been on just such a tropical island when she received the letters that Kierkegaard had sent to her in the time of the engagement, when he had come to sense in earnest the scope of his artistic powers and was therefore forced to recognize that life with Regine, on which the letters so animatedly focused, had to remain just an idea and would never amount to more than an aching dream.

History does not tell us what Fritz's reactions were to Brandes's biography. But that he may have become reconciled to his strange fate is supported by a particular remark: Fritz was Chairman of the Board for the Refsnæs Hospital at Kalundborg for tubercular children from poor families. When the hospital was opened on the 17th of October 1875, he and his wife were invited on a tour with the hospital's inspector, N. C. Ottesen, in whose office there hung side-by-side portraits of Grundtvig and Kierkegaard. Fritz stood there and said to those around him: "Long after Grundtvig's influence is over and done, his will still be alive!"[46] The comment is said to have pleased Regine immensely, and there can of course be many reasons for that, but her pleasure might just have been due to Fritz's acknowledging in public that he had now overcome his Kierkegaard crisis. As for Fritz himself, he may have been a little proud at the thought that, thanks to his wife's amorous past, he was sure of going down in history in celebrated company.

FIREBURN: FRITZ'S REENCOUNTER
WITH THE WEST INDIES

When the thirty-five-year-old Brandes published his biography in 1877, Fritz had just a few months before reached sixty and was now a gentleman beyond his best years. But there was still use for this cultivated, experienced, and efficient man. Fritz occupied positions in management, contributed to several philanthropic undertakings, and had positions of honor, including, as we have seen, chairing the Relief Fund in 1864. He was also appointed alderman in Copenhagen's magistracy's second department, which oversaw the city's finances, and in 1873 became the same department's prefect. Even though uncertain health forced him to leave that post a few years later, Fritz continued to take part as municipal representative in the administration of local affairs. He had also retained his interest in the Danish tropical colonies, so when in 1878 there was a rebellion in St. Croix, it was natural to appoint Fritz chairman of the commission which went out early in 1879 to the West Indian islands to form an impression of the conditions after "Fireburn," as that rebellion is usually called.[47]

It was against this tragic background, then, that after almost twenty years in his motherland, Fritz had an opportunity to see again the three islands of which for five problematic years he had been governor. It was hardly a sentimental journey, but that the visit was in many ways affecting is apparent from a letter, in which Regine, on the 3rd of March 1879, gives Cornelia a summary of the travelogue she had received that same morning from Fritz. We understand that Fritz had first been at Barbados from where the journey proceeded to

44. "Centerline" is what the just over fifteen-mile stretch connecting Christiansted in the east and Frederiksted in the west is called. It was down this string-like, king-palm-lined avenue, cutting through some of the island's most profitable plantations, that Peter von Scholten rushed off on the night of the 3rd of July 1848 and not many hours later proclaimed freedom for the slaves in front of the fort in Frederiksted. The action occasioned Frederik VII's "most extreme displeasure" and led to von Scholten's dismissal.

St. Thomas. The voyage had been "remarkably fine," but when Governor Garde, who had invited Fritz to stay at Government House, described the state of the islands to him in the most dismal terms, Fritz had to confess to Regine that his "heart sank." The members of the commission had a tight agenda, from nine in the morning until half past seven in the evening, and it included inspection of

45. On Saturday the 31st of March 1917, at a solemn ceremony on St. Thomas, Danne-brog, the Danish flag, was lowered for the last time and the Stars and Stripes raised on high. The Danish West Indian Islands changed their name to the Virgin Islands of the United States and are now referred to informally as the US Virgin Islands. The transfer sum was twenty-five million dollars.

the burnt plantations. Regine became much concerned—"it is almost too much for a man of his age."

On his homecoming, Fritz was awarded the Grand Cross of the Order of the Dannebrog. The commission was effective and put forward a range of practical proposals: policing should be strengthened, the laborers' conditions improved, and the labor rules liberalized; correspondingly, the level of education in the black community and school attendance in general were to be increased; finally, as a preventative measure the commission proposed that a warship should again be stationed on the islands and a new barracks erected in the middle of St. Croix.[48]

Most people saw the value of these proposals, but few knew how they were to be financed. Not even Fritz. Like many others at the time he must have felt that Fireburn was the beginning of the end for Denmark as a colonial power. The three small Virgin Islands were sold to the United States in 1917 for twenty-five million dollars, and with that two hundred and fifty-one years of Danish colonial history came to a close.[49] What might today be found shocking, shortsighted, and, in sentimental moments well nigh unforgivable, evoked only limited in-terest at the time. For generations the islands had presented a moral problem and since the middle of the nineteenth century they had been running at a decided loss.

When, on the 14th of December 1916, a referendum was held on the sale, only a little over a third of those entitled to vote took the trouble to do so—and among those 283,670 were for and 158,157 against. True to tradition, the islanders themselves were not asked for their preference, maybe because the majority of the whites had in a Gallup poll already acknowledged their desire to belong to the United States. How free Danish hands really were is debatable. After the outbreak of the First World War the Americans feared that Germany would invade Denmark and then place military units on these small tropical islands so close to the Panama Canal. Power politics of this kind were something the population of a small country like Denmark should not meddle with.[50]

EXIT TO ETERNITY

In 1880, steam-miller Emil Winning disposed of his life's project and returned with Cornelia to the capital, where they settled in Bredgade. Since the two sisters no longer had any need to write to each other but could at last talk together arm in arm, our main source for their activity ran dry. What we know of the Schlegels' lives in the 1880s is therefore very limited and in the nature of incidental glimpses. One such glimpse is captured by the local historian Gunnar Sandfeld, who reports that during these years they holidayed in Vedbæk, where for the summer they rented a villa "Strandlyst," north of Vedbæk Kro:

> Here they swam in Øresund, that is, it was, to be sure, only Regine who did so. Every morning she took a dip. The villa's garden abutted an inn's garden, in whose straw-roofed pavilion the poet Holger Drachmann regularly partied with his friends. Regine was no doubt unable to avoid hearing what went on there (speeches, poetry readings, etc.).

We can only guess at what the "etc." conceals, but Drachmann was a sensual Renaissance man, so the merrymaking was unlikely to have been of the purely intellectual kind. That it was Regine who ventured into the waves while Fritz preferred solid ground fits quite well with the picture that the letters have conveyed of these two over the course of time. The temporary neighbor-relations there at Vedbæk, between the quiet married couple and the modern poet who celebrated British socialism, present also a picture of the transition between the nineteenth and twentieth centuries and of the colossal upheavals in the offing, or already under way in a reality visible if one peeked out of the window.

46. One of the last letters that Olivia Olsen wrote from St. Croix before her death was addressed to her brother-in-law and introduced with a loving backward glance: "Dear sweet Fritz! That is what you were always called, when with my usual vehemence I would insist I was right, and you with your usual Indian calm sat and looked at me and finally exclaimed, 'Yes but you are plain, damned crazy, and you will keep on seeing things from such a twisted side.'" He has taken his Indian calm with him in this undated photograph, in which hair no longer manages to hide his rather low-set, protruding ears, which Regine would tease him about when she was in the mood.

In the 1880s Fritz was several times high bailiff, or prefect, of Copenhagen, and in 1886 he received the honorable and honorary title of *Geheimekonferentsraad* (Privy Councillor). A long and active life came to an end on Monday the 8th of June 1896, when Fritz died at the age of seventy-nine. On the following day this death notice could be read in *Berlingske Tidende*:

That *Geheimeconferentsraad* **J. F. Schlegel**, Grand Cross of the Order of the Dannebrog and Dannebrog's Man, has died on the 8th inst., is announced by his wife.

Regina Schlegel

Interment is set for Saturday the 13th of June, **12 o'clock**, from the **Church of Our Lady**.

On Saturday the 13th of June, the evening edition of *Berlingske Tidende* reported on the burial that had just taken place:

> **Burial**. Today noon at 12 o'clock, interred from the Church of Our Lady *Geheimeconferentsraad J. F. Schlegel*.
> The coffin was arranged between green plants and *guéridons* with lighted candles and was covered with fine wreaths and palm decorations. There was a wreath from the children at the coastal hospital at Refsnæs, from the Sisterly Benevolent Society, and the University Jubilee's Danish Society.

"Guéridons" are tall, column-shaped or three-legged decorative tables with a circular surface area on which candelabra are usually placed. Sometimes a Negro supports the *guéridon*'s surface, which in this case would have been grotesque considering the deceased's West Indian past, though it would have harmonized well with the "palm decorations" that provided a tropical leavening in the classically chilly church space.

> While a farewell sounded from the organ, the coffin is carried out of the church, after which the burial took place at Assistents Cemetery.

As the century ran out, so too did Regine's circle of friends and acquaintances. Maria Olsen died, eighty-three years old, in 1892. On Monday the 22nd of January 1900—it was the day before Regine's seventy-eighth birthday—her beloved brother-in-law Emil died at eighty-two. Cornelia, the wise bosom friend, tactful confidante, the favorite sister, died on the 26th of March 1901 at the age of eighty-three and was buried at Vestre Cemetery beside her Emil. The following year it was the turn of Jonas, the good-hearted theologian and big brother, who was eighty-six. Oluf, the last of the Olsen siblings, the correct civil servant who was treated so harshly by life but yet survived his brothers, sisters, and brothers- and sisters-in law, first found peace on Wednesday the 11th of July 1906, on the way to being ninety-two.

47. "She was of a rare, genuine femininity," remarked Kierkegaard in his notebook from 1849 of Cornelia, who was Regine's favorite sister and bosom friend. Cornelia's remark that "Mag. K" was in her eyes a "good person" in spite of the break with Regine was something he never forgot. It is not known when F. W. Schmidt in Horsens photographed Cornelia, but the picture was presumably taken at the end of the 1860s. With flowers in her hair and wild head ornaments, she singularly anticipates the hippie culture of a century later.

PART 3

1897–1904

⌒∞⌒

"THEN COMES A DREAM FROM MY YOUTH'S SPRING . . ."

In his rather strange book *Repetition* (1843), Kierkegaard has a young unnamed person seek out a gentleman by the name of Constantin Constantius in order to ease a heart bursting with love. This love is of the complex romantic kind that never succeeds, and the young man paces restlessly up and down the floor reciting over and over again the same strophe from Poul Martin Møller's "Den Gamle Elsker" (The Old Lover):[1]

> Then comes a dream from my youth's spring
> > In my chair reclining,
> For you, I with all my heart am longing
> > You sun of women shining![2]

Constantin Constantius, a man of some experience, admits that the scene with the young man has made a deep impression on him. He doubts not for a second that the youth is deeply and sincerely in love but, psychologist that he is, he soon realizes that because the young man has started to recollect his love, he has, in effect, already brought his relationship to the young girl to an end, so that she must cede place to the realization of the strong artistic forces she has aroused in the young man. What was at work here was something Constantin Constantius called a "strange dialectic,"[3] but he is convinced that if anyone can talk of the "love of recollection," it has to be this young man.

It is hardly a wishful misrepresentation to read this little episode with Constantin Constantius pacing the floor as a piece of poetically re-worked autobiography. In his letters from the time of the engagement, Kierkegaard would also weave in a line from Poul Martin Møller's poem about the old lover, so that the young Regine might perhaps in this sad whisper form some intimation of the scope of the dark fate awaiting her.

Now, these many years later, there was no disturbed young man pacing up and down the floor but an elderly Regine sitting in her armchair and thinking back to that time long ago when, as the "sun" of women, she was yearned for by the young Kierkegaard. It was she, therefore, who could talk in earnest of a recollection's love that grew with time and, in the end, filled everything. If we allow ourselves a glance at the years in which Regine survived Fritz, it seems almost as if she wanted to break the silence that the decorum of marriage had imposed on her. When she now began to talk about Kierkegaard he was not someone from a far-off past, but a loved one who throughout the years had been invisibly by her side.

In other words, Regine seems to have had no difficulty in being simultaneously Schlegel's wife and Kierkegaard's fiancée. And although it was he, Kierkegaard, who had taken her into history, there was something that it was at last her turn to say![4] In any case, she was not allowed to stay alone with her history for long. With the letters of condolence there also came direct inquiries about the possibility of talking with the small widow in black about her enigmatic young love. At first rather reserved, she came to see that, as the last survivor of the three, she had to be heard while there was time. She had been so shyly evasive when Brandes visited her while Fritz was still alive, but once a widow she became just as amiably accommodating should someone ask about him—that is, about the other him.

Purely practical matters provided the first occasion. One day in the late summer of 1896, Regine opened the door to the librarian Julius Clausen, who recalled their first meeting in these words:

> A rather small, white-haired old lady with the friendliest of expressions opens the door for me the first time I ring the doorbell at the house on the corner at Nørrebrogade and Sortedamsdossering. She is dressed in a black silk dress and wears a fringed cap. Just about a year ago she was left the widow of Privy Councillor *Schlegel*, a highly respected civil servant, who was recently prefect in Copenhagen, and formerly the governor of the Danish West Indies. The councillor left a very large library—a sort of universal library including all sorts of books—the type of library established before this era of specialized knowledge. Mrs. Schlegel's agent has asked me to organize and catalog this library before it is sent to auction. That is why I am here.[5]

Fritz had left roughly seven thousand books, which Julius Clausen was to catalogue for the auction that opened on the 5th of October that same year. This inventory was compiled in the most enchanting summer weather, and when Clausen was finished with each day's work around nine o'clock in the evening, Regine would come into the library and offer refreshments, usually a glass of guava rum, which she mixed with ice water and served to the exhausted librarian. "You must be tired now. You could certainly use a little something cool to drink," she said—and of course it was just what Clausen could use.

> And so we sat there in the large rooms, warm from the summer heat, while the cool of the evening fell and the conversation began. I, of

course, knew who she was, but naturally did not presume to make any allusions. But the old lady was less reticent. It always began with Schlegel, whose excellent qualities she praised in high-toned fashion, but it always ended with—Kierkegaard.[6]

Julius Clausen was not yet thirty years old and approached Regine with as much respect as curiosity—just as Brandes earlier. One also understands that he had an urge to question the elderly woman about "the dream of her young days" but "naturally" had enough tact to suppress his curiosity, which we may now regret. Yet Regine could sense that the young man sitting there was straining to converse about everything else while politely sipping his drink, so she didn't mince matters and told him about the men in her life, first Fritz and then this Søren. What she had to say Clausen does not tell us, but in Regine's stressing Fritz's "excellent qualities," there is an emotional sobriety that might just have suggested to him something of the character of their relationship, for qualities are not the kind of thing one loves, one loves a person.

Clausen appears to have been a master of this discreet form of indiscretion. In connection with the embarrassments that Kierkegaard's sealed letter occasioned, he remarks: "I cannot say whether this played a role in Schlegel's seeking the post in the West Indies. His wife said nothing about that."[7] But, thanks to a kind of intimation, Clausen has as it were received whispered acknowledgment that Fritz might well have had other than purely career motives for applying for a job outside Denmark—among them, and not least, the intense presence of this Kierkegaard, from whom his wife continued to have difficulty in freeing herself.

THE RIGHT TO REGINE'S LOVE STORY

During 1897 Regine moved out of her "place on the corner" and in with Oluf, who lived in a villa at Frederiksberg. The address was 10 Alhambravej. Four years earlier, sometime in 1893, while Fritz was still living, Regine had visited Kierkegaard's niece Henriette Lund to tell her that on Regine's death she would have custody of the letters and entries that had to do with her relationship to Kierkegaard. The arrangement took Henriette rather by surprise, since for her it meant that Regine was not able to "bring herself to destroy" the documents in question and so wanted another "to take on that task." Regine brought up the matter again on a later visit, but Henriette was still of several minds, and it was only after the intervention of an unnamed "cousin" that she began to see the unique importance of the material for future biographies of Kierkegaard. In order to avoid possible misunderstanding, she chose however to contact Regine once more:

> I went then to her and asked if I had been mistaken in once regarding the decision to send me the letters in question as a reluctance on her part to destroy them herself, and therefore almost a prayer to me that I should carry out the sad action. She seemed for a moment undecided; but I soon came to see that this had been wrong, and that something more lay behind it, which she herself expressed as a feeling of duty to the departed—not least in consideration of his great religious significance—to pass on, without reservation, whatever could serve to throw light also on this period of his life.[8]

The moment's indecision that Henriette thought she detected in Regine was probably due not to Regine's being in doubt about the value of preserving the letters, but to her momentary horror that it might have occurred to Henriette to destroy them. On the contrary, Regine wanted them to come to wider public attention. Some time in the fall of 1895, she gave the rest of the material to Henriette, who supplemented it with relevant quotations from Kierkegaard's journals. A year later she read her account aloud to Regine, who according to Henriette expressed her "entire satisfaction." The two women then made an agreement that the material be held by Henriette, who after Regine's death would arrange for the account to come out in book form.

A few years later, in 1898, Regine approached Henriette again, this time in order to retract the first part of their agreement. She didn't like the idea that the material lay in a private home, where it might be exposed to "fire and other accidents." So, on the 12th of November that same year, the papers were handed over to the university library on Fiolstæde, something that particularly pleased Regine, but about which Henriette was not especially enthusiastic. It was not only that there was a more or less blatant expression of mistrust in Regine's decision, but that the new place of safekeeping gave others access to material over which Henriette understandably enough felt she had some ownership rights. That this in particular worried Henriette appears in a letter that she wrote to Regine shortly before the material's transfer to the university library, and in which she repeated the contents of the promises Regine had made:

> Since everything had already been given to me "as my rightful property," as the expression goes, it will not surprise you if I now remind you of the promises you made when we parted earlier today: 1) that you yourself will remove none of the materials upon which I have in good faith based my presentation; and 2) that the package will be sealed

48. A self-consciously lounging Henriette Lund—daughter of Kierkegaard's favorite sister, Petrea Severine—poses in the photographer's studio. She just happens to have a book with her that could well be by her beloved "Uncle Søren." She helped to ensure his reputation through her memoirs and a number of conversations that she held with Regine, included in *My Relationship to Her: From Søren Kierkegaard's Posthumous Papers*, which appeared in 1904.

in your presence for preservation in the library. As number 3, I would like to ask if you would agree to add the condition that the package remain unopened for the first ten years after your death? That is what I had intended, and I have very much wished that it could be arranged in this fashion. *After all, everything about which people might want to know is set forth in my presentation.* But even though I carefully and conscientiously adhered to the truth, a certain caution was nonetheless necessary. I am not delighted at the thought that everyone—thus also including the crudest hands—could get hold of his posthumous papers so quickly and perhaps distort them *from the very beginning.*[9]

Henriette's letter betrays a peculiar mixture of genuine concern for the material's future fate and a fussily throbbing self-interest that aims at monopolizing the moving love story lest it fall into the hands of the wrong people, which really means anyone but Henriette herself. As a consequence of this *double entendre* she points out that her presentation on the one hand gives an exhaustive account of the engagement but is, on the other hand, marked by a "certain caution," which is appealing enough, but hardly a strong argument from the point of view of historical biography.

The reason why the now seventy-four-year-old Regine chose to ignore Henriette's request to stipulate a ten-year moratorium was supposedly that she wanted her story told and told by more people. Within the same year Regine thus engaged in intense discussions with Hanne Mourier, her contemporary in years, who later summarized what Regine had to tell her. This commitment to paper was, according to Mourier in an account addressed directly to Regine, done on Regine's express initiative, but not with publication in view; the intention was to produce a document that could, if needed, form a counterbalance to "inaccurate accounts of your own and your husband's attitudes toward, and views of, Søren Kierkegaard."[10] Mourier's account includes a short postscript dated the 1st of March 1902, in which Regine declares herself "satisfied" with the "present version" of what she had reported. [11] The full account amounts to seven pages in print and includes a range of important information about the history of the engagement, chronological as well as biographical; but the fact that the relationship had extensive emotional repercussions is touched on only peripherally, and so far Regine's riddle remains intact.

"... HE IS THE RIDDLE, THE GREAT RIDDLE"

Brandes failed to give a satisfactory account of the nature of the Kierkegaardian forces that from their artistic launching-pad in accidental earthly constellations resulted in immortal works and managed to elevate an impossible infatuation within the Copenhagen ramparts to gripping global art. Like many others since, Brandes came to the laconic conclusion: ". . . in other words he is the riddle, the great riddle."[12] Perhaps it was a not dissimilar solution that Regine was left with: Kierkegaard was the riddle in her life, the great riddle, which she bore for the rest of her life, whereby she went on to become a riddle for herself—and for us others: Regine's riddle.

And perhaps it was the desire for someone to solve this riddle, or at least sense its character, that had the aging Regine further engaging her Copenhagen circle of acquaintances. A month before the transfer to the university library, she contacted the librarian, Raphael Meyer, with an offer that he "listen to what 'an old lady' had to tell."[13] Meyer soon realized that he had been summoned not because Regine needed some chatty diversion, but because she wanted to make sure that her enigmatic story would survive her, which is why she also requested of Meyer that after her death, "when the matter of Søren Kierkegaard's engagement would again become a burning issue," he use the information "he had obtained in conversations with her."[14]

So during the winter and all the way to May 1899, Meyer paid weekly visits to Regine at Alhambravej, and like Hanna Mourier he wrote down the content of their conversations immediately afterward. Regine, says Meyer, was immeasurably happy about the growing, now also international interest being shown in her former betrothed—even if the French, she thought, would never understand him. That the French existentialists, with Sartre and Camus at their forefront, were to contribute to Kierkegaard's world fame was something Regine could not, of course, know. Nor could she be reconciled to the Danish priests' reservations about Kierkegaard; indeed one day, coming upon a Copenhagen priest who had no knowledge of Kierkegaard, she clenched her little fist and took him properly to task: "This is unacceptable in an educated man in the country where Kierkegaard was born and worked, and especially so with a pastor in the Danish Church." She suspected the negligent priest subsequently got down to some reading.[15]

Raphael Meyer prepared the conversations for publication with Regine and had them included in his 1904 *Kierkegaardske Papirer, Forlovelsen. Udgivne for Fru Regine Schlegel* (Kierkegaard's Papers, the Engagement. Published for Mrs. Regine Schlegel). In the preface he tells how, after Kierkegaard's death, the papers were sent, as we know, to the West Indies in two sealed packages that also contained Regine's own letters, which according to herself she had "luckily" burnt; after which Meyer tells us:

> The remainder she hid away as a valuable treasure. According to her testimony, later, during her husband's final illness, when she was very

much affected, partly by sorrow and partly by repeated attacks of influenza, she presented the letters [from Kierkegaard to herself] to S.K.'s niece Miss Henriette Lund.[16]

It is uncertain whether Raphael Meyer, who in his introduction mentions that the material was to be "opened and published" only after Regine's death, had himself respected the clause, or had given in to the temptation to peek into the material that was in the library where he worked daily. Nor can it be excluded that Regine felt that the material would be best taken care of by Meyer, and therefore made known by word of mouth that he could ignore the clause. In any case, the contest for the right to Regine's love story had begun, even while the old lady was still going about in Frederiksberg as large as life. She was decidedly not without a share in the growing interest in her own fate. The readiness with which she opened the door after her husband's death to those who wanted to hear her tell about Kierkegaard can be interpreted either as an expression of old-age narcissism or as an enduring concern to understand why passion in platonic love can be as intense as in consummated eroticism, that indeed platonic love can in certain cases be much stronger and significantly deeper than the erotic variety.

In his memoirs, the theater historian and actor Robert Neiiendam, whose acquaintance Regine made when young Neiiendam was apprenticed at a bookshop in Gammel Kongevej, a stone's throw from Alhambravej, mentions in passing the conversations he had with Regine playing the double role of Schlegel's wife and Kierkegaard's fiancée. Neiiendam describes Regine as a "small, amiable, and very attractive lady with kind eyes, which must once have been full of life."[17] She had precise diction and a tactful tone, marked by many years in diplomacy, and when Neiiendam one day asked if a picture of Kierkegaard in a not further specified *History of Literature* resembled the portrayed, he received what was also a very diplomatic answer. "Both yes and no," was Regine's reply. "Kierkegaard's exterior was easy to caricature, and people exploited that." Neiiendam thought that Kierkegaard was always presented as stiff-backed, but to that Regine said only:

> "Yes, he was somewhat high-shouldered and his head tilted forward a bit, probably from all the reading and writing at his desks."[18]

Regine was loyal and loving to the last, happy to have been taken over into history. And just this thought compensated, according to Neiiendam, for what she had suffered: "Time had smoothed away the pain, and what remained was the memory of *the experience* in her life."[19] Interestingly, it is the very word "experience" that Julius Clausen fastens on when he mentions the epoch-making chapter in Regine's youth. "Regine never forgot the great experience of her early youth," he writes, and he defines it as "the sense of having been face to face with the exceptional, the rare."[20] Clausen kept in contact with Regine when, "up in her eighties," she had moved out to Frederiksberg. He notes with a distinctive candor that practically speaks for itself, "I visited her there often; and now she no longer spoke of Schlegel but only of Kierkegaard."[21] Still, neither Clausen nor any of the other diligent jotters succeeded in coaxing the riddle from the enigmatic widow. And old age's greedy decay then swallowed the remainder: "Aren't you the one I gave the ring to, the one I got from Søren," she asked him one day. "Unfortunately not," he had to admit.

"'OUR OWN DEAR, LITTLE REGINE'"

On Friday the 18th of March 1904, the small, sensitive woman with the snow-white hair died. She died, at home, eighty-two years old. She had been seen of late by her highly esteemed physician, Mads P. Buhl, who was married to Cornelia's daughter Mathilde. According to Frederiksberg parish's burial records, the cause of death was influenza. The following day Oluf had this death notice printed in *Berlingske Tidende*'s morning edition:

> My dear sister, **Regine Schlegel**, widow of Privy Councillor F. Schlegel, died yesterday, 82 years old.
>
> Alhambravej, the 19th of March

On Sunday the 20th of March, the newspaper *Politiken* had a somewhat unhelpful obituary that first mentions a traffic accident of which the Privy Councillor's wife had been a victim some years previously, then cites her relationship to Kierkegaard, and finally touches on the marriage with Schlegel, which once more comes last.

Gehejmekonferensraadinde

Schlegel

Gehejmekonferensraadinde Schlegel died on Friday at the advanced age of more than 82.

We will recall the elderly lady's name from a few years ago, when she was run over on the street, she broke, if memory serves, a hip on that occasion, but recovered from this accident so dangerous for a lady of her age.

But Mrs. Schlegel's name has another and much greater claim to be mentioned, now that she has died, for it is no secret that she, who was the daughter of Councillor of State and Departmental Head Terkel Olsen, was at one time engaged to Søren Kierkegaard.

Young and cheerful, she became engaged in 1840 to the later so famous philosopher. But 13 months later he broke off the engagement. As he later wrote: "She could not break his melancholy's silence." It is well known how, in order to soften the break for her, Kierkegaard did everything possible to show himself to her in the worst possible light, and after standing up to the gossip for 14 days—as he himself says— traveled in despair to Berlin, where he stayed for some time.

Miss Regine Olsen married 6 years later Head Clerk Schlegel, who later had a brilliant career, became governor in the West Indies, Prefect, and rose to the highest honors in the State.

Regine was buried at Assistens Cemetery beside her husband. The funeral was conducted on the 24th of March by Dean Juul Bondo, who had also officiated at Fritz's funeral. On the gravestone we read:

Here rests Johan Frederik Schlegel, Privy Councillor S. K. DBMD. Born 22nd of January 1817, died 8th of June 1896. And his wife Regine Schlegel, née Olsen, born the 23rd of January 1822, died the 18th of March 1904.

One notes the initials "S. K." and associates them inevitably with those of his rival, who seems to have been fated to follow Fritz all the way into the realm of the dead. But then on second thought it is obvious that "S. K." does not stand for Søren Kierkegaard, but is an abbreviation for "Stor Kors" (Grand Cross), the honor Fritz received for his contribution in the West Indies, while "DBMD" is a compressed form of "Dannebrogsmand."

Just as in the hectic real world Regine and Søren were seldom far from each other, so too the distance between them in the silent world of the dead became very surmountable, roughly fifty meters, if that. And just as old Mrs. Schlegel, having stood by her consort's gravestone, presumably found her way just as quietly to the Kierkegaardian gravestone to lose herself there in her own thoughts, so do those visitors, who on occasion now wander inquisitively along the narrow paths between the graves, bind Søren and Regine together again and thus help to place them in the same lineage of ill-fated lovers as Pyramus and Thisbe, Dante and Beatrice, Abelard and Héloise, Romeo and Juliet, Kafka and Felice, who will forever belong together, because they could not be united in the world of time but had to wait patiently for eternity. For as Søren once said: "You see, Regine, in eternity there is no marriage; there both Schlegel and I will be happily together with you."[22]

It can look like a strange augury of this heavenly bigamy that in one of his letters from the time of the engagement the same Søren had mentioned his fiancée in the plural form of "our Regine"—did he know already, then, that Regine would never belong to him, but always to more, many, all? When, in 1849, he wrote the sealed letter, he used the expression "our Regine" again and put it in quotation marks to show that he was quoting himself:

> Beloved she was. My existence was to accentuate her life absolutely, my activity as an author could also be viewed as a monument to her praise and honor. I am taking her with me into history. And I who, melancholy, had only one wish, to enchant her: *there* it is not denied me; there I walk by her side; as a master of ceremonies I escort her in triumph, saying: please make a bit of room for her, for "our own dear little Regine."[23]

So make room for little Regine! For even though she was, according to Fritz, no bigger than that she could run dry-shod between the raindrops, she made her presence richly felt. Likewise her riddle, which is no easier to solve than all the other riddles whereby love at any time teases and blesses those who love in earnest.

Postscript and Acknowledgments

Since Regine's letters have not been indexed, it is not possible to give them references. Unless otherwise stated, the letters in part 1 belong to the year referred to in the chapter in which they appear. Where the letters from another year are included in a chapter, the relevant chronological data are given. Due to the much longer time span covered by part 2 and part 3, letters here are dated only when and where this is judged important. Orthographic variations in the originals are of course not preserved in translation, while abbreviated words have been written out in full.

Regine's letters contain only a few corrections, additions, or inked-out lines. In certain cases I have inserted a missing word or letter to facilitate reading, just as I have sometimes added an explanatory comment. Underlining in the letters is rendered here in italic.

Regine writes in what in professional circles is called a "Latin" hand—that is, her handwriting reminds us very much of our own and is therefore relatively easy to read. Cornelia's handwriting is much harder to decipher, not only because it is "Gothic," but because the ink is in certain places so faded that the words are almost illegible. Anne Mette Hansen's offer to transcribe Cornelia's letters, using her expertise as a PhD in Nordic philology, has therefore been of vital importance. For her skilled and conscientious work I owe her a great debt of gratitude.

When a grant from the Gad Foundation made possible a visit to the former colonies, I was given a lively tour round Saint Croix by the author Nina York, who introduced me to people whose professional knowledge has been of benefit to this book. In this regard I want to extend my thanks to the historian Michael Sheen and his wife Jane, who opened their home to me and showed me their outstanding collection of stereographs, and to the historian George Tyson and his Danish wife Camilla Jensen, who received me at their home in Cane Garden and made it possible for me to go inside Schlegel's former summer residence, which is today owned by Richard H. Jenrette. Thanks to Arnold R. Highfield and his wife Shirley, to Myron Jackson, Ronald Lockhart, David Knight, and Eleanor Gibney—all, jointly and severally, have confirmed that the legendary West Indian hospitality is in the best of health.

I will always remember with a special gratitude Agnete and Torben Tryde, the married couple from Søllested who entrusted me unquestioningly with

Postscript and Acknowledgments

Regine and Cornelia's correspondence. After the couple died, I kept in contact with their daughters, Ingeborg and Eva Tryde, to whom I likewise owe a big debt of gratitude. Special thanks are due also to Gad's Forlag in the persons of Project Manager Henrik Sebro and the company's director, Ulrik Hvilshøj, the latter of whom readily and generously undertook to be the book's editor. Poul Olsen, head consultant at the National Archive, and Anne Walbom, chair of the Danish West Indian Society, have done me the favor of reading through the manuscript. Thanks are due to Erhard Bruun for letting me use his miniature portrait of Regine as an illustration in the book, and also to Hans Fonsbøll and Erik Fonsbøll for their helpfulness and for the loan of Emil Bærentzen's drawing of Regine. Thanks, too, to my son Adam Garff for photographing Regine's letters as well as other things for the book.

Finally, I would extend my sincere thanks to Assistant Editor Hannah Paul and Senior Production Editor Natalie Baan of Princeton University Press. They have both been a pleasure to work with and have lent to the work a refreshing thoroughness and inspiring enthusiasm. Last, but unconditionally not least, I want to thank Alastair Hannay, who is not just an experienced and excellent Kierkegaard translator, but also an internationally acknowledged Kierkegaard researcher with a comprehensive body of work. His willingness to take on the translation of the book I regard as a gift.

Notes

PREFACE

1. Georg Brandes, *Levned* [Life], vol. 1. Copenhagen and Kristiania: Gyldendal, 1905, p. 207. With minor modification the translation is from Bruce H. Kirmmse, *Encounters with Kierkegaard* [*EK*]: *A Life as Seen by His Contemporaries*, collected, edited, and annotated by Bruce H. Kirmmse, tr. Bruce H. Kirmmse and Virginia R. Laursen. Princeton, NJ: Princeton University Press, 1996, pp. 51–52*. References to this work where the translation is emended are marked, as here, with an asterisk.

TUNING IN

1. *Kierkegaard's Journals and Notebooks* [*KJN*], vol. 8., ed. Niels Jørgen Cappelørn, Alastair Hannay, Bruce H. Kirmmse, David D. Prossen, Joel D. S. Rasmussen, and Vanessa Rumble. Princeton and Oxford: Princeton University Press, 2015, NB22:146. References where the translation is emended are marked with an asterisk.
2. *KJN* 8, NB25:109*. The following unreferenced quotations are from this entry.
3. S. Kierkegaard, "Two Upbuilding Discourses," in *Eighteen Upbuilding Discourses*, tr. Howard V. Hong and Edna H. Hong. Princeton, NJ: Princeton University Press, 1990, preface ("himself" changed to "themself" to preserve in this case the convenient neuter gender of the Danish).
4. *KJN* 3, Notebook 15:4.
5. *KJN* 8, NB25:109. The following unreferenced quotations are from this entry.
6. *KJN* 9, NB27:21.
7. *KJN* 9, NB27:58.
8. *EK*, p. 42.

1855

1. Cf. Alfred Jeppesen, *Rejseliv i Danmark. Fra oldtidsvej til dampferge* [Travel in Denmark: From Ancient Way to Steam Ferry]. Copenhagen: Gyldendal, 1978, p. 145.
2. Constantin Constantius, *Repetition: An Essay in Experimental Psychology*, in *Søren Kierkegaard, Repetition and Philosophical Crumbs*, tr. M. G. Piety, with introduction by Edward F. Mooney. Oxford: Oxford University Press, 2009, p. 20.
3. H. C. Andersen, *I Spanien* [In Spain]. Danske Klassikere. Det Danske Sprog- og Litteraturselskab, Valby: Borgen, 2005, p. 10.
4. *EK*, pp. 45–46.
5. *KJN* 2, JJ:300.
6. *KJN* 8, NB22:146.
7. *KJN* 3, Notebook 15:4*.
8. *EK*, p. 34.
9. *KJN* 1, AA:53.
10. H. F. Rørdam, *Peter Rørdam. Blade af hans Levnedsbog og Brevvexling fra 1806 til 1844* [Peter Rørdam: Pages from his Life History and Correspondence from 1806 to 1844], vol. 1. Copenhagen: Karl Schønberg, 1891, p. 78.

11. *KJN* 3, Notebook 15:4.

12. *KJN* 1, AA:54.

13. *KJN* 2, FF:54.

14. *KJN* 2, EE:128.

15. *KJN* 2, EE:7.

16. *KJN* 3, Notebook 15:4.

17. *EK*, p. 40.

18. *KJN* 3, Notebook 15:4.

19. Bodil and Heino Døygaard, *Dansk Vestindien—i dag. Fra dansk koloni til turistparadis* [The Danish West Indies—Today: From Danish Colony to Tourist Paradise]. Copenhagen: Munksgaard, 1987, p. 29.

20. Cf. Thorkel Dahl and Kjeld de Fine Licht, *Kunstakademiets Vestindienstudier. Opmålimger 1961 af bygninger på St. Thomas and St. Croix* [The Academy of Art's West Indian Studies: Surveys in 1961 of Buildings on St. Thomas and St. Croix]. Copenhagen: Kunstakademiets Arkitektskole Forlag, 2004, p. 82.

21. Cf. Dahl and de Fine Licht, p. 82.

22. Cf. Sophie Petersen and Arne Ludvigsen, *Vore gamle Tropekolonier* [Our Old Tropical Colonies]. Copenhagen: Thaning and Appel, 1948, p. 82.

23. Søren Kierkegaard, *The Moment and Late Writings*, *Kierkegaard's Writings* [KW] XXIII, ed. and trans. Howard V. Hong and Edna H. Hong. Princeton, NJ: Princeton University Press, 1998, pp. 5–6* (*Fædrelandet* [The Fatherland], February 1854). References where the translation is emended will be marked with an asterisk.

24. *KW* XXIII, p. 21 (*Fædrelandet*, January 26, 1855).

25. *KW* XXIII, p. 33* (*Fædrelandet*, 22 March 1855, 2nd day of Pentecost 1854).

26. *KW* XXIII, p. 35* (*Fædrelandet*, January 1855).

27. *KW* XXIII, p. 39 (*Fædrelandet*, January 26, 1855).

28. *KW* XXIII, p. 186* (*Øieblikket* [The Moment] no. 5, July 27, 1855).

29. *KW* XXIII, p. 204* (*Øieblikket* no. 6, August 23, 1855).

30. *KW* XXIII, p. 123 (*Øieblikket* no. 2, June 4, 1855).

31. *KJN* 11 (forthcoming), Loose Paper 591* (1855).

32. Søren Kierkegaard, *Letters and Documents*, trans. Henrik Rosenmeier, *Kierkegaard's Writings* [KW] XXV. Princeton, NJ: Princeton University Press, 978, doc. XX, p. 28. References where the translation is emended will be marked with an asterisk.

33. *EK*, p. 117.

34. *EK*, p. 118.

35. *EK*, pp. 121–22.

36. *EK*, p. 125.

37. *EK*, p. 124.

38. *EK*, p. 119.

39. *EK*, pp. 257 and 259; cf. *KJN* 6, NB14:108.

40. Cf. *KJN* 6, NB14:108, and *KJN* 7, NB15:82.

41. *KW* XXV, p. 31.

42. *EK*, p. 128.

43. *EK*, p. 124.

44. Carl Weltzer, *Peter og Søren Kierkegaard* [Peter and Søren Kierkegaard] vols. 1–2. Copenhagen: G.E.C. Gads Forlag, 1936, p. 271.

45. *KW* XXV, p. 28.

46. *KW XXII, The Point of View*, trans. Howard V. Hong and Edna H. Hong. Princeton, NJ: Princeton University Press, 1998, p. 97.

1856

1. *EK*, pp. 47–48.
2. *KJN* 8, explanatory note, p. 846.
3. *Søren Kierkegaards Skrifter* (*SKS*), ed. Niels Jørgen Cappelørn et al. Copenhagen: Gads Forlag, 1994–2011, *K*(Commentary) 27, p. 5.
4. The letter is lost; cf. *EK*, p. 282n5.
5. *EK*, p. 48.
6. Weltzer, op. cit., p. 285.
7. Flemming Chr. Nielsen, *Alt blev godt betalt. Auktionen over Søren Kierkegaards indbo* [Everything Went for a Good Price: The Auction of Søren Kierkegaard's Household Contents]. Lyngby: Holkenfeldt 3, 2000, p. 60.
8. *KJN* 3, Notebook 15:4.
9. *EK*, p. 44.
10. *KW* XXV, p. 61. Letter 15.
11. *KW* XXV, pp. 62–63. Letter 17.
12. *KW* XXV, pp. 61–62. Letter 16.
13. *KW* XXV, p. 72. Letter 26.
14. *KW* XXV, pp. 72–73. Letter 27.
15. *KJN* 2, JJ:145.
16. *KJN* 4, NB5:109.
17. *KW* XXV, p. 83.
18. That the letters were sent on Wednesdays (cf. Henning Fenger, *Kierkegaard-Myter og Kierkegaard-Kilder* [Kierkegaard Myths and Kierkegaard Sources]. Odense: Odense Universitetsforlag, 1976, pp.149ff.) is uncertain and their chronological order is given differently in *SKS*.
19. *KJN* 3, Notebook 7:36.
20. *KW* XXV, p. 77, Letter 31*.
21. *KW* XXV, p 78, Letter 32.
22. Fenger, op. cit., pp. 158f.
23. *KW* XXV pp. 74–75. Letter 29.
24. *KW* XXV, p. 81. Letter 36.
25. *KW* XXV, p. 85. Letter 40*. See also *KJN* 3, Notebook 8, explanatory note, p. 616.
26. *KW* XI, *Stages on Life's Way*, trans. Howard V. Hong and Edna H. Hong. Princeton, NJ: Princeton University Press, p. 330, translator's translation here.
27. *KJN* 6 NB12:122.
28. *KW* XI, p. 306.
29. *KJN* 3, Notebook 14:4.
30. *EK*, pp. 213–14, 217.
31. *KW* XXV, p. 86. Letter 42.
32. *KJN* 3, Notebook 15:4.
33. *KJN* 3, Notebook 15:4.
34. *KJN* 3, Notebook 15:4.
35. *KJN* 3, Notebook 15:4.

36. *EK*, p. 36.

37. *KJN* 3, Notebook 15:4.

38. *EK*, p. 53*.

39. *EK*, p. 220.

40. *KJN* 3, Notebook 25:4.

41. *KJN* 2, JJ 107.

42. *KJN* 3, Notebook 15:4.

43. The first Danish railroad connection, between Kiel and Antona, opened in 1844. Kierkegaard traveled by train in May 1843, when returning from Berlin on the newly opened line to Angermünde, halfway to Stettin. *Adresseavisen* (a newspaper devoted to public announcements), no. 109, 10 May 1843, could report that this allowed the journey from Stettin to Berlin to be made in from nine to ten hours. Cf. *SKS*, K 10, 79, 19.

44. *KW* XXV, p. 150. Letter 79*.

45. *KW* XXV, p. 151. Letter 80.

46. *KW* XXV, pp. 154–55. Letter 82.

47. *KJN* 2, JJ:115.

48. *KJN* 2, JJ:115.

49. *KJN* 2, JJ:115.

50. *KJN* 3, JJ:116.

51. Søren Kierkegaard, *Repetition* and *Philosophical Crumbs*, tr. M. G. Piety. Oxford: Oxford University Press, 2009, p. 48.

52. *Repetition*, pp. 7 and 9 ("his beloved" changed to "the beloved").

53. *Repetition*, pp. 9–10.

54. *Repetition*, p. 12.

55. *Repetition*, pp. 12–13.

56. *Repetition*, p. 15.

57. *Repetition*, p. 15.

58. *Repetition*, pp. 12–13.

59. *Repetition*, p. 3.

60. *Repetition*, p. 19.

61. For the manuscript texts before alteration, see *Pap*. IV B 97,3,24, and 13.

62. Cf. *Repetition*, p. 74. Translator's translation here.

63. In the manuscript. See *SKS, K4*, p. 25. The image of a "darkened tooth" is from the Roman poet Horace's *Odes*, Book 2, viii, "Faithless Barine."

64. In the manuscript. See *SKS*, K4, p. 24.

65. *KJN* 2, JJ:155. "Exchange" is preferred here to "Dialogue."

66. *Repetition*, pp. 54–55.

67. *KJN* 4, NB3:43 and 44.

68. *EK*, pp. 35 and 40.

69. *EK*, pp. 162–163*.

70. *KW* XXV, p. 94. Letter 50.

71. *KW* XXV, p. 137. Letter 68.

72. For Henrik Lund's participation, see the commentary on *On My Activity as an Author*, in *SKS* K 13, p. 45.

73. *EK*, p. 192.

74. *KW* XXIII, p. 117 (*Øieblikket* no. 2, June 4, 1855).

75. *EK*, p. 134.

Notes to 1856

76. Weltzer, op. cit.

77. Cf. Raphael Meyer, *Kierkegaardske Papirer* [*KP*]. *Forlovelsen. Udgivne for Fru Regine Schlegel* [Kierkegaardian Papers: The Engagement. Published on Behalf of Mrs. Regine Schlegel]. Copenhagen and Kristiania: Gyldendalske Boghandel Nordisk Forlag, 1904. p. 142.

78. *KP*, pp. 142f.

79. *KJN* 5, NB10:191.

80. *KJN* 3, Notebook 15:6*.

81. *KP*, p. 144.

82. *EK*, p. 280n.

83. *KP*, p. vii.

84. *EK*, pp. 280n and 38.

85. Søren Kierkegaard, *Either/Or: A Fragment of Life*, tr. (abridged) Alastair Hannay. London: Penguin Books, 1992, p. 306.

86. *KJN* 3, Notebook15:6.

87. *Søren Kierkegaards Papirer* [Søren Kierkegaard's Papers] [*Pap.*], second and enlarged ed. by Niels Thulstrup, vols. 12–16, Copenhagen: Gyldendal, 1968–1978, *Pap.* XI 3 B 87, pp. 429f.

88. Alastair McKinnon, "*Hun* and *Hende*: Kierkegaard's Relation to Regine," *Kierkegaardiana* 22 (2002), p. 24.

89. Søren Kierkegaard, *Philosophical Crumbs*, in Søren Kierkegaard, *Repetition* and *Philosophical Crumbs*, tr. M. G. Piety, p. 101.

90. *KJN* 2, JJ: 115.

91. *KJN* 5, NB7:10.

92. *KJN* 6, NB12:29.

93. *KW* XXV, p. 335.

94. *KW* XXV, p. 330. Letter 236*.

95. *KJN* 6, p. 643n; cf. *KW* XXV, p. 335.

96. *KJN* 8, NB22:146.

97. *KW* XXV, p. 325. Letter 235.

98. *KW* XXV, p. 336.

99. *KJN* 1, AA:12.

100. *EK*, p. 37.

101. *H. C. Andersens Dagbøger, 1873–1875* [H. C. Andersen's Journals], ed. Tue Gad. Copenhagen: Det Danske Sprog- og Litteraturselskab, 1974, vol. 10, p. 38.

102. Cf. Villads Christensen, *København i Kristian den Ottendes og Frederik den Syvendes Tid, 1840–1875* [Copenhagen in the Time of Christian VIII and Frederik VII, 1840–1875], vol. 10. Copenhagen: G.E.C. Gads Forlag, 1905, p. 38.

103. The passage is quoted in *SKS K* 2–3, p. 180.

104. *SKS* 2, p. 235. Translator's translation here.

105. *KW* XXV, p. 325, Letter 235.

106. *KW* XXV, p. 334. Letter 238*.

107. *KJN* 6, NB12:29*.

108. *KJN* 8, NB22:146.

109. *KJN* 6, NB12:150.

110. *KJN* 5, NB7:10.

111. Søren Kierkegaard, *Fear and Trembling*, tr. Alastair Hannay. London: Penguin Classics, 2014, pp. 124–125.

112. *Fear and Trembling*, pp. 125–126.

113. *Fear and Trembling* pp. 125–126fn.

114. Weltzer, pp. 285f. The following five quotations are from the same source, pp. 312, 287, 288, and 291f.

115. Finn Gredal Jensen, "To genfundne breve. Fra J. C. Lund til P. C. Kierkegaard og fra-Regine Schlegel til Henrik Lund [Two Recovered Letters: From J. C. Lund to P. C. Kierkegaard and from Regine Schlegel to Henrik Lund]," *Dansk Studier*. Copenhagen: C. A. Reitzel, 2005, pp. 194–200.

116. *KP*, p. 145.

117. *KP*, p. 146.

118. *KP*, p. 146.

119. *Søren Kierkegaards Papirer*, ed. P. A. Heiberg, V. Kuhr, and E. Torsting, vols. 1–11, Copenhagen 1909–1948, *Pap.* X 5 B 262–263, pp. 429f.

120. *Pap.* X 5 B 263.

121. *Pap.* X V B 264.

122. *Pap.* X 5 B 263.

123. *KJN* 6, NB13:4.

124. As announced in *Departementstidenden* [Departmental News, henceforth *Dept.*], nos. 9–10, 1860, pp. 134f. These official reports are to be found in an edited version published by State Councillor J. Liebe. Cf. the relevant Danish State Archives at: http://www.virgin-islands-history.dk/a_wicomp.asp.

125. Weltzer, p. 305.

1857

1. Søren Kierkegaard, *Either/Or: A Fragment of Life*, tr. Alastair Hannay, abridged. London: Penguin Classics, 2004, p. 256.

2. *KJN* 3, Notebook 15:4.

3. *EK*, p. 57.

4. *EK*, p. 58.

5. Heiberg, *Intelligensblade*, no. 24, Copenhagen, 1843.

6. *Either/Or*, p. 250.

7. *Either/Or*, p. 112. "The Immediate Erotic Stages," not the Diary itself.

8. *Pap.* V B 53,26; cf. *SKS* K4, p. 434.

9. This reading draws its inspiration from Jean Baudrillard's *De la séduction* (English tr. by Brian Singer, *Seduction*, New York: St. Martins Press, 1990).

10. *Either/Or*, p. 265.

11. *Either/Or*, p. 358.

12. *Either/Or*, p. 251.

13. *Intelligensblade*, op. cit., pp. 285f.

14. *Pap.* V B 53,26.

15. Søren Kierkegaard, *The Concept of Anxiety: A Simple Psychologically Oriented Deliberation in View of the Dogmatic Problem of Hereditary Sin*, tr. Alastair Hannay. New York and London: Liveright Publishing Corporation/W.W. Norton & Company, 2014, p. 58.

16. *KJN* 6, 12:116.

17. *Either/Or*, p. 251*.

18. Leif Svalesen, *The Slave Ship Fredensborg*, tr. Pat Shaw and Selena Winsnes. Bloomington: Indiana University Press, 2000, p. 101.

19. Ibid., p. 110.

20. *KW* XXII (*SKS* 13:26).

21. Hornby, *Kolonierne i Vestindien*, pp. 273ff.

22. Hornby, *Kolonierne i Vestindien*, p. 275.

23. *KW* XXV, p. 140. Letter 69.

24. *KW* XXV, pp. 90–91. Letter 49.

25. *KW* XXV, pp. 102 and 104. Letter 54*

26. *KW* XVV, p. 105. Letter 54.

27. *KJN* 3, Notebook 8:42*.

28. *KW* XXV, p. 90. Letter 49.

29. *KW* XXV, p. 89. Letter 49.

30. *KW* XXV, p. 99. Letter 52.

31. *KW* XXV, p. 97. Letter 51 (to Pastor P. J. Spang).

32. *KJN* 3, Notebook 8:9.

33. *KW* XXV, p. 118. Letter 61 (to Pastor P. J. Spang).

34. *KW* XXV, p. 120. Letter 62.

35. *KW* XXV, pp. 133–134. Letter 68*.

36. *KW* XXV, p. 104. Letter 54.

37. *KW* XXV, p. 138. Letter 68.

38. *KW* XXV, p. 123. Letter 62.

39. *KW* XXV, pp. 134–135. Letter 68.

40. *KW* XXV, p. 139. Letter 69.

41. *Either/Or*, p. 463*.

42. *Either/Or*, p. 350*.

43. *Either/Or*, p. 54.

44. *KW* XXV, p. 120. Letter 62.

45. *Either/Or*, p. 367*.

46. *Either/Or*, p. 448.

47. This and the following three quotations from *Dept.* no. 52, 1857, pp. 792f.; nos. 65 and 66, 1857, p. 1008; nos. 73 and 74, 1857, p. 1140; nos. 77 and 78, 1857, p. 1201.

48. *H. C. Andersens dagbøger, 1851–1860*, vol 4, pp. 253 and 254.

49. *H. C. Andersens almanakker*, 1833–1873 [H. C. Andersen's Almanacs, 1833–1873], ed. Helga Van Lauridsen and Kirsten Weber. Copenhagen: Det Danske Sprog- og Litteraturselskab/ G. E. C. Gads Forlag, 1990, pp. 23 and 24.

50. *KW* I, *Early Polemical Writings*, trans. Julia Watkin. Princeton, NJ: Princeton University Press, 1990, p. 84.

51. *KJN* 4, NB: 156*.

1858

1. *KW* XXI, *For Self-Examination/Judge for Yourself*, trans. Howard V. Hong and Edna H. Hong. Princeton, NJ: Princeton University Press, 1990, p. 47.

2. *KW* XXV, pp. 327–328. Letter (draft) 236.

3. *KW* XXV, p. 328*. Letter (draft) 236.
4. *KW* XXV, p. 328*. Letter (draft) 236.
5. *KW* XXV, p. 329*. Letter (draft) 236.
6. *KW* XXV, p. 239*. Letter (draft) 236.
7. *KW* XXV, p. 329. Letter (draft) 236.
8. *KW* XXV, p. 330. Letter (draft) 236.
9. *KW* XXV, p. 330. Letter (draft) 236.
10. *KW* XXV, p. 331. Letter (draft) 236.
11. See *KJN* 6, p. 622. "Dating and Chronology" of NB 14.
12. *KJN* 6, NB14:44.
13. *KJN* 6, NB14:44.
14. *KJN* 6, NB14:44, original in italic.
15. *KW* XXV, pp. 322–323. Letter (draft) 235*.
16. *KW* XXV, p. 324*. Letter (draft) 235.
17. *KW* XXV, p. 325*. Letter (draft) 235.
18. *KW* XXV, p. 326. Letter (draft) 235*.
19. *KW* XXV, pp. 326–327. Letter (draft) 235.
20. *KW* XXIII, p. 207 (*Øieblikket*, no. 6, August 23, 1855).
21. *KW* IX, p. 150.
22. *KW* XXIII, p. 233 (*Øieblikket* no. 7, August 30, 1855).
23. Ibid., pp. 234–235.
24. See http://tom.brondsted.dk/genealogi/CharlotteIbsen.php.
25. Morten Borup, *Johan Ludvig Heiberg*. Copenhagen: Gyldendal, 1949, vol. 3, p. 101.
26. Borup, op. cit., p. 126.
27. *Dept.*, nos. 3 and 4, 1858, p. 50.
28. *KJN* 3, Notebook 8:2.
29. *KJN* 3, Notebook 8:4.
30. *KJN* 3, Notebook 8:5.
31. *KJN* 2, FF:93.
32. *KJN* 9, NB27:71.
33. *KW* XVI, *Works of Love*, trans. Howard V. Hong and Edna H. Hong. Princeton, NJ: Princeton University Press, 1995, pp. 9–10. Translation emended.

1859

1. Regine alludes to a Danish saying: "Uden mad og drikke duer helten ikke," for which an English rhyming equivalent might go: "Without a good luncheon, the hero won't function."
2. *KW* XXV, p. 66. Letter 20*.
3. *KW* XXV, p. 82. Letter 36*.
4. *Either/Or*, p. 349.
5. *Either/Or*, p. 323.
6. *KW* V, Søren Kierkegaard, *Eighteen Uplifting Discourses*, trans. Howard V. Hong and Edna Hong, Princeton, NJ: Princeton University Press, 1990, p. 399.
7. *KW* XXIII, p. 73 (*Fædrelandet*, December 1854).
8. *KW* XXIII, pp. 157–158* (*Øieblikket*, no. 4, July 7, 1855).

1860–1896

1. "Dannebrog" is the name of the Danish national flag.
2. *Dept.*, nos. 29–30, 1860, p. 415.
3. *Dept.*, nos. 9–10, 1860, pp. 134f.
4. Regine writes that the cakes say "Sparto" to the baker's, a reference to L'Hombre, the traditional trick-taking card game popular in Denmark, in which the two of spades is a high-ranking card.
5. See previous note.
6. Cf. Steen Tullberg, *Søren Kierkegaard i Danmark. En receptionshistorie* [Søren Kierkegaard in Denmark: A Reception History]. Copenhagen: C. A. Reitzel, 2006, p. 127, n. 26.
7. For this reference and the following three, see Aage Kabell, *Kierkegaardstudiet i Norden* [The Study of Kierkegaard in Scandinavia]. Copenhagen: H. Hagerup, 1948, pp.124f.
8. *KP*, p. vi; *EK*, p. 37.
9. *KJN* 3, Notebook 8:24.
10. *KJN* 3, Notebook 8:25.
11. *KJN* 3, Notebook 7:45*.
12. *KJN* 3, Notebook 8:20*. The word used is "Smørrebrød."
13. *KJN* 3, Notebook 8:31.
14. *KJN* 3, Notebook 8:18.
15. *KJN* 3, Notebook 8:20.
16. Aage Kabell, *Kierkegaardstudiet i Norden*, pp. 126 and 131.
17. *KJN* 3, Notebook 8:32.
18. *KJN* 8, NB22:148.
19. *KJN* 8, NB22:146.
20. *KJN* 8, NB22:146.
21. *KJN* 8, NB22:146*.
22. *Either/Or*, p. 259.
23. *KJN* 8. NB22:146.
24. *KJN* 6, NB12:198.
25. *KJN* 6, NB13:16.
26. *KJN* 6, NB13:16.
27. *KJN* 6, NB13:16.
28. *KJN* 6, NB12:198.
29. See Matthew 25:16 for right and left in connection with sheep and goats.
30. Roar Skovmand, "Folkestyrets Fødsel 1830–1870," *Danmarks Historie*, vol. 11. Copenhagen: Politikens Forlag, 1980, p. 479.
31. *KJN* 6, NB12:122.
32. *Stages on Life's Way*, p. 331 Translator's translation here.
33. *KJN* 4, NB:131.
34. *KJN* 6, NB12:138.
35. *KJN* 6, NB12:138.
36. *KJN* 6, NB12:138.
37. *KJN* 6, NB12:138.
38. *KJN* 6, NB12:138.

39. Henning Fenger, *Den unge Brandes. Miljø, Venner, Rejser, Kriser* [The Young Brandes: Environment, Friends, Travels, Crises]. Copenhagen: Gyldendal, 1957, pp. 108–109.

40. Georg Brandes, *Levned*, vol. 1, pp. 207f.

41. Georg Brandes, *Søren Kierkegaard. En kritisk Fremstilling i Grundrids* [Søren Kierkegaard: A Critical Presentation in Outline]. Copenhagen: Gyldendal, 1877, pp. 61f.

42. Brandes, *Søren Kierkegaard*, p. 66.

43. Brandes, *Søren Kierkegaard*, p. 66.

44. Brandes, *Søren Kierkegaard*, p. 69.

45. Brandes, *Søren Kierkegaard*, p. 77.

46. *EK*, p. 38.

47. Cf. Hornby, *Kolonierne i Vestindien*, pp. 312f.

48. Cf. Hornby, *Kolonierne i Vestindien*, p. 318.

49. Cf. Heino Døygaard, *Fra det nu forsvundne Dansk Vestindien*, Strandberg, 1987, pp. 9f, 50f.

50. Hornby, *Kolonierne i Vestindien*, p. 377.

1897–1904

1. Poul Martin Møller, *Efterladte Skrifter* [Posthumous Papers]. Copenhagen 1839–1843, vol. 1, p. 12.

2. Cf. *Repetition*, p. 7. Translator's translation here.

3. *Repetition*, p. 8.

4. *EK*, pp. 33 and 39.

5. *EK*, p. 52. Clausen's memory fails in so far as Fritz died on the 8th of June 1896, not the 18th.

6. *EK*, p. 52.

7. *EK*, p. 53.

8. This and the following from Henriette Lund, *Mit Forhold til Hende* [My Relationship to Her]. Copenhagen: Gyldendal, 1904, pp. 5, 6, 8,11, and 12.

9. *EK*, p. 281n.

10. *EK*, p. 33.

11. *EK*, p. 39.

12. Georg Brandes, *Søren Kierkegaard*, p. 80.

13. *EK*, p. 280n.

14. *EK*, p. 280n.

15. *EK*, p. 40*.

16. *EK*, p. 280n.

17. *EK*, p. 54.

18. *EK*, p. 54. "desk" altered to "desks."

19. *EK*, p. 54.

20. *EK*, p. 54.

21. *EK*, p. 54.

22. *EK*, p. 42.

23. *KJN* 3, Notebook 25:14.

Illustration Credits

1. Undated photograph. The Royal Library, Denmark.
2. Photograph from 1865. The Royal Library, Denmark.
3. Photograph from c. 1855. The Royal Library, Denmark.
4. Photograph from c. 1865. The Royal Library, Denmark.
5. Drawing by N. C. Kierkegaard, c. 1840. The Royal Library, Denmark.
6. Painting by Emil Bærentzen, 1840. The Copenhagen Museum, Denmark.
7. *Illustrated Times*, March 1870. The Royal Library, Denmark.
8. Map of Saint Croix, 1856. The Danish National Archives.
9. Photograph by Joakim Garff, 2012. Private collection.
10. Photograph by Joakim Garff, 2012.
11. Undated photograph. The Royal Library, Denmark.
12. Letter from Kierkegaard, 1840. The Royal Library, Denmark.
13. Photograph from c. 1860. The Copenhagen Museum, Denmark.
14. Letter from Kierkegaard, c. 1841. The Royal Library, Denmark.
15. Letter from Kierkegaard. The Royal Library, Denmark.
16. Lithograph from a drawing by C. Winsløw, 1825. Courtesy of Hans Fonsbøl.
17. Painting by E. Bærentzen, c. 1847. Photograph: Kit Weiss. The Museum of National History, Frederiksborg Castle.
18. Photographs by Joakim Garff, 2012.
19. Photograph by Joakim Garff, 2012.
20. Photograph from 1896. The Royal Library, Denmark.
21. Undated photograph. The Danish West Indian Society.
22. Photograph from the 1870s. Private collection.
23. Photograph by Adam Garff, 2012. Private collection.
24. Undated photograph. The Royal Library, Denmark.
25. Lithograph by E. Bærentzen.
26. Undated photograph. The Royal Library, Denmark.
27. Undated photograph. Horsens City Archive, Denmark.
28. Drawing by Emil Bærentzen, c. 1840. Courtesy of Hans Fonsbøl.
29. Etching, c. 1788. Library of Congress Rare Book and Special Collections Division.
30. Painting from nineteenth century.
31. Undated photograph. The National Museum of Denmark.
32. Undated photograph. Courtesy of Thorkel Dahl and Kjeld de Fine Licht.
33. Undated photograph. The Royal Library, Denmark.
34. Drawing by N. C. Kierkegaard, 1838. The Museum of National History, Frederiksborg Castle.
35. Undated photograph. The Royal Library, Denmark.
36. Photograph by Adam Garff, 2012. Private collection.
37. Photograph by Adam Garff, 2012. Private collection.
38. Photograph from c. 1900. The National Museum of Denmark.
39. Photograph by Adam Garff, 2012. Private collection.

Illustration Credits

40. Photograph from 1860. The Royal Library, Denmark.
41. Photographs from 1863. The Royal Library, Denmark.
42. Photograph from c. 1875. The Royal Library, Denmark.
43. Photograph from c. 1886.
44. Undated photograph. Courtesy of Michael Sheen.
45. Photograph from 1917. The Royal Library, Denmark.
46. Undated photograph. The Royal Library, Denmark.
47. Undated photograph. Private collection.
48. Undated photograph. Private collection.

Name Index

A, the Aesthete, 127
Aagaard, Charlotte, 212
Aagaard, Dr., 119, 121, 122, 125, 168, 184, 186, 217, 218, 241
Abelard, 60, 294
Abraham, and Isaac, 132
Adam, and Eve, 152
Adamine, 262
Aeneas, 80
Agnete, and the Merman, 132–135
Andersen, Hans Christian, 14, 44, 123, 148, 189–190, 214
Anny, the black maid, 85, 165
Arc, Joan of, 60

Bærentzen, Emil, 22, 23, 174, 213
Baggesen, Jens, 56
Bahneberg, Niels Anthon and wife, 93
Barfod, H. P., 17, 252–253, 256
Beatrice, 294
Beecher Stowe, Harriet, 163–164
Bernhard, Carl, 61
Birch, Frederik Christian Carl, 92, 235
Birch, Vilhelm Ludvig, 92, 168–169, 170, 235
Bismarck, Otto von, 260
Bjerring, A. N., 243, 246
Bjørnson, Bjørnstjerne, 255
Boesen, Emil, 44–48, 66, 71, 73, 98, 106, 127, 138, 144, 172–173, 178, 236
Bøgh, Erik, 252
Bondo, Juul, Pastor, 294
Borchsenius, Otto, 256
Borries, Catharine Christiane, 8
Bøttger, C. J., 250
Brandes, Georg, xi–xii, 271–276, 287, 290
Brandt, Pastor, 40
Bryde, Niels, 189
Buhl, Mads P., 293

Camus, Albert, 291
Cathala, housekeeper, 265
Christian IV, 15, 249
Christian VIII, 158
Clausen, Julius, 68, 286, 287, 292–293

Collin, Theodor, 123
Columbus, Christopher, 25, 29, 272
Constantius, Constantin, 14, 73–76, 77, 79, 285
Cordelia, 15, 16, 146–150, 231

Dante 294
de silentio, Johannes, 132, 133
Dickens, Charles, 189, 214
Dido, Queen, 80
Don Juan, 132
Dorré, Louise, 271
Drachmann, Holger, 279
Dyppel, Jørgen Iversen, 27

Elvira, Donna 175
Esmit, Nicolai 27
Eve, and Adam 152
Ewald, Johannes 56, 60
Exner, Julius 89, 90

Feddersen, H. D. F., 169, 194, 241
Feddersen, Mrs., 185, 227
Felice, 294
Ferdinand, King, 25
Fibiger, Mathilde, 214
Forsberg, Mrs., and her son William, 121
Frederik V, 29
Frederik VI, 32
Frederik VII, 124, 187, 225
Freund, H. C., 30
From, Ludvig, 210–211

Gammeltofte, O. C., 244
Garde, J. A., 277
Gardelin, Philip, 157–158
Garlieb, Johann Gottfried, 218, 219
Grundtvig, N. F. S., 47, 208–210, 276
Gyllembourg, Thomasine, 214

Hall, C. C., 102
Hansen, C. F., 30
Hansen, Peter, 170
Hauch, Carsten, 44

Name Index

Heiberg, Johan Ludvig, 127, 148–149, 151–152, 215–216
Heiberg, Johanne Louise, 215–216
Héloise, 60, 294
Henck, Miss, 236
Hertz, Henrik, 69
Hjaltelin, J. J., 248
Høedt, Frederik Ludvig, 215

Ingemann, B. S., 44
Isaiah, 81

Janus, 222
Jenrette, Richard H., 84
Jesus, 90, 112, 268, 269
Job, 76
Johannes the Seducer, 107, 148–151, 153, 231, 257
Juliet, 294

Kafka, Franz, 294
Kierkegaard, Ane, 96
Kierkegaard, Michael Pedersen, 20, 113
Kierkegaard, Niels Andreas, 96
Kierkegaard, Niels Christian, 22, 174
Kierkegaard, Peter Christian, 2, 47, 51–52, 54, 67, 70, 101, 102, 105, 135–136, 144, 174, 268, 269
Klein, police officer, 100
Knudsen, Adrian Benoni Benzon, 185
Kolthoff, Ernst Vilhelm, 110
Krebs, Miss, 213
Kuntzen, Councillor, 216

Læssøe, Signe, 148
Lassen, Captain, 168
Laura (married to Oluf Olsen). *See* Winning, Laura Isidora
Laura Henriette (married to Jonas Olsen), 181, 182, 186, 187, 262
Løvmand, Albert, 87
Lumby, H. C., 216
Lund, Carl Ferdinand, 2, 98, 176
Lund, Henriette, 96–99, 287–290
Lund, Henrik Ferdinand, 96
Lund, Henrik Sigvard, 53, 54, 96, 97, 99–107, 128, 135–139, 141–144, 172, 201, 211, 243
Lund, Johan Christian, 47, 52, 96, 144
Lund, Michael Frederik Christian, 47, 100
Lund, Nicoline Christine (née Kierkegaard), 96

Lund, Peter Christian, 97
Lund, Peter Severin, 97
Lund, Peter Wilhelm, 99
Lund, Petrea Severine, 96, 289
Lund, Vilhelm Nikolai, 97

Maag, Attorney, 52
Malling, Regine Frederikke, 14, 80, 82, 119
Martensen, H. L., 35, 34, 47, 102, 237
Meidell, Frederik, 252
Meineke, Mrs., 194–195, 213
Meyer, Raphael, 106–107, 291, 292
Meza, Julius de, 260
Møller, Poul Martin, 18, 89, 285
Monigatti, Johan, 173
Monrad, H. C., 156
Moth, Frederik, 30
Mourier, Hanne, 121, 290, 291
Mynster, J. P., 8, 34, 35, 60, 70

Neiiendam, Robert, 292
Neukirch, Dr., 235–236
Newton, John, 155
Nietzsche, Friedrich, 272

Oehlenschläger, Adam, 56
Ohsten, C. F., 94
Olivarius, H. T. P., 184
Olsen, Jonas Christian, 70, 81, 90, 181–183, 208, 218, 251, 262, 281
Olsen, Maria, 14, 15, 33, 42, 81, 93, 186, 211, 281
Olsen, Mathilde (Thilly), 24, 29–30, 40, 85–88, 129, 138, 153, 194, 213, 217, 247, 248, 271–273
Olsen, Olivia Christiane, 94, 166, 185, 229, 263, 266, 271, 280
Olsen, Oluf Christian, 24, 29–30, 33, 40, 81, 86–88, 96, 125, 129, 158–162, 167, 171, 172, 218, 219, 224, 242, 251, 281, 287, 293
Olsen, Regine. *See* Schlegel, Regine
Olsen, Regnar, 42, 85, 247
Olsen, Sigrid Marie Cornelia, xii, 13, 15, 16, 33, *passim*, 281, 282
Olsen, Terkild, 14, 17, 29, 67, 69, 82, 92, 109–110, 197, 265
Ottesen, N. C., 276

Paludan-Müller, Frederik, 205–207
Paul, the Apostle, 36, 63
Paulli, Just, 6, 49

Name Index

Philip V, King of Spain, 178
Pontavice, Emilie de, 94, 95, 196
Pontavice, Jean de, 95
Pyramus, 294

Quidam, 268

Reitzel. C. A., 179
Riise, A. H., 123
Romeo, 294
Rømer, Ludvig Ferdinand, 156
Rørdam, Bolette, 17, 20, 95, 211–212, 232
Rørdam, Cathrine Georgia, 17
Rørdam, Elisabeth, 17
Rørdam, Emma, 17
Rørdam, Peter, 20, 212
Rørdam, Thomas Schatt, 17
Rousseau, Jean-Jacques, 148

Sand, George, 214, 229
Sarah, 193
Sartre, Jean-Paul, 291
Schanshoff, Josephine, 24, 85, 93, 114, 125, 165, 242, 246
Scheherazade, 190, 193
Schelling, Friedrich von, 177–178
Schlegel, Augusta, 16
Schlegel, Clara, 16, 40, 171, 243–244
Schlegel, Dorothea Maria, 16
Schlegel, Emma, 16
Schlegel, Johan Frederik (Fritz), xi, *passim*
Schlegel, Regine, xi, *passim*
Schlegel, Wilhelm August, 16, 249
Schmidt, F. W., 282
Schmidt, Mrs., 217
Schmidt, Mr., 31, 41, 243, 264
Scholten, Peter von, xiv, 31, 87, 159–162, 277
Schopen, John William, 33
Schubothe, J. H., 127
Schulze, Hedwig, 175
Schwartz, Mrs., 194–195, 213
Scribe, Augustin Eugène, 127–128

Shahriyar, King, 190
Sibbern, F.C., 6, 65, 176
Simmelkjær, Miss, 213
Skrike, Adolph, 219, 241
Smed, Erik Nielsen, 26
Søbøtker, Johannes, 31
Socrates, 112, 221
Soldenfeldt, Ferdinand Vilhelm, 15, 262
Solodenfeldt, Joseph Carl, 15, 262
Stow, David, 87
Stylites, Simeon, 273

Thisbe, 294
Thomas, a sailor, 109
Thorvaldsen, Bertel, 32
Trier, Seligmann Meyer, 43, 49, 81
Tryde, E. C., 100, 102
Typhon, 221

Unna, Camilla Marie, 225
Ussing, A. S., 208

Vater, Daniel Christian, 225

Wiedewelt, J., 30
Wiehe, Michael, 215
Wilhelm, Assessor, 179, 181
Willumsen, Niels, 251
Winning, Frederik Emil, 15, 45, 85, 86, 91, 124–126, 128, 147, 158, 181, 186, 193, 234, 242, 251, 279, 281
Winning, Frederikke Mathilde, 15, 293
Winning, Johanne Marie, 15, 42, 193
Winning, Laura Isidora, 15, 29, 85,160, 162, 166, 204
Winning, Olivia, 15
Winning, Paul Thorkild, 15
Winsløw, Carl, 69
Winther, Christian, 56
Wittgenstein, Ludwig, 232
Wulff, Henriette, 214

Zerlina, 132